2 47

.2

RETAIL MERCHANDISE MANAGEMENT

PRENTICE-HALL, INC., Englewood Cliffs, New Jersey

RETAI

JOHN W. WINGATE

Professor of Marketing, Emeritus
City College
The City University of New York

ELMER O. SCHALLER

Associate Dean
Institute of Retail Management
New York University

F. LEONARD MILLER

Vice President and General Merchandise Manager
Jordan Marsh of Florida

MERCHANDISE
MANAGEMENT

RETAIL MERCHANDISE MANAGEMENT

John W. Wingate, Elmer O. Schaller, and F. Leonard Miller

ISBN: 0-13-778753-7

Library of Congress Catalog Card No.: 73-168617

10   9   8   7   6   5   4   3

PRENTICE-HALL INTERNATIONAL, INC., *London*
PRENTICE-HALL OF AUSTRALIA, PTY. LTD., *Sydney*
PRENTICE-HALL OF CANADA, LTD., *Toronto*
PRENTICE-HALL OF INDIA PRIVATE LIMITED, *New Delhi*
PRENTICE-HALL OF JAPAN, INC., *Tokyo*

CONTENTS

part II
PRICING

part III
INVENTORY

part IV

MERCHANDISE PLANNING AND CONTROL IN DOLLARS

The Formula for Staple Stock Control
The Rate of Sale

PREFACE

It is widely recognized that changes in the past two decades have profoundly affected the field of retailing. Examples are: the wealth of data now available through the computer; the increasing importance of return on investment due to more public issues of retailing companies' stock and the high cost of money; the proliferation of branch stores, changing one-store operations into mini-chains and multi-unit organizations; and the split of the buying and selling functions in many larger companies.

There is a need to meet these and other contemporary problems, especially as they relate to the merchandising and management executives in the retailing industry. *Retail Merchandise Management* is designed to fill that need in the study and treatment of major retailing problems and systems. It supercedes *Techniques of Retail Merchandising*, long considered the classic in its field by academicians as well as by retailing executives. Its principles and procedures for profitable manipulation of a merchandise investment, including planning, pricing and inventory control, have successfully stood the test of time. In this updated version, most of the material has been rewritten, with an emphasis on the management point of view, *i.e.* planning, coordination, supervision, and control. Furthermore, there are additional chapters on the merchant's long-range objectives and on profit return on the investment, particularly regarding merchandise and physical space.

The sections of the book are grouped in logical sequence, beginning with the *objectives* and *philosophy* of the store's management, particularly as they are expressed in the actual merchandise *assortment plan*. Pricing of the merchandise is followed by a section on inventory, which includes a chapter on *stockturn*. Two complete sections are then devoted to *planning* and *control* in *dollars* and then in *units*.

The authors have deliberately geared the presentation of the subject matter to be of direct value to the merchant or merchandising executive who may require guidance in the solution of a particular management problem. Virtually every topic treated is as important to the small merchant as to the large one. Even advanced practitioners in stores of all sizes will find that a study of the text will organize and sharpen their own thinking and make them better merchants. And manufacturers and wholesalers who sell to retail merchants, as well as agencies that provide retailers with a consultation service, will find that this book enables them to view their customers and clients in the light of the latters' challenges and problems. This knowledge will make it possible for them to service better, not only their immediate customers, but also the great body of ultimate consumers upon whose favor all business must depend.

As a *training guide* for young promotional buyers and junior merchandising executives, this text provides a comprehensive course of instruction, whether formal or home study. It is well suited to an intensive course in retail merchandising offered in either the community or the senior colleges. For a two-semester course, Parts I, II, and III will provide sufficient material for the first semester's work since they thoroughly cover retail profit and loss, retail pricing, and inventory analysis. Parts IV and V on Planning and Control then provide for the second semester's work.

At the end of every chapter, probing discussion questions are presented. Few of these have rote answers, nor are the answers more than merely suggested in the test. Most of them call for a management decision that demands rational, sensitive, and often, original thought.

It is recommended that this text be used in conjunction with *Problems in Retail Merchandising* by Wingate, Schaller, and Goldenthal, also published by Prentice-Hall, Inc. The latter book provides many mathematical problems of a nature suggested in this present text but without the philosophy and rationale that this text provides. These problems are important because they assure that the student has mastered the basic merchandising relationships that may be expressed in figures rather than to have simply acquired a general knowledge. Students who hope someday to be store buyers, merchandise managers, or merchants in their own right need to master the specifics as well as the general concepts. A third book, which may be thought of as a companion to these, is *The Management of Retail Buying* by Wingate and Friedlander, also published by Prentice-Hall, Inc.

In addition to the many who over the years have contributed to the concepts developed in this book, the authors wish to express their special indebtedness to Dr. Theodore D. Ellsworth, Professor of Retail Management, New York University Institute of Retail Management, and to Dr. Robert W. Bell, Professor of Marketing, University of Arkansas. Both have made many suggestions that have been incorporated in the text.

JOHN W. WINGATE
ELMER O. SCHALLER
F. LEONARD MILLER

part **I**

Part I introduces the subject of retail merchandising, presenting the importance for all merchants of a knowledge of the techniques involved. In view of the fundamental economic and social changes taking place today, a clear-cut managerial philosophy is becoming essential for success. Accordingly, a special chapter is devoted to this subject. The elements of the profit and loss statement are then explained with emphasis on the effect of its various elements on the profit goal.

MERCHANDISING: THE BASIS FOR SUCCESSFUL STORE OPERATION

1

RETAIL MERCHANDISING

THE PLANNED ASSORTMENT

"I'll take that shirt, please. Do you have it in blue, size sixteen, and thirty-three sleeve length?" If the salesman can answer yes to this question from the customer, the sale is made. If the answer is no, the sale is lost and the store has wasted a part of a large investment in merchandise, advertising, training, personnel, physical plant, and goodwill.

Simple as the consummation of a sale may seem, the preparation for it is decidedly complex. To be assured of having just the shirt the customer wants, the assortment available must include different materials (cotton and synthetic), different weaves (oxford and broadcloth), different colors (white, blue, and others), a variety of collar styles (spread, button-down, and others) at least two cuff styles (french and barrel), two or more brands, six different neck sizes, and at least three long-sleeve as well as a short-sleeve length. In fact, the average shirt classification in a store of medium size may be required to carry some one thousand different stockkeeping units in its assortment.[1]

The challenge of keeping such a large assortment in stock is enhanced by the strict dollar limits set on the amount that the buyer may spend in meeting the varied demands of many different customers.

Take the case of the young man who has just been appointed buyer of men's shirts for a group of department stores. The man to whom he reports, the merchandise manager of men's wear, has asked him to prepare a fall assortment plan that will provide for a total stock to be valued at $15,000 retail. This inventory is to provide a markup of 42 percent; this means that it is to cost about $8,700. The buyer's problem is to spend this sum in such a way as to satisfy the particular demands of the customers who wish to buy shirts in his department. First, he must analyze the component parts of these demands and then plan for their purchase. He starts by determining the major classifications he will have to carry: dress shirts, knit shirts, sports shirts, and formal dress shirts. Under each class, he selects the prices at which he believes shirts in that class would sell readily and still provide an adequate markup. Within each price, he decides on fabrics, such as broadcloth, oxford, and batiste. He then brings into his plan other selection factors including collar and cuff styles, neck sizes and sleeve lengths, and, of course, colors. After he has lined up all the variations necessary to satisfy the special requirements of most potential customers, he must decide how many of each variety to stock to minimize the danger of being out of stock before reorders can be provided. The job is an exacting one, but once properly organized, it will guide the buyer in his purchasing activity.

This planning process is an important part of the function of retail merchandising.

WHAT IS MERCHANDISING?

The term merchandising has been given different meanings by various business groups. Some manufacturers think of it as a synonym for marketing; others treat it as the function of product planning and development. The retailer associates the term with the planning

---

[1] A stockkeeping unit, or SKU, is either a single item of merchandise or a group of items for which separate sales and stock records are kept. In the case of shirts, for example, it may be a dress shirt made from a particular fabric in a particular style, with a particular collar size and sleeve length, and in a particular color, or it may include all dress shirts of a particular material and style, with no attempt to maintain separate records of differences in color, collar size, and sleeve length.

and control of his merchandise assortment. A broad definition, approved by the American Marketing Association, describes it as "the planning and supervision involved in marketing the particular merchandise or service at the places, times, and prices, and in the quantities that will best serve to realize the marketing objectives of the business."

For purposes of this text, retail merchandising is viewed as the planning and control of a stock assortment so as to meet predetermined objectives. While the primary objective may be profit, there are, as we shall see, other objectives that may be paramount over the short run.

A well-planned assortment must contain a merchandise mix attuned to both expressed and latent needs and wants of potential customers. From the customers' point of view, the mix must include goods of the right (1) *type*, (2) *quality*, (3) *price*, in (4) *quantities* adjusted to expected demand, available at the (5) *time* customers are ready to inspect and buy, and at the (6) *places* in an individual store or in a multi-unit system where customers would expect to find such an assortment. Any failure to achieve these six *rights* will lead to lost sale opportunities or to unbalanced inventories with heavy handling or carrying costs, including depreciation.

A well-planned assortment must not only meet customer demand advantageously, it must also provide the merchant with a markup adequate to cover costs and expenses of operation and contribute to the overhead expenses and profits of the organization as a whole.

Retail merchandising requires the setting up of planning units that are under the supervision of a buyer or a department manager. These may be merchandise departments such as men's furnishings, dairy products, or beauty aids. Or they may be merchandise classifications within department groupings, such as white shirts, cheeses, and shampoos, each with its distinct end use.

MERCHANDISING SERVICES

Today merchants are giving increased attention to the sale of services, not only to the sale of merchandise. This is because customers in our relatively affluent society are devoting an increased proportion of their income to the purchase of services. Some of the services that retailers are selling profitably include leasing tools, equipment, cars, and special occasion clothing; supplying beauty treatments; repairing furniture and appliances; conducting training courses in specialized activities such as cooking, painting, and bridge playing; and providing the services of insurance, travel, and entertainment ticket agencies.

While such selling units may not require a merchandise assortment (except in leasing), they do require a careful adjustment of the service to customer demand and the astute setting of prices for each unit of service so as to provide for costs and expenses and a contribution to profit. They require planning that is very similar to the merchandise plan. Thus, the term merchandising may be broadened to include the planning and control of units of service to achieve sales and profit goals.

ORGANIZING FOR MERCHANDISING

IN THE SMALL STORE

Every merchant must perform the merchandising function adequately in order to survive. Even the peanut vendor with sales of a few dollars a day is subject to the same kind of penalties for failure to perform his merchandising functions properly as are the tremendously large grocery chains and mail-order houses. The job of maintaining merchandise in the six right relationships is the central function of the merchant himself in the small store and of the merchandise division in the large one. While the small merchant must direct personal selling, must advertise, must provide a suitable space in which to operate, and must record transactions, he usually allocates these duties to subordinates. He seldom delegates, however, the planning necessary to balance his stocks to customer demand in order to achieve his objectives.

IN THE LARGE STORE

The merchandising function is assumed by the merchandise division, which is set off from the store management, publicity, and control divisions. This division is sometimes headed by the store president. Where there is a separate merchandise manager, he is generally the second in authority in the store.

This merchandise division does more than merchandising, that is, it does not limit its activities to planning and control. It is also responsible for buying—and usually for selling. Buyers or department managers are appointed for each major line of goods: they buy, they direct sales, and they merchandise—they plan and control their activities in view of customer demand and profit possibilities. Divisional merchandise managers supervise buyers under them and coordinate their activities so that all departments will reflect the basic character that top management wishes to develop. Thus, much of the time of the merchandise managers is given to merchandising, with the execution of the plans left largely to the buyers. There is a tendency, nevertheless, to develop buyers who can merchandise their own departments, requiring fewer merchandise managers who specialize in coordination, since they need devote only a minimum of time to supervision.

IN THE CHAIN STORE SYSTEM

The division of responsibility within the chain organization is somewhat different. Buying and selling are separated. Central buyers develop standardized assortment plans, determine the resources from which purchases may be made, negotiate the terms of sale, and usually make the decisions in regard to new items to be added to an approved buying list and old ones to be dropped. The actual placing of orders for specific items and quantities then becomes the duty of the store managers.

In the purchase of private brands and in some apparel chains, however, the central organization may perform all buying and reorder functions. The central buyer orders the specific styles in the quantities deemed necessary for the chain as a whole, and merchandise distributors allot the incoming goods to the store units. Under this arrangement, the major duty of the store managers is merchandise presentation and sale, with the attendant customer services. In such a central merchandising operation, the planning is done by merchandise controllers, each of whom is attached to one or more buyers. They plan purchase requirements for the chain as a whole, based on sales forecasts as well as the stock requirements of each individual unit. In a larger multi-unit operation, with buying highly centralized, there may be a merchandise planner or a controller who devotes all his attention to the overall needs of the chain and district merchandise managers who take care of the needs of the individual stores in each district. Under their supervision, there may be "paper" planners, or distributors, who allot a portion of each style or lot number received to each selling unit.

IN THE BRANCH SYSTEM

A branch organization differs from the typical chain operation in that the assortment and service offered in each store is more closely tailored to local requirements rather than to a standardized assortment mix. Such variations are necessary in the retailing of better grades of clothing, home furnishings, and other types of general merchandise, where fashion, distinctiveness, and the particular needs of each community must be considered. Such variations are not necessary for chains that handle staples such as foods and housewares or bargain-priced general merchandise. Here the assortments can be planned and controlled centrally, with each unit carrying a virtual duplicate of a standardized assortment.

In the branch organization, the managers in each unit must be given the authority to deviate from a centrally devised standard, since the demand for shopping goods differs in different locations. While it is difficult to draw a clear-cut line between the responsibilities of the central buying staff and those of the unit managers, the central merchandisers usually plan the initial assortment, set the prices, and select the new merchandise to be added to the stock and the items to be withdrawn. The unit managers control the reorders and thus adjust the quantities and the mix to meet the special requirements of the local market. They may also be permitted to make price changes, after consultation with the central buyers.

The position of branch department managers in centrally merchandised multi-unit operations is still relatively new, and store administrators have not wholly solved the problem of how to free them to use their initiative and creativity in taking advantage of local opportunities and yet maintain the advantages of having central buying specialists that serve all units.

PERSONAL QUALIFICATIONS FOR MERCHANDISING

The merchandising function in retailing is, as indicated, commonly spread among several executives: the *merchandise manager* is responsible for forecasting sales for his division and for planning in dollars the stock required to support these sales at an adequate markup. He breaks down these overall plans into various departments under his supervision and consults with buyers and department managers as to the means of achieving the planned goals. The *buyer*, in consultation with his superior, makes merchandising plans for his own department in terms of dollars and converts the dollar plans into units of merchandise. In practice he may plan his unit sales and his unit assortment first and convert them into dollar figures to check against his merchandise manager's plan. The branch manager controls his own stock assortment so as to adhere to the buyer's plans or to modifications of them approved to meet the peculiar requirements of the local market.

The qualifications for these positions differ in degree. The *merchandise manager* must first be a good leader with the ability to analyze merchandising figures, especially those expressed in dollars, and to make sound judgments and to inspire aggressive performance in buying and selling. He must be sensitive to changes in customer demand and familiar with the peculiarities of the wholesale markets. The *buyer* must be able to develop balanced unit assortment plans for his line and to appraise quality and customer acceptance for the many items offered on the market and must always be prepared to take advantage of profitable pricing opportunities. If he is a fashion goods buyer, he will be flexible in deviating from his assortment plan to accommodate what is new and potentially salable. He will be a good judge of color, line, and design, especially in their commercial aspects, and he will be creative in developing and recognizing new combinations to which significant segments of his customer clientele will respond. If he is a buyer of staple goods, he will be a good trader for merchandise values and services provided by competing suppliers and will be adept in suggesting the most appropriate arrangement and display of his merchandise on the sales floor. A *department manager* in a selling unit must have the broad qualifications of a merchant: he must be an aggressive leader of his sales force, a sympathetic customer adviser, and an astute merchandiser in adapting his merchandise mix and the depth of his assortments to local demand.

With the unprecedented rapidity of change taking place today, with technology spewing out a flood of new products, and with customers ever ready to try something new, yet discriminating in their choice, all merchandisers must avoid relying too heavily on statistical data of past demand. They must become sensitive to the changes that are currently evolving and be quick to modify assortments by relating what is new on the market to current changes in the living and thinking habits of customers.

MASTERY OF FIGURE RELATIONSHIPS

When we realize that the qualities of the merchandise manager, the buyer, and the department manager are similar, it becomes clear that a thorough technical training in the computation and interpretation of figure facts—particularly as they relate to a profitable operation—is a prime requisite for the would-be merchandiser of tomorrow.

The person starting a study of merchandising is often surprised by the extent to which business judgments depend upon figures. It is true that merchandisers do much of their planning in terms of dresses, shoes, or toasters, but they must express their thinking in specific quantities, and these involve numbers. Again, the goal of the merchandising operation is twofold: serving the public well and making a profit for the retail store. Profits can be figured only in dollars, not in merchandise. Every potential buyer and merchandise manager must understand the interrelation of the many factors that enter into profits so that he may intelligently adjust them. The study of retail merchandising logically begins with the setting of objectives that find their financial expression in a *profit and loss statement*.

Since profits are chiefly the results of markup, inventories, sales volume, and expenses, it is logical to continue the study of retail merchandising with a careful investigation of *markup* and an explanation of how it is interrelated with sales and expenses in yielding a profit. The problem of price is perhaps the central one, for retail prices, if properly set, have a dynamic power to move goods. Frequently a small difference in price makes a large difference in both sales volume and profits.

The next phase of the study is *inventories*, since inventories provide the stock from which sales materialize and the valuation of the inventory has a decided effect on profits.

Since profits depend upon sales volume as well as upon markup and inventories, the study of retail merchandising must include the *analysis of sales possibilities* and the planning and *control of stocks and purchases* required in view of the demand. Attention must also be given to stockkeeping to insure (1) that maximum sales are realized by properly replenishing fast-selling stock and promptly clearing slow-selling stock and (2) that merchandise depreciation and theft are reduced to a minimum.

Profits cannot be realized by a consideration of markup, inventories, and sales volume possibilities only. Expenses associated with various sales and markup objectives must also be planned and controlled.

PROFIT AS A MOTIVATING GOAL

Profit-mindedness is an essential ingredient for success in retailing. Merchants are in business to serve the community, it is true, but they are also in business to make a profit. Buyers are judged by the sales volume they achieve, but probably even more by the profit they earn for their employers. Profits are a measure of the degree of success with which the public is served, and they provide the motivation to drive merchandisers to provide even better service. We believe that under a philosophy of free and independent enterprise human beings are spurred to maximum achievement. The striving for profits will continue to be a major constructive force so long as merchants realize that as the complexity of our society increases, so must their obligations to their customers, their employees, their suppliers, and even their competitors.

CRITICISM OF PROFIT GOAL

Many ethical thinkers in our Judeo-Christian society feel that the preoccupation with profits is egocentric and incompatible with the ideal of service to others. They tend to think of profit as an unearned toll that business is able to exact from buyers. At this point a distinction may be made between the goals of an individual and those of a business enterprise. A person can successfully engage in the merchandising business, moved by a desire to make his life count by distributing fairly priced goods and services that appeal to the physiological or sociological needs of customers and help build their sense of well-being. Like workers in any field, he will expect a fair return for his services commensurate with his contribution. This might be in the form of wages, bonuses, and/or a share in profits.

The business enterprise, however, must make profits over the long run if it is to survive and grow and if it is to continue to employ people, serve customers, and attract capital. We live in an age of amazing technological change and of inflation. Buildings, furniture, and fixtures wear out and must be replaced, usually by more expensive ones. Replenishment of stocks has to be made at continuously higher prices, and the stock assortment has to be expanded to meet the demands of increasingly exacting customers. Multi-units have to be created to serve a growing but shifting population. All such growth requires massive additions of capital. Profits are essential, not only to provide some of this capital but also to attract outside capital. Investors will not commit additional capital unless they are confident that profits will be large enough to assure them dividends or to protect the firm's ability to pay them contractual interest and provide for the ultimate repayment of the loan.

Today a business must grow or perish. Standing still is really slipping back toward failure, for the rest of the economy is growing rapidly and the company that accumulates no profits for reinvestment and for eventual dividends to equity investors will become a shrinking factor in its community. It must grow to continue to serve. Thus, retail merchants must insist on expert merchandisers who can generate profits from their activities.

MAXIMIZING PROFITS

Some students of business are convinced that business must aim not simply at earning profits but also at maximizing them. The attempt to respond to sales opportunities most effectively to keep the cost of such response to a minimum and to develop an assortment mix that will yield more profit than any other is believed to provide the combination of resources that will best serve society.

While this may theoretically be true over the long run, it is not true in planning for a short time ahead. The specific objectives of a company have to vary with circumstances. Sometimes a substantial rise in sales volume must be achieved to establish the store in the mind of the community. The low markup and high expense that this move may entail may yield less profit than could be achieved with a lower sales volume. Again, it may take a few years for a new retail selling facility or the addition of a new merchandise line to achieve its potential, even though it adds heavily to current expenses.

Sometimes the immediate objective may be to maintain or increase one's market share to hold or improve the store's standing in the community. Current profits may deliberately be sacrificed to achieve such goals.

The current crises in our great cities and the demands of disadvantaged groups for equal opportunity have made it imperative that merchants recognize a social responsibility toward these groups; otherwise the city may become one vast ghetto. Stores that have outlets in poorer neighborhoods should perhaps lower prices, improve assortments, and forgo tricky but successful installment selling schemes, even though present methods of operation would yield much more profit currently. A merchant may be well advised to operate some units unprofitably for the present, if by so doing he can help eliminate the ghetto and bring the community into the mainstream of America's middle class.

While the attempt to maximize profits over the long run is attractive, in practice it is not possible to evaluate the results of any proposed decision in terms of its precise effect on sales, costs, and goodwill. Accordingly, merchandising decisions that will hopefully achieve the immediate objectives of the operation and also contribute to profit over the long run may be as satisfactory as an attempt to choose from a number of possible actions the one that will be more profitable than any other.

Something is to be said for deliberately attempting to achieve profits somewhat below the maximum possible in order to create an enduring and attractive image. For example, a product may sell as well today at twenty dollars as it does at nineteen dollars, but those who buy at twenty dollars may conclude that they failed to obtain outstanding value, whereas purchasers at nineteen dollars may be very favorably impressed and associate the store with excellent values. As already suggested, goodwill building is often a wiser goal than near-term profit, and this may be thought of as an attempt to optimize profits—to make them as favorable as possible over the long run rather than to maximize them.[2]

THE CHALLENGE OF MERCHANDISING

The student who is exploring the field of merchandising will discover a great personal challenge. To serve the consumer well in a rapidly changing world, he must be both creative and analytical. He must learn how to determine what features in goods and in related services appeal to the life-styles of his various customer groups and how to obtain from the computer the information essential for profitable operation. He must learn how to weigh potential sales against costs and how to achieve profits while he provides a merchandising service of excellence. He must become a true professional and not an opportunist.

Today, a new dimension has been added to the merchant's task. He must involve himself in the urgent social problems of his community. His executives must function on planning committees, and he must implement a development program for employees from minority groups.

Even those who are not planning a career in retail merchandising will find the study of the subject enormously worthwhile. The success of all workers in a retail organization depends to a consider-

[2] For a vigorous defense of the profit motive, see Milton Friedman, *Capitalism and Freedom* (Chicago: The University of Chicago Press, 1962), also his article in the *New York Times Magazine*, September 13, 1970. Mr. Friedman, professor of economics at the University of Chicago, states that although individuals have social responsibilities, business corporations—as distinct from individual entrepreneurs—do not. The goal of the corporation, he argues, must be to increase profits for its principals, the stockholders. When an individual becomes a decision maker in a business corporation, he must act as an agent of the corporation with its profit goal. Any other approach, he believes, is socialism, for if the corporate executive attempts to assure a social goal, he is assuming a function properly reserved for government without having been given any such authority by those he claims to represent. For example, if he raises prices in order to assume the cost of a social good, he is in effect taxing his customers for a goal that he deems laudatory. He would be spending someone else's money, not his own, for a purpose he thinks desirable, with the consent of neither his customers nor his stockholders. The whole subject is a highly controversial one today, with some businessmen giving lip service to the concept of social responsibility but acting in practice as agents for their stockholders.

able extent upon their comprehension of the merchandising function. For example, the personnel director must hire and must help train people for merchandising positions; the advertising executive must work closely with the buyers and must understand their objectives; the fashionist, likewise, must have an appreciation of the profit-mindedness of the buyer if she is to succeed; and the controller must see the merchandise realities behind the figures and symbols if he is to exert an influence in policy making and planning. All members of the store team must make their contribution to a sound merchandising operation; to do this they must be well versed in basic merchandising concepts.

It is not only store workers who must comprehend merchandising techniques. Manufacturers and wholesalers who sell to retailers, trade-paper editors who analyze retail operations, resident buyers who represent stores in central wholesale markets, management engineers who survey store data and store practices, all must understand merchandising relationships if they are to serve their retail accounts effectively.

QUESTIONS FOR DISCUSSION

1. (a) How do the definitions of merchandising given in the text agree with your own conception of the meaning of the term? Have you thought of it as a synonym for retailing?
   (b) Over fifty years ago, an authority on merchandising explained it as follows: "The purpose and function of merchandising is the providing of merchandise, or 'goods' as they are generally known in the trade, in such quantities, of such quality, and in such assortments as will supply the wants, desires, and tastes of the ultimate consumers for whose use they are intended."[3] Is this still a satisfactory definition of retail merchandising? Can you improve upon it?

2. What do you understand by *merchandise mix*?

3. In view of the increasing variety of goods on the market and of the availability of computers for analysis, would you expect planning units to become larger or smaller assemblages of merchandise?

4. Compare the duties and qualifications of a specialized central buyer for a multi-unit operation with those of a department manager for a single selling unit. Which has a greater variety of responsibility? Which probably receives the greater remuneration? Why?

5. Which must be given more freedom of authority: the manager of a supermarket or the manager of an equally large unit of an apparel branch system? Why?

[3] A. W. Douglas, *Merchandising* (New York: The Macmillan Company, 1918).

6. Is leadership ability essential for a central buyer of a specialized line, sold in many separate outlets?
7. Suggest five major topics in the study of retail merchandising and present them in a logical order.
8. How can merchandise planners obtain current information about changes in customer demand that are not yet reflected in sales?
9. What are the attributes of a science and do you believe that retail merchandising is approaching a science? Does it continually test hypotheses? If so, how?
10. Do you agree that profit is essential to survival and growth?
11. Can the profit motive be reconciled with the motive of service to others?
12. (a) Should a merchant attempt to maximize profits over a reasonably long period of time?
    (b) Is there a real difference between the concept of maximizing profit and that of optimizing profit?
13. Is the management of a retail corporate chain justified in making substantial grants to collegiate schools of business without the express consent of the corporation's stockholders? Defend your position. Would your answer be different in the case of grants to charitable organizations?
14. What kinds of people find merchandising challenging?
15. What are some of the specific ways in which a young merchandising executive can serve his community in a period of social tension?
16. Is the lack of a merchandising background on the part of the chief executive likely to be injurious to the success of large-scale retailing over the long run?

2

MERCHANDISING PHILOSOPHY AND OBJECTIVES

Although a profitable operation is a motivating goal for merchants, the route toward this goal is determined by the philosophy or preconceived concepts of each store's management as to the kind of store it wants to operate. Differences in merchandising methods are not simply the result of outside factors affecting customer demand; they grow out of differences in the thinking of each store's management team and its degree of willingness to plan ahead in a systematic way.

THE NEW EMPHASIS ON PLANNING

Retailing, until recently, has primarily been a day-to-day—relatively small scale—business. True, there existed short-range seasonal merchandising plans and monthly advertising plans, but most merchants were more urgently concerned with "Did we beat last year TODAY?" The very nature of retailing, until recently, did not require in-depth written plans. The store manager was the owner and he was responsible for only one store. As proprietor, he knew every counter and corner and called each salesperson by name. He knew by intuition how much to buy, and often for which customer. Intuition is still a valuable asset to any merchant. But his survival today requires him to make far-ranging decisions based on objective data regarding new locations, new merchandise lines, new services, executive development programs, and a reorganization of duties and lines of authority.

In this age of planetary exploration, accelerated technological advancement, and television in nearly every home, the tempo of dramatic change in retailing is increasing rapidly. If there is one certainty in modern retailing, it is that of change. The successful merchant must learn to ride on the crest of change rather than be buffeted about by forces he has not anticipated.

Thus, management is forced to evaluate trends and predict in what ways the store will need to change direction. Prophesy is always fraught with hazards; yet, prediction is a required function of management. Add to this the complexity of multi-unit organizations, geographically dispersed, and there emerges an urgent need for a plan that fits the countless pieces together. Management must plan ahead if it is to survive and maintain its position against aggressive competition. However, a plan is not in itself an end. It should stimulate decision making which, in turn, leads to action.

The material that follows provides an orderly way to proceed: it consists primarily of questions that management must answer.

THE PHILOSOPHY OF THE COMPANY

A merchant's philosophy relates to his concept of the kind of store he thinks he is best equipped to operate successfully. This has many aspects, including the segment of the entire consumer market to be served and the demands of this segment, the sharing of this market with competitors, the merchandise assortment to be provided, the store's relationship with sources of supply, and the attitude of management toward consumerism and community involvement.

SEGMENTS OF THE CONSUMER MARKET TO BE SERVED

No store can attempt to cater to every segment of the public. Differences in customers' incomes, in their occupations, in their social class groupings, and in their interests make it desirable for management to seek actively the patronage of only a certain portion of the buying public.

Most stores attempt to cater to a considerable portion of the great middle class who are price conscious, yet ready to make discretionary expenditures. A store may, however, elect to serve the much smaller group of upper-income customers or the still large lower-income group close to the poverty line, even those who are dependent upon public welfare.

Management may envision itself in any one of many retailing roles. For example, it may consider itself a prom. tional store, perhaps of the discount variety, catering to those consu ner groups who are always on the lookout for low prices, even though many of them may not be in the lower-income group. Perhaps management sees itself as a specialist, serving those customers who want assortments selected with discrimination and offering them personal service.

Management's goal may be to operate a popularly priced dominant department store, catering to a wide variety of the needs of the great middle class. This does not mean, however, that the store should refrain from catering to affluent customers willing to pay high prices. Many popular-priced stores have developed deluxe and boutique departments, and some discount stores excel in high-priced gourmet foods. At the other extreme, to sell to the value-conscious, low-income consumer may require a budget floor, a basement store, or a discount annex.

Consistent income-group appeal. If the merchant elects to operate a departmentized store, he is faced with the problem of catering to the same typical customer in his different departments. Does he accept the theory that the best-selling price in each major merchandise line should appeal to the same income-level customer so that the typical customer attracted might become a customer for the merchandise in all departments? Or does management permit department managers to set prices that are unrelated to prices in other departments, a policy that leads to each department having its own clientele which may not patronize other departments? Is there an organized, deliberate attempt to identify the middle-price range of each major commodity sold in the store? For example, if the average man's suit sold costs ninety-five dollars, what price should the average shirt be to appeal to the ninety-five-dollar suit buyer? Is this philosophy of price line coordination uniformly understood by all in the store responsible for making these determinations?

One company that recognizes the importance of this fundamental principle is Sears, Roebuck and Company. It is its apparent policy to offer at least three price points for each major item carried in stock. There is a lower, a middle, and an upper price point, spaced far enough apart to justify the selling features of each differently priced item. As the assortment in a classification expands, the cluster of price points added will be in balance above and below the middle price point.

Customer services.   The degree of services offered customers must depend both on the management's philosophy and on the wishes of the selected customer clientele.

To say "our store should offer the best service possible" is not always the best philosophy. A wide variety of services may be desirable, but each has its cost to the store and often, ultimately, to the customer.

Management should try to offer services that make shopping easy and pleasant within the framework of what is expected of a store of its particular character but should ask itself: What do our customer really want? What do we have space available for, after all the selling departments are planned? For example, how much profit-producing selling space will have to be sacrificed for an auditorium, which may produce little or no revenue? What can we afford?

The importance to the consumer of traditional selling services must be reexamined. Do customers truly desire overattentive, ever-present, eager salespeople in every department? Are there some areas, even of a quality operation, where customers prefer self-selection fixtures, where merchandise is exposed to the touch, and where customers want no help in making their buying decisions? Is the store open at the hours customers would like to shop? If customers prefer to shop in the evening and on Sunday, is it necessary to open the store in the slower early morning hours? Many merchants are currently discarding established practices in regard to store hours to meet the shifting demands of the consumer groups they wish to serve.

Physical appeal of the store.   The appearance and atmosphere of a store usually reflect the concept of management, as management evaluates the reaction of its intended segment, of the consumer market. The *look* and *feel* of a successful store do not just happen—they are the result of planning. For example, a quality department store commonly has a wide, high entrance, wide aisles, a preponderance of closed showcases, with emphasis on display rather than on stock. It has many expensive counters and wall dividers, distinctive color schemes and decor, and a high proportion of merchandise-feature presentations and display fixtures rather than gondola-type shelf units that hold a mass of merchandise. This quality store may use carpeting rather than terrazzo, and unique fixtures rather than a profusion of standard fixtures that are interchangeable.

Multiple locations.   Traditionally, retailers have operated from one location, catering to those customer groups who had ready access to the single store. Convenience goods chains were the major exception. But with the growth of metropolitan trading areas, shopping goods stores in downtown locations have opened branches in new regional shopping centers in the same trading area and even in other cities in other localities.[1] If management is ready for geographic expansion, should all units emulate the main store and be very much alike in merchandise assortments and services, or should they be tailored to the particular consumer communities in which they are established? And should the downtown store remain the dominant "headquarters" store or simply one large unit in the multi-unit complex? And is it conceivable that the downtown store can be eliminated because of all the stores in suburban areas?

The established preconceptions of management tend to determine whether a multi-unit operation should be controlled closely from headquarters or whether a great deal of freedom should be given to branch managers and department heads. When stores started to add branches, the central organization dominated, with branch executives acting as assistants to their counterparts in the main store. But as branches multiplied in number and distance from headquarters, management was forced to move in one of two directions: (1) to insist that the manager of each unit operate his store on a basis of detailed standards set up centrally or (2) to permit each store manager to control his own merchandise assortments and service features. The acute problem has to do with the employment of central buyers to assure complete coverage of wholesale markets and mass buying and yet permit branch department managers to replenish their own assortments geared to the particular local demand. The trend is in the direction of decentralization, but in some cases it has been retarded by the biases of central management and by the difficulty in developing efficient branch personnel.

STORE'S POSITION IN THE COMPETITIVE MARKET

In catering to a distinct consumer market, management must decide what share of this market to capture.[2]

---

[1] Barney's, the large men's wear store in New York City, recently nearly doubled the size of its only store at Seventh Avenue and Seventeenth Street rather than add new units elsewhere.

[2] *Market share* may be expressed as a percentage of total retail sales in a trading area. Such information is available from census data. It is more useful, however, to relate sales to the total sales in the area of the kind of goods the store carries. The federal reserve banks supply for many communities data on the sales of general merchandise, apparel, and furniture, called the *G.A.F.* This may be used to determine the merchant's share. Department stores in many localities also have data made available to them on total department store sales which are used to determine market share. Both percentages are important: A department store may be holding its own relative to other department stores but may be dropping in its share of the G.A.F. This indicates that customers are turning to other types of stores to satisfy their demand for the lines carried by department stores.

In its class—whether a traditional department store, a specialty store, a discount house, or a supermarket—should the store seek to maintain or enhance its position if it is already the dominant, number-one store? If it is second or third, should it seek to overtake the dominant store? What change in its basic character would have to be effected to accomplish this? Or should it choose to be dominant or superior only in a selected number of merchandise areas for which it is noted? Many stores that were once leaders in their community have slipped to third or fourth position. Their planning was poor, their direction obscure, they failed to adjust adequately to shifting trends and, as a result, lost their niche in the midst of thriving markets. The retailing graveyard is full of once great names.

Competitive pricing policy. Some managements take an aggressive view toward pricing, insisting that all retail prices be as low or even lower than those of competitors. But competition is variously defined. Does it include all stores in the trading area that handle similar goods or simply a handful of the store's major competitors? Does it include the special sale prices of competitors or only their regular prices? And how effective is the store's stated policy of comparison shopping?

Many merchants, while zealous to meet direct competition, deliberately stock as much exclusive merchandise as they can and meet competition only on identical items. Thus it may be possible to achieve a high markup on the average and still maintain a competitive price policy.

In planning ahead, markdown practices also need careful review. Are buyers and department managers being restrained from moving slow-selling goods by rigid markdown budgets? Are reasons for markdowns being carefully analyzed and are organized efforts being made to minimize the causes of markdowns?[3]

ASSORTMENT OF MERCHANDISE AND SERVICES

Lines of merchandise. The list of merchandise lines or departments can no longer remain static, since customer demand is undergoing change. For example, although most department stores carry the traditional lines in apparel and accessories, they vary a great deal in the "hard lines" they carry. Some eliminate furniture, major appliances, home repair products such as paint, hardware, and electrical supplies. Even in clothing and accessory lines, millinery, fine jewelry, work clothing, and Boy Scout attire may be omitted. On the

[3] Pricing policies are so important that Part II of this text is largely devoted to them.

other hand, specialized merchandise lines of growing importance may be expanded into separate shops, such as a shop for goods with a common geographic origin or for goods made of a particular material, such as leather. With the increase in leisure time available to consumers, stores are giving more attention to lines that contribute to leisure activities. One great department store chain's policy is to specialize in three categories of merchandise and service: apparel, leisure, and home.

The personal standards of the merchant often limit the lines he will permit his store to carry. Some merchants will not stock liquor or cigarettes even though their customers would buy them readily. In the past, some merchants have even refused to sell playing cards, and today many will not carry pornographic literature, even in localities where public authorities exercise no police power.

Many retail managements are committed to selling only merchandise, but the trend is in the direction of adding departments engaged primarily in selling services at a profit. Customers today are spending an increasing proportion of their income for services of many kinds and relatively less for goods. Accordingly, astute merchants are revising the concept of their task to include the distribution of both merchandise and services to the ultimate consumer. Services that are being successfully sold in retail stores include car rentals, equipment leasing, clothing rentals, home repair services, beauty shops, travel and insurance agencies, restaurant service, and recreational and educational facilities. On the other hand, if any of these services cannot be offered profitably, they may be avoided.

Breadth versus depth. Within the merchandise lines a store elects to carry, it must decide whether to have a wide variety to satisfy most shades of demand or whether to concentrate on the best sellers in each line in depth, those that satisfy the requirements of the majority of its clientele. To stress breadth may lead to a sacrifice in depth with loss of sales; to stress depth may sacrifice breadth with loss of sales to customers who feel that stock assortments are inadequate. Management must decide on the emphasis that seems best to meet the requirements of the intended clientele. A key determinant in this decision is often the amount of space available for that category of merchandise.

Promotional merchandise. Many customers today respond favorably to *specials*. Even though many merchants are convinced that the maintenance of a deep stock of basic items for which there is a recurring demand is the key to good merchandising, promotional merchandise may make the difference between an exciting and a drab store. Promotional merchandise includes goods that have a strong fashion appeal at the moment, opulent merchandise that appeals to the sophisticated, affluent customer, and goods in popular demand made available at bargain prices. Leading stores in many cities are successfully promoting expensive imports, such as Belgian chandeliers, gilt French sofas, and one-of-a-kind toys.[4] *Limited editions,* in such products as porcelain figures, tufted wall hangings, towels in exotic designs, scarves, and jewelry, are proving to have great drawing power even though they do not sell in large quantities. If management has a sense of showmanship, it may develop an atmosphere of merchandise extravaganza that acts like a magnet for a large portion of the buying public. Promotional emphasis centered on bargains may be developed in the same store that stresses opulence.

Questions such as the following should be asked if management decides to develop a promotional store: Is there an attempt to control actively the proportion of promotional merchandise to the total assortment (i.e., through a seasonal unit assortment plan)? Are certain items in the assortment designated as basic items which will be continuously in stock to insure a day-to-day rightness? Is there a staple stock unit control system that is well defined, scheduled, and supervised? Can purchase orders be processed for these selected items regardless of open-to-buy conditions in the total department?

If there is a heavy emphasis on promotions, there must also be a well-supervised procedure to dispose rapidly of unsold promotional merchandise. Is the initial markup on these promotions high enough to offset the markdowns necessary to liquidate those remainders?

Emphasis on new merchandise.   Management may be conservative in its attitude toward new merchandise, preferring to stock and promote established best sellers, but customers are increasingly responding to new merchandise. Merchants dedicated to fashion merchandise welcome change and new merchandise appearing on the market, often introducing it experimentally before it has become an accepted fashion. The store may employ a fashion director for home furnishings, one for apparel, and perhaps a teen coordinator as well. There may be frequent fashion shows in the store and out, model rooms in the store and in new housing developments, frequent storewide fashion meetings, and fashion bulletins. Is there a deliberate program to emphasize fashion merchandise in nonapparel depart-

---

[4] While some managements are committed to domestic merchandise, an increasing number are recognizing the promotional value of foreign goods and their above-average markup. In fact, some department stores realize nearly 10 percent of their volume from such merchandise.

ments (housewares for example), to buy it in depth, display it, and present it with fashion flair? Is merchandise in home furnishings departments presented by color and style, recognizing these primary shopping factors in many customers' minds? Does management continually police opportunistic purchases and new items to insure that they do not conflict with the desired level of goods taste?

RELATIONSHIP WITH THE MERCHANDISE SOURCE

Many merchants procure their merchandise requirements from any reliable manufacturer or wholesaler who carries merchandise suitable to their consumer clientele and who sells at prices that make an adequate markup possible. But some retailers deliberately favor small manufacturers who are flexible in meeting the specific requirements of each store. In such organizations as Sears, many of the once small resources have grown large with the expansion of the retail establishment with which they have been associated for years.

Some merchants select from the assortments presented to them by vendors with preference for national brands for which the manufacturers have already created a demand. But many retailers today are tending to cooperate with key resources to develop special items, often to be sold under a store's private brand. The specifications for such items are jointly developed by the vendor and the store buyer who may be assisted by laboratory technicians. Frequently, the store makes monetary advances to manufacturers to finance the production process.

In general, retailers have avoided owning and/or controlling manufacturing operations. They treasure the freedom of choice in the marketplace. Among the items sometimes produced are household drug products and some outer apparel. Some retailers have their own laboratories for household drugs, and others operate custom-made workrooms. Some companies have both manufacturing and retailing subsidiaries, with the manufacturing units providing a considerable portion of the retail requirements of their affiliates. This integrated approach to retail distribution tends to gear production closely to customer demand and to reduce the cost of negotiation between store buyer and resource.

Leasing. While most store organizations own and merchandise all the lines of goods they elect to carry, a great deal of expansion has taken place where management has been willing to lease certain lines to outside owners and operators. Recently, for example, Kresge expanded its assortments in its fast-growing K-mart stores by leasing to others lines in which management was not expert, such as foods, footwear, and fashion accessories. However, such decisions are often temporary, with management taking over the merchandising of these lines as relatively short leasing arrangements run out.

ATTITUDE TOWARD CONSUMERISM AND COMMUNITY INVOLVEMENT

Consumerism. An important aspect of today's rapid change —public dissatisfaction with past policies and practices—is consumerism. This is the demand by consumer groups for better protection in the marketplace and for more complete information on which to base buying decisions. Some retail managements see this as a passing phase and see no need to change current practices that affect the consumer. But to an increasing degree, merchants are taking consumerism seriously, recognizing that the new consumer is shrewd, articulate, informed, and young in spirit, with high expectations but with little tolerance for shoddy merchandise, unsatisfactory service, and misleading advertising claims. The consumer is entranced with the merchandise wonders that technology has wrought but resents the failure of products to perform adequately in use and the disinterested service on the part of store personnel, is keenly aware of what inflation is doing to buying power, and is even ready to participate in a consumer boycott if prices seem too high.

Accordingly, enlightened managements give more than lip service to the slogan, "To serve the public to its complete satisfaction." They recognize the need to develop rigid merchandise specifications, to test products, to simplify merchandise warranties, to improve repair service, to prepare more informative and forthright advertisements, and to develop among all employees an attitude of personal commitment to satisfy every customer.

Involvement in social and economic community problems. Does management accept the thesis that it must contribute to resolving the problems of the community or does it limit its responsibility to serving its customers with merchandise? Until recently, most retail managements took the narrow view, fearing that involvement might antagonize certain customer groups and would dissipate their own energies. But changes for the worse, particularly in the great urban centers that are the strongholds of retailing, are altering this belief. Among the major problems are the pollution of land, water, and air; lack of adequate housing, job opportunities, and educational facilities for disadvantaged minority groups; unreliable and poorly maintained mass transportation services; militant social unrest; and crime in the streets.

More and more, enlightened business leaders recognize the urgency to cooperate with public authorities in solving these problems. They realize that urban life, as we now know it, may cease to exist, leaving instead a blighted environment unhealthy for human life, as well as for business.

Planning, therefore, may include a resolution to employ and train a larger proportion of the minority groups, particularly the underprivileged. Social involvement also requires that executives join civic and action committees engaged in improving the local community. A modest portion of the store's expense budget may be allocated to activities that do not immediately contribute to sales and profits but do contribute to a healthier economic and social environment for the future.

STORE IMAGE TO BE DEVELOPED

As management attempts to set an exact profile of the kind of store it now operates, the kind of store it plans for the future, and its place in the community, it must give careful attention to the store's image as seen by the major groups of customers it attempts to serve. Customers are likely to view the store very differently from the way store management views itself. What is important in planning is to make changes that will improve the customer's image of the store rather than satisfy the ego of management.

By means of recognized research techniques, various segments of the buying community should be surveyed in regard to their attitude toward the store's merchandise, prices, services, and advertising and other promotional devices. A key question to ask is whether customers feel that the store is truly dedicated to acting as a purchasing agent for them or is it primarily interested in its own immediate welfare.

SPECIFIC OBJECTIVES OF THE COMPANY

The objectives of a company grow out of its philosophies of store management and operation and should be expressed in concrete terms, commonly as figure goals.

SALES PLAN

Every facet of a retail business is planned in relation to sales. But to utilize *only* the sales history of a particular store in predicting future sales can be extremely dangerous. For example, for a store with a recent historical growth of 5 percent a year, it may be incorrect to plan the same 5 percent growth rate in future years because local competitors' sales are increasing at a 15 percent rate. If this is so, the leading store in the community may quickly find itself in second or third place.

Therefore, sales planning should be approached from the point of view of *potential*—How much *should* our sales be and what should be our market share? These may require professional research.[5]

PROFIT OBJECTIVES

A store's objectives are not limited to sales; they include goals for markup, markdown, gross margin, operating expense, and resultant profit. A long-range plan is often used to point up deficiencies in factors affecting margins and expenses. Management must be determined to resolve these deficiencies and thus improve margin and profit. The adequacy of the profit projected should be determined by relating it not only to sales but also to the investment in the business and especially to the merchandise investment and to space occupied.[6]

In short, plans should include a spread sheet that predicts a complete operating statement for each of the years covered.

All managements are not equally dedicated to the profit motive. As already mentioned, the time-honored goal of profit for the stockholders is being subjected to careful scrutiny.

STOCKTURN OBJECTIVES

Does management believe in, and effectively communicate to subordinates, the profound effect that stockturn has on profit? Does it set up this factor as a standard of performance for its managers, periodically checked and reported? If there are merchandise programs to which the store is committed (i.e., private brands, imports, staple stocks), which may serve to reduce stockturn, is there a counteracting determination to identify slow-selling stocks and to liquidate them expeditiously? Are the advantages of this policy emphasized (i.e., fresh stocks, continuous fashion flow, ever-present open-to-buy, ability to react quickly to customer preferences, lower interest charges, and less investment)?

---

[5] One such approach is presented in chapter 15 in connection with sales planning for a new branch.

[6] This is discussed fully in chapter 13.

DEPARTMENTAL GOALS

Sales, profit, and stockturn goals should not be limited to the store as a whole or to the business as a whole. Each department must receive individual attention.

Management should adopt the policy of seasonally or annually reviewing each department's sales and profit performance for the purpose of selecting certain departments for intensification programs. The selection should be based on the "big payoff" of departments that are performing grossly under their potential. A careful analysis of such neglected departments should lead to management's approval of specific needs which may include changes in merchandise investment, advertising, floor space, and sales force coverage and supervision, along with a built-in follow-up procedure to report results to management.

PRODUCTIVITY GOALS

Perhaps the major task of management is to utilize scarce resources in such a way as to insure the healthy growth of the company with an increase in profitability. Three major resources are merchandise, space, and people. Management should set goals as to the productivity to be achieved year by year in each of these areas, such as gross margin per dollar of merchandise cost investment and gross margin per square foot of selling space.

OUTSIDE FACTORS LIMITING OBJECTIVES

The setting of specific objectives depends to a considerable degree upon factors beyond the control of the store. Some of these are outlined below.

GENERAL BUSINESS OUTLOOK

What are the prospects for the national economy? What is the current stage of the business cycle and what may it be during the next five or ten years? What effect might the following have: the political party in power, war, defense spending, continued inflation, and the labor market? As will be indicated, many such developments cannot be foreseen; nevertheless, probabilities have to be weighed.

LOCAL ECONOMIC CONDITIONS

Changes in size and type of population, land availability, deterioration of the downtown area, unemployment rates, attraction of new industries, income distribution and cost of living—these are all factors to consider in planning.

It is especially important to obtain available information from city, state, and federal authorities concerning projected new highways and mass transit systems. There may also be city programs and other projected renovation projects that may bring about profound changes in residential and business areas, including the speed and convenience of travel from one part of the trading area to another.

COMPETITION

A survey should include a listing of all competing stores by size, location, and estimated volume as well as a projection of sales growth, physical expansion, and proliferation. This can then serve to indicate whether or not the area is "overstored" in relation to future sales potential in the trading area. This realistic approach should obviously be taken when considering any expansion.

UNFORESEEABLE FACTORS

It should be observed that many of the outside factors that determine sales are not only uncontrollable but also unforeseeable. Wars here and abroad, strikes, earthquakes and fires, shifts in government policy, and new decisions of major competitors—all have the potential to upset calculations based on the projection of trends and current economic data. Accordingly, intuition and the willingness to assume a calculated risk must play an important part in planning ahead.

IMPLEMENTING THE OBJECTIVES

With a clear picture of the store character that management wishes to express and of its particular objectives, limited by the changes in the environment, the planner is ready to determine the requirements for future operation.

NEW STORE AND FACILITIES

Most retail industry expansion in recent years has involved the opening of additional stores by established retailing firms. Its implication for the future of most companies is obvious. It is one of the key requirements in today's planning. In presenting a plan for building future stores, the following facts should be determined:

1. *Location*—may be a general area or a pinpointed site
2. *Sales projections* (for the unit or units planned)
3. *Size of store*—should include both gross space and estimate of net selling space
4. *Sales per square foot*—productivity figure should be planned to meet the standards set by the company
5. *Required investment*—may include the cost of land, building, fixtures, and merchandise
6. *Return on investment*—projection of the operating profit on estimated sales of a unit compared to the investment required

Expansion or renovation of existing units should be subjected to the same standards of return on investment. However, certain valuable historical data can be used to justify the need, such as sales and sales per square foot.

Service facilities may also be required for increased capacity and/or efficiency which may lead to expense savings.

The expense savings and benefits must be compared to the investment cost and to their ultimate effect on total company profit.

ORGANIZATION STRUCTURE

To achieve the expansion planned, management must provide specific answers to the following questions:

Is there a need for centralization (example: all receiving and marking functions)?

Is there a need for decentralization (example: local buyers for remote regions)?

Who assumes replenishment responsibility? (Should this remain in central control?)

To whom do store managers report?

Is there a need for an executive in charge of all branch stores in the organization?

What is the authority of the central buyer over the department manager in the store?

Who is responsible for the merchandising and operation of the downtown store?

Does the problem of sales supervision require a type of store executive in the branch different from the one in the main store?

What are the qualifications for buyers?

How are these changing?

Is there a pressing need for a mangement development director in the organization of the personnel division?

Is the store large enough to support a staff for research and comparative shopping?

PEOPLE

A plan should be introduced that will enhance the quality level of merchandising personnel by the application of the newer management development techniques.

The plan might include giving department managers both responsibility and authority to make decisions that have local implications primarily, so that only major decisions are passed up to the higher administrative levels. It should include the supervisory technique known as *management by objective* whereby each supervisor sets his own goals for the period ahead; once these are approved, he is rated on his success in reaching his own objectives. Management should also train each supervisor to realize that every store employee has personal goals and a self-image quite different from company goals and the store image that management wishes to create. To try to reconcile the two sets of goals is one of the central problems of today's management.

The personnel plan also requires management development programs to broaden the interests and extend the horizons of managers. These are aimed at developing the conceptual skills that will permit managers to see themselves and their jobs in the broadest perspective of human interaction within a system or field of activity.

Management must also take an inventory of its present personnel and future requirements by answering such questions as the following:

Is there an inventory of present merchandising executives (This should list all executives, summarizing management's evaluation of them and their possible growth.)

Is there a prediction of future growth patterns for all key executives?

Is there a determination of projected new merchandising posts to be filled?

Is there a determination of projected needs that cannot presently be filled from within the organization?

PROJECTED NEED FOR BUYERS (1970–75)

- What is the total number in present organization?   50
- What is the number required to replace attrition, based on historical data?   15
- Estimate needs for "growth splits."   5
- New buyers required   20
- Determine how many openings can be filled from within.   18
- Derive balance that must be recruited from the outside.   2

QUESTIONS FOR DISCUSSION

1. What are the differences between short-range and long-range planning?
2. Is the trend in the direction of single- or multi-line stores? Why?
3. Are department and departmentized specialty stores faced with an excellent opportunity to increase their sales of services as distinct from their sales of merchandise? Why?
4. Under what conditions should the units of a multi-unit operation be standardized?
5. Is a downtown main store essential for a branch store system? Explain.
6. What are the relative advantages of centralized versus decentralized control of inventories in multi-unit operations?
7. For a particular store of your choice, suggest the desirable ratio of promotional merchandise to total inventory. Defend your suggested ratio.
8. Can a store be successful with a wide and deep assortment of staple merchandise but with no fashion or novelty emphasis? Explain.
9. Under what conditions is a retail organization wise to (1) associate itself with well-known national brands, thus depending for patronage partly on the reputation engendered by these brands, or (2) develop and promote its own private brands?
10. (a) Are most retailers right in not integrating their sphere of activity to include manufacturing?
    (b) Under what conditions is the integration of manufacturing and retailing likely to be successful?
11. Is management's image of its own store likely to differ materially from the customers' image of the store? Discuss.
12. What are the chief demands of modern consumerism to which

merchants should give serious attention? Suggest a program to meet these demands.

13. In evaluating job opportunities in different stores, do young people give much weight to the degree of each store's involvement in social action? Discuss.

14. What are the major types of figure goals that management should set for itself?

15. Are outside factors such as economic conditions and competition more important in determining the success of a store than internal factors over which management has control? Explain.

16. In what respects is the planning of personnel requirements a merchandising activity?

17. Are any important merchandising "philosophies"—beliefs and attitudes of management—omitted in this chapter? Explain.

3

ELEMENTS
IN
PROFIT

PROFIT DETERMINATION

Profit may be defined as a gain a business enterprise realizes over a period of time, measured in terms of money. The gain realized from trading operations alone, that is, from buying and selling goods, is called *operating profit*.[1] This is the difference between the sales on the one hand and the *cost of merchandise sold* and the *expenses* of store or department operation on the other. Operating profit is distinguished from *net profit* (also called *net gain*) in that the latter figure is the sum of operating profit and *net other income* (also called *financial income*). This is the income from sources not directly related to merchandising and operating the store, such as interest and dividends on outside investments less interest paid on borrowed funds.

The net profit is the result of the interplay of four basic factors: (1) sales volume, (2) cost of merchandise sold, (3) expense of doing business, and (4) other income (see following table).

[1] Departmental profit and loss statements normally end with *operating profit* or *loss*, with *other income* reserved for the store as a whole. Operating profit is sometimes called *trading profit*, or *merchandising profit*, and net profit is also called *net gain*.

			Percentage of net sales[a]
(1)	Net sales	$100,000	100
(2)	Cost of merchandise sold	63,000	63
	Gross margin	$37,000	37
(3)	Operating expenses	30,000	30
	Operating profit[1]	7,000	7
(4)	Net other income	1,000	1
	Net profit	8,000	8

[a] See figure 3.1 for a graphic portrayal of these relations.

PERCENTAGE COMPARISONS

Net sales, as the major source of income, are logically the basis upon which most other figure facts are expressed. Thus, if sales are $100,000 and expenses $30,000, the expense percentage is 30 percent. For comparison purposes, this ratio is even more significant than the dollar figures themselves. It allows a comparison of expenses with those of other stores doing a greater or smaller volume, and it

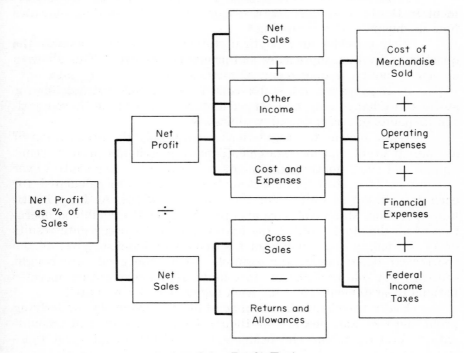

FIGURE 3.1 Profit Factors

allows a comparison with former expenses in the same store. The important fact for next year's planning is not that expenses were $30,000 but that they were 30 percent of sales. If sales next year are $120,000, there would be no occasion to try to hold expenses at $30,000, but there would be cause for concern if they exceed 30 percent of $120,000, or $36,000.

Again, the expense percentage allows a comparison with the gross margin obtained. Obviously the gross margin rate obtained month by month must average more than the anticipated expense rate if the store is to make a profit. Goods that must, over the year, produce a dollar margin of at least $30,000 are not all bought at once. The pricing of goods must be guided by the minimum rate of margin required to cover expenses and costs rather than by the dollar margin needed in the aggregate.

THE PROFIT AND LOSS STATEMENT

A profit and loss statement has it least three specific advantages for the merchant.

1. It allows an accurate determination of whether his investment in the business has increased or decreased and thus indicates how the business is progressing.

2. It provides an analytical statement that helps answer the question, Why were more sales and profits not realized? This allows a change in policy, management, or methods before it is too late.

3. If prepared in a standardized way, it makes it possible for stores to exchange data and for each store to determine by comparison its points of strength and weakness.

While income tax regulations require only the preparation of an annual profit and loss statement, many merchants prepare semiannual and even monthly statements to provide a closer control over operations. If a store is departmentized, profits are calculated for each department as well as for the store as a whole. As for a multiunit operation, statements are also prepared for the combined operation of all the store units in the group and for the aggregate results of all the selling departments of a specific merchandise type: all the sportswear departments, for example, where the goods are bought centrally but sold in different store units. If the corporation operates nationally, statements covering each region are also prepared.

Every merchant should understand the principles underlying profit and loss statements, even though he may hire trained accountants to prepare them. The businessman's ability to interpret these statements and to act on them wisely is a basis for successful merchandise management.

SALES

Table 3.1 elaborates on the four basic profit elements and warrants detailed analysis.[2]

Gross sales are normally recorded at the prices actually charged customers or employees for their purchases, even when a discount is granted. They consist of both merchandise sales and sales of services that are intended to yield a profit and not simply as an accommodation to customers.

TABLE 3.1   Operating Statement

Sales		Percentage
Gross sales	$110,000	
Less returns and allowances	10,000	9.09
Net sales	$100,000	100.00
Cost of Sales		
Inventory—first of period	20,000	
Gross purchases (billed cost) $73,000		
Less returns and allowances (vendor) 4,000		
Net purchases *costomer returns*	69,000	
Transportation charges	1,000	
Total merchandise handled	$90,000	
Inventory—end of period at cost or market[a]	25,000	
Gross cost of merchandise sold	65,000	65.0
Cash discounts earned	3,000	3.0
Net cost of merchandise sold	62,000	62.0
Net alteration and workroom costs	1,000	1.0
Total merchandise costs	$63,000	63.0
Margin and Expenses		
Gross margin ($100,000–$63,000)	$37,000	37.0
Operating expenses	30,000	30.0
Operating profit	$7,000	7.0
Other Income[b]		
Miscellaneous other income 2,000		
Deductions from other income 1,000	1,000	1.0
Net profit before federal income tax[c]	$8,000	8.0

[a] Under the retail method, this figure is obtained departmentally from the retail inventory figure by complement of markup, as explained in chapter 11.
[b] "Other income" would not appear in departmental statements. It is included here so that both types of statement may be explained with one example.
[c] Net profit after federal income tax is also computed.

[2] Table 3.1 and the accompanying description are based on the recommendations appearing in the *Retail Accounting Manual* of the Controllers' Congress of the National Retail Merchants Association. While not accepted as standard by all retailing groups, they are the best available for stores handling general merchandise.

RETURNS AND ALLOWANCES

The net sales figure in table 3.1 ($100,000) is derived by subtracting returns and allowances from the gross sales of a period.

Returns from customers represent cancellations of sales. Merchandise that has previously been credited to gross sales is returned to stock, and the customer gets her money back or it is credited to her account. If the resale price of the goods returned is less than the original sales price, the difference is handled as a markdown (see chapter 8).

If a customer exchanges merchandise for goods of different value, the goods brought back may be treated as a return and the new goods as a new addition to gross sales. Even exchanges, however, in which a customer returns one article for another of the same value, are not usually included in either gross sales or returns.

Some stores treat occasional trade-ins in the same way as returns from customers. Thus, if a customer buys a refrigerator for $300 and is allowed $50 on her old refrigerator, gross sales are recorded as $300 and returns as $50. If the trade-in cannot be resold for $50, a markdown is taken to the actual resale price, just as any other return may require a reduction in price before sale. In other stores where trade-ins are frequent, they are sometimes handled like merchandise purchases.

In addition to returns, allowances to customers must be deducted from gross sales to find net sales. An allowance represents a reduction in price after the sale has taken place. For example, a customer may have bought for $10 a blouse that faded. She may complain to the store and be granted a cash refund or a credit of $4. This is the amount of the allowance. Where a perpetual dollar inventory is kept, it is necessary to take a markdown whenever an allowance is granted a customer in order to keep the stock records correct. Allowances, then, usually require two entries: (1) subtraction from gross sales and (2) inclusion in the markdown record.[3]

The returns and allowance percentage.   Although the net sales figure is the usual basis for comparisons, returns from customers and allowances to customers are regularly expressed as a percentage of gross sales rather than net sales. Thus, if gross sales are $110,000 and returns plus allowances are $10,000, the resultant net sales are $100,000, and the returns and allowance percentage is 9.09 percent rather than 10 percent. This is the logical comparison, since $10,000

---

[3] Without the markdown, the subtraction of net sales from the total retail purchases to date (including beginning inventory) would yield a figure of retail stock on hand in excess of actual.

worth returned is not a part of the $100,000 worth retained by customers but rather of the gross sales of $110,000, the amount originally purchased.

THE COST OF SALES

As table 3.1 reveals, total merchandise costs, which àre the cost equivalent of sales, are calculated by adding net cost purchases (including transportation costs) to opening inventory and subtracting the closing inventory.

PURCHASES AT BILLED COST

Billed cost, as used above, represents invoice cost less trade and quantity discounts.[4] For example, goods may be bought at a list price of $1,000 with a trade discount of 40 percent and a cash discount of 2 percent. The goods should be charged in as purchases at a "billed cost" of $600.

The usual practice is to disregard cash discounts in accumulating purchase and inventory figures and to take credit for them as an adjustment downward of the "cost of merchandise sold."

If the P and L statement is for a department or a store unit within a chain, transfers in from other units of the organization are included as purchases, and transfers out as returns for the sending unit and as purchases for the receiving unit.

Merchandise repossessed from customers at depreciated cost is also properly included in purchases. If this figure is less than the amount the customer owes, the difference is a bad-debt expense.

Returns to vendors and allowances from vendors are subtracted to get net purchases.

Net Purchases

TRANSPORTATION CHARGES

Transportation charges, including insurance in transit, are added to the net cost purchase figure because the true cost of merchandise, it is generally agreed, is the cost at the store, not the cost at the place of origin. All express, freight, cartage, and parcel-post charges on incoming merchandise paid for by the store rather than by the shipper are added to the net purchase figure. Although the

[4] Consignment purchases are commonly treated as regular purchases even though the store has the right of return.

transportation charges on each shipment may be recorded as a purchase along with the merchandise amount, a more common practice is to accumulate charges each week or month on a separate record and to add this amount to net purchases of this weekly or monthly period.

MERCHANDISE INVENTORY

The merchandise inventory figure includes the value of goods on hand at a specified inventory date. The goods do not have to be in stock, however. They may be in one of various nonselling departments of the store (for inspection, for example), in the hands of the manufacturer (for repair), or even in the hands of the customer on approval. It follows that goods belonging to customers but in the store for repair or inspection are not a part of the inventory. Goods on hand belonging to the manufacturer but purchased on consignment are to be treated as a part of the inventory. Supplies on hand to be consumed in running the business are excluded.

Cost or market valuation.   The principle of inventory valuation that is generally followed by mercantile enterprises is known as "cost or market, whichever is lower."[5] This means that whenever a stock on hand is worth as much or more today than the amount paid for it, it is valued at the amount it cost the store; whenever it is worth less today then the amount paid for it, it is valued at today's lower price—this is the current price for identical goods in the wholesale market. Since stocks tend to depreciate in value between the time they are bought and the time they are sold, inventories are often evaluated at less than they originally cost the merchant.

The supporting rationale for the "cost or market" principle is that competition usually prevents selling goods at the originally intended retail price whenever the market cost for identical goods has fallen. Thus, the goods on hand are no longer worth what was paid for them. On the other hand, when the replacement (market) price for a present inventory is likely to be at a higher cost price, the merchandiser does not as a matter of course raise his retail prices. The forces of competition tend to prevent prices from being adjusted upward until the higher price is actually paid for replacement. Thus, a higher market price does not assure a larger profit on present stocks.

There are two ways to determine the cost or market value of

[5] See chapter 11 for other methods of inventory valuation.

an inventory: the cost method and the retail method. Under the first, the inventory is counted at billed cost and depreciation is estimated. Under the second, the goods are counted at current retail prices and reduced to "cost or market" by applying a markup percentage.[6]

GROSS COST OF MERCHANDISE SOLD

The total merchandise handled at cost (TMH) consisting of opening inventory, net purchases, and transportation costs less the cost or market of the closing inventory is called the *gross cost of merchandise sold*. Again refer to table 3.1 for an example.

CASH DISCOUNTS

In most stores, one or two adjustments have to be made in the value of the cost of goods sold before it is subtracted from net sales to obtain gross margin. One has to do with cash discounts on purchases and the other with workroom and alteration costs.

If purchases are charged in at billed rather than at actual cost, as is usually the case, and if no effort is made to remove cash discounts in evaluating the cost price of the inventory, it should be clear that the cost of merchandise sold is somewhat overstated and that it should be reduced by the amount of cash discounts earned on purchases during the period. In our example, the TMH is $90,000, the closing inventory $25,000, and the cost of merchandise sold $65,000. Since cash discounts have not been deducted from either the $90,000 or the $25,000, it is obvious that the cost of goods sold is also overstated. Our example shows the discounts earned to be $3,000.[7] By subtraction, the *net cost of merchandise sold* becomes $62,000.

ALTERATION AND WORKROOM COSTS

A second adjustment in the cost of goods sold figure is to account for "alteration and workroom costs."[8] This is the cost of operating merchandise service workrooms, maintained for the purpose of completing the sale of merchandise already retailed.

---

[6] These methods are discussed in detail in chapters 9 and 11.

[7] *Anticipation on purchases* and the *loading of invoices* are discussed in the companion book, Management of Retail Buying.

[8] Occasionally certain other merchandise costs are included along with workroom costs, such as the cost of special containers and of repairing and altering goods still in stock.

The amount must include materials, supplies, labor, and all expenses in which service departments directly participate. The net cost of these departments, after any income received from customers has been deducted, should obviously be borne by the regular selling departments they serve. Examples of areas that are generally operated as service workrooms are the women's apparel alteration department, men's busheling room, and corset, carpet, silver engraving, furniture polishing, and drapery workrooms. These areas are not regular selling departments making sales to customers and attempting to make a profit. They may be called subsidiary departments in that they exist primarily to assist regular departments to complete sales by fitting the merchandise to the needs of customers. The women's alteration room services the women's ready-to-wear departments, the busheling room the men's wear departments, the corset workroom the corset department, and so forth.

Whether alteration costs should be treated as a part of the operating expenses of the store and departments involved or as an addition to the cost of merchandise sold is debatable. The recommended procedure is to treat them as additions to merchandise cost because they provide "form utility," which is not true of store-operating expenses that provide place and time utility.

Alteration costs are more akin to manufacturing costs than to the distribution expenses of a store. However, many types of retail stores commonly include alteration costs in expenses in the interest of simplicity.

These costs might have been included along with purchases, but since they take place after merchandise has been put into stock and retailed and since they apply to goods that have been sold and not to all purchases, it has been found desirable to add them to the cost of merchandise sold. The new figure is called total merchandise costs (see table 3.1). When this is subtracted from net sales, the difference is *gross margin*.

GROSS MARGIN AND EXPENSES

GROSS MARGIN

Gross margin, sometimes called *gross merchandise margin*, is simply the difference between net sales and total merchandise costs. Ordinarily it calls for no adjustment (but may in the case of installment sales). It represents what is available for operating expenses and profit.

It may be distinguished from *maintained markup*, which is the difference between the net sales and the gross cost of merchandise sold—in our example, $100,000 less $65,000, or $35,000.

The relation between the maintained markup and the gross margin may be illustrated as follows, using the same figures:

Net sales	$100,000
Gross cost of merchandise sold	65,000
Maintained markup	$35,000
Cash discounts earned (add)	3,000
Alteration and workroom costs (subtract)	1,000
Gross margin	$37,000

The gross margin is generally larger than the maintained markup because cash discounts ordinarily exceed alteration costs. The maintained markup is a useful analytical device (see chapter 4).

Gross margin is commonly called *gross profit*, a term that is misleading. Frequently, all of the margin is required to pay expenses and there is no profit and perhaps a loss. Margin is simply what is left after costs have been deducted but before operating expenses have been considered. The name given to this difference should not suggest that most of it is profit.

OPERATING EXPENSES

Natural divisions. The expenses of operating a business may be classified for purposes of analysis in a great many different ways. The most common classification is by natural division, that is, by the nature of the services that are being purchased. Examples are payroll, advertising, rentals, and supplies. Most of the expenses under these headings represent cash outlays, but some represent charges made against current operations even though no cash outlay is made at the time. These include not only debts incurred but also depreciation on fixed assets and on accounts receivable (bad debts).

Owner's salary. In a corporation, each of the owners engaged actively in the business draws a salary, which appears in the expense payroll figure; but the owner-manager of an unincorporated store generally treats all his earnings as profits. His profit is thus both a salary for his personal efforts as manager and a reward for the risk and responsibility he assumes in bringing together capital, labor, and managerial skill.

To separate these two sources of profit, an independent merchant may impute his salary. He may estimate what he can earn by working for another merchant in a similar capacity and include this amount in expenses. He does this to determine whether the business is paying him more than a reasonable salary for his managerial services and to compare the expenses of the proprietorship fairly with those of corporations in which owners engaged actively in the business do draw salaries. The amount charged as expense must be included in the merchant's other income because he must pay taxes on total earnings. The government is not interested in distinguishing between a merchant's wages and his purely business profits.

If all of the earnings of a merchant exactly equaled his wages, he would show no operating profit. If the outlook were for no improvement in circumstances, he might be wise to sell his store and accept employment elsewhere. Thus, he would eliminate the risks of being in business for himself without curtailing his income. It is true, of course, that by nature many merchants prefer to be their own bosses, even though they could earn as much or more by working for someone else.

Interest paid.   Interest paid on borrowed funds should not be included in operating expense. It should be treated as a financial expense deducted from "other income" of the store as a whole. Years ago, stores generally treated it as an operating expense but found that this practice distorted interstore comparisons.

Expense centers.   In large stores, expenses are classified by functional divisions, called *expense centers*, as well as by natural divisions. Pertinent natural divisions are set up under each expense center. An expense center is a grouping of the expenses for performing a measurable function. For example, *accounts receivable* is typically set up as an expense center and charged with the following natural divisions of expense: payroll, supplies, services purchased (collection agency), unclassified, communications, postage and phone, and equipment costs. The function of this center is measured in terms of the number of credit sale transactions handled, and the productivity of the center may be expressed in terms of the number of such transactions handled by one worker in one hour.

OTHER INCOME AND NET GAIN

The *operating profit*, found by deducting all operating expenses from gross margin, is the final figure in departmental and divisional analysis but is not the final net profit or net gain upon which a store must pay income taxes.

Financial *income* largely from investments and the sale of capital assets and financial *outgo*, such as interest on borrowed funds, have to be brought into the picture.

The sum of the operating profits for all selling units combined plus the net other income for the operation as a whole, or less the net financial loss, gives the final *net profit*, or *net gain*, which becomes the basis for figuring income tax liability.

It should be observed that net gain is frequently less than operating profit because interest paid on borrowed capital can readily exceed interest and dividends received and the other minor sources of other income.

The student of merchandising is frequently at a loss to understand why so much emphasis is placed upon an exact and rigid arrangement of the many factors entering into the operating statement. He may correctly observe that any one of the many arrangements will yield the same final net-profit figure. In fact, since the computations involve addition and subtraction primarily, it is possible to put all the pluses in one column and all the minuses in another and draw off the correct profit result.

But a study of the figures involves more than an attempt to obtain the correct profit answer. A standard arrangement provides an analytical picture of results that makes possible a determination of points of strength and weakness and comparisons with other stores. Again, profit finding involves much more than adding and subtracting figures. A complete collection of all the pertinent data is essential, and the inventory must be evaluated to reflect market value when it is less than cost.

ANALYZING PROFIT

The dollar-operating profit realized from trading operations is, as we have seen, the result of sales, cost of sales, and expense relationships, but its adequacy cannot be determined from its dollar amount alone. The profit figure takes on significance only as it is related to other factors. There may be:

1. The previous year's profit
2. The net sales
3. The average merchandise investment
4. The number of transactions realized
5. The amount of space occupied
6. The amount spent for people—the payroll

7. The net worth, which is the owner's equity in the business
8. The number of shares of corporate stock outstanding

COMPARISON OF PROFIT (EXAMPLE)

Given: net sales, $100,000; operating profit, $5,000; net profit, $6,000; last year's operating profit, $4,000; average merchandise investment at cost, $15,000; number of gross transactions, 20,000; number of feet of selling space, 1,000 sq. ft. and 15,000 cu. ft.; net worth of the store, $60,000; total payroll, $18,000; shares of stock ownership, 500.

1. Relative to last year's operating profit:
$$\frac{\$5,000}{\$4,000} = 125\%$$

2. Relative to net sales: $\frac{\$5,000}{\$100,000} = 5\%$

3. Relative to merchandising investment: $\frac{\$5,000}{\$15,000} = 33\,1/3\%$

4. Relative to transactions: $\frac{\$5,000}{20,000} = 25$ cents

5. Relative to space occupied: $\frac{\$5,000}{1,000} = \$5$ per sq. ft.

and $\frac{\$5,000}{15,000} = 33\,1/3$ cents per cu. ft.

6. Relative to payroll: $\frac{\$5,000}{\$18,000} = 28$ cents per dollar of payroll

7. Relative to net worth: $\frac{\$6,000}{\$60,000} = 10\%$

8. Relative to shares of stock: $\frac{\$6,000}{500} = \$12$ per share

All of these relationships are significant in determining the adequacy of the profits. For example, if profits on a class of merchandise average twenty-five cents a transaction, the merchant will hesitate to promote ten-cent merchandise even though 5 percent profit could readily be earned; he would prefer to devote his energies to items that would contribute larger dollar profits per transaction. Again, if selling space is very limited, it should be allotted to items that can earn a large profit relative to the space they occupy. And with funds scarce, it is more important to invest in merchandise that will earn a high return on the investment rather than a high return on the sales. These relationships will also have to be compared with the performance of the group of stores that have characteristics similar to the store in question.

DEPARTMENTAL PROFIT AND LOSS

CONTROLLABLE PROFIT

As already observed, stores that have a number of selling departments work out operating statements for each. These are similar to the statement in table 3.1 that we have been using as a frame of reference but do not go beyond the figure for operating profit. In fact, some departmental statements do not go beyond the gross margin figure. In others, only direct expenses that are at least partially under the control of the department manager (selling and buyer's payroll, advertising, delivery, etc.) are charged against the departments. The difference between the department's gross margin and its direct expenses is called *department contribution,* or *controllable profit.* The department contributions for all departments may be totaled and the overhead or joint expenses of the store subtracted to determine the store's operating profit.

Were the data appearing in the operating statement (table 3.1) limited to a single department, from the gross margin of $37,000 would be subtracted the direct departmental expenses. Were these to be $17,000, the controllable profit would be $20,000. The department's share of joint expenses might or might not be subtracted from the controllable profit to obtain an operating profit for the department.

KINDS OF SELLING DEPARTMENTS

There are two major kinds of selling departments in large retail stores: owned departments and leased departments. The former are owned and operated by the store's own management, whereas the latter are operated by outside management in space rented by the store. Owned departments are usually subdivided into owned retail departments and owned cost departments.

Owned retail departments. The typical small store has only one kind of selling unit: the owed retail department, which buys and sells goods without changing their form. Most food, clothing, and home furnishings departments are of this type. The retail method of inventory, discussed in chapter 11, is suitable for such departments, and when this method used, they are called *retail inventory departments.*

Owned cost departments. Owned cost departments, with representation in most large stores, also deal directly with customers on a profit-making basis, but they do not carry inventories at retail prices; they produce goods and services and also deal in them. Their inventories, if any, include very little finished goods—mostly ingredients. Examples are the baked goods shop, public restaurant, beauty salon, custom-made millinery and drapery departments, and some repair departments. These carry such inventories as they may require at cost prices and compute their cost of merchandise or service sold, as do manufacturers, to include materials, direct labor, and other production costs. Operating expenses—those having to do with distributing the products or services produced—are then subtracted to yield the operating profit or loss.

A variation of the owned cost department is the *contract department*, which sells at wholesale prices to business and institutional buyers, often by the bidding device. Inventories, if any, are usually carried on a cost basis. A separate buyer may manage the department. Because of the large unit of each sale, it can operate at a much lower markup than can departments dealing with the typical household consumer.

Leased departments.   Leased departments are the opposite of owned departments. They are merchandised and operated by outside management, which contracts to pay an agreed percentage of net sales to the store as a commission to cover a reasonable charge for space and other services the store provides lessors.

It is now standard practice to regard the sales of such units as sales of the store, although at one time it was customary to regard the commission as "other income" and to exclude the lessees' sales from store sales. This practice distorted the productivity of space and treated a merchandising function as though it were a financial one.

There is a problem in determining cost of merchandise sold and gross margin for leased departments. For example, net sales of a leased millinery department may be $100,000 and the store's commission 15 percent, or $15,000. The $85,000 paid over to the lessor includes not only the true cost of the merchandise sold but also the expenses that the lessor assumes in merchandising and operating the department: buying, selling, advertising, and administering the department, often from a central source. Some stores attempt to reconstruct a cost of merchandise sold and gross margin, but the job is cumbersome and involves estimating data not available to the store management.

Accordingly, the practice that is becoming prevalent is to treat the commission earned as the gross margin on leased department sales and to charge against it the operating expenses assumed by the store; the difference is operating profit.[9]

But a special adjustment is desirable because the commission, approximating 15 percent, is considerably less than the gross margin earned on owned departments. Leased department sales are sometimes higher than 10 percent of total sales and their low gross margin tends to reduce the aggregate gross margin of the store. To avoid error in analysis, it is common practice to calculate separately the gross margin for (1) all owned retail departments, (2) all owned cost departments, and (3) leased departments.[10] The three are then combined to yield an overall gross margin percentage that is lower than that of owned departments.

The franchise operations.   The franchise operation is somewhat similar to the leased department but usually includes an entire store unit, not a single department. An outside firm arranges a deal with a retail merchant involving the use of a name owned by the franchiser, the carrying of an inventory determined by the franchiser, and maintenance of a specific standard of service. The franchisee owns his own business and accordingly has considerable freedom of action in selling and store management, but the franchise may be withdrawn if he fails to follow standards set by the franchiser and to buy enough of the franchiser's products and services to make it worthwhile for him to maintain the arrangement. The merchant pays a considerable fee to be given the privilege of being franchised, sometimes more than $25,000, and he buys his major merchandise and service requirements from the franchiser. Many expenses that he might have were he operating alone are absorbed in his purchases from his exclusive merchandise supplier, but in general his operating statement will look like that of other stores.

COMPARISONS OF OPERATING DATA

In analyzing the figures that enter into a store's or a department's profit and loss statement, comparisons are more important than the figures themselves; figures take on significance only as they are related to other figures. Internally, it is important to compare the

[9] If direct expenses only were charged against the gross margin of leased departments, the difference would be controllable profit.

[10] Percentages reflecting markons, markdowns, shortages, cash discounts, and alteration and workroom costs are calculated only for owned retail departments.

major profit elements month by month or even week by week as the year progresses.

Comparisons with results in other stores are also necessary

TABLE 3.2   Composite Operating Statement for 217 Men's Stores, 1969[a]

	Range of Common Experience		Median Store	Your Store
SALES				
1. Net sales, excluding leased departments, percentage of total net sales	98.0% to 100.0%		100.0%	——%
2. Net sales of leased departments, percentage of total net sales	0.0 to 2.0		0.0	——
COST OF GOODS SOLD (Percentage of net sales, excluding leased departments, except as noted.)				
3. Beginning inventory as cost	18.4 to 31.4		26.3	——
4. Net purchases at cost including transportation charges	57.4 to 66.1		61.7	——
5. Cost of total merchandise handled	78.4 to 96.3		86.3	——
6. Ending inventory at cost	18.0 to 33.3		27.0	——
7. Gross cost of merchandise sold	57.2 to 65.1		60.0	——
8. Cash discounts earned	0.1 to 1.3		1.1	——
9. Net workroom costs	1.1 to 3.3		2.2	——
10. Total cost of merchandise sold	58.7 to 65.4		61.5	——
11. Gross margin, excluding leased department income and sales	34.6 to 40.8		38.5	——
12. Gross margin, including income from leased departments, as a percentage of total net sales	34.7 to 41.7		38.4	——
OPERATING EXPENSES (Percentage of total net sales.)				
29. Total Expenses	27.8 to 36.7		32.5	——
NET GAIN (Percentage of total net sales, except as noted.)				
30. Operating profit, including income from leased departments	2.5 to 9.8		5.8	——
31. Net other income and expenses	0.0 to 2.5		1.3	——
32. Net profit, before Federal income taxes	3.9 to 12.0		6.9	——
33. Net profit before Federal income taxes as a percentage of net worth	9.4 to 35.1		20.8	——

[a] Details of expense data (lines 13–28) omitted. The range of common experience is the inter-quartile range. Courtesy: Menswear Retailers of America, Washington, D. C. The use of medians does not give exact mathematical relationships among the figures.

but usually involve the comparison of ratios rather than of actual dollar results. The adequacy of any single performance ratio, such as that of gross margin, may be judged only as it is compared both with figures of the store's own past performance and with those of similar stores. If the store's or department's gross margin has been running 29 percent of sales and is now raised to 30 percent, some improvement has occurred, but there is no sound basis for judgment until the margins of others similarly situated are known. If the latter figure is 35 percent, it is clear that the margin problem is far from solved, even though there has been some improvement.

Comparisons with other stores are possible (1) by subscribing to publicly available statistical services that report typical figures for an industry and (2) by participating in a private figure exchange association consisting of a group of stores of similar size and similar operating methods.

Table 3.2 presents a summary from an annual report of an industry survey of men's wear stores; note the space provided for each store to enter its own figures for comparison. This group of stores also provides breakdowns by size of store, Federal Reserve District, and merchandise composition (whether or not women's wear as well as men's wear is carried).

Limitations of comparisons. There has been a tendency for store executives to place too much reliance on outside standards and to exert pressure to achieve a typical or a goal figure that does not really apply to the store in question. Typical figures are essentially *medians*—that is, the data are arranged into an *array*, from smallest to largest, and the midpoint (with possibly some adjustment) is taken as the typical figure. Thus, with a typical figure of 40 percent for markup, the data may have ranged from 35 percent to 45 percent.[11] It is clearly wrong to assume that the stores reporting markups between 35 percent and 40 percent have markups too low and that the others with markups between 40 percent and 45 percent have markups too high. Markup may vary with differences in size of store, and usually with differences in policy. A store that makes low prices its major appeal and that sells on a self-service basis would obviously have a smaller than *typical* markup. Conversely, a store providing the acme of personal service for its customers must have a higher than typical markup. Again there is some evidence that department stores have accepted as reasonable higher markdowns than are really desirable because the typical figures have been allowed to become the

---

[11] Initial markup, as distinct from gross margin, is not included in table 3.2 because the majority of stores did not report it.

target. Since there are many respects in which the stores or departments making up a group are heterogeneous, the averages, whether they are typical or goal figures, are inadequate standards for any but a very few stores in the group. To attribute to the averages the quality of the ideal may lead to very wrong merchandising action.

Nevertheless, in the hands of the trained analyst, comparison of one store's data with the averages assists materially in the diagnosis of weak departments or sections or stores. If a department's markup, for example, is considerably below the typical, there is need for a careful investigation at this point to determine whether store policy or unsurmountable obstacles cause the apparently low markup. If these factors do not seem to explain the markup, the analyst is then ready to explore the thesis that the buying or pricing practices of the buyer may be inadequate and that improvement is possible by positive action.

The situation is similar to the diagnosis of a physician who knows normal temperature, heart beat, blood pressure, blood count, and weight. He does not necessarily judge a patient sick if the patient deviates from the norm. He tries to find the factors in the individual that justify a variation even when the person is well. A good doctor judges a patient even more in relation to his past performance than in relation to standards obtained from humanity at large. Similarly, the merchandising analyst gives more emphasis to variations over a period of time than he does to comparisons with the averages. Yet he does note the former and often uncovers weak spots that the internal comparisons alone would not have revealed.

QUESTIONS FOR DISCUSSION

1. If sales of $27,000 this year are reported to be 10 percent below those of last year, what would last year's sales have been?
2. If a store's sales have tripled since 1950, what is the percentage of increase?
3. Why is a transfer of merchandise out of a selling department not a sale for the department?
4. If net sales are reported as $45,000 and returns and allowances as 10 percent of gross sales, how would you find the dollar value of the gross sales and of the returns and allowances?
5. Why should not transportation on incoming goods be treated as an operating expense?
6. (a) Why should selling departments be credited with cash discounts on purchases, since their realization depends upon the availability of cash and care in making prompt payment, both matters beyond the control of department managers and buyers? (b) If a departmentized store loses, through failure to pay for

a purchase on time, a cash discount that the manufacturer had made available to a certain department within the store, how should the loss of the discount be handled? Consider at least two possibilities: (1) to include in the cash discounts earned and credited to the department's gross cost of merchandise sold only the cash discounts actually realized or (2) to include all cash discounts made available as earned by the department and to charge the cash discounts lost as a deduction from the *other income* of the store as a whole. Present a defense of the method you recommend.

7. (a) What is the effect of a merchandise shortage on the cost of merchandise sold?
   (b) The effect of a cash shortage?

8. If a store or department has a gross margin of $80,000 with cash discounts earned of $4,000 and alteration costs of $1,000, what will its maintained markup be?

9. Why are federal income taxes excluded from operating expenses? Should not other income taxes (state and local) be handled the same way?

10. Do you see much point in an independent merchant charging himself a salary?

11. Why should not interest paid on borrowed capital be included in operating expenses?

12. What is the logic in differentiating between sales income and other income?

13. Do you expect cost selling departments to increase in importance? Why? Leased departments?

14. If a store compares its current performance carefully and in detail with its past performance does it really need to make comparisons with outside data?

15. What organizations are engaged in compiling comparative store data? Determine by name at least five organizations that do so.

16. (a) Which figure would normally be the larger: the gross margin percentage where leased departments are excluded or where they are included? Why?
    (b) Do the numbers reported on table 3.2 bear out this relationship?

17. It has been suggested that operating expenses should include interest on certain assets (imputed interest), such as on the merchandise inventory, irrespective of whether or not the interest is actually paid out. What merits and demerits do you see to this suggestion from a management point of view?

part **II**

PRICING

Price is the central problem in economic theory, and, along with sales and expenses, it bears a central position in the merchants' search for profit. This section presents, first, the techniques involved in setting markup goals and then considers the pricing of individual items and the establishment of policies having to do with pricing and repricing.

4

DETERMINATION
OF
MARKUP

ELEMENTS IN INITIAL MARKUP

The woman who pays $15 for a new fall hat knows, if she stops to think, that it must have cost the store less than $15. If she is reasonably familiar with the expenses involved in running a store and the losses that have to be taken on hats that fail to sell, she may estimate the cost at approximately $8. The difference between the cost and the original retail price of merchandise (the $7 in the example) is technically known as the initial markup. In the aggregate, the markup must be sufficient to cover the following items:

1. The expenses of the store or department.
   a. Direct expenses, such as expenses of handling the article and selling it.
   b. A share of the store or department overhead (joint or indirect expenses).
2. A possible price reduction that may be taken before the goods are sold, or the possibility of physical losses due to theft and breakage.
3. A contribution to operating profit.

For example, a store expecting to sell $65,000 worth of millinery at cost may have expenses of $30,000 and may estimate markdowns and physical losses at $10,000. With a $5,000 profit goal, the goods should be marked to sell at $110,000.

It is neither common nor desirable, however, to require that the markup on every item allow a profit over and above direct and indirect expenses and probable price reductions. Custom, competition, and desirability of goods to customers often result in prices above or below a mathematically determined price based on costs. This problem will be treated at length in later chapters.

THE MARKUP PERCENTAGE

THE RETAIL BASE

Reasons for the retail base. The dollar markup, the difference between cost[1] and retail, may be expressed for comparative purposes as a percentage either of the cost or of the retail. For example, if an article costs $0.60 and is retailed at $1.00, the markup of $0.40 is 66⅔ percent of cost and 40 percent of retail. Likewise, if the total purchases at cost are $10,000 and the total at retail is $15,000, the purchase markup is 50 percent of cost and 33⅓ percent of retail. In the interests of uniformity, it is desirable to agree on either the cost or the retail basis for the markup percentage. In exchanging merchandising data among stores, it would be confusing if two stores with like markup reported them on different bases—one as 66⅔ percent of cost and the other as 40 percent of retail. One basis or the other should always be used in order to insure fair comparisons among departments and among stores.

The retail basis has been generally accepted as the more desirable of the two for the following reasons:

1. The percentage of retail is nearly always less than the percentage of cost. The casual reader who notes that stores get a markup of 50 percent on their goods (based on cost) may judge this to be exorbitant because of lack of knowledge of retail expenses. If the figure is reported as 33⅓ percent (based on retail), however, the reasonableness of the markup is less likely to be challenged by representatives of the public. Since in many stores the net profit approaches the vanishing point, there is no just cause for the cry of profiteering.

2. The use of the retail percentage channels the retailer's thinking along retail lines rather than along cost lines. He tends to do his planning in terms of retail price lines and retail stocks and

---

[1] For discussion of technical meaning of "cost," see pages 67–69.

thus can keep better in tune with customer demand, which is a demand for retail, not cost, values.

3. Net sales have generally and logically been used as a basis for expressing expense figures, and it is desirable to have markup figures as nearly comparable as possible. Were the markup expressed as 33⅓ percent of the cost of purchases and the expenses as 25 percent of sales, it would not be obvious whether a profit were being earned. The markup would have to be converted into a percentage of retail (25 percent) or the expenses into a percentage of cost (33⅓ percent) to determine that there would be no profit even if the goods should sell without any markdowns. The basing of expenses on sales is preferable because sales are always available for comparison.

TWO BASES FOR MARKUP

A merchant purchased some aprons for $15.75 a dozen to fit into his $1.95 retail price line and wanted to determine what markup he would be getting. He figured it two ways as follows:

$1.95 × 12 = $23.40 Total retail
15.75 Cost
_____
$ 7.65 Markup

$7.65 ÷ $23.40 = 32.7% markup percent on retail
$7.65 ÷ $15.75 = 48.6% markup percent on cost

The danger of failing to make correct percentage comparisons is evidenced by the following experience. A hardware merchant was in the habit of adding 50 percent of the cost to the cost prices of merchandise to determine his retail prices. This he regarded as a markup of 50 percent. At the end of each year, he observed that his expenses were about 25 percent of his sales. He assumed these two figures to be comparable and thought that there was a large profit margin between cost plus expenses, and selling price. Actually his markup on retail was only 33⅓ percent, and, after markdowns, it probably did not exceed 30 percent. This misinterpretation led the dealer to decide to cut his markup to stimulate volume. He proceeded to add about one-third to his cost in the belief that he still had an adequate margin above his expenses. Actually his markup rate just equaled his expense rate, with no allowance for markdowns. The sales volume increased considerably under the stimulus of low prices, but the merchant found that he was losing money, whereas formerly he had made money. It was not until he called in a merchandising expert that he realized the fundamental difficulty: his markup, expressed on cost, was too low to cover his expenses and markdowns.

Applying the markup percentage of retail. With a goal for his initial markup percentage on retail, a merchant must be able: (1) to compute his retail when his cost is known, (2) to compute his cost when his retail is known, and (3) to compute both when his dollar markup is known. Such computation is based on the following markup equation:

Cost + Markup = Retail, or C + M = R

This equation may also be written as follows:

Retail − Markup = Cost.
Retail − Cost   = Markup,

Since all three factors in the equations may be expressed either in dollars or in percentage of retail, a good method of solution is to write the appropriate equation and to insert the dollars above and the percents below and then solve.[2] For example, the cost is $6 and the markup 40 percent of retail; find retail. Since the markup is given as a percentage of retail, the retail must be 100 percent and the cost must be 60 percent of the retail. Since this is $6, the retail must be $6 divided by 60 percent or $10.

Dollars $6
Equation .... C + M = R
Percentages............ (60)   40   100

$$60\% = \$6$$
$$1\% = \frac{\$6}{60} = \$.10$$
$$100\% = \$.10 \times 100 = \$10[3]$$

Likewise, the retail may be $20 and the markup 35 percent of retail; find cost:

[2] Some prefer an algebraic solution:
Problem: Cost: $6, Markup: 40 percent of retail. Find retail.
Solution: Let x = Retail.
Since Retail−Markup = Cost
$$x - .40x = \$6$$
$$.60x = \$6$$
$$x = \frac{\$6}{.60} = \$10$$

[3] Some may find the explanation clearer in this and the following calculations by arranging the three factors vertically rather than horizontally as on the bottom of the next page.

Since the retail is 100%, the cost must be 65% of the retail and 65% of $20 is $13.

Dollars.................. $20
Equation.............. Cost + Markup = Retail
Percentages .... (65)   35   100
Since 100% = $20, Cost = 65% of $20 = $13

Again, the dollar markup may be $4 and the percentage markup 40 percent of retail:

Since $4 equals 40% of retail, the retail may be found by dividing $4 by 40%. This yields $10. The cost, then, must be $6.

Equation.................. $C + M = R$
Percentages ....(60)   40   100
$$40\% = \$4$$
$$1\% = \frac{\$4}{40} = \$.10$$
$$R = 100\% = \$10$$
$$C = R - M = \$10 - \$4 = \$6$$

The great frequency with which markup is figured in stores suggests the need for shortcut methods. From the above calculations, it will be observed that the retail may be found quickly by dividing the cost by the complement of the markup percentage (100 percent −M %):

$$R = \frac{C}{100\% - M\%}$$

In like manner, the cost may be found by multiplying the retail by the complement of the markup percentage:

$$C = R \times (100\% - M\%)$$

And the retail may be found by dividing the dollar markup by the markup percentage:

$		%
	Retail	100
	Markup	40
6	Cost	60

If 60% of retail = $6
$$1\% \text{ of retail} = \frac{\$6}{60} = \$.10$$
100% of retail = $.10 × 100 = $10

$$R = \frac{\$ \ M}{M \ \%}$$

These three relationships are fundamental, and every retailer should drill until he can solve for cost and retail by making one division or one multiplication, as the case may be. He should form the habit of thinking *complement* whenever he has a markup to apply. Thus, the *complement* of 40 is 60 and of 25 it is 75. Since the complement is less than 1, or 100 percent, dividing by it gives a larger

TABLE 4.1   Examples of Calculation—Markup on Retail

Given	*To Find*	*Procedure*
a. Cost and retail $1.00 $1.50	Markup percent	Divide Markup by Retail Divide 50¢ by $1.50
b. Retail and markup percent $2.00 40%	Cost	Multiply Retail by (100% — M. %) Multiply $2.00 by (100% — 40%)
c. Cost and markup $5.00 $3.00	Markup percent	Cost + Markup = Retail $5.00 + $3.00 = $8.00 Markup divided by Retail = M. % $3.00 divided by $8.00 = M. %
d. Markup and markup percent $1.05 35%	Retail	Divide Markup by Markup % and multiply by 100 Divide $1.05 by 35 and multiply by 100
e. Cost and markup percent $1.50 40%	Retail	Divide Cost by (100% — M. %) and multiply by 100 Divide $1.50 by (100 — 40) and multiply by 100
f. Retail purchases and markup percent $10,000 35%	Cost pur- chases	Multiply Retail purchases by (100% — M. %) $10,000 multiplied by (100% — 35%)
g. Cost purchases and markup percent $6,600 40%	Retail purchases	Divide cost purchases by (100% — M. %) $6,600 divided by (100 — 40) multiplied by 100

quotient; this is the calculation to apply when solving for the larger retail. Multiplying by the complement gives a smaller product, the calculation to apply when solving for the smaller cost. Some examples of computations that are frequently made appear in table 4.1.

Where the markup is in round numbers, the calculation of retail—when cost is known—may be somewhat simplified as follows:

To secure a 20 percent markup, divide cost by 8.

To obtain a 25 percent markup, divide cost by 7.5.

To obtain a 30 percent markup, divide cost by 7.

To secure a 33⅓ percent markup, divide cost by 2 and multiply by 3.

To secure a 40 percent markup, divide cost by 6.

To secure a 50 percent markup, divide cost by 5.

After each division, the decimal point must be moved one place to the right. For example, an article may cost $2.80, and a selling price based on a 30 percent markup may be desired. Divide $2.80 by 7, move the decimal point one place to the right, and arrive at a selling price of $4.00.

THE COST BASE

Reasons for the cost base. In spite of the logic of the retail basis for expressing markup, some merchants, particularly small ones, still adhere to the cost basis for the following reasons:

1. Custom. The cost basis is the older one and is accordingly better understood by men of the "old school."

2. Many people find it easier to multiply and add than to divide and make use of the markup complement. Thus, if the cost is $12 and the markup on retail is 33⅓ percent, it is necessary to divide $12 by the complement of the markup, 66⅔ percent, to find the retail of $18. If the cost basis were used, the markup would be 50 percent, which could be added to the cost: 50 percent of 12 is $6, and $6 plus $12 is $18.

Applying the markup percentage of cost. As in the case of markup on retail, the user of markup on cost must be able: (1) to compute his retail when his cost is known, (2) to compute his cost when his retail is known, and (3) to compute both when his dollar markup is known. The basic equation is again used, with the dollars above and the percents below.[4] For example, if the cost is $1.00 and the markup 50 percent of cost, find retail:

---

[4] As explained earlier in the chapter, the data may be arranged vertically in bar chart form.

Since the markup is given as a percentage of cost, 100 percent must be the cost and the retail must be 150 percent of the cost—150 percent of $1.00 is $1.50.

$$\text{Dollars} \dots\dots\dots\dots \$1$$
$$\text{Equation} \dots\dots\dots\dots \; C + M = R$$
$$\text{Percentages}\dots\dots\dots100 \quad 50 \; (150)$$
$$100\% = \$1.00$$
$$150\% \text{ of Cost } (\$1) = \text{Retail or } \$1.50$$

The retail may be $1.50 and the markup 50 percent of cost, find cost:

Since the retail is 150 percent of the cost, the cost is $1.50 divided by 150 percent or $1.00.

$$\text{Dollars} \dots\dots\dots\dots \qquad \$1.50$$
$$\text{Equation} \dots\dots\dots\dots \; C + M = R$$
$$\text{Percentages}\dots\dots\dots100 \quad 50 \; (150)$$
$$150\% \text{ of } C = \$1.50$$
$$1\% \text{ of Cost} = \frac{\$1.50}{150} = \$.01$$
$$100\% = 100 \times \$.01 = \$1.00 = \text{Cost}$$

The markup may be $5 and the markup on cost 25 percent, find cost and retail:

Since $5 equals 25 percent of the cost, the cost is $5 divided by 25 percent, $20, and the retail is $25.

$$\text{Dollars} \dots\dots\dots\dots \qquad \$5$$
$$\text{Equation} \dots\dots\dots\dots \; C + M = R$$
$$\text{Percentages}\dots\dots\dots100 \quad 25 \; (125)$$
$$25\% \text{ of Cost} = \$5$$
$$1\% \text{ of Cost} = \frac{\$5.00}{25} = \$.20$$
$$100\% = 100 \times \$.20 = \$20$$
$$\text{Retail} = \text{Cost} + \text{Markup} = \$20 + \$5 = \$25$$

From the above calculations, it will be observed that retail may be found by multiplying the cost by the *supplement* of the markup (100 percent plus the markup):

$$R = C \times (100\% + Mc\%)$$

The cost may be found by dividing the retail by the *supplement* of the markup:

$$C = \frac{R}{100\% + Mc\%}$$

And, the cost may be found by dividing the dollar markup by the percentage markup:

$$C = \frac{\$M}{Mc\%}$$

Table 4.2, analogous to table 4.1, gives examples of calculations commonly made when markup is on cost.

It should be observed that in solving for either cost or retail, when markup is based on cost, it is the *supplement* that it used, rather than the *complement* used when markup is based on retail. Since the

TABLE 4.2   Examples of Calculation—Markup on Cost

Given	*To Find*	*Procedure*
a. Cost and retail $1.00 $1.50	Markup percent	Divide Markup by Cost Divide 50¢ by $1.00

b. Retail and markup
   percent
   $2.00   40%
	Cost	Divide the retail by (100%
		+ Markup %)
		Divide $2.00 by 140%

c. Retail and markup $5.00 $2.00	Markup percent	Retail − Markup = Cost $5.00 − $2.00 = $3.00 Markup divided by Cost = Mc % $2.00 divided by $3.00 = Mc %

d. Markup and markup
   percent
   $1.05   35%
	Cost	Divide Markup by Markup
		% and multiply by 100
		Divide $1.05 by 35 and
		multiply by 100

e. Cost and markup
   percent
   $1.50   40%
	Retail	Multiply cost by (100% +
		Mc %)
		Multiply $1.50 by 140%

f. Retail purchases and
   markup percent
   $10,000   35%
	Cost pur-
	chases
		Divide Retail purchases by
		(100% + Mc %)
		Divide $10,000 by 135%
		(1.35)

g. Cost purchases and
   markup percent
   $6,600   40%
	Retail
	purchases
		Multiply Cost purchases by
		(100% + Mc %)
		Multiply $6,600 by 140%
		(1.40)

supplement is more than 1 or 100 percent, multiplying by it gives a larger product, and this is the calculation to apply when solving for the larger retail. Dividing by the supplement gives a smaller quotient, the calculation to apply when solving for the lower cost.

Conversion.   Markup percentage on cost may be converted to markup percentage on retail, even though the dollar quantities involved are not available. For example, a markup of 60 percent on cost may be converted to a retail basis as follows:

$$100\% = \text{Cost}$$
$$\underline{60\% = \text{Markup on cost}}$$
$$160\% = \text{Retail}$$
$$\frac{60\%}{160\%} = 37\tfrac{1}{2}\% = \text{Markup on retail}$$

Conversely, a markup of 40 percent on retail may be converted to a cost basis as follows:

$$100\% = \text{Retail}$$
$$\underline{40\% = \text{Markup}}$$
$$60\% = \text{Cost}$$
$$\frac{40\%}{60\%} = 66\tfrac{2}{3}\% = \text{Markup on cost}$$

Table 4.3 shows the differences of the two bases. It is interesting to note that, with low markups, there is very little difference. The two move farther and farther apart, however, as dollar markups increase until the theoretical maximum is reached; this is 100 percent

TABLE 4.3   Markup Equivalents

Markup on Cost	*Markup on Retail*
$11\tfrac{1}{9}\%$	10%
25	20
$33\tfrac{1}{3}$	25
60	$37\tfrac{1}{2}$
$66\tfrac{2}{3}$	40
100	50
150	60
300	75
400	80
900	90
Infinity	100

at retail and infinity (∞) at cost, since 100 percent (the markup) divided by 0 percent (the cost) equals infinity.

In all such calculations the essential points to bear in mind are (1) that 100 percent should be set equal to cost whenever markup is given as a percentage of cost and (2) that 100 percent should be set equal to retail whenever markup is given as a percentage of retail.

MEANING OF COST IN MARKUP COMPUTATIONS

In the discussion thus far, it has been assumed that the cost figure to be subtracted from the retail to determine markup is a specific, clearly indicated figure. In practice this is not so. The hat costing $8 is marked $15, but it does not follow that $8 is the true cost of the hats to the store.

A buyer may purchase two hundred hats in the market at a billed price of $8 each, a total of $1,600. From this figure, he may be allowed to deduct cash discounts of $90, but he must pay transportation charges of $20 on the incoming shipments. Is his cost, for markup purposes, $1,600, $1,510, $1,530 or $1,620? If his retail price is $3,000, is his purchase markup $1,400, $1,490, $1,470, or $1,380? The usual basis is the billed cost plus transportation charges paid by the store without the subtraction of the cash discount. In this instance, the cost would be $1,620 and the markup $1,380. In defining billed cost, however, trade and quantity discounts have already been subtracted. For example, goods bought at a list price of $1,600 with a trade discount of 25 percent and a cash discount of 2 percent would have a billed cost of $1,200. To this the buyer must add the transportation charges in order to figure the cost for markup purposes.

Since transportation is regarded as an element in merchandise costs, it is important that the buyer include transportation in the total cost of each invoice when he sets his retail prices rather than lose sight of transportation by including it with departmental expenses that bear no specific relation to each article purchased.

Some stores take out the cash discount from the billed price and use the true cost figure in computing markup on inventory and purchases, but it is standard practice to use the inflated billed figure, making a correction for cash discounts in the "cost of merchandise sold" figure. Customarily, then, the first three of the four markups listed in table 4.4 are based on billed cost figures with transportation charges added. Gross margin, however, is based upon actual cost, since the cost of merchandise sold is reduced by the amount of the cash discount, before it is computed.

BILLED-COST CONCEPT

There are several reasons why the billed-cost concept generally prevails in calculating all markups except the gross margin:

1. Customary office procedure in which invoices are charged at billed cost and cash discounts computed only when payments are made.

2. Lack of assurance that cash discounts available will be realized. Some bills may not be paid on time, in which case the billed cost becomes the actual cost.

3. The theory that discounts available on purchases should not be treated as earned, but rather only those discounts that apply to the goods sold.

4. Deliberate desire to inflate costs so as to allow a "cushion" to protect profits in case of contingencies. Some merchants like to be guided by overstated costs so that, should they fail to reach plans made, they may still show a profit in the form of cash discounts earned. Should plans be based on actual costs, failure to realize them would result in a loss. The use of billed figures is one of the methods of setting up a profit reserve.[5]

5. Desire to obtain slightly higher selling prices by regarding the billed price as the true cost. For example, a merchant may purchase an article at a billed cost of $1.00. When the discount is deducted, the cost is $0.94. If it is marked on a basis of $1.00 cost, he may mark it $1.50, but if it is marked on a basis $0.94, he may erroneously think that a retail price of $1.40 is adequate.

6. Fear of errors in making historical comparisons, if a change were to be made to a net basis. For example, a store or department may have an established record of a 40 percent markup, with cash discounts averaging 5 percent of billed cost. If the goods formerly charged in at $0.60 cost were now charged in at $0.57 (5 percent less), the markup would jump to 43 percent, assuming no change in retail prices. This jump might cause confusion in the analysis of trends: a merchant who for years has had 40 percent as his objective might be under pressure to increase his volume. Suddenly, he finds he is getting a 43 percent markup and he may forget or not know about the change in procedure instituted in the office. As a result, he might cut the retail price of his merchandise to stimulate volume. Thus, he would reduce his true markup below former levels and thus jeopardize his profits.

---

[5] Initial markups are usually planned to yield a profit in excess of cash discounts expected. Thus, even if this profit is not realized because of low sales or unexpectedly high expenses, the cash discount still provides some profit.

INITIAL VERSUS MAINTAINED MARKUPS

Even though the retail is the generally accepted basis for the markup percentage, it should be noted that there are two kinds of retail: purchase retail and sales retail. When goods are given a retail price at the time of purchase, the markup percentage is based on the retail price of the goods that the merchant hopes to realize. But price reductions may be necessary before the goods are sold, so that the store realizes a lower markup. This *maintained markup*, as it is called, is the difference between the actual sales price and the gross cost of the goods sold, expressed as a percentage of the sales. Initial retails are frequently higher than retail prices at which goods are ultimately sold, since some depreciation in the form of markdowns may occur before sale. For example, a stock of goods may cost $600 and be marked originally to retail at $1,000. The initial markup is $400 or 40 percent of retail, but the goods may eventually be sold for a total of $900. The maintained markup is $300, or 33⅓ percent. Because of these two types of retail, care must be taken in comparing initial with maintained markups. Even though both are on retail bases, they are not percentages of the same thing.

TABLE 4.4　Kinds of Markup

The bookkeeper in a clothing store provided the owner-manager with the following figures reflecting a month's operation:

	Cost	Retail
Beginning inventory	$13,000	$20,000
Purchases	25,000	40,000
Sales	18,200	28,000
Cash discounts earned	800	
Alteration costs	520	

The merchant figured four markup percentages as follows:

(1)　Markup on month's purchases:

$$\$40,000 - \$25,000 = \$15,000$$
$$\$15,000 \div \$40,000 = 37\tfrac{1}{2}\%$$

(2)　Initial markup

	Cost	Retail
Beginning inventory	$13,000	$20,000
Purchases	25,000	40,000
Total	$38,000	$60,000

$$\$60,000 - \$38,000 = \$22,000$$
$$\$22,000 \div \$60,000 = 36\tfrac{2}{3}\%$$

(3)　Maintained markup $= \$28,000 - \$18,200 = \$9,800$
$$\$9,800 \div \$28,000 = 35\%$$

(4)　Gross margin $= \$9,800 + \$800 - \$520 = \$10,080$
$$\$10,080 \div \$28,000 = 36\%$$

Table 4.4 shows four ways of expressing markup. The first two are based on goods purchased and the last two on goods sold. The relationship between the last two, gross margin and maintained markup (explained in chapter 3) should be reviewed:

1. Gross margin = Maintained markup + Cash discounts − Alteration costs.
2. Maintained markup = Gross margin − Cash discounts + Alteration costs.

When there are no cash discounts or alteration costs, the two figures are the same.

The two most talked about markups in retail discussions are the initial markup and the gross margin. The first (initial markup, or markon) represents the adequacy of a merchant's asking price, and the second (gross margin, or gross merchandise margin) the adequacy of the realized price. The difference is the loss due to price reductions and alterations, less cash discounts.

Although initial markup and gross margin may be calculated for individual items, they are more commonly used to report markup over a period of time, such as a year or the season to date. Initial markup over such an extended period is commonly called *cumulative markon*. This is the way it is used in table 4.4.

PLANNING INITIAL MARKUP

At the beginning of this chapter, it was indicated that initial markup should be adequate to cover the factors of expense, reductions, and profits. This may be done by rule of thumb growing out of past experience or it may be worked out mathematically on a basis of expected sales, reductions, and expenses.[6]

For example, a merchant may estimate that to sell a quantity of merchandise costing $6,000, he will have to incure expenses of $3,000, suffer markdowns and shortages of $700, and be able to realize a profit of $300. The merchandise, then, must be offered for sale at an original retail price of $10,000 ($6,000 + $3,000 + $700 + $300) in order to assure that the profit goal of $300 will be earned.

In practice, data regarding expenses, markdowns, and the other factors involved are seldom available for each purchase, and it becomes necessary to plan the initial markup *percentage* required on all of the merchandise handled during a period, such as a six-month season.

---

[6] Price reductions include markdowns, stock shortages, and discounts to employees and customers.

Steps in Planning

The standard method of computing the necessary markup percentage is as follows:[7]

1. The total sales for the coming year or season are forecast.
2. An estimate is made of the expenses and price reductions that will be necessary to reach the sales plan.
3. A profit goal is set (operating profit or department contribution).
4. The estimated expenses, price reductions, and profit are added together to find the dollar markup necessary over the cost of merchandise sold.
5. The original retail price of the goods to be sold is determined by adding to the planned sales the planned price reductions.
6. The dollar markup as computed (step 4) is divided by the original retail price (step 5).

For example, sales may be planned at $100,000 for the year, with probable operating expenses of $30,000, price reductions of $10,000, and a profit goal of $5,000. The necessary markup, then, is the sum of the last three figures, or $45,000. Next, the price reductions of $10,000 are added to the sales $100,000 to determine the total retail at which goods must first be put into stock. This is $110,000. Finally, $45,000 is divided by $110,000 to determine the necessary markup as a percentage of initial retail price. This is 40.9 percent.

As an equation,

$$\text{Initial Markup } \% = \frac{\text{Expenses} + \text{Profits} + \text{Reductions}}{\text{Sales} + \text{Reductions}}$$

In the example,

$$\text{Initial Markup } \% = \frac{\$30,000 + \$5,000 + \$10,000}{\$100,000 + \$10,000} = \frac{\$45,000}{\$110,000}$$

$=40.9\%$

When expenses, reductions, and profits are planned as percentages of sales rather than in dollars, the equation may be used equally well. In this case, sales become 100 percent in the equation. Expenses in the example above average 30 percent of sales, the profit goal 5 percent, and price reductions 10 percent. Converting these percents to decimals:

$$\text{Initial Markup} = \frac{.30 + .05 + .10}{1.00 + .10} = \frac{.45}{1.10} = 40.9\%$$

By means of this equation it is possible for a merchant to

---

[7] Where cash discounts on purchases and alteration and workroom costs are involved, these factors also have to be considered in the calculation, as explained later in this chapter.

determine what percentage of markup he must realize on his purchases if he is to cover all expenses and the necessary markdowns and
still make a planned profit. It does not follow, however, that he will
always plan this markup for his store or department or attempt to
realize it on each purchase. Sales possibilities may make it necessary
to deviate considerably in actual pricing, but the formula does provide
a useful guide in showing what markup is necessary on an average
to realize a wanted profit.

EXPENSE AND PROFIT DATA USED IN THE MARKUP EQUATION

The expense figure used in the equation may be the operating
profit in dollars or percentage for the entire store, probably handling
only a specialized line of goods. In this case, the profit figure is the
operating profit goal. In the case of the individual selling department,
again total operating expenses charged to the department and the
department's operating profit may be used. But if only direct expenses
are charged selling departments, the expense figure will be limited to
those expenses, and the profit goal will be that for the department's
contribution, explained in chapter 3. Thus, expenses would be relatively low and profits high in the application of the equation.

EFFECT OF ALTERATION AND WORKROOM COSTS ON THE MARKUP EQUATION

In chapter 3 we found that alteration and workroom costs and
cash discounts earned on purchases are elements in the cost of merchandise sold.[8] Accordingly, the markup equation must allow for them
when they exist. Obviously, markup must cover net alteration and
workroom costs as well as expenses; therefore, they must be added to
the numerator of the equation. They have no effect on the denominator, since they must be paid for out of net sales income and do not
represent an addition to sales.

EFFECT OF CASH DISCOUNTS EARNED ON THE MARKUP EQUATION

Cash discounts earned, on the other hand, are *subtracted* from
the numerator of the markup equation for the following reason: They
represent additional income received from suppliers, which contri-

---

[8] As already indicated, the net alteration and workroom costs represent
the difference between the total cost of operating workrooms (that finish goods
at the time of sale) and the charges made customers for the work.

butes to the profits without requiring a markup for the purpose. Another way to explain the handling of the cash discounts is to note that the profit figure in the equation represents *all* the operating (or department contribution) profit, including what is earned in the form of cash discounts, but the markup percentage is calculated over the billed cost, not over the actual cost. The markup, then, does not have to provide for all of the profit but only for the difference between the total profit and the profit earned from the cash discounts. For example, goods having a billed cost of $60,000 may involve expenses of $30,000, reductions of $5,000, and cash discounts of $3,000. A profit of $8,000 may also be sought on this merchandise. It is necessary to add the expenses and the reductions but not all of the profit to the $60,000, since $3,000 of the profit is coming from the discounts. Only $5,000 of the $8,000 profit goal need be added, along with $30,000 for expense and $5,000 for reductions. Thus, the original retail at which the goods should be stocked is $100,000 and the markup is $40,000, or 40 percent.

THE COMPLETE EQUATION

Where alteration costs and cash discounts exist, then, the markup equation appears as follows, with the elements in the *reduction* figure spelled out in full:

$$\text{Initial markup } \% = \frac{\begin{array}{c}\text{Expenses} + \text{Profits} + \text{Alteration costs} - \text{Cash}\\ \text{discounts} + \text{Markdowns} + \text{Stock shortages}\\ + \text{Employee and customer discounts}\end{array}}{\begin{array}{c}\text{Sales} + \text{Markdowns} + \text{Stock shortages}\\ + \text{Employee and customer discounts}\end{array}}$$

The above expression may be simplified, since:

Expenses + Profit = Gross margin, and since:
Markdowns + Stock shortages + Employee and customer discounts = Reductions

$$\text{Therefore: Initial markup } \% = \frac{\begin{array}{c}\text{Gross margin} + \text{Alteration costs} -\\ \text{Cash discounts} + \text{Reductions}\end{array}}{\text{Sales} + \text{Reductions}}$$

A further simplification is possible, since:

Gross margin + Alteration costs − Cash discounts = Maintained markup[9]

$$\text{Therefore: Initial markup } \% = \frac{\text{Maintained markup} + \text{Reductions}}{\text{Sales} + \text{Reductions}}$$

[9] This relationship was developed in chapter 3.

When Maintained markup and Reductions are expressed in percentage of sales rather than in dollars, the equation becomes:

$$\text{Initial markup \%} = \frac{\text{Maintained markup \% + Reduction \%}}{100\% + \text{Reduction \%}}$$

This is the basic equation for planning.

The application of this equation may be illustrated as follows: Expenses 28 percent, Profit 7 percent, Cash discounts 3 percent, Alteration costs 2 percent, Reductions 5 percent,

Find: (a) Gross margin
       (b) Maintained markup
       (c) Initial markup

Solution:

Gross margin = Expenses + Profits = 28% + 7% = 35%
Maintained markup = Gross margin − Cash discounts + Alteration costs = 35% − 3% + 2% = 34%

$$\text{Initial markup \%} = \frac{\text{Maintained markup \% + Reductions \%}}{100\% + \text{Reductions \%}}$$
$$= \frac{34\% + 5\%}{100\% + 5\%} = \frac{39\%}{105\%} = 37.1\%$$

PLANNING INITIAL MARKUP—AN EXAMPLE

The proprietor of a men's shop had made the following estimates for his fall season business:

Sales	$80,000
Reductions	4,000
Expenses	25,000
Profit goal	8,000
Cash discounts on purchases	2,000
Alteration costs	1,120

With this information, he computed his necessary markup on purchases for the season (including his opening inventory) as follows:

$$\text{Needed markup \%} = \frac{\begin{array}{c}\text{Expenses + Profits + Reductions} \\ \text{+ Alteration costs} \\ \text{− Cash discounts on purchases}\end{array}}{\text{Sales + Reductions}}$$

$$\frac{\$25,000 + 8,000 + 4,000 + 1,120 - 2,000}{\$80,000 + 4,000} = \frac{\$36,120}{\$84,000} = 43\%$$

SOLVING FOR PROFIT WHEN MARKUP IS KNOWN

In practice, the markup equation is often used in reverse to find what maintained markup, what gross margin, and what profit will be achieved with a predetermined initial markup percentage. This is most useful in making estimates of profit possibilities under various combinations of sales volume, initial markup, and expense ratios.

If all but one factor in the initial markup equation is known, it is easy to solve for the unknown one. This is frequently the profit. A merchant or department buyer must frequently test what profit he can hope to achieve if he aims at an initial markup percentage that seems reasonable to him in view of past experience and the competitive situation.

Thus, a buyer may have been operating at a 40 percent initial markup and wish to continue; his probable reductions this year may be 8 percent and his expenses 30 percent. There may be no cash discounts or alteration costs. He wishes to determine what profit he may hope to realize. This may be done by applying the basic equation:

$$\text{Initial markup } \% = \frac{\text{Maintained markup } \% + \text{Reductions } \%}{100\% + \text{Reductions } \%}$$

Applying this method, calling the maintained markup M, and making use of decimals rather than percentages,

$$.40 = \frac{M + .08}{1.00 + .08}$$
$$.40 \times 1.08 = M + .08$$
$$.432 = M + .08$$
$$M = .432 - .08$$
$$M = .352 \text{ or } 35.2\%$$

Since no cash discounts or alteration costs are involved, the maintained markup is the same as the gross margin. Therefore, the gross margin minus expenses (35.2 percent–30 percent) equals 5.2 percent, the profit.

The equation used above may be transposed as follows to facilitate the calculation of the maintained markup:[10]

[10] The steps in the transposition are

$$I = \frac{M + R}{1 + R}$$
$$I + IR = M + R$$
$$M = I - R + IR$$
$$M = I - R (1 - I)$$

Maintained markup % = Initial markup % − Reductions ×
(100% − Initial markup %)
Thus, Maintained markup % = 40% − 8% (100% − 40%)
= 40% − (8% × 60%)
= 40% − 4.8% = 35.2%, as above

OPERATING AT AN INITIAL MARKUP THAT YIELDS AN APPARENT LOSS

It must not be concluded that the markup finally set for a classification of goods, for a department, or for a store is simply the result of a mathematical calculation. The demand side, the markup at which goods will sell readily, is fully as important as the cost side. If the markup finally set is less than the mathematical markup, an attempt may be made to operate on a lower expense rate and to reduce markdowns. The originally planned profit figure may also suffer, but every effort should be made to protect it. At times, however, a department or merchandise classification may be operated at a markup that yields an apparent loss and yet it may be continued under one more of the following circumstances:

1. If the lines involved are essential for the completeness of the store. Goodwill and the patronage of other lines would be lost if the ones in question were discontinued. For example, women would expect to find boys' clothing in a department store and would resent the inability to buy clothing for their boys in the place they buy girls' clothing and men's furnishings.
2. If the line is a traffic builder that attracts customers to purchase other goods.
3. If the insufficient markup represents a temporary condition that may be rectified as the season progresses, as outside conditions improve, or as management is improved.
4. If the markup is sufficient to cover losses from markdowns and the direct expenses of the department and to contribute to the indirect expenses. For example, a department may have a stock costing $10,000 and retailing at $15,000. Because of depreciation in the form of markdowns and shortages, only $14,000 may be realized for the goods. The direct expenses that could be eliminated, were the department discontinued, might be $3,000, and the indirect expenses might be $2,000. The latter represents a share of the joint expenses for the store as a whole and would continue whether or not the department were operated. The markup of $5,000 on the stock is obviously insufficient to cover markdowns and shortages of

$1,000, direct expenses of $3,000, and indirect expenses of $2,000. Not only is there nothing left for operating profit, but there is a $1,000 operating loss. But at least the department brings in sufficient income to cover direct expenses and to contribute $1,000 to the joint expenses of the store. Were the department discontinued, this $1,000 would not be received, the indirect expenses would continue, and the store profits would be $1,000 smaller than with the "losing" department in operation. When charged with what seems to be a fair share of joint expense, the department is unprofitable, but from the broader viewpoint, it is profitable, since it shoulders some of the indirect expense burden. Unless the management sees a more productive use (a) for the space occupied by the department, (b) for the merchandise investment, or (c) for the personnel investment, the department will be continued, even where there is no prospect for improvement.

LIMITATIONS OF THE MARKUP PERCENTAGE AS A GUIDE TO PROFITS

Although the markup percentage is a useful index of the ability of a buyer to obtain a markup high enough to cover expenses and reductions and still show a profit, there are times when it is misleading. For example, a buyer may realize an initial markup of 40 percent on goods to be sold during a period: $10,000 at retail and $6,000 at cost. This $4,000 markup should cover expenses and reductions. If expenses are $3,000, and reduction $800, the 40 percent markup allows a $200 profit margin:

Expenses	$3,000
Reductions	800
Total	$3,800
Initial markup	4,000
Profit margin	$ 200

With the reductions $800, the sales would be $10,000 less $800, or $9,200.

Were sales to fall off, however, a 40 percent markup on purchases might prove wholly inadequate to yield a profit. For example, a 25 percent decline in sales would reduce the original retail price of the goods to be sold to $7,500. With the same markup percentage,

only $3,000 rather than $4,000 would be available for the three factors enumerated. If prices are declining, it may not be possible to
lower reductions (largely markdowns), and expenses as a general
rule cannot be reduced as rapidly as the decline in sales. The situation
would then be somewhat as follows:

Expenses—down 12½% (½ rate of sales decline)	$2,625
Reductions—same rate	600
Total	$ 3,225
Initial markup	3,000
Profit margin	− $225 (loss)

The 40 percent markup that had proved a satisfactory guide
to profits now yields a loss, owing to declining volume and to the fixed
nature of many items of expense.

During periods of declining sales, more attention should be
given to the dollar markup and not simply to the percentage, for the
former percentage of markup may now be insufficient for a profit.
Conversely, as sales increase, the dollar markup may be maintained
at an adequate level even though the percentage of markup declines.
Expenses are paid in dollars, not in percentages, and the dollar figure
should not be lost track of in the endeavor to adhere to fixed percentage relationships.

The philosophy of low margin retailing.   The importance of
markup dollars rather than percentages is inherent in the discounter's
philosophy. This means that if lower prices with a reduced markup
percentage yield more sales and if enough units are sold, the net
dollar markup may be increased. And if total expenses do not increase
proportionately, greater profits will result.

Referring to the prior example of the traditional 40 percent
markup, a discounter may choose to reduce his markup to only 28
percent and succeed in doubling his sales to $20,000. The result might
be:

Expenses:	up only 25% because many are fixed and fewer costly services are offered	$4,000
Reduction:	also up only 25% in view of quicker sales	1,000
Total		$5,000
Initial markup:	28% of the original retail (the sum of $20,000 sales plus $1,000 reductions)	5,880
Profit margin		$ 880

QUESTIONS FOR DISCUSSION

1. Would you urge a merchant who figures his markup at cost to change to the retail basis?
2. (a) Of the seven types of calculation given in table 4.1, which two is a store buyer likely to find most useful?
   (b) Answer the same question with regard to table 4.2.
3. If a buyer retails an imported item that costs only fifty cents at ten dollars, what will be his markup on cost? On retail?
4. Were you to go into the retail business, would you instruct your bookkeeper to enter merchandise purchases at billed cost or at net cost with cash discounts available deducted?
5. (a) Why is the maintained markup in a department or store nearly always less than the initial markup?
   (b) Why is the gross margin often larger than the maintained markup?
6. Do you feel that the initial markup formula is actually a practical way of planning initial markup or is it more useful in estimating profit probabilities at different markups that are under consideration?
7. In a men's sportswear department, you are aiming at a departmental contribution, after direct expenses, of 24 percent of sales. Direct expenses are estimated at 13 percent. Estimate additional data for markdowns, shortages, cash discounts earned, and alteration costs and calculate the necessary initial markup.[11]
8. In a glassware department, you plan to achieve an initial markup of 49 percent. Estimate reductions (markdowns and shortages), cash discounts, and direct expenses (selling and buying salaries and advertising) and calculate by means of the initial markup formula the probable contribution of the department.
9. If a selling department shows an initial markup of 41 percent and a maintained markup of 35.1 percent, what must the reductions have been? Is this a satisfactory way to determine the reduction figures for guidance in operation?
10. Why is an initial markup goal that has been a satisfactory guide in the past often inadequate when sales volume declines?
11. What three results should be obtained to justify the discounter's philosophy of a low markup?

[11] Reference to a recent MOR report of the National Retail Merchants Association will help determine reasonable estimates.

5

THE PRICING
OF
INDIVIDUAL
ITEMS

The discussion so far has had to do with the planning of an average markup for a department or merchandise classification that is set to yield a profit objective. But it does not answer the question of how to price the individual articles of merchandise that make up the assortment.

PRICING METHODS

In practice, a variety of concepts have been applied in the retail pricing of merchandise.

PRICES DETERMINED BY THE VENDOR

The merchant can accept the retail price either set or suggested by the vendor, but this practice gives him little or no control over his markup. He has to try to adjust his expenses and price reductions to whatever markup the retail prices determined by the vendor provide. He has no advantage over his competitors because his prices are standard. Furthermore, this method is limited to those lines where the sellers customarily set or suggest retail prices for their customers. Although it might provide an adequate overall markup for the average convenience goods store, it would not normally provide for the expenses associated with special services that the store may wish to offer.

PRICES DETERMINED BY CUSTOMER ACCEPTANCE

In some merchandise lines, the retail prices are largely determined by the customer whose degree of knowledge about customary market prices greatly limits the merchant's freedom of decision. Goods that are commonly priced this way may be classified as follows:

Class A. Products whose market price is well known to most customers. These include staple and standard convenience goods. The retail prices set are based on competitive market price. However, they may be priced somewhat above the market price if the store offers unusual service or provides an atmosphere of opulence. They may be priced somewhat below the market price if the store is streamlined in its service and depends largely on a bargain price appeal. A product in this class might be dropped entirely if the retail market price would not produce a contribution to profit above direct expenses.[1]

Class B. Products of which customers know only the approximate prices. For example, the customer may be able to evaluate a dress as retailing somewhere between $15 and $25. Such merchandise would be marked at a predetermined price line set within this range.[2]

Class C. Novelties, new products, replacement parts, and confined goods of which customers have little knowledge of retail prices. Such merchandise will usually be priced to provide a high markup percentage. The retail price will depend upon rough estimates of sales opportunities and margin at different price points. Usually, the new product will first be sold at a high markup to skim the cream off the market. If it catches on, it is likely to be reduced to a price that yields a normal markup, since the goods now fall into the Class B group. A large retailer might try to penetrate the market in depth right at the start by taking a normal markup. While this practice is sometimes a wise one for the manufacturer, it is not likely to work out well for the retailer unless he has complete control over the product.

[1] See the discussion of market plus and market minus pricing in chapter 7.

[2] See the discussion of price lining in chapter 6.

On some goods, a store may have something of a monopoly. A good example of this is special parts for particular equipment, such as for a car or a sewing machine. Since the replacement of worn parts is essential to the use of the articles as a whole and since there is little competition in the retail distribution of these parts, the parts can often be priced high, with little consideration to costs, and still suffer no loss in sale opportunity. The limited yet persistent demand allows a high markup over a long period of time. On the other hand, standardized parts usable on varied equipment are generally sold at competitive prices.

PRICES DETERMINED BY THE MARKUP FORMULA

The merchant may adopt a customary markup percentage goal or he may mathematically calculate an initial markup for his store or department that is designed to yield a planned profit goal. This is then applied to most purchases, except those that are price fixed. For example, if the goal is 40 percent, the item costing sixty cents is marked at one dollar and the item costing six dollars is marked at ten dollars. Small merchants are likely to simplify the arithmetic for themselves by using fractions. A 40 percent markup means adding two-thirds to the cost; a 33⅓ percent markup means increasing the cost by one-half, and so forth.

This practice gives no consideration to the degree of customer acceptance at various price points and, in practice, is not likely to achieve the markup goal. Competition simply will not allow the sale of many items at the desired level of markup. Markdowns will have to be taken, even if the goods are first introduced into stock at the goal markup. A merchant must take a larger markup where competition permits to offset the lower markup where competition does not permit. The late Lew Hahn, president of the National Retail Dry Goods Association,[3] put it like this: "If you want to get by car to a spot 400 miles away in 10 hours, you will never get there in 10 hours if you attempt to keep going at 40 miles an hour. You will pass through congested places where you can only crawl and must step on the gas when you hit the open road."

PRICES SET TO MAXIMIZE THE CONTRIBUTION OF EACH ITEM TO PROFIT

The merchant may attempt to forecast the probable sales of the item at various price points and also the direct handling costs

---

[3] Now National Retail Merchants Association.

associated with sales at each point.[4] He then calculates the item's contribution to other expenses and profits and selects the price that provides the largest contribution. For example:

Cost per Unit	Possible Retail Prices per Unit	Estimated Sales in Units	Margin	Direct Handling Cost 50¢ per Unit	Contribution to Profit
$6.00	$7.00	100	$100	$50.00	$50.00
	8.00	90	180	45.00	135.00
	9.00	80	240	40.00	200.00
	10.00	75	300	37.50	263.50
	11.00	60	300	30.00	270.00
	12.00	40	240	20.00	220.00

cost-retail

Although the margin is the same at the $10 and at the $11 retail prices, the $11 price is the optimum one because direct expenses are lower. Under this concept, it would be chosen as the retail price.

This method has the germ of a great truth: Volume opportunities at various price points must be considered wherever the merchant has any freedom in pricing. To pinpoint sales at different price points, however, and to estimate closely the direct expenses at each point are beyond the skill of even the most intuitive and astute merchant. Perhaps the true volume opportunity at $9 is one hundred twenty units, not eighty. This result would yield a margin of $360 and a profit contribution of $300. Furthermore, the method concentrates on short-term considerations. Perhaps the particular item would be more profitable at $11 than at $10, but at the $11 price it might not enhance a desired image of giving the customer exceptional value.

Because of such difficulties, most planners give considerable attention to the overall markup percentage goal and try not to deviate very far from it unless they have a strong intuition that the product is exceptional in that it is very likely to sell extremely well at a high markup or, on the contrary, that it is likely to an outstanding seller at a very low markup.

PRICES SET BY MEANS OF MERCHANDISE MANAGEMENT ACCOUNTING

The method of setting prices by management accounting puts primary emphasis on the costs and expenses to the store or depart-

---

[4] Advertising costs may also be considered.

ment of handling the goods that fall into various classifications or subclassifications of merchandise.[5] The accountant determines for each class of units the costs of the various functions performed upon it in connection with handling and selling it. This is not strictly unit cost accounting, since no effort is made to determine the precise expenses associated with each item. Instead, items are grouped into narrow categories, depending upon estimates of differences in handling, selling, and servicing requirements, and expenses are estimated for the different groupings. Some of the expenses are called *flat* expenses, that is, they do not vary with the value of the unit; they are stated in dollars and cents. Others, those stated in percentages, are called *value variable expenses*; they tend to vary with the retail value of the item.

For goods in a particular merchandise classification, the costs appearing in table 5.1 may be determined and then used to find the break-even retail prices for goods costing various amounts. The break-even retail is the price that provides a margin that will just cover costs and expenses and make no contribution to profit.

If an appliance costs $140.00, for example, there will be added

TABLE 5.1   Cost Elements for a Major Appliances Classification

	A Flat Costs	B % of Retail Price
Receiving	$0.65	
Warehousing	1.45	
Selling		6.0
Advertising		2.5
Carrying charges		(2.75)
Credit expense	2.00	
Delivery	3.63	
Installation	3.50	
Warranty	2.10	
Markdowns		4.0
Other costs		1.17
Total	$13.33	10.92

Courtesy: Journal of Retailing, Spring, 1958, p. 23. Carrying charges are minus because of vendor rebate.

[5] For a thorough analysis of this method see Robert Matthew Beall II, "Merchandise Management Accounting: An Inquiry into the Impact on Department Store Merchandising Practices" (MBA thesis, Graduate School of Business Administration Library, New York University, 1969).

to this the *flat* expenses of $13.33 and the value variable expenses of $10.92 percent of the break-even retail price. The break-even price can then be calculated as follows:

Break-even retail = $140.00 (cost) + $13.33
(flat expense) + 10.92% of break-even retail
(value variable expense).
Break-even retail − 10.92% of break-even
retail = $153.33.   89.08% of break-even
retail = $153.33.   Break-even retail = $153.33 ÷ .8908
= $172.00 (approx.).

At any price above $172.00, the appliance will make a contribution to profit; below, it will show a loss. At a retail of $200.00, for example, the contribution would be $24.83 ($60.00 gross margin −$13.33 "flat" expense −10.92 percent of $200.00).

When introduced some years ago this method caused a considerable stir in retail circles, but in practice it has seldom been employed. Actually to pinpoint expenses and costs to each unit in a narrow classification of merchandise is an accounting problem of the first magnitude. Most of the expenses singled out to charge to the unit are really joint costs allocated to units. There is no assurance that the handling of any unit actually generates that much expense or that the dropping of an item will cut expenses by the amounts indicated. Again, any unit expenses based on the average of past experience might not be applicable to an item now to be handled. Even if receiving plus warehousing expenses have averaged $2.10 per unit in the past, it does not mean that the handling of this $140.00 item will make any addition to the actual expense figure. The employees involved may not be working at maximum capacity and there may be unused storage space. On the other hand, were people and space used to capacity, the handling of an additional line might require expansion that would cost much more than $2.10 for each of the additional units to be handled.

Even more seriously, the plan gives no direct attention to the sales opportunities that may greatly reduce some of the expenses per unit and also turn a small unit contribution into a very large aggregate.

Even though merchandise management accounting is not used in a strict sense today, it has had an important impact on the thinking that goes into pricing decisions. The approach reveals an important fact: High-priced merchandise can generally be sold profitably at a lower markup percentage than can low-priced goods. This is because many expenses vary with units rather than with dollars. The following example explains the reasoning. Here a doubling of the flat expenses (handling and storage) is provided for, but they are still very low relative to the high cost of the mink coats.

However, the low markup on high-priced goods would have to be offset by a higher than the required average on low-priced goods. Competition doesn't usually permit this because customers generally have a better knowledge of values in the low-priced area. There are two ways out of this dilemma: (1) to drop the low-priced goods from stock, if they are making a negative contribution to indirect expense and profit, or (2) to increase the sales of high-priced goods to make it possible to operate profitably at a lower markup than formerly thought necessary.

PRICING A HIGH UNIT-VALUE ARTICLE

In a fur store with a planned 35 percent markup, the merchant purchased some mink coats at $2,000 each. The average-priced coat in his store was $400 retail with expenses per unit as follows: $60 handling expense, $30 occupancy expense, and $10 store indirect expenses. The mink coats were expected to sell more slowly than the rest of the stock—in fact, at a turnover one-half as great. It was also estimated that each sale of the mink would cost about twice as much to handle as the other merchandise because of the extra selling time and effort required. Markdowns on the average sale averaged $25 a unit but on expensive mink coats about fifteen times as much. There was a great *demand* on the part of customers for mink, but few could afford to pay more than $2,750. The question was whether the buyer could afford to sell them at that price. He reasoned as follows:

Normal Unit of Sale		*Mink Coat*	
Cost ($400×65%)	$260	Cost	$2,000
Handling expense	60	Handling expense	120
Occupancy expense	30	Occupancy expense	60
Indirect expense	10	Indirect expense	10
Markdowns	25	Markdowns	375
Total cost	$385	Total Cost	$2,565
Retail	400	Retail	2,750
Profit	$ 15	Profit	$ 185

He concluded that if he looked to each transaction for his *average* indirect expense per units of $10, he could make $185 profit by selling mink coats at $2,750, a markup of only 27.3 percent. Even were he to charge fifteen times as much indirect expense ($150) to the mink as to the typical transaction, he would still make a larger dollar profit than on his typical sale. Of course, if he could sell the coats in reasonable quantity at a regular markup—at $3,077—there would be no point in the price cut. Since many more would sell at $2,750 than at $3,000 plus, however, he decided to take the low markup.

JUDGMENT METHOD OF PRICING

Still another method of pricing involves an analysis of each item in reference to both customer demand and expenses of handling and selling to the customer.

The merchant begins with the average percentage markup goal for the department or classification and applies it to the item. He then moves up or down from this price depending on his analysis of whether the item incorporates more of the conditions that warrant a high markup or more of those that warrant a low markup.

Conditions justifying a high markup.   The conditions under which a buyer is usually able to obtain a higher markup than the average required are as follows:

1. When the risk of price reduction is unusually great. If the danger of obsolescence, deterioration, breakage, and theft is greater than that associated with most of the merchandise carried, the markup taken should normally be high to protect profit.

2. When the expenses of handling and storage are likely to be abnormally great relative to the price of the goods: (a) goods may be bulky and require delivery to customers, or they may require more expensive packing than usual, and (b) goods may have a very low stock turnover, necessitating more occupancy expense for a considerably longer period than that for most goods carried. For example, it may take two months to sell out most purchases, whereas the goods in question, occupying equal space, may take four months. Normally, they should have a higher markup to offset the doubling of the cost of space.

3. When cash discounts on the merchandise in question are lower than the average.

4. When alteration and workroom costs are abnormally high.

5. When the goods are exclusive and not subject to direct competition. The merchant takes advantage of such opportunities to

sell at a higher markup and thus offset the lower than average markups he frequently takes.

6. When the price that customers expect to pay is well above the normal markup. For example, a merchant may procure a lot of goods normally costing $4.80 at a bargain price of $3.00, and his normal markup may be 40 percent. To mark the goods $5.00 rather than $8.00 may make customers suspicious of their quality. A price of $6.95 or more may be necessary to convince customers of the genuine value.

7. When a retail price line has been established and the goods cost somewhat less than the average cost price that the merchant can afford in order to resell at this retail price. Thus, the markup of the department may be 40 percent and the established price $25.00. On an average, then, the merchant can pay $15.00 ($25 × .60), but he may set up a buying range of $13.50 to $16.50, pricing any goods bought within this cost range at $25.00. Thus, any article costing between $13.50 and $15.00 will enjoy a higher than average markup.

Conditions justifying a low markup. Goods often warrant a lower than average markup in situations the reverse of those just explained:

1. When the danger of price reduction is very small, as in the case of much staple merchandise.

2. When the expenses of handling are relatively small: (a) no packaging or delivery needed; (b) very high turnover, resulting in low space cost per unit; and (c) high unit of sale, as explained in the mink coat example.

3. When cash discounts are higher than average.

4. When alteration and workroom costs are very small.

5. When the goods are carried by most dealers and are therefore subject to much price competition.

6. When the customary price is lower than the price necessary to yield an average markup. This is a corollary to point 5.

7. When a retail price established by the vendor provides less than the average markup. This often occurs when the manufacturer sets a resale price under the fair trade laws. Conceivably, this contract price may provide a higher than average markup.

8. When the volume possibilities at a lower than average markup will yield a larger dollar profit than could be obtained with an average markup. For example, a millinery store may need a 40.9 percent markup with estimated sales of $100,000 and reductions of $10,000. Yet, the buyer might pay $4 each for a lot of 1,000 hats to sell at $5 provided the sales of the lot will be an *addition* to the $100,000 planned:

	Cost	Ratail	Markup
Planned purchases	$65,000	$110,000	$45,000 (40.9%)
Additional purchases	4,000	5,000	1,000 (20.0%)
Total purchases	$69,000	$115,000	$46,000 (40.0%)
Markdowns (all on originally planned purchases)		10,000	
Sales (all merchandise sold)		$105,000	
Cost of sales		69,000	
Gross margin		$ 36,000	

The gross margin figure of $36,000 is $1,000 more than what would have been realized with a markup of 40.9 percent but with only $100,000 in sales.[6]

The operating profit may not be quite $1,000 larger because of additional expenses of handling the extra sales, but these additional expenses would probably be less than 10 percent of the additional sales of $5,000. Thus, the low markup percentage may increase profits if *extra* volume can be achieved.

A low markup, where it means increased volume, does not necessitate a higher markup on other goods and may actually lead to a decrease both in the average markup and in the markup on other goods.

SETTING LIMITS ON MARKUP

In permitting long markups on exclusive and novelty goods, as distinct from staples, it may be necessary to set certain markup limits. In one department it was concluded that any markup above 50 percent of retail, that is, more than double the cost, is dangerous. As a rule of thumb it was concluded that the profit possibilities at a higher markup are seldom as good as those below. The small sales volume that could generally be realized at a higher markup cut down on total margin. The department had a great deal of competition and carried goods of the same type that all its competitors carried; accordingly, every attempt to "get away" with a high markup was likely to lead to the discovery by customers that someone else was selling comparable goods cheaper. The department thus found by trial and error that in the long run the best adjustment was a price no more than double the cost.

[6] With only regular merchandise, cost of sales would have been $65,000 and gross margin $35,000.

On the other hand, stores that handle really exclusive goods of the specialty class need not be limited to a set maximum percentage in setting prices—that is, the volume and margin combination may be greater at a very large markup than at a moderate one. For example, one shop makes a specialty of seashells and dinosaur bones, which can be sold many times above cost. A lower price would probably have no effect on volume, for the store has no competition and the few who want these curios buy as much at one price as at another, so long as it is within the zone of their buying power—a shell costing $0.15 may sell just as fast at $1.00 as it would at $0.25.

Even as it may be desirable to set a maximum markup percentage, so it is sometimes desirable to set a minimum markup. For example, it may be found that direct expenses per transaction are nearly always at least 5 percent of the cost value; thus a $1.00 cost item should not be sold for less than $1.05 regardless of volume possibilities at a lower markup.

To avoid unprofitable extremes in the markup percentage, some stores have set limits for the buyer. Markups outside of these limits have to be authorized by the merchandise manager or owner. These limits are expressed in one of two ways: (1) as a markup range and (2) as a cost range for certain fixed retail prices. Under the first plan, with an average planned markup of 40 percent, a range of 30 percent to 50 percent may be allowed.

Under the second plan, a range of cost prices is set for every regular retail price line. For example, where an average markup of 36½ percent is planned, goods for retail at $2.95 must be bought between $20.00 and $24.00 a dozen. The intention may be to buy most of the goods for $22.50 a dozen but to allow some leeway.

AVERAGING MARKUP IN PRICING

The opportunities to average high and low markups so as to yield a desired goal are found largely in apparel and home furnishings lines when fashion is involved. In the case of staples (Class A merchandise as described earlier in this chapter) the buyer has little control over his markups, but even here he can give increased promotional emphasis to lines carrying the higher markups.

Procedure Involved

An example of the problem of averaging is as follows: A dealer plans to spend $6,000.00 for merchandise on which he should realize a markup of 40 percent of retail. Among the articles he buys, he purchases one thousand units costing $1.00 each, which he finds it necessary to retail at $1.20 each, a much lower markup than the aggregate desired. If a 40 percent markup is to be realized on the aggregate purchases, the balance must carry a markup higher than 40 percent. The exact markup necessary is computed as follows:

	Cost	Retail	Percent of Markup
Total planned purchases	$6,000	$10,000	40
Purchases made	1,000	1,200	16⅔
Purchases to be made	$5,000	$ 8,800	43.18

$$\$8,800 - \$5,000 = \$3,800$$

and
$$\frac{\$3,800}{\$8,800} = 43.18\%$$

　　On the balance of his purchases the merchant will attempt to realize a markup of over 43 percent. The opposite situation may occur where the buyer has purchased $5,000 worth of goods out of $6,000 planned and had realized a markup of 43.18 percent on the purchases thus far. He may wish to procure $1,000 worth of merchandise as a leader on which a very low markup will be realized. If he gets a markup of only 16⅔ percent on this $1,000 purchase, the desired average will still be attained. Thus, he is enabled to hold a special promotion at a bargain price. Buyers are always on the lookout for items on which long markups are possible, so as to set up reserves for necessarily short or low markups.

　　Common error.　An error commonly made is to attempt to average markup percentages of retail, weighting them by cost quantities. In the example, the total markup of 40 percent would be weighted erroneously by the 6($6,000), giving 240 percent. The markup of 16⅔ percent would be weighted by 1($1,000) and subtracted, giving 223⅓ percent as the weighted markup on 5/6 of the stock. Dividing by 5 gives 44.67 percent, over 1½ percent larger than the correct figure. The difficulty is that markup percentages of retail should be weighted only by retail quantities, in this instance by 10 and 1.2 rather than by 6 and 1.

　　Seasonal adjustment.　Some merchants attempt to balance their high and low markup purchases each day or each week so as to adhere to the average planned, but it is sometimes necessary to strike a balance only over the entire season. For example, a buyer may plan an initial markup of 40 percent for a spring season, February through

July. On June 1, when two-thirds of the season is past, the actual markup to date may be computed as follows:

	Cost	Retail	Markup Percent
Inventory, Febuary 1	$ 6,200	$10,000	38
Purchases, February 1–May 31	18,200	30,000	39⅓
Total merchandise handled	$24,400	$40,000	39

The buyer may be planning to make purchases at cost during June and July of $8,000. He may compute his desired purchase markup for this two-month period as follows:

	Cost	Retail	Markup Percent
Total merchandise handled to date	$24,400	$40,000	
Planned purchases June and July	8,000	(14,000)	
Total	$32,400	($54,000)	40

$32,400 ÷ .60 = $54,000, the total retail value of the season's planned merchandise handled.

Since, of this total, $40,000 has already obtained, planned purchases must have a retail value of $14,000. Since the cost is $8,000, the dollar markup desired is $6,000, or 42.86 percent.

Many stores plan purchases at retail rather than at cost. For example, the retailer may plan to buy $15,000 worth of goods at retail in June and July. The question is: How much can he pay for them in order to realize a 40 percent initial markup for the season?

	Cost	Retail	Markup Percent
Total merchandise handled to date	$24,400	$40,000	
Planned purchases	(8,600)	15,000	
Total	($33,000)	$55,000	40

$55,000 × .60 = $33,000, the aggregate cost. $33,000 − $24,400 = $8,600, the desired cost of the planned purchases. $15,000 − $8,600 = $6,400, the purchase markup, or 42⅔ percent.

Varying Monthly Markup Plans

To achieve a predetermined markup percentage over a season or year is one of the merchant's major objectives. If he fails, his profits will be adversely affected unless he can sell more goods than planned or reduce expenses or markdown losses. Since attainable markups may vary not only on different merchandise but with the season of the year, an even more elaborate calculation is sometimes required.

For example, one buyer of coats had a markup goal for the six-month spring season of 42 percent. The markup on his opening retail inventory of $18,000 was 41 percent. During February, he achieved a purchase markup of 44 percent on $5,000 worth of retail purchases; during March, a purchase markup of 43 percent on $7,000 worth of retail purchases; and in April, 42½ percent on $8,000 worth. He was directed to take part in a big special sale to take place in June with the goods coming into stock in May. In order to present very good values to the public, the buyer decided to aim at a markup of only 35 percent on his May purchases, which would total $9,000 at retail. His planned retail purchases for the entire spring season were $40,000 and the question was: What markup should he attempt to obtain during the other two months (June and July), so as to end up with an aggregate markup of 42 percent? He solved the problem first by estimating the total merchandise handled for the season, reducing it to cost, and subtracting the opening inventory at cost.

	Cost	Retail	Markup Percent
Opening inventory	($10,620)	$18,000	41
Planned season purchases	($23,020)	40,000	
Total merchandise handled (planned)	($33,640)	$58,000	42

Thus, he established that his $40,000 planned retail purchases should cost no more than $23,020.

Second, he accumulated his cost and retail purchases to date plus the plan for the month of May.

	Cost	Retail	Markup Percent
February (actual)	$ 2,800	$ 5,000	44
March (actual)	3,990	7,000	43
April (actual)	4,600	8,000	42.5
May (estimated)	5,850	9,000	35
Total, 4 months	$17,240	$29,000	

The next step was to subtract the four-month total from the plan for the six months:

	Cost	Retail
Planned season purchases	$23,020	$40,000
Four-month total	17,240	29,000
Planned purchases for June and July	$ 5,780	$11,000

Thus, the markup needed in June and July was $5,220 ($11,000–$5,780) and the markup percent 47.5 ($5,220 ÷ $11,000).

This figure is so much higher than the markup achieved in any month so far as to seem virtually unattainable. Accordingly, consideration should be given to revising the May planned markup upward; otherwise the season's objective of 42 percent is hardly to be achieved.

PRICING, AN ART

The pricing of merchandise is an art, not a science. The merchandiser's goal is to obtain not as high a percentage markup as possible but as high a dollar contribution to joint expenses and profits as is compatible with goodwill building and customer loyalty. For example, a $0.60 cost item retailed for $1.00 (40 percent markup) may sell at the rate of ten a week, yielding a gross margin of $4.00. If direct expenses of handling each unit are $0.05, or $0.50 on the ten, the item will contribute $3.50 a week.

If the merchandiser senses that a price of $0.90 (33⅓ percent markup) would result in sales of twenty a week, he would earn at this point a total gross margin of twenty times $0.30, or $6.00. With unit handling expenses of $0.05 or $1.00 for twenty, the item would contribute $5.00 a week; the 33⅓ percent markup would be immediately more profitable than the 40 percent markup. Of course, some other combination of sales volume and markup might prove better yet, and profits may deliberately be sacrificed today to assure future patronage. In many instances, however, a high markup percentage will not cut into sales volume materially and will yield a higher dollar profit than a normal markup without sacrificing goodwill. The astute merchant is continually searching to find these *optimum* prices at which markup and volume combine to provide the largest dollar profit. But he often prices somewhat below them so that customers will be well satisfied and will continue to buy.

Because of the difficulty of forecasting volume at different price levels, however, the merchant hesitates to deviate too far from a planned initial markup percentage that gives consideration to his total probable expenses, probable reductions, and normal profit. A further discussion of pricing policy appears in the next chapter.

QUESTIONS FOR DISCUSSION

1. Is the classification of goods according to the degree of customer knowledge as to their worth a sound basis for pricing?

2. Is it justifiable to apply a planned markup percentage to all purchases within a merchandise classification?

3. Would there be any merit in applying a fixed dollar markup rather than a fixed percentage markup to each item? For example, if unit sales are estimated at one thousand and the total dollar markup required to cover expenses and price reductions is $4,000, the average markup to break-even is $4 per unit. Are there instances where this dollar markup, with an added profit margin, should be applied to items having different cost prices?

4. Even though sales volume at any proposed price cannot exactly be forecast, is it not better to estimate the price providing the optimum profit or contribution rather than rely on a planned percentage of markup?

5. For what kind of item or under what circumstances may a high retail price result in a greater sales volume in units than a lower price on exactly the same merchandise? Why?

6. What are the chief lessons to be learned from the merchandise accounting approach to pricing?

7. Is it practical for the buyer to relate every new product to be priced to a checklist of conditions associated with high and low markups?

8. Demonstrate how a less than average markup can increase the total gross margin in dollars.

9. In attempting to attain his goal markup should the buyer seek to average his markup every day (when in the wholesale market) every week, every month, every season, or every year?

10. If you have obtained a markup of 40 percent on three-fourths of your retail purchases and require an average markup on all purchases of 42 percent retail, what markup would you have to achieve on the remainder of your purchases?

11. In connection with the example on pages 93–94, what markup would you recommend for May?

6

PLANNING PRICE LINES

PRICE LINES AND ZONES

A pricing policy of considerable importance for merchants who deal in apparel and home furnishings is whether to mark each item at any price that seems likely to give the desired sales and profit results or to set up distinct retail price lines or ranges and to insist that every item be marked at one of these prices and not at points in between. Price lining is based on the belief that customers are grouped into rather narrow purchasing power zones; for example, there may be a large number of women who pay between $5.00 and $7.00 for a handbag. Within these limits the demands of members of each group are flexible; if a store establishes a single price somewhere near the center of the zone, it may be able to satisfy the price demands of most customers in the zone. Thus, a price line of perhaps $5.95 might be established. Where the zone is broad, two or three price lines may be necessary in the zone.

Price lining is primarily suited to shopping goods, that is, to merchandise of which the customer wishes to inspect an assortment of styles, patterns, or colors before selection (see table 6.1). It is particularly adaptable to apparel, apparel accessories, and home furnishings in the popular price ranges, but it has only a limited application to convenience and specialty goods. There is no need for a grocery store to maintain price lines of canned peas or of coffee—the customer does not wish to compare an assortment in a price line before buying. The demand is for specific articles or brands rather than for a class from which a choice is to be made. Thus drugs, notions, and housewares do not generally need price lines. It is true that individual prices must be set to realize a free flow of sales, but there is no need to have a variety of items all at the same price.

THE PRICE ZONE VERSUS THE PRICE LINE

Price Zone: A range of prices all appealing to customers in a certain demographic group. It is also called a *price range*.
  Example: $17.95 to $25.00 dresses.
Price Line: A specific price within a price zone at which a representative stock is carried.
  Example: $19.95 dresses.
Note: There may be more than one price line within a zone. Example: $17.95, $19.95, $22.95, and $25.00 within the $17.95 to $25.00 zone.

Nor are price lines necessary in high-priced goods where the price is a minor consideration in selection. In real jewelry, as distinguished from novelty and costume jewelry, the customer is not looking for assortments in certain price zones but rather for one-of-a-kind merchandise of a specialty nature. The same logic applies to high-priced apparel. Likewise in expensive antiques, price lines do not fit into the customer's buying psychology. However, in the case of inexpensive antiques and gifts, price lines may be very important, for the customer may be seeking something in a price zone that will fill a general need and he wants an assortment to choose from in that range.

THE PROS AND CONS OF PRICE LINING

ADVANTAGES

The chief advantages of price lining for shopping goods are as follows:

1. Increased sales because of (a) bigger assortments in each price line made possible by elimination of in-between prices; (b) greater ease in getting a customer to come to a decision when her selection is limited to goods all at one price and to recognize readily the difference in values at different prices; and (c) more effective advertising and promotion, since the store can concentrate interest at a few price points. The customer gets to know the store's price lines and knows she can usually find complete assortments at these prices.

2. Easier-to-maintain stocks that are balanced to demand, because the merchant can focus his attention on a few prices rather than spread it over a great many.

3. Smaller total stocks, resulting in higher stockturn and lower markdown risk.

4. Price coordination of merchandise in different lines simplified. This point is discussed on page 102.

5. Easy to set the retail price. With price lining, the choice is generally limited to marking the goods at only one or possibly two retail prices in view of the cost price of the goods. If retailed at the higher price line the goods would not be attractive to the customer; if retailed at the next lower price line, the markup would be inadequate to cover expenses.

LIMITATIONS

In spite of the obvious advantages, there are some limitations to a policy sharply restricting the number of price lines:

1. Considerable jumps between prices make it difficult to trade up. For example, a store may have a $1.00 price, a $1.35 price, and a $1.75 price. There may be some customers who would pay more than $1.00 but not so much as $1.35, or more than $1.35 but no so much as $1.75. Chances to make a $1.50 sale rather than a $1.35 sale, for example, may be foregone in establishing price lines. To avoid the loss of such opportunities, some stores have substituted price zones for price lines. For example, $1.20 to $1.50 may be regarded as one zone centering at $1.35. Most goods in the zone may be marked at $1.35, but the manager is allowed to mark some items higher or lower. For merchandise control purposes, the zone may be treated as a single price line, and the goods in the zone are generally grouped together for customer convenience.

Although there is danger of curtailing the average sale by rigidity in price lining, particularly if the prices are far apart, it must be recognized that a few strong prices are just as likely to lead to trading up as to trading down. With a strong $1.35 price line, many

TABLE 6.1   List of Price Lines in Three Departments in one store—
an Example[a]

Medium-Priced Dresses		Popular-Priced Coats		Millinery	
Cost	Retail	Cost	Retail	Cost	Hetail
$10.75 {	$16.95	$29.95	$49.95	$3.00	$5.95
	17.95	35.00 }	59.95	3.50	6.95
11.75	19.95	39.75 }		4.00	7.95
12.75	22.95	39.75 }		4.50	8.95
14.75	25.00	42.75 }	69.95	5.50	10.95
16.75 }		45.00 }		6.50	12.95
17.75 }	29.95	45.00 }	79.95	7.50	15.00
18.75 }		49.75 }			
18.75 }	35.00	49.75	89.95		
19.75 }		59.75	98.00		
22.75 }		69.75	110.00		
23.75 }	39.95				
24.75 }					
26.75 }	45.00				
27.75 }					
29.75	45.95				

[a] It should be noted that there is considerable variation in markup at different points, except in the case of millinery. Thus, an $18.75 cost dress marked $29.95 provides a markup of only 37 percent, but if marked $35.00 provides a markup of 46 percent. Likewise, a $59.95 coat costing $35.00 provides a markup of 42 percent compared with a $69.95 coat costing $45.00 that provides a markup of only 36 percent, but the dollar markup at both prices is identical.

customers who intend to spend about $1.25 will spend $1.35 rather than drop to the $1.00 price line when they see that they can get better goods for an additional ten cents. The opportunity to offer complete assortments at a few prices probably more than offsets the advantage of complete flexibility, with prices a few cents apart. This leaves a continual question in the customers' minds to whether one item is worth the few cents more or not. The differences in price lines should be large enough so that customers can easily recognize the differences in quality and style.

2. Another limitation of price lining is that the arrangement is inflexible on a rising or a falling market. For example, a store may have one price line of $1.35 and a lower one of $1.00. Goods retailed at $1.35 may average $0.80 at cost and at $1.00, $0.60. A 10 percent decline in wholesale prices brings the cost of the former to $0.72 and makes the $1.35 price too high in view of competition. If the goods are marked at the lower price line, the markup is only 28 percent compared with a former 40 percent. There is no doubt that during

recessions stores that have established price lines find it difficult to adjust retail prices in the same ratio as the decline in wholesale prices. Likewise, on a rising wholesale market, to jump retail prices to the higher regular price line may harm sales; accordingly, there is a danger of holding to existing retail levels for a time after the wholesale has risen.

PLANNING BY ZONES

In weighing the importance of the limitations of price lining, it should be borne in mind that changes in wholesale price levels are bound to present a difficult problem whether price lines exist or not. During transition periods, new and intermediate price lines may have to be established and a careful analysis may have to be made of the relative merits of the former markup percentage at a restricted volume or maintained volume at a restricted markup. As suggested above, planning by price zones rather than by price lines often proves the better plan. Knowing, for example, that a representative assortment of dresses must be carried between $35.00 and $50.00, the store can change the price line emphasis within the zone in view of market offerings. Rather than be under any commitment to maintain a complete assortment at $40.00 for example, the buyer can move up or down within the range, selecting the point at which he can offer the most attractive merchandise at the moment, consistent with adequate markup.

Ordinarily, in most small stores and in departments of large stores, three price zones are sufficient: a middle-volume zone accounting for at least 50 percent of the total dollar sales volume, a lower-promotional zone accounting for 15 percent to 40 percent of the sales volume; and an upper-prestige zone accounting for 10 percent to 25 percent. In a large store that caters to many income groups, more than three zones may prove necessary. In these cases, it is desirable to establish separate budget or basement departments and possibly deluxe departments in addition to the regular upstairs departments. Thus it would be possible to have nine zones, even though there would be some overlap.

SETTING SPECIFIC PRICES AND ZONES

NUMBER OF PRICE LINES AND JUMPS BETWEEN

There is no categorical answer to the question of how many price lines should be carried. Some shoe stores and some men's clothing stores in the past have been successful with only one price in a major merchandise category, but most stores carry a number of price lines, breaking down customer demand into zones and subzones and carrying at least one price line within a subzone.

Example of price zones and common price lines. An example of price zones is given in table 6.2. It is a reasonable conclusion that at least one price line is necessary in each of the subzones that the store wishes to have represented in stock. A large popular-priced department store may carry C_3 merchandise up to A_3. Seven price lines, then, would be the minimum, but it might be wiser to have two price lines in every subzone.

An apparel chain may operate in zone C, with its peak unit volume at C_3. A better department store may operate in B and C, with its peak unit volume in C_1. A Fifth Avenue specialty shop may operate in zones A and B.

In general, the jumps between price lines should increase as one moves up the price scale, with the percentage increases remaining more nearly constant. Thus, a customer who normally pays $30 for a dress may be "traded up" to $40, which to her represents a dress and a third. It may be no more difficult to "trade up" a $60-dress customer to $80.

Again it should be observed that manufacturers' wholesale price lines have a great deal to do with the setting of retail price lines and that the relative emphasis on the price lines within the zone must fluctuate with changing market conditions.

Special Prices for Marked-Down Merchandise

It may be desirable to plan two sets of price lines—one for regular price lines, at which points new goods are added to stock, and another for goods that are being reduced in price. The special markdown prices become associated with bargains, in the customers' minds, and the segregation makes it possible to analyze the drawing power of goods as originally priced. For example, one shoe department established the following prices:

Regular	Markdown
$ 5.94	$ 4.94
7.94	6.44
9.34	8.44
11.74	10.74
13.89	11.89
16.89	13.74

The sales at regular prices are better guides as to the effectiveness of the regular prices than are all the sales, many of which may have been clearances from higher prices.[1]

TABLE 6.2   Example of Major Price Lines and Zones for Street Dresses[a]

Price Line	Subzone	Major Zone
Above $150 150	......................................A_1	
125 100 90	......................................A_2	......................................A
80 70 60	......................................A_3	
50 40 35	......................................B_1	
30 25	......................................B_2	......................................B
23 20	......................................B_3	
18 17	......................................C_1	
15 14 13	......................................C_2	C
11 10 9 8	......................................C_3	
7 Below 7	......................................C_p[b]	

[a] In practice, the price lines commonly end in odd cents, such as $29.95, rather than in even dollars, such as $30.00.
[b] Promotional prices, not regular price lines.

CORRELATION OF PRICE LINES AMONG DEPARTMENTS

It is generally agreed that price lines carried in related departments should be correlated with price lines in others so that customers

[1] See chapter 8 for a further discussion on markdowns.

shopping in one department will find goods in other departments that fall within their buying range. If customers who normally pay $100 for a winter coat expect to purchase a dress at $25, these price points should be carried in the two departments involved. Were the dress department to carry little or no assortments below $30, it would mean that satisfied $100-coat customers would have to shop elsewhere for their dresses.

One store concluded that the customer who would pay $100 for a coat would pay approximately the following prices for related items:

Daytime dress	$25
Evening dress	45
Hat	9
Shoes	13
Bag	7

Analysis in terms of zones rather than specific prices would probably have been more satisfactory. Also, it should be observed that store research along this line has not been conclusive because any one store's assortments at all price points are incomplete and many customers buy one item, such as shoes, in one store and hats in another. Thus, the best selling prices in the various departments are not necessarily those that appeal to the same typical customer. Again, even when charge accounts are analyzed, purchases for different members of a family distort the picture of what price lines in related departments really apply to the same person. Data on total production by price lines or zones would probably be the most accurate guide for analyzing the problem.

STEPS IN SETTING PRICE LINES

The steps in setting price lines are approximated as follows:
1. List all prices at which stock is carried or at which sales have been made during the past year.
2. Determine the sales at each price by means of a unit-control system. If possible, the sales made at original prices should be segregated from the sales of reduced merchandise, perhaps by establishing special markdown prices at which no new goods are marked.
3. Analyze the sales at each price in relation to (a) the stock that has been available at that price, (b) the customer requests submitted for goods at that price, and (c) the promotions at that price.

The price line showing the greatest sales may not be the most desirable. Another price may potentially be a much greater volume getter, but it may have suffered from starved stocks and lack of promotional emphasis.

4. Make an estimate of the income and the budget of expenditures of the average family to whom the store caters. This will help determine how much customers can afford and how much they will wish to spend for the line in question.

5. Group nearby price lines that seem to appeal to the same class of customers into zones and determine the relative importance of each zone. The establishment of correct zones of demand is more important than the setting of individual price lines within each zone.

6. Study price lines and zones in related departments to determine the type of customer to whom the department can best appeal and to realize correlation among offerings of related lines of goods.

7. Study competitors' prices both as to number and as to price points. The prices finally set should be near enough to those of others to be competitive.[2]

8. Have the dollar jumps between price lines in the high-priced zones greater than those in the medium-priced and lower-priced zones.

9. Consider store policy in regard to price endings. (This matter is discussed in the next chapter.)

10. Consider wholesale prices at which good values are available in the wholesale market. Although, over the long run, the price lines the retailer prefers in view of customer demand will become established, over the short run he is dominated by the existing wholesale price lines and must adjust his retail prices to points that will provide the approximate markup he requires. Thus, if there is an established wholesale price for coats at $49.75 and the buyer needs about a 45 percent markup, he will establish a retail price at $90.00 or thereabouts.

11. Set cost ranges for each retail price line. For example:

Retail Price Line	Cost Range
$2.00	{ $1.00 1.40
3.00	{ 1.55 2.00
5.00	{ 2.75 3.50

[2] In this connection, a store should compare its price lines with those reported annually in Neustadt's *Red Book of Seasonal Patterns*, Neustadt Statistical Organization, 31 Union Square, New York.

These avoid extremes in markup and may aid in bargaining if the manufacturer's quoted cost is between two buying ranges.

REVISING PRICE LINES

After price lines or price zones have been set, there should be a careful analysis of sales, stocks, and "wants" at each to determine whether they are proving adequate for the demand. Normally, the greatest unit volume in a store should be enjoyed at a middle price or zone. For example, if dresses are only sold at $9.95, $12.95, and $16.95, the greatest volume should be realized at $12.95. If $9.95 should prove the more popular price, this would be an indication that many customers would favorably respond to a lower price, perhaps $7.95. However, the possible lack of suitable merchandise in the wholesale market to sell at this price might make it unwise for the store to introduce the lower price line.

Similarly, should the greatest unit volume be realized at $16.95, this would be an indication that many customers would readily pay more for still better quality and a $19.95 price might be introduced.

In periods of deflation, a middle price line or zone that has been the most popular may become the highest price at which goods sell actively, and the need for a price below the former lowest price may become apparent. Likewise, in inflation, the middle best-selling price may become the lowest price at which any substantial volume is realized, indicating the need for a higher price than the highest one formerly in use.

During the downward course of a depression, every merchant is faced with the following alternatives in regard to price lines and quality of shopping goods handled:

1. Maintain present price lines but offer better quality than before at these points.
2. Lower price lines and offer the same quality as before.
3. Lower price lines drastically and carry lower quality than before.

During a period of rising prices, each of the alternatives is reversed.

ON A DECLINING MARKET

During periods of declining prices, all three of these alternatives have been tried. The first has not generally been successful.

With the decline in incomes, it is impossible for people to pay former prices even though they get more for their money.

The second policy, that of lowering prices but maintaining quality standards, is most praiseworthy and conducive to the maintenance of customer goodwill, but it frequently fails to sustain volume adequately. Incomes are in many cases cut so drastically that customers find it necessary not only to buy at lower price levels but also to buy lower quality than they would have considered before. As a result, stores that reduce standards of quality sometimes enjoy a considerable patronage. However, the dissatisfaction with some of the purchases made impairs customer confidence. The store that is adequately financed to ride through the depression on reduced volume is probably better off by maintaining quality.

ON A RISING MARKET

On a rising market, the offering of lower quality at a pre-existing price is exceedingly dangerous. Should it seem desirable to adjust retail prices upward more gradually than cost prices, it would be better to take a temporary cut in markup than to offer lower quality at established prices.

There is no doubt that rising real income brings a demand for better quality merchandise at higher prices. Since many of the expenditures of a typical customer are of a relatively fixed nature, a 10 percent rise in income allows more than a 10 percent increase in the expenditure for general merchandise and automobiles. Thus, a policy of stocking and promoting better quality goods at prices above the former best-selling levels may prove the most desirable. This policy is much easier to defend than one of simply adjusting prices upward on the same quality. With a 10 percent rise in prices, a customer who paid $20 for a tire does not like to feel that he is getting no more for his money at $22. But if the store offers him an improved tire at $22 he is more likely to be satisfied. In brief, to offer better quality at higher prices in periods of rising prices and to offer the same quality at higher prices in periods of falling prices—these seem to be the preferable policies.

DANGER IN "TRADING UP"

Some stores and their suppliers have made the mistake of replacing or deemphasizing well-established low-price zones because of ready acceptance of higher-priced zones by their more affluent customers. The extra sales of better-priced goods carrying a higher dollar markup proved most attractive, even though considerable unit volume at lower prices was being sacrificed to the great mass merchandisers such as Sears and Penney. Whenever the more affluent customers restrict their buying, perhaps because of a recession, the stores catering to them are faced with a sharp loss in volume, since they have relinquished the mass market. For example, at a time when over 58 percent if the entire women's skirt business was at retail prices of $8 and less, many stores stressed the $12 to $20 zone with virtually no assortments to appeal to the mass market.[3] It may be concluded that stores that cater to the middle-income market should carefully watch the price lines of the mass merchandisers and maintain adequate assortments in ranges that are competitive.

BUILDING ACCEPTANCE FOR PRICE LINES

The technique first expounded by the late Edward A. Filene in his book *Model Stock Plan*[4] was that at every planned price line there should be two especially selected items: a Best Buy and a Most Profitable purchase. The former, or B.B., is an article of great intrinsic worth at the price, a value gained if necessary by lowering the markup on that item below the average necessary for the line as a whole. The latter, or M.P., is an article that provides a high markup to the store but incorporates certain style features that appeal to fashion-conscious customers. The bargain seekers who recognize good material and workmanship will buy the B.B. and spread the news of the excellent values the store affords at the price. The fashion conscious customers, on the other hand, will locate the M.P. in the price line assortment, with its extra features of novelty that have not added to its cost. Between B.B. and the M.P., the store can maintain an adequate markup on the price line.

AVERAGING MARKUPS ON PRICE LINES

ONE COST AND TWO RETAILS

The manipulation of markup frequently involves (1) buying different items at the same cost to retail at different prices and (2) buying items at different cost prices to retail at the same price.

There are two reasons for pricing different goods that cost the same amount at different retail prices. One is that goods of like wholesale price are not all of the same value, even when bought from the same manufacturer. Some manufacturers make up goods in different materials and with different labor cost and put them all out

---

[3] *The New York Times,* July 5, 1970, Sec. F, p. 9.
[4] Reprinted by the Puckett Foundation, Allied Stores, Inc., New York.

at the same price, making a larger profit on some styles than on others. If a buyer detects these differences in value due to differences in materials, workmanship, and style and believes that the observant customer could detect them too, he may mark the better merchandise at a higher price.

A second reason for having different retail prices for a single cost is in order to achieve an average markup necessary for a profit. For example, as a result of competition and custom, it may be that most $2.00 cost merchandise in some line retails for $3.00, giving a markup of 33⅓ percent. But the markup required for a reasonable profit may be 35 percent. Rather than drop the $3.00 price and mark all the goods at a higher price, it may be wiser to mark that portion of the goods that are least competitive at $3.25. Such adjustments are frequently necessary when a manufacturer raises his wholesale price and the retailer is loath to revise his established retail price.

Procedure for one cost and two retails.   The proportions in which to price a lot of goods costing the same may be calculated as follows in a simple case with only two retails.

A buyer of handbags may have to average a 35 percent purchase markup but may find it necessary to retail at $3.95 some goods for which he pays $2.75 each, a markup of only 30.4 percent. He may find it possible, however, to retail some of the best $2.75 items at $5.00, a markup of 45 percent. As already indicated, these may be of greater value to the customer, even though sold by the manufacturer at the same price, for they may have fashion features that make them more desirable or may actually have cost the vendor more to produce. The immediate problem is to determine in what proportions to mark the goods costing $2.75.

The average retail price requires a markup of 35 percent. It is found, therefore, as $2.75/.65, or $4.23. This average retail may then be compared with the planned retails of $3.95 and $5.00 as follows:

	$3.95 Price	*$5.00 Price*
Average retail required	$4.23	$4.23
Actual retail planned	3.95	5.00
Under in markup	$ .28	
Over in markup		$ .77

The buyer "loses" $0.28 on every $3.95 item, but "gains" $0.77 on every $5.00 item. In order that unders may just equal overs, he must mark 77 at $3.95 (where he loses $0.28) to every 28 items at $5.00 (where he gains $0.77).[5] Since 77 items plus 28 items equals

[5] 28 (cents) $\times$ 77 (items) $=$ 77 (cents) $\times$ 28 (items).

105, the answer in percentage is 73 percent at $3.95 to 27 percent at $5.00. If the buyer were to buy a dozen or less, this ratio could be approximated at 3 to 1. Some may wish to solve the problem algebraically.

Two Costs and One Retail

It is more common to set up one retail price for goods that cost different amounts than to set different prices for goods that cost the same. No store would find it wise to carry as many different retail prices as there are wholesale cost prices. The small variations would confuse the customer, delay closing sales, and necessitate a very large stock assortment. It is better to set a range of cost prices for a single price line. For example, instead of deciding that merchandise for the $12.50 price line must cost $8.12½ (when a 35 percent markup is needed), it may be decided that all goods costing between $7.00 and $9.00 may be retailed at $12.50. If within this range there are only two major cost prices—$7.75 and $8.75—the question arises as to the proportions in which to buy $7.75 and $8.75 merchandise in order to average a 35 percent markup.

Procedure for two costs and one retail. As in the case of one cost and two retails, there are two ways to solve the problem: the ratio one and the algebraic one.[6] The ratio solution is the simpler.
65 percent of $12.50 = $8.125, the average cost price the buyer can pay.

	$8.125	$8.125
Average cost required	$8.125	$8.125
Actual costs	7.75	8.75
Over in markup	$ .375	
Under in markup		$ .625

The buyer should purchase more at $7.75 than at $8.75 to offset the larger loss at the higher price. He should buy 625 at $7.75

---

[6] The algebraic solution is as follows:

Quantity	Cost	Weighted
100	$7.75	775
x	8.75	8.75x
$100 + x$	$8.125 (Av.)	$812.5 + 8.125x$

$$775 + 8.75x = 812.5 + 8.125x$$
$$.625x = 37.5$$
$$625x = 37{,}500$$
$$x = 60$$

For every 100 items bought for $7.75, 60 may be bought at $8.75. This is in the ratio of 5 to 3, or 62.5% to 37.5%.

to 375 at $8.75. This is the same ratio as 62.5 to 37.5, or 5 to 3. In practice, approximations are satisfactory. For example, if 5 dresses are to be purchased, 3 could be bought at $7.75 and 2 at $8.75.

Such mathematical analysis does not answer the question as to whether all the articles costing $7.75 will sell readily against those costing $8.75. If most of the $7.75 merchandise has to be marked down from $12.50 to move it, nothing will be gained by stocking in the planned proportions. The merchant must give the public good values even when his markup is high.

DIFFERENT COSTS AND RETAILS

The averaging process may also be used when neither the cost nor the retail prices of two different items are the same. For example, a store may have a private brand that costs $1.00 and retails for $1.69 and also a national brand that costs $1.25 and retails for $1.95. On the two brands combined an average markup of 37½ percent may be sought. At a 37½ percent markup, the average retail for the private brand would be $1.60 and for the national brand $2.00. The solution would proceed as follows:

	Private Brand	National Brand
Average retails	$1.60	$2.00
Actual retails	1.69	1.95
Over in markup	$ .09	
Under in markup		$ .05

Therefore, nine should be bought of the national brand for every five of the private in order to achieve a 37½ percent markup.

Where there are more than two costs and/or two retails involved in the averaging prices, there is no neat mathematical solution, for a great many different quantitative proportions could yield the desired average. Which set of proportions to aim at would be a matter of judgment, not of arithmetic.

QUESTIONS FOR DISCUSSION

1. Do you recommend price lining for toiletries, for small electrical appliances, for frozen orange juice?
2. For a ready-to-wear line, which would you recommend to govern the pricing and control of merchandising: price lines or price zones?

3. What price lines would you suggest for men's shirts in a high class men's shop? For lamps in a large department store? For women's skirts in a discount house? Would you have special markdown prices also?

4. If you were a merchandise manager would you place any limits on the number of price lines that might be set up in a merchandise classification?

5. Should the jumps between price lines be about the same percentage of each price below? If so, what percentage would you recommend? Why?

6. The typical customer for a seventy-five-dollar man's suit is likely to be interested in what price ranges in the purchase of each of the following: overcoat, car coat, slacks, sports shirt, hat, shoes?

7. Do you think that for every retail price line there should be a predetermined cost-buying range? Why?

8. Is the Filene concept of B.B. and M.P. in each price line still a sound one?

9. Which is probably the more common practice: to buy at one cost for two retail prices or to buy at two costs for a single retail price?

10. If it is determined that three units of a private brand must be handled to every one unit of a national brand in order to achieve a desired markup on both combined, what can be done to adhere to this proportion without becoming overstocked on one brand or the other?

7

COMPETITIVE
PRICING
POLICIES

There are generally two ways to compete for customer patronage: to rely on a low price appeal or to depend upon nonprice competitive devices. The latter include emphasis on broad assortments, high quality, fashion leadership, exclusive offerings, and/or extensive or personalized service. While the store that can attract patronage upon the basis of such features is in a strong competitive position, the typical store that caters to the mass market must feature price, if not continually at least much of the time.

The underlying price policy of a store is an outgrowth of its basic merchandising policy, that is, of the character or personality it is attempting to create and the lines it intends to carry. If its main appeal is low price, it will try to give bargains every day at low markups and will sacrifice service and broad assortments to do it. If its main attraction is the reputation of having many product variants, it will set prices that will provide a markup that will compensate for the expense of stocking the slow sellers. If its main attraction is fashion leadership, it will set initial markups high enough to allow for markdown losses inherent in short-lived fashion merchandise.

PRICING RELATIVE TO THE MARKET

As indicated in chapter 5, where customers have a fairly accurate knowledge of market prices, goods should be priced close to the market price.[1] Nevertheless, the merchant does have a choice of three policies: (1) to price goods *at* the market price, (2) to price goods above the market price, and (3) to price goods *below* the market price.

For example, a recognized quality of hosiery costs approximately $0.83 and is usually sold at $1.35, but some merchants sell this hose at $1.50 and others at as low a price as $1.09.

PRICING AT THE MARKET

Where competitors deal in identical or closely comparable items, they tend to settle on market prices that all observe, at least until some economic factor upsets the equilibrium. To sell for more would adversely affect sales, and to sell for less either would be unprofitable or would lead to a price war. However, a competitive advantage is often sought at the market price by the offer of an extra inducement to the customer. For example, in the food and grocery fields, it is common to offer trading stamps and other premiums, such as free drinking glasses and participation in contests and games largely based on chance. While these devices have been effective, they are subject to considerable criticism. They add to expenses and, unless the increase in sales is material, they may lead to retail prices that are no longer competitive with those of others who do not offer such inducements.

PRICING ABOVE THE MARKET

A policy of marking goods above the market is most likely to be attempted where the markup at the market price is inadequate, but for the highly competitive store the practice is likely to prove disastrous. Ill will may be engendered and sales of other merchandise reduced. Again, the loss of volume on the item in question is likely to cut down the contribution the item is making to store overhead. For example, the $0.30 drug item retailed at $0.39 may sell one hundred a week and thus contribute $9.00 to expenses. If marked at $0.50,

---

[1] Some inexpensive fashion goods produced at standardized cost prices also fall into the staple category. For example, $4.75 cost dresses are typically sold at $6.95, but some stores sell them for $7.95, and others for $5.95.

only ten may sell a week, a contribution of only $2.00. Even though some allowance should be made for the difference in direct expenses of handling one hundred rather than ten items, the $0.39 market price is still likely to prove more advantageous.

Some stores attempt to obtain a satisfactory level of sales volume at a price above the market by offering more service to customers, by evolving elaborate displays, or by establishing a reputation of exclusiveness. Types of stores that are particularly successful in this regard are the installment credit store and the exclusive specialty shop. The credit store sells on the installment plan almost entirely. Customers are more interested in the amount of their weekly or monthly payments than in the price of the goods. Such a store can price staples above the market without serious injury to volume, and the extra markup is necessary to cover the extra costs of credit and collection. In addition, stores that open at unusual hours or that are especially convenient to their clientele may be able to sell above the market even in the case of highly competitive goods such as groceries.

The shop with a somewhat spendthrift clientele can also price goods above the market. Its customers do not compare values—and they may be patrons of the "right" stores. Even if they know the same thing can be procured for considerably less elsewhere, they get satisfaction in paying more. However, the extra margin that stores catering to such a clientele enjoy is not all added profit. Their customers, even though they do not question price, demand expensive personal service and an opulent store atmosphere. Nor do they hesitate to return goods bought carelessly.

PRICING BELOW THE MARKET

The policy of pricing below the market, or at cut rates, is practiced chiefly by discount stores and other mass merchandisers.

Discount houses grew amazingly by offering goods *regularly* at less than market prices. They were able to do this profitably by cutting expenses and concentrating on best sellers that provided a large volume with a low stock level and low markdowns. The expense ratio was cut by reducing services and by keeping the work of the nonselling departments at a minimum; activities that did not contribute to immediate sales were eliminated. Thus, early in the discount era, goods were sold at a much lower markup than that obtained by the typical, conventional retailers.

The differential in the markup has narrowed greatly, due partly to the tendency of discount houses to add services and to broaden assortments.

Traditional stores were faced with three alternatives: (1) to change into discount stores, (2) to drop the lines in which the discount stores were strong, and (3) to meet the competition on comparable goods stocked.

Because of the demand on the part of the affluent middle class for wide assortments, quality, and service, the first alternative was not attractive to established stores, except that some traditional department stores developed their own discount subsidiaries. The second alternative to drop lines—such as major appliances—meant the loss of a great deal of volume and tarnished the image of the complete store. Most stores found that as long as the lines challenged by the discount houses could be sold competitively at a price slightly in excess of cost and direct expenses, they would make some contribution to the overhead and profit of the store as a whole. There was also the possibility that increasing volume would increase the dollar margin at a lower markup percentage.

In general, the policy of meeting competition, with some reduction of service perhaps (or extra charge for it) in those lines that are heavily discounted, has proven the best policy for many.

PRICING PRIVATE BRANDS

The introduction of private brands is an important way of selling below the market price established by well-known national brands and yet of improving the markup percentage. There is some evidence that if the private brand in foods is to attract a large body of customers it must be offered at a price approximately 15 percent to 20 percent below the price of the competing national brand.[2] Thus, if a national brand of frozen cut green beans sells at $0.25, the private brand would be made available at $0.20 to $0.21. At either of these low prices, the markup percentage, but not the dollar markup, may be higher that that obtained on the national brand, due to a lower cost price.

Some private brands, particularly those sponsored by a reputable store group, sell readily at prices very close to those of competing national brands. For example, a national brand broiler may cost the store $19.21 and sell for $30.00. A comparable private brand item may be obtainable at $16.98 and sell in reasonable quantities

---

[2] Some food products bought frequently may readily sell without a price differential as large as 20 percent. For example, a private brand of applesauce may find ready acceptance at $0.43 against a national brand at $0.49, a difference of 12 percent. But private brands of staple clothing items may require even more than 20 percent off.

also at $30.00, yielding a markup of 43.4 percent against 36 percent. The merchant must decide whether a price on the private brand below $30.00 will stimulate enough extra volume to warrant a markup of less than 40 percent. Even if it would, the merchant might nevertheless decide to sell at $30.00 if his goal were to convince customers that his private brands were equal in quality to competing national brands. Thus, he may decide for a higher markup rather than for a retail price advantage.

Dual Pricing to Facilitate Price Comparisons

Manufacturers and dealers in packaged goods, especially in the food field, have sometimes attempted to avoid direct comparison of their prices with those of similar products by packaging them in odd quantities. Thus, applesauce brand A may be packed in a sixteen and one-half ounce jar and priced at $0.20, whereas applesauce brand B is put in an eight and one-quarter ounce jar and priced at $0.16. Because customers are not adept at making correct price comparisons in a case like this, brand B that actually costs $0.30 a pound may attract considerable patronage even though the cost per pound of the A brand is only $0.19.

From the consumer point of view, either of two methods is desirable: (1) that containers for convenience goods be uniform in weight or quantity of contents or (2) that dual pricing be observed, each package carrying both a package price and a price per standard unit of measure. This may be the price per pound, per pint, per quart, or per square foot (for example, aluminum foil).

Packages of standardized weights are becoming more common and are required in many localities for such items as bread and milk. Where such standardization is currently not feasible, regulations are being introduced to require dual pricing for a wide variety of packaged goods sold in packages of unstandardized weight. This plan is already widely required for meats. Supermarkets are beginning to adopt the plan more generally. In one instance, the computer is called upon to perform the necessary arithmetic and to print out price labels bearing both the package price and the price per standardized unit. If this policy is generally adopted, convenience goods will be priced closer to a single market price level than they are today.

PRICING FOR PROMOTIONAL EVENTS

Although a special sale may primarily attract because of the unusual nature of the merchandise offered, a special price is usually necessary.

If the usual price of the goods is well known to the buying public, the goods must be offered at prices below market, probably at least 10 percent and perhaps as much as 20 percent below the usual price in order to make customers react. If customers know the approximate value only of the goods within a range of prices, the price reduction must be relatively greater to induce action. For example, goods would have to be brought down into the next subzone of demand. Thus, the item that would usually be retailed at $20.00 might be offered at about $14.00. In fact, assortment merchandise of this kind offered for special sale is usually retailed at slightly above the normal cost price, that is, 30 percent to 40 percent below the regular retail price. Novelty goods, for a special sale, would have to be offered at no more than normal cost price, and often at as much as 50 percent off.

Such cuts in the usual price do not necessarily mean that markups must be cut accordingly. The manufacturer may reduce his price in proportion to the cut at retail. The regular $12.00 cost item, retailing for $20.00, may temporarily be available at $8.40. At a $14.00 retail, there will be no cut in the markup percentage. Such opportunities may be the result of a manufacturer's end-of-season closeout of a model or style, his need for quick liquidation to obtain capital, or his savings in production and selling costs, where the buyer purchases a very large quantity.

Even where the manufacturer does not reduce his cost in proportion, goods may still be offered at a special price in order to build volume.

LEADER MERCHANDISING

A variation of the special sale policy is to offer certain items as *leaders*, with some such items nearly always available.

The leader policy is one that combines high and low markups; instead of marking goods at the price that is expected to yield the largest aggregate dollar margin above costs and direct expenses, some items are deliberately sold at a lower, less profitable price to attract customers to the store and to other goods on which a larger profit may be made. The low markup goods are used as leaders, that is, as a promotion device to attract trade for other goods. When goods are deliberately sold at a loss—below cost—they are referred to as loss leaders.[3] It must not be concluded that the marking of some goods at less than the average markup required in a department always represents a leader policy. A low markup may be more profitable than a normal one because of volume possibilities.

[3] Cost may be considered to be either invoice cost or invoice cost plus direct handling expenses.

DEGREES OF PRICE CUTTING

The difference between routine merchandising, dynamic merchandising, leader merchandising, and loss leader merchandising may be explained by the following example of an item costing $0.60 with $0.02 handling costs in a store with a normal markup of 40 percent.

	Billed Cost	Unit Handling Cost	Unit Retail	Margin per Unit	Weekly Rate of Sale	Total Margin
Routine merchandising (40% over billed cost)	$.60	$.02	$1.00	$.38	1	$.38
Dynamic merchandising (point of greatest total margin)	.60	.02	.66	.04	20	.80
Leader merchandising (to attract customers to other merchandise)	.60	.02	.63	.01	25	.25
Loss leader merchandising (goods are deliberately sold at a loss)	.60	.02	.59	−.03	30	−.90

CRITERIA FOR SUCCESSFUL LEADERS

One research investigator has set forth certain criteria for successful leaders. Successful leader items are those that will appeal to a large proportion of potential clientele. It would be foolish to use some item that is purchased by only a few people, such as pickled watermelon rind in a food store. The item should be sufficiently familiar to the public so that they can recognize the reduction as having created a bargain. If the item is currently being used as a leader by a competitor it will not be as effective and may lead to a price war as well. Also, those items that have their retail prices controlled by the vendor cannot be used without the vendor's permission. The amount of price reduction will also have an important effect upon the success of a leader. It must be great enough on one or on a number of items to justify special effort on the part of the prospective customer to come to the store.

LIMITATIONS OF LEADER POLICY

The leader policy has probably caused more criticism of retail stores than any other. It may tend to mislead customers in that it gives the impression that all of the store's prices are low, whereas the store may actually be taking extra high markups on other goods to offset the less profitable low prices. The leader is simply an inducement to get the customer to the store with the intention of selling her other goods in addition to the leader.

Soft-pedaling leaders.   In some stores, a practice is followed of trying to avoid the sale of the leader and substituting the sale of a profitably priced article. For example, in one chain organization, it was found that the large volume of sales in leader merchandise was seriously cutting down profits, even though a 33 percent markup was realized on nearly all other stock. Yet the company felt that competition forced it to continue the leader policy. To minimize volume on these items, however, it established the following rules:

> First, each store was to have leaders in every department, but salespeople were instructed not to use them for any other purpose than for "prys" or "openers." Previously there had been no restrictions on leaders, and salespeople could get their day's "book" easily by concentrating on the leaders, or nonprofitable merchandise.
> Second, through the educational department of the organization a course in salesmanship was given to all salespeople. Unless a salesman was willing to take the course, he was not encouraged to stay with the company. The problem of leaders was thoroughly discussed in the course, and reasons were given as to why leaders should not be used for anything other than "prys." Advantages of properly used leaders were stressed, showing how they could assist in increasing net profits. In this course, the merits of the company's own brands of merchandise carrying normal percentages of markup were emphasized, and salespeople were urged to support these brands when selling. To stimulate salespeople to concentrate to an even greater extent on merchandise with a normal markup and use leaders only when necessary, the company worked out a bonus plan for employees in stores where they attained a markup above a certain percentage.

To urge salespeople to soft-pedal leaders is a common but questionable practice, and some stores have gone to extremes. Frequently, stores claim to be sold out on the leader, and salesmen are sometimes told to criticize the leader and urge the customer to buy a substitute described as being much superior. Such attempts to withhold the sale of advertised or featured leaders are generally conceded to be unfair, and the practice may subject the store to a court order to desist, at the instigation of the district ·attorney and the Better Business Bureau.

Effect on the trade.   The leader policy may not only mislead customers but also work a hardship on competitors and vendors. The cutting of a price below cost or even to a point less profitable than a higher one may force others to do the same to maintain their reputation for reasonable prices and to get a share of the business. Thus many items, especially well-known national brands, become "footballs" in the trade and unprofitable to all retailers either permanently or for long periods. Manufacturers and other suppliers of these brands can also be hurt by retailers who attempt to switch customers from the unprofitable leaders to more profitable substitutes. In some instances, the retailer may drop from his line entirely those items subject to ruinous price wars.

A Substitute for Advertising

Although a leader policy may be attacked from the standpoints of customer, competitor, and supplier, it has its defenders. It is pointed out that a leader is a substitute for advertising. It may cost a store one thousand dollars to attract one thousand people through the newspapers, whereas the offer, through a display of goods that cost the store one dollar each for sixty cents each may be equally effective. It costs the store only four hundred dollars if each customer is limited to a single purchase. Thus, if both types of promotions resulted in an equal quantity of regular markup sales, loss-leader policy would be the more profitable. In practice, however, many customers who are attracted by leaders may tend to buy the leader and nothing else. Although the leader policy may attract people to the store more cheaply than other methods, the percentage of those attracted who actually buy profitable goods is much higher when advertising is used. Thus, the contention that a leader policy is a desirable substitute for advertising is open to question. It may be a cheaper substitute but also one less productive of results.

It is probably a fair conclusion that even though a loss leader policy may yield profits to the store employing it, it is likely to be injurious to others and prove less and less profitable to its practitioners over a period of time. This does not mean, however, that all offerings at lower markups are to be avoided. As already pointed out, volume possibilities at a low markup may yield the store a larger profit than a normal markup.

Legal Aspects of Loss Leaders

The loss-leader practice has caused so much friction in the trade that some states and the federal government have passed laws to curb or eliminate it. These are of two types: (1) prohibition of sales below cost and (2) authorization of resale price agreements. The first, called *unfair practice acts*, includes regulations found in many of the states that prohibit selling nonperishable and undamaged goods below cost. Cost is often defined as purchase or replacement cost, whichever is lower, plus the cost of doing business. The cost of doing business in some states is set at 6 percent of the purchase price to cover direct handling. These laws are difficult to enforce not only because of the difficulty in defining cost but also because of the requirement that there be proof that the price-cutter intended to hurt competition and restrain trade.

In addition to state laws aimed at selling below cost, section 3 of the Robinson-Patman Act prohibits sales below cost where there is an intent to injure competition or an attempt to restrain trade. Since intent is hard to prove, this prohibition is difficult to police by court action.

The second legal method of coping with the loss-leader problem is the authorization of resale price maintenance contracts. Most states have such laws, and the federal Miller-Tydings Act recognizes such contracts in interstate commerce.[4]

CHIEF FEATURES OF FAIR TRADE LAWS

Purpose: To provide sellers the right to fix minimum resale prices.

Coverage: All states except Missouri, Texas, Vermont, and the District of Columbia.

Prices covered: Usually the minimum resale price.

Who bound: Those who have signed contracts agreeing to the minimum resale prices set. In most states, non-signers also bound.

Frequent provisions:
- Only trademark owners and their authorized distributors are permitted to establish contract resale prices.
- Gifts, premium offers, coupons, trading stamps, and combination sales are prohibited if the effect is evasion of contract prices.
- Secondhand goods and goods from which trademarks have been removed are not subject to resale price agreements.
- Producer or distributor must be given reasonable notice of clearance or closeout sales and opportunity to repurchase stock at original invoice prices.

---

[4] The student who wishes to study price maintenance in depth should refer to a recent text on marketing.

ODD PRICE POLICY

A common way to give the impression of low prices without resorting to leaders is to end prices in uneven amounts rather than in round numbers. The original reason for introducing them was apparently to force salespeople to obtain change and thus make it less easy for them to pocket the customer's remittance without recording a sale. The scheme was thus a deterrent to dishonesty, but state and city sales taxes have changed this situation. Today the chief reason for the odd price is a belief that it sells goods more readily than the even price. It is said that a $2.95 price draws attention to $2.00, not $3.00, and that psychologically it is much less than $3.00; accordingly, sales volume may be materially increased.[5] Also, it is believed that customers like to get change back.

There are certain odd prices that are frequently considered more fruitful than even prices, but there are certain even prices that are better. In general, odd prices are more compelling in the lower ranges. For example, a $1.95 price seems to many merchants to be better than a $2.00 price for an item that sells in greatest volume at higher prices, but a $10.00 price in the same category may be just as good as a $9.95 price, probably because the even price emphasizes quality, which the customer is looking for at the higher price.

The relative acceptance of odd and even prices in different price zones probably varies with communities and with merchandise. A store must experiment to determine what odd prices are actually preferred. But it is wrong to assume that odd prices are generally more conducive to sales. They have probably been overdone. They are particularly adaptable to a store whose central policy is low price. When the chief emphasis is placed on assortments, quality, or service, round prices may be used.

To adhere to odd prices where round ones would do just as well is like throwing a mountain of pennies out the window. Within a year, a large store may make one hundred thousand sales at $1.95 when they might have been made at $2.00. This would mean an unnecessary loss of $5,000.00. Probably many stores are paying a high price in continuing to use odd prices on a broad scale. Furthermore, the higher degree of sophistication of the average customer today may lead one to believe that few people would be swayed by a differential of one to five cents when comparing, for example, the price points of $19.95, $19.99, and $20.00.

---

[5] Some experts feel that a price must be much lower than $2.95 to give the customer the impression of a $2.00 price. But note that gasoline prices nearly always end in 9/10 of a cent, with the 9 in small type.

DETERMINING SALES VOLUME REQUIRED TO JUSTIFY A PRICE CUT

THE UNIT VOLUME FORMULA

A major problem in connection with pricing is to determine what increases in volume would be necessary to justify cuts in retail prices or in markups. This problem applies particularly to staples that can be sold in increasing volume if the price is lowered or that are being diverted to discount houses. But before a lower than normal retail price is attempted, the merchandiser should know how much sales would have to increase above those at a normal markup to justify the cut. For example, an article costing $0.60 in a store with a 40 percent markup will normally sell for $1.00, and sales at this price may average ten a week, providing a total of $4.00. Were the price to be cut from $1.00 to $0.80, the markup on each sale would be only $0.20. To yield $4.00 a week, then, twenty sales a week would be necessary. Unless there is good reason to believe that such a price cut would more than double volume, it would not be justified except on the theory that it would build a wanted image and build store volume over the long run.

$$\text{Ratio of New Unit Volume to Old} = \frac{\text{Old dollar markup per unit}}{\text{New dollar markup per unit}}$$

Thus, in the above example,

$$\text{Ratio of New Unit Volume} = \frac{\$.40}{\$.20} = 2 \text{ or } 200 \text{ as an index}$$

As indicated, the unit volume must be doubled. See figure 7.1 for increases in unit volume that would be required to offset various price cuts.

The same formula may be used if a higher retail price is contemplated to determine how much volume can decline without curtailing total dollar markup. For example, it may be proposed to sell the $0.60-cost item for $1.20 rather than $1.00:

$$\text{Ratio of New Unit Volume} = \frac{\$.40}{\$.60} = .66\tfrac{2}{3} \text{ or } 67 \text{ as an index,}$$

indicating that if the number of sales at $1.20 falls off no more than one-third, there will be no loss in aggregate margin.

THE DOLLAR VOLUME FORMULA

The calculations above provide an answer in terms of changes in *number of items sold*, not changes in *dollar sales*. Thus, a cutting of prices from \$1.00 to \$0.80 requires that twice as many articles be sold but not twice as many dollars. Where one item formerly sold for \$1.00, now two items must sell for \$0.80 each, a total of \$1.60. Thus, *dollar sales* need increase only 60 percent to maintain as large a margin as before.

Conversely, with the \$1.20 price, at least two-thirds as many units must be sold: 66⅔ units at \$1.20 each amounts to \$80.00, whereas 100 units at \$1.00 amounted to sales of \$100.00. Thus, *dollar volume* may decline 20 percent (while unit volume is declining 33⅓ percent) without impairing total margin.

Rather than multiply the index of unit volume by the new price to find the change in dollar volume, this change may be determined directly from the following formula:

$$\text{Ratio of New Dollar Volume} = \frac{\text{Old markup percent}}{\text{New markup percent}}$$

In the first example, the former markup was \$0.40, or 40 percent of \$1.00. At the \$0.80 price, it is \$0.20, or 25 percent of \$0.80. Thus:

$$\text{Ratio of New Dollar Volume} = \frac{40\%}{25\%} = 1.6 \text{ or } 160 \text{ as an index,}$$

indicating that dollar volume must increase 60 percent.

IF YOU CUT THE PRICE			5%	10%	15%	20%	25%	30%	35%	40%	45%	50%
ON	25%	THE	25.0%	66.7%	150.0%	400.0%						
	30%	ADDITIONAL	20.0%	50.0%	100.0%	200.0%	500.0%					
MER-	35%	UNIT	16.6%	40.0%	75.0%	133.0%	250.0%	600.0%				
CHANDISE	40%	VOLUME OF	14.3%	33.3%	60.0%	100.0%	166.6%	300.0%	700.0%			
THAT	45%	BUSINESS	12.5%	28.6%	50.0%	80.0%	125.0%	200.0%	350.0%	800.0%		
HAS	50%	REQUIRED TO MAKE UP	11.1%	25.0%	42.8%	66.6%	100.0%	150.0%	233.0%	400.0%	900.0%	
BEEN	55%	THE SAME	10.0%	22.2%	37.5%	57.1%	83.3%	120.0%	175.0%	266.0%	450.0%	1000%
NORMALLY	60%	DOLLARS	9.0%	20.0%	33.3%	50.0%	70.2%	100.0%	140.0%	200.0%	300.0%	500%
MARKED	65%	AND CENTS	8.3%	18.2%	30.0%	44.4%	62.5%	85.7%	116.7%	160.0%	225.0%	333%
	70%	MARGIN	7.7%	16.6%	27.3%	40.0%	55.5%	75.0%	100.0%	133.3%	180.0%	250%
UP	75%	WILL BE	7.1%	15.3%	25.0%	36.3%	50.0%	66.7%	87.5%	114.3%	150.0%	200%

COURTESY NOTION AND NOVELTY REVIEW

FIGURE 7.1   Increases in Unit Volume Needed to Offset Price Cuts

Conversely, with a new price of \$1.20, the new markup is \$0.60, or 50 percent of \$1.20. Then,

Ratio of New Dollar Volume $= \dfrac{\$.40}{\$.50} = .80$ or 80 as an index, indicating that dollar volume may decline 20 percent.[6]

CHANGES IN PRICE AND CHANGES IN MARKUP

The examples above indicate that an increase or decrease in price is quite different from an increase or decrease in markup. A 20 percent decrease in price decreases the markup from 40 percent to 25 percent.

Every buyer should recognize the difference between these two concepts. For example, in a line with a 35 percent markup, it may be proposed to increase markup to 38.5 percent, with wholesale prices constant. This is not the same thing as increasing prices either 3.5 percent or 10 percent. The increase in price may be calculated as follows:

Let $\$1.00 =$ retail, and
    $.65 =$ the cost

Then, the new retail is $\dfrac{\$.65}{1.00 - .385} = \dfrac{\$.65}{.615} = \$1.056$, an increase of 5.6 percent.

Conversely, a cut in markup from 35 percent to 31.5 percent is not the same thing as either a 3.5 percent or as a 10 percent cut in prices:

Let $\$1.00 =$ former retail, and
    $.65 =$ cost

Then, the new retail is $\dfrac{\$.65}{1.00 - .315} = \dfrac{\$.65}{.685} = \$.949$, a decrease of 5.1 percent.

ALLOWANCE FOR DIRECT EXPENSES

When the expense of handling each unit of sale and the outlay for advertising are known, it is possible to plan the volume necessary to achieve a "controllable profit" goal and not stop at the gross margin level. For example, a store may be selling a certain brand of tooth paste, costing $0.30, for $0.50 retail. At this price one dozen may

---

[6] The discussion above is an oversimplification because it does not include changes in expense resulting from changes in volume; it centers on margin and does not consider the direct expenses and the contribution of the item to the entire operation.

sell a week with about $52.00 spent a year to advertise the brand—or $1.00 a week. Direct handling expenses (costs of ordering, receiving, selling, and wrapping) may be estimated at $0.05 a transaction. The weekly contribution of this item toward joint expenses and profit of the store may then be estimated as follows:

Weekly sales ($.50 × 12)		$6.00
Weekly cost ($.30 × 12)		3.60
Gross margin		$2.40
Advertising expense	$1.00	
Handling expense ($.05 × 12)	.60	
Total direct expense of the item		1.60
Item's contribution		$ .80

The merchant may be considering reducing the price of this brand to $0.45 and doubling the amount of advertising. The question arises as to how many units he would have to sell to justify the changes. Clearly, he would have to realize a contribution from this brand of at least $0.80 a week and his margin after handling expenses would have to cover his advertising outlay, in this case $2.00. The $2.80 he needs each week for "contribution" and advertising is to be realized by selling goods costing $0.30 for $0.45, a margin of $0.15. But $0.05 of this margin must go to handling expense, leaving only $0.10 from each transaction for "contribution" and advertising. Since $2.80 in total is to be realized at the rate of $0.10 per item, twenty-eight items will have to be sold each week. Since twelve are selling now at the $0.50 price, the cut in price cannot be justified over the short run unless it increases unit volume more than two and one-third times.

The reasoning above may be expressed as an equation:

$$\text{Unit volume needed} = \frac{\text{Contribution} + \text{Advertising expense}}{\text{Unit markup} - \text{Unit handling expense}}$$

This equation allows for four variables and accordingly can be applied to many variations in plans. For example, an article costing $0.75 may be selling for $0.95 at the rate of one hundred a week. Handling costs may be $0.03 each and advertising $10.00 a week. The contribution, then, is:

Sales ($.95 × 100)	$95.00	
Margin ($.20 × 100)	20.00	
Advertising	$10.00	
Handling	3.00	13.00 (expenses charged against the item)
Contribution	$ 7.00	

The merchant may deem this contribution too small in relation to the sales of $95.00 and may contemplate increasing the price to $1.00 and spending no more for advertising than before. The question is how much volume can he afford to lose if he aims at a minimum "contribution" of $10.00 a week from this item:

$$\text{Unit volume needed} = \frac{\$10 + \$10}{\$.25 - \$.03} = \frac{\$20}{\$.22} = 91, \text{ compared with}$$

100 units currently.

Thus, if the increase in price from $0.95 to $1.00 will reduce volume only 9 percent, the change will be profitable. The maximum loss in volume—the point at which the increase in price gives the same contribution as before—may be calculated as follows:

$$\text{Unit volume needed} = \frac{\$7 + \$10}{\$.25 - \$.03} = \frac{\$17}{\$.22} = 77, \text{ compared with}$$

100.

Thus, if the price increase resulted in a 23 percent loss in volume, the same contribution as before would be realized.

The formula may also be used to allow for changes in handling expenses per unit.

QUESTIONS FOR DISCUSSION

1. Will competition permit a store to sell regularly and consistently above the market? Below the market?
2. How can a traditional service store meet discount prices on identical or closely comparable goods without suffering a loss?
3. In a department store of your choice, compare the prices of a few private brands with those of competing national brands. About how much lower are the private brand prices? Do you think that the differences are about right? Defend your stand.
4. (a) Is it essential that a private brand be offered for sale at a considerably lower price than that of a competing national brand? Defend your stand.
   (b) Currently, what is the approximate price differential between national and private brands of packaged foods?
5. Why does the ratio of price reductions required for special sales increase with a decline in the customer's knowledge of values?
6. Is there a clear-cut distinction between a leader and a loss leader?
7. Are the arguments in defense of leaders valid?
8. Do you agree with the conclusion in regard to loss leaders given in the chapter?
9. Distinguish between *unfair practice* acts and *fair trade* acts.
10. (a) In what lines has *fair trade* been reasonably successful?
    (b) Why is enforcement difficult?
    (c) Do you expect *fair trade* to increase or decrease in importance? Why?

11. If you were a merchandise manager, would you insist on the use of odd prices for goods priced under a certain figure, such as $10.00?

12. If a price line of $8.95 is reduced to $8.50 with no change in the cost price of $5.25:

(a) What is the change in the markup percentage?

(b) How much would unit sales have to increase to provide the same dollar margin as before?

(c) How much would dollar sales have to increase to provide the same margin?

(d) If handling costs are $0.50 a unit, how much would unit sales have to increase to provide the same *contribution* as before?

(e) Is it reasonable to expect that the increases you have calculated can be realized?

13. Suggest a set of pricing policies for a specific store with which you are well acquainted.

8

MARKDOWNS

The need for lowering prices to move goods causes the retailer much concern. He would prefer to sell everything he buys at the price he originally sets, but he is forced to make downward adjustments in price on a significant portion of his sales. These reductions, taken to achieve prompt sales, are called *markdowns*.[1]

Fortunately, the retailer occasionally finds it possible to offset markdowns by price increases. He may find that he has initially priced goods below a retail price at which they will readily sell and perhaps so low as to make customers question their quality. But these opportunities are relatively rare.

A markdown is, in effect, the merchant's way to correct a price on an item so that it reflects its current value. Thus markdowns represent the loss in the value of the goods reduced. Markdowns are not all bad, however, and, because they are considered a necessity, can be turned to good advantage. For example, they help

[1] Certain reductions in retail price are not classified as markdowns. These include discounts to employees and certain customer groups, stock shortages (where the price may be thought of as a reduction to zero), policy allowances that are charged off as expenses, corrections of clerical errors at the time of the original pricing, and reductions taken when a rebate from the vendor reduces the cost price at which the goods were originally put into stock.

maintain a "clean" stock, create open-to-buy for a new flow of fresh merchandise, and foster goodwill by giving a bargain to a store's customers.

In this chapter we shall explore the causes for markdowns in an effort to minimize them and describe the proper procedures to follow to maximize their effectiveness.

CAUSES OF MARKDOWNS

Because of large markdowns, the maintained markups of many stores fall far short of their initial markups. In other stores, because of failure to take markdowns, sales fall short of possibilities. These markdowns are of three major types: (1) those that are taken to correct retail prices to which customers are not responding satisfactorily, (2) those that are operational, representing shopworn goods, remnants, and broken lots, and (3) those that are used as a merchandising device to increase sales. The first type may be thought of as corrections of three types of errors that have been made—errors in buying, in pricing, and in selling.

MERCHANDISING ERRORS

Buying errors.   The merchant may fail to analyze trends in customer demand and to make buying plans. Accordingly, he buys the wrong styles, sizes, colors, patterns, prices, or types—or too large quantities of otherwise desirable merchandise. Many buyers spread their investment too thin, buying a wide assortment of many items that allows for no depth of stock of the items in popular demand. Another error is the reorder of excessively large quantities of successful styles at the peak of the season which cannot be disposed of during the waning season except at a loss.

BUYING ERRORS LEADING TO MARKDOWNS

- Overbuying
  a. Failing to plan sales and purchases in accordance with demand in specific classifications and price lines
  b. Failing to buy in small experimental quantities prior to placing large orders
  c. Buying more goods than necessary in view of stock on hand and on order

- Buying of the wrong styles, colors, fabrics, and sizes (too many mediocre items)
  a. Carelessly analyzing sales records
  b. Overbuying "novelty" goods
- Failing to anticipate reductions in wholesale prices
- Poor timing
  a. Ordering goods too early
  b. Ordering goods too late—at height of selling season—at regular prices
  c. Receiving goods too late after ordering
  d. Failing to plan stocks and resultant purchases in relation to expected sales each week or month
- Failing to develop a close working relationship with key resources whose advice can help avoid mistakes
- Overdepending on a few pet resources, with a high proportion of the stock invested in their mistakes
- Failing to examine incoming merchandise carefully for defects, workmanship, and fit

---

Pricing errors.   A second reason for markdowns is errors in pricing. Goods may be bought in the right styles, at the right time, and in the right quantities but may be improperly priced. The buyer may be overoptimistic, pricing goods too high. For example, a couch costing $120 may be retailed at $240, even though it may not sell in reasonable quantities for more than $200.

PRICING ERRORS LEADING TO MARKDOWNS

- Setting initial price too high
- Setting initial price too low, with customers suspicious of value
- Failing to check competitors' prices for the same or similar goods
- Consolidating price lines
- Deferring price reductions too long
- Making first markdown too small

When the initial price is too low and customers are suspicious of quality at the unexpectedly low price, the solution would seem to be to mark the goods up; but if they have already been held at the low price until late in the season, markdown for clearance may still be necessary.

Consolidation of price lines sometimes leads to markdowns. If a buyer has twenty price lines and finds he can get along with ten, it will generally be necessary to mark down goods from the intermediate prices to be dropped rather than from the ones to be retained. To mark up goods to the higher prices to be retained would lead to customer criticism in many cases.

Even when initial pricing is properly done, errors may be made in repricing. Some buyers don't like to admit errors. Ostrichlike, they sometimes put the goods physically out of sight and leave them there until ultimately a successor junks them. Or buyers try to minimize their errors by taking a smaller markdown than necessary to move a substantial portion of a style no longer selling at its original price. For example, a portion of $59.95 slow-selling suits might readily sell for $39.95, a 33⅓ percent reduction from the original retail price. But to mark them first $55.00, then $49.50, and later $39.95 may leave most of the supply still to be sold at even lower prices. Like cutting off the dog's tail, each slash is sure to hurt, but the first cut should be large enough to achieve the sales objective. It does not follow, however, that every markdown should move all the goods reduced. If a cut from $59.95 to $39.95 moves over half the supply, the results are generally satisfactory. To be sure that every style, color, and size would sell at the first reduction might mean offering the goods at half price, $29.95 or even less—and the total markdown loss would be much larger than necessary.

Selling errors.   A third reason for markdowns springs from improper salesmanship and display. One of the major causes of customer returns is careless selling or high-pressure selling, and returned goods are an important source of markdowns—changes in style and price and physical deterioration while the goods are out of stock result in markdowns. Again, there may be no adequate follow-up system to keep salespeople aware of aging stock that should receive special attention.

SELLING ERRORS LEADING TO MARKDOWNS

- Failing to show and display merchandise adequately
- Placing merchandise in the wrong selling location
- Failing to inform salespeople about the types of customers for whom certain styles were designed
- Not providing follow-up of salespeople to keep them interested in showing old stock as well as new stock (show an old style with every two new styles)

- Poor stockkeeping and failing to maintain a periodic checkup of slow-selling styles
- Careless handling leading to damaged merchandise
- High pressure or careless selling leading to customer returns and eventual markdowns

---

Placing merchandise in the wrong location on a selling floor may also contribute to higher markdowns, especially for highly seasonal merchandise with a short life. For example, bermuda shorts should be presented near the front of a department or store at the beginning of the hot-weather season, not buried in a rear corner or in a stock drawer.

OPERATIONAL AND UNCONTROLLABLE CAUSES

In addition to markdowns caused by errors, normal operations and unforeseeable developments may lead to them. Reductions must be taken to weed out goods that become unsalable as a result of normal handling. Goods become shopworn; individual pieces in sets are sold separately or become damaged and the remaining items require a reduction to move them; in yard goods remnants shorter than dress lengths are left at the ends of bolts. Markdowns are also caused by unforeseeable developments such as inclement weather and strikes that curtail customer buying response.

MARKDOWNS RESULTING FROM SELLING POLICIES

After every effort has been made to reduce unwise buying, pricing, and selling practices and operational losses, markdowns will still remain significant, particularly in fashion merchandise, owing to the existence of certain store policies introduced in the interests of sales volume.

SALES POLICIES LEADING TO MARKDOWNS

- Meeting price competition
- Having special sales of regular stock (unsold balance may be restored to regular price)
- Having frequent special sales of promotional merchandise leading to promotional remainders

- Being obligated to customers to maintain reasonable assortments late in the season
- Having a policy of large initial markups coupled with large markdowns so as to exploit the comparative price appeal
- Taking markdowns prematurely
- Having a policy of carry-over to the next season
- Having a multiple-sale policy (for example: ten cents each, three for twenty-five cents)
- Carrying prestige merchandise (model pieces and "fashion show" merchandise originally purchased primarily for display purposes and "fashion umbrella" departments, such as design dresses, which are often deliberately carried at a loss)
- Giving customers goods free of charge, such as samples

Price competition and sales.   Obviously, if a store has a policy of meeting all price competition, the unforeseeable action of other stores will force markdowns even though goods have been properly bought, priced, promoted, and controlled. This is the price paid for a reputation that builds goodwill.

Special sales policy.   A promotional policy of frequent special sales is sure to lead to larger markdowns than a nonpromotional policy of carrying regular stock assortments. Some stores reduce regular stocks once or twice a year to induce extra traffic and sales volume to help carry joint store expenses. After the sale, the goods are restored to regular prices.

A common practice is to obtain manufacturers' closeouts for special sales and to obtain normal markups on them. But later markdowns on such goods are generally in excess of normal reductions: The time is usually late in the season with a short selling period; the assortments of sizes and colors are often unbalanced; the goods may be soiled and damaged, and they do not fit into stock assortments regularly carried.

While for some stores a policy of frequent special sales is of questionable value because of the high extra expense and markdowns usually necessary, other stores thrive on it. A large store in a large city may have established itself throughout the trade as receptive to closeouts and is offered specials first and can choose the best of them. If this store is organized to handle crowds, the very volume engendered will yield a profit, in spite of promotional and other direct costs, since overhead is spread thin.

Maintaining assortments. A sound policy that most stores follow, and yet one that leads to markdowns, is to maintain complete assortments through the greater part of the selling season in order to obtain maximum volume. Customers demand a variety from which to select, and unless a store carries more items in stock than it can possibly dispose of before the clearance season, it will be unable to realize maximum sales. For example, a merchant may have found that, after a late Easter, the only way to dispose of suits is to mark them down to appeal to the bargain seekers and to those who expect to wear them only a few weeks. Even if he were able to anticipate exactly how many suits and the type of suits he would be able to sell up to Easter, he could not realize this figure unless he purchased a larger quantity. The customers who come in to buy shortly before Easter insist upon the privilege of choosing from an assortment. To sell one tailored suit in size sixteen, it may be necessary to have three in stock. If only one were carried, the potential sale would probably be lost as the customer would exercise her privilege to shop further. Paradoxically, stores deliberately buy more than they can sell without markdowns to realize maximum sales before markdowns. Also, they will purchase to maintain assortments in the face of a probable price decline to obtain maximum sales and retain customer goodwill.

High initial markup policy. A somewhat questionable but common promotion policy is that of setting a price on new goods at which only a small portion of the stock can be sold; after a few sales have been made at these "plus" prices, the balance of the stock is marked down to what is frequently a reasonable markup, but the price appeal attracts a different class of customers. For example, some stores buy a piece of occasional furniture for $75 and put it into stock at $200. Soon it is offered in a departmental special sale at "33⅓ off," or $133; this is a markup of nearly 44 percent, which may be a normal one. Again, an evening shoe costing $10 may be priced $29 early in the fall season, reduced to $17 in midseason, and closed out for $8 in January. The average price may be about $18, providing a satisfactory markup on the entire operation and selling more shoes than would have sold at a single $18 price. Here there are attempts to cater to several classes of customers with the same goods. Those who are unmindful of price and primarily interested in style are sold first at a large margin over cost, and the remainder of the purchase is then reduced to appeal to larger groups who insist upon getting their money's worth. There is a marked difference of opinion in regard to this policy of taking very high markups and offsetting them quickly with markdowns for special sale purposes. The store catering to a transient trade and with a considerable number of wealthy customers who care little about price may find the policy of high initial markup coupled with large markdowns profitable, but most stores find that customers soon become suspicious of original prices and buy only after markdowns are taken; customers even question the reasonableness of marked-down prices. On the other hand, it is often a wise policy to buy somewhat more than can probably be sold before the waning season requires markdowns. This is done not only to maintain assortments as long as possible but also to obtain the increased business that can be obtained only by offering bargains. For example, a buyer may be reasonably sure that he can sell one hundred items costing $6.00 at an original retail of $10.95 but may deliberately buy one hundred twenty-five. The twenty-five marked down may be sold at an average price of $8.00, an extra margin of $50.00. There is likely to be only a small increase in expenses; accordingly, the department may increase both sales and profits by buying a quantity that requires some markdowns. Of course, it may be argued that the extra sales could be obtained by buying only one hundred and later buying twenty-five of a new style at which the regular markup could be obtained. But in most communities, there is a large body of bargain hunters who put chief emphasis on value, not style. Their patronage can sometimes be obtained only at markdown prices at which the store cannot afford to sell the entire quantity.

Premature taking of markdowns. It is suspected by some analysts that the policy of taking markdowns very early in the season, as soon as the sales fail to come up to expectations, is a cause of markdowns. In fashion merchandising, operators may live in a continual state of the jitters and tend to slash prices before it is really necessary.

Policy of carry-over. On the other hand, some merchants adopt a policy of carrying over goods from one season to the corresponding season next year—winter goods to the next fall, for example. While this plan may be satisfactory for some seasonal staples, for shopping merchandise it is usually bad because new styles, even though varying only in minor details from older ones, are more attractive to the customer. Furthermore, it is costly to carry over stock in view of storage, handling, and investment costs.

Other policies. There are still other sales policies that lead to markdowns: the policy of multiple pricing, where a number of articles bought together are sold for less than the sum of their unit prices; the policy of carrying high-priced merchandise for atmosphere but with the expectation of a big reduction in price before the goods can be sold; and the policy of making price allowances to complaining customers for goodwill purposes, even though the merchandise is not at fault. Such policies may be justified as volume and profit builders, notwithstanding the fact that the potential markup is reduced by their application.

MARKDOWNS BY MERCHANDISE LINES

Some large stores keep records of the amount of markdown taken for each line. Whenever the price of a group of goods is reduced, the buyer must decide what reason necessitates the markdown. He indicates this reason on the markdown form. The strict accuracy of such entries may be questionable as the buyer may be inclined to attribute the necessity for the markdown to a relatively innocuous reason such as "special sales" or "broken assortments" rather than to the actual reason, which may be that he bought the wrong fabrics, sizes, or styles. This, however, will vary with the degree of discipline and executive follow-through in each organization. It will also depend on top management's commitment to the philosophy of controlling markdowns by determining and correcting their causes rather than by arbitrarily limiting the markdown dollars that can be taken in any period.

TIMING OF MARKDOWNS

An important problem in connection with markdowns is the matter of timing. There are two chief possibilities: (1) to take markdowns early—that is, on individual styles as soon as their rate of sale slows down or after they have remained in stock a set length of time, and (2) to take markdowns late—that is, to leave goods at original prices until nearly the end of the season and then to hold a clearance sale.

EARLY MARKDOWNS

Most department stores and popular-priced specialty stores follow the policy of early markdowns. For women's ready-to-wear a two- three- or four-week time limit is often set depending on the stockturn goal. In other lines, goods are marked down as soon as the rate of sale is deemed inadequate. They are sometimes placed into regular lower price lines and sometimes collected on special sales racks. The advantages of these early individual markdowns are as follows:

1. The amount of markdown per unit is less. Since the reduction is taken while there is still an active demand for the goods, a small reduction is generally sufficient to move them. Should they fail to sell, there is still time before the end of the season to take a more drastic cut. It should be observed, however, that a small percentage off the original price of goods reduced is not synonymous with small dollar markdowns over a period. It is possible that many small early markdowns may cause more loss than a few large late ones.

2. Reducing the stock through early markdowns makes room for the purchase of more salable goods, particularly of manufacturers' special offerings right after the peak of the season. The sale of the reduced goods makes room for new goods that increase volume and make the merchandise investment more productive.

3. Lower price lines may be replenished from higher ones, thus maintaining assortments at the lower prices without additional purchasing.[2]

4. Selling expense is reduced because the goods marked down early generally sell quickly and because extra salespeople do not have to be employed for a clearance sale.

5. Fashion integrity is maintained. Unsatisfactory or out-of-season styles are not shown to customers again and again at regular prices. This practice can be especially dangerous when more alert competitors have marked down the same merchandise much earlier.

6. Goodwill is enhanced. There is much to be said about the goodwill a store gains whenever the customer who loves a bargain tells all her friends about the good buy she found.

Some stores have developed the early markdown policy to the extent not only of marking goods down a certain number of days after they are put into stock but also of marking them down a fixed percentage. This is called an *automatic markdown plan*. In one store, for example, goods that fail to sell in the first two weeks after being put into stock are marked down 25 percent; if they fail to sell at the reduced price by the end of one week more, they are marked down another 25 percent of original retail. This process is repeated the next week, and finally anything left at the end of five weeks is given to charity. This plan insures very careful buying, for a buyer must be reasonably sure that he can sell out each lot purchased within two

---

[2] See page 141 for a discussion of the practice of putting markdown goods into regular price lines.

weeks without a markdown. On the other hand, the plan may be too rigid and may keep buyers from taking enough chances in stocking desirable lots that may require a longer time for disposal.

LATE MARKDOWNS

Although a considerable number of merchants insist that the preponderance of argument is in favor of early markdowns, many high-class stores with a clientele that is interested throughout the season in quality and style, and many small stores with little traffic, follow the policy of late markdowns. They often hold two annual clearance sales a year, in January and July, and take very few markdowns in between.

The advantages of this plan are as follows:

1. The store attracts lower-end customers only twice a year to clean out its stocks. It avoids the bargain appeal entirely the rest of the year and thus maintains a policy of exclusiveness with the established clientele. Since the sales are held at times when regular customers are inactive, bargain hunters are attracted at a time when the store is not busy handling regular patrons.

2. The sale of regular goods is not disrupted. Where markdowns are early, customers are likely to become suspicious of original prices and to wait until midseason, knowing that there will then be substantial reductions. Thus, early season volume at good markups may be retarded. Fear of such early breaks in prices has led certain groups of high-class stores to set rigid rules to the effect that markdowns cannot be advertised before certain specified dates, late in each season, but some of these stores do take markdowns on a current basis but segregate the merchandise in a separate clearance room, where it is sold without benefit of advertising.

3. The quantity of stock for clearance accumulated in a season allows the store to make the clearance an advertised event that is looked forward to by bargain seekers.

4. The late markdown allows a long trial period; the goods are given every opportunity to sell without a markdown. In a small shop, particularly, it frequently happens that certain articles fail to sell for some time, not because they have mistakenly been bought but because by chance the customer who would be interested in the article has not yet come in—before the end of the season, she is likely to come in and buy.

Some stores have attempted a compromise between the early and the late markdown policies by holding a monthly clearance sale on the last day of every month. This method has its limitations—

some styles may even then be held too long, in some months certain departments may have almost nothing to contribute to the sale, and the effect of such sales during the height of a season may not be desirable.

AMOUNT OF THE MARKDOWN

Since the one reason for marking down merchandise is to sell it without further delay, the markdown should obviously be large enough to yield this result. As already indicated, it does not necessarily follow that the first markdown should be large enough to move the entire supply. One specialist in markdown control is of the opinion that the first markdown is satisfactorily large if it moves from 35 percent to 50 percent of the entire lot. On the other hand, too many small reductions taken during a period of rapid obsolescence may increase the total loss.

It is difficult to generalize on percentage reductions necessary to move different kinds of goods. It depends on the nature of the merchandise, the original markup, the time in the selling season, the quantity on hand, and the pressure on the store to turn inventory into cash.

Goods that are going out of fashion, including styles that have found little acceptance at the original price or that are slowing up in selling tempo, are commonly reduced 30 percent to 50 percent. The percentage reduction is usually higher on high-priced goods to bring them to the attention of bargain seekers. For example, a $19.75 coat that fails to sell may be cleared at $13.95, a reduction of about 30 percent, whereas a $250.00 coat may have to be reduced to $125.00 to appeal to a group that is uninterested at the higher price.

As already indicated in connection with price lines, customer demand is grouped into price zones. In general, it may be concluded that a markdown from one price in a zone to a lower price in the same zone is adequate only when the supply to be cleared is small and when it is believed that the same people who rejected it at the original price will find it a good value at the reduced price. But when the supply is large and the style questionable, the goods should be marked down into a lower zone, where a new customer group will be attracted to the unusually good quality now available in this price range.

Staples that are reduced temporarily for special sale purposes and that will be soon restored to the regular price may require about a 10 percent reduction to achieve a considerable speedup in the rate of sale. Thus, five cents off on $0.49 margarine, fifty cents off on

$4.95 sheets, and two dollars off on a $16.00 battery are likely to be effective.

In the electrical appliance field, many markdown are taken in anticipation of new models about to make their appearance. Since they will give many years of service and will vary only slightly from the former model, a small reduction will usually suffice. Thus, a mailorder house may reduce a $205 washer to $190 and a $450 refrigerator-freezer to $420, both reductions of only 7 percent but representing substantial savings to the buyer.

Automobiles are a special case. Because of the forced obsolescence in annual style change, a car is *used* if driven only a few miles and is subject to a year's depreciation. In the summer, early users of that year's models, especially salesmen, often trade for the next year's models. Cars priced new in the year of manufacture within the $3,000 range tend to depreciate about as follows:

> by end of first year, 25 percent of the original price
> by end of second year, 40 percent of the original price
> by end of third year, 50 percent of the original price

After this, the rate of depreciation varies widely with the condition of the car, but after ten years few cars would have a market value of as much as 10 percent of the original price.

Special markdown prices.   There is difference of opinion as to whether to put markdown goods into a regular price line or to segregate the goods into special prices reserved for markdown goods. Since customers may roughly be classified into two groups: those who primarily seek style and those who primarily seek value, it would seem wise to segregate the markdowns in the case of fashion merchandise such as dresses and millinery. Thus the bargain seeker who knows values finds an assembled assortment from which to choose, whereas the style seeker looking over the assortment in her price zone is not forced to inspect garments of questionable style, the chief attraction of which is materials and workmanship at a price.

If separate prices are set for markdowns, both salespeople and customers get to recognize bargains. Also stock and sales analyses are facilitated; in determining the relative importance of regular price lines, the merchant does not find the sales and stock figures distorted by marked-down goods.

There are times when it is unwise to segregate marked-down goods. For example, early in the season a store may have put into stock suits at $129 and $145. The $129 price may be much more popular and may seem to be a limit above which the store can obtain little business. Accordingly, it is wise to reduce the $145 suits to $129, but it is not desirable to segregate them as marked-down bargains. Here they are not being marked down because they are wrong in style but because the original price was above the price limit of the group of customers on whom the store has to depend.

Again, segregation may not be necessary for shopping goods that do not frequently change in style. For example, in marking down an article of house furnishings, such as a rug, it may be wise to reprice the item into a regular price line. Here there is not the marked distinction between bargain hunters and style hunters, so it is not necessary to keep new stocks separated from old.

It may be concluded that early season markdowns taken to consolidate price lines and markdowns on semistaples do not require segregation, whereas midseason and late markdowns taken to dispose of fashions that are questionable in style or that are becoming unseasonable may well be segregated.

BARGAINING POLICY

An important aspect of markdown policy has to do with taking a price reduction on the spot in the presence of the customer at the time of sale rather than in advance, thus giving the customer the impression that she is getting a special price not offered to others. Some stores recognize preferred customer groups such as the clergy, teachers, and employees, who receive preferential prices. Customers who have charge accounts are often given advanced opportunity to buy at reduced prices and may exhaust the supply before the general public is given a chance to participate. Over sixty years ago, bargaining with individual customers was a frequent practice in retail stores, and it is still more common than generally supposed. In some stores, minimum selling prices are indicated in code on price tickets, and salespeople's remuneration depends upon how high a price they can get above the minimum. In a number of specialty stores that engage in high-pressure selling T.O. (turnover) men are employed who have authority to reduce a price quoted by the first salesman contacting the customer. For example, a fur coat costing $100 may be offered at $250. If the customer shows interest in the coat but objects to the price, the salesperson calls a T.O. man, who poses as an important executive. The T.O. man handles the sale, agreeing to sell the coat for $200 as a special concession to gain a new customer. If the customer still refuses, a second T.O. man may be called who makes a further concession, and a sale may finally be consummated at a price that seems to be a great bargain but still represents an adequate markup for the retailer. In some foreign countries, customers regularly offer a third of the retailer's asking price. It is said that in one store the buyer and seller throw dice to see which of the two prices is to prevail; the seller is insulted if his asking price is accepted without providing him the chance to participate in his game of dice.

CONFIDENCE IN THE ONE-PRICE POLICY

Although the opportunity to bargain is welcomed by customers endowed with a trading or sporting instinct, there is no doubt that the majority of customers lose confidence in such a store. They recognize their own inability to judge values and are by temperament unwilling to enter into a battle of wits upon every purchase. If a store depends upon repeat patronage rather than upon catch-as-catch-can transient trade, it must at least approach a policy of adhering to prices it quotes customers. With the possible exception of shops in the amusement centers of metropolitan cities, a store must create in the customer's mind a belief that the price quoted him is the same as the price quoted every other customer, that the price is fair, and that it is not subject to reduction by haggling.

Such a policy, however, does not preclude price reductions. It simply means that the reduction will not be made at the time of sale. If a number of customers refuse to buy, the price will be reduced between attempts to sell, and new customers will be quoted a lower price.

There is danger of some customer dissatisfaction at the moment the price is reduced. For example, in April, a customer may buy a suit for $39.50, and the next day the remaining suits may be marked down for clearance to $27.50. When the customer comes in again, perhaps to take delivery on her suit purchased the day before, she may notice the same merchandise selling at $27.50. Should the store refuse a reduction to her, she could generally insist upon a return and refund of $39.50 and then buy the same garment for $12.00 less. To handle such situations, a store may adopt the following rules:

1. Plan the time to take markdowns on each different class of goods, and for a few days before the reduction is effective remove the goods to be marked down from the selling area. Thus, a customer does not see the duplicate of her purchase offered the next day or hour at a lower price. The time interval of a few days justifies a lower price.

2. Where price reductions occur within a week of sale or within some other specified time, refund the difference without argument to any customer who complains. This does not mean, however,

that the store will take the initiative and make refunds to all customers who bought shortly before a price reduction.

Some deviation from a strictly one-price policy may be necessary in the case of quantity purchases. For example, a man who wanted a piano found two friends who were also in the market. They went to one of the largest stores in New York and offered to make a group purchase if a special price could be arranged. This was readily accomplished. Such transactions in a big store are best handled through a contract department to which the quantity buyer is referred. Such a department works with each selling department to set a lower price than the regular retail price. Stores frequently outfit hotels and public institutions this way as well as individual customers who buy in large quantities.

MARKDOWN CALCULATIONS AND RECORDS

MARKDOWN PERCENTAGES

Markdowns may be expressed in two different ways: (1) as a percentage of sales and (2) as a percentage off the original retail price.

Thus, if during a month a store's net sales are $10,000 and its markdowns $500, the markdowns are 5 percent of sales.

If the markdowns of $500 were all taken on a lot formerly priced at an original retail of $1,500 and sold for $1,000 (included in the total sales of $10,000), the percentage off is 33⅓ percent of the former retail price. This is the figure commonly used in advertising price reductions to the public. For internal record purposes, if goods retailed at $50,000 are reduced $10,000 and sold for $40,000, the markdowns are stated as 25 percent, not 20 percent. If a merchant reduces his retail prices 20 percent during a period, it does not mean that his markdowns will be 20 percent. If all the goods sell, the markdowns will be 25 percent:

$$\text{Let } \$100 = \text{original retail and}$$
$$\underline{\$\ 20} = \text{reduction}$$
$$\$\ 80 = \text{sales}$$
$$\text{Markdown percent} = \frac{\$20}{\$80} = 25\%$$

On the other hand, if only one-half of the goods are sold, thereby bringing in $40, the markdowns will be $20 ÷ $40, or 50 percent of the sales.

It does not follow that markdowns as a percentage of sales are usually larger than markdowns as a percentage off original retail. Thus, a merchant may slash one-quarter of his retail stock 50 percent of the original retail price and sell all the reduced goods and half of the nonreduced goods:

Total stock	$100.00
Amount of stock reduced	25.00
Markdown (50 percent of $25.00)	12.50
Sales of reduced goods	$ 12.50
Sales of regular goods (1/2 of $75.00)	37.50
Total	$ 50.00

Markdown percent ($12.50 ÷ $50.00) = 25%

ESTIMATING MAINTAINED MARKUP

In the purchase of high fashion and experimental goods, it is important to estimate what portion of a lot is likely to have to be reduced for clearance and to what level. It is then possible to forecast the unit maintained markup that will probably be realized from the purchase.

For example, a purchase may be contemplated of one hundred units of a new style in assorted sizes and colors that costs $5.80 an item and is to retail at $10.00, a 42 percent markup. But the probabilities may be that only 70 percent of the lot will sell at the original retail price, that 20 percent will be sold just above cost at approximately $6.00 a unit, and that 10 percent will have to be sold at half price, or $5.00 a unit. The following calculation may then be made:

Estimated Retail Sales Price per Unit	*Estimated Units Likely to Sell at Each Price (Probabilities)*	*$ Sales Estimate*	*Cost $5.80 × 100*	*Maintained Markup*
$10	70	$700		
6	20	120		
5	10	50		
Total	100	$870	$580	$290

Maintained markup percent: $\dfrac{\$290}{\$870} = 33\ 1/3\%$

If on goods of this sort a maintained markup of 35 percent is considered a minimum objective, the lot may be passed up unless a 44 percent initial markup is deemed feasible.

RECORDING OF MARKDOWNS

To enable merchandising executives to review the markdown practices pursued by their buyers it is important that the store introduce an efficient system of recording and reporting markdowns. Such a system is also necessary in the calculation of inventory records and the determination of stock shortages (see chapter 10). Small stores on the cost method of inventory commonly keep no markdown records, but they would probably buy and control their stocks more intelligently if they did.

Control of repricing.   The usual procedure requires the buyer or department manager to fill out a markdown form indicating the old price, the new price, the quantity reduced, and the reason for the reduction. In many instances this is simply a request that must be approved by a superior before the markdown is taken.

Old versus new price tickets.   In repricing the merchandise, there are two possibilities: one is to note the new prices on the old tickets and the other is to replace all old-price tickets with new ones. The first is the simpler plan and allows the customer to note the amount of the price reduction and thus have greater interest, if bargain conscious. But it is so easy to re-mark a price ticket that there is danger of unauthorized markdowns being taken. Various ingenious ways to guard against this have been devised: Some stores allow the use of a specially colored ink or pencil only; others use a hand-printing device that can be applied to a price ticket without removing it.

The policy of removing old tickets and attaching fresh ones that show only the new price provides excellent control and an air of authenticity to all prices. Also, many stores believe that it is unwise to attempt to sell merchandise on a basis of comparison with former prices. The value of merchandise fluctuates over time; the fact that a suit was once offered for $79.50 provides no reason, it is argued, why, customers should buy it today for $59.50. Many stores prefer to give the impression that all prices are as low as present conditions warrant and to give no extra preference to marked-down goods. On the other hand, many customers do exhibit interest in former prices, and some stores feel the customers have a right to the information.

It should be noted that even when a new ticket is attached, an old price can be shown with a printed line drawn through it.

QUESTIONS FOR DISCUSSION

1. Does it make any real difference whether or not all price reductions are classified as markdowns?
2. Which is probably the most common type of buying error: (1) to buy too much of the right goods at the right time, (2) to buy the right goods but either too early or too late in their cycle of acceptance, or (3) to buy the wrong goods?
3. Do you attribute the necessity for markdowns more to the action or lack of action by management or to the failure of salespeople to sell aggressively the goods in stock?
4. Is it a wise policy to take a relatively high markup on new goods with the express purpose of repricing them at a normal markup at midseason?
5. How late in the summer should reasonable assortments of hot-weather goods be maintained? (In tropical climates, the "summer" season may not be the same as that in temperate climates).
6. Do the arguments for taking markdowns early (such as three weeks after receipt of fashion goods) outweigh the arguments for taking them late?
7. (a) A store advertises national brands of women's underwear as follows:

Regular	Sale Price
$ 3.00	$ 2.39
4.00	2.99
4.50	3.59
7.00	5.99
10.00	7.95
11.00	8.99

    Are the reductions adequate to attract shoppers in volume? Assuming that the original price lines correctly reflect differences in value, which sale prices suggest better bargains than others?

    (b) A store advertises a well-known brand of women's shoes as follows:

    "$13.95, were $16.95 to $23.95—Save up to $10.00"

    Is the markdown adequate? In what respect may shoppers be disappointed?
8. If the markdowns in a department were 12 percent and if goods had to be reduced an average of 30 percent to move them, what portion of the sales must have been made at marked-down prices? Of what practical value is such a calculation? Note: Assume sales of $100 and markdowns of $12. This $12 markdown is 30 percent of the original retail price of the goods reduced. This original retail price less the dollar markdowns is the sales price of the goods reduced.
9. A style is introduced into stock at a 44 percent initial markup,

but only half of the quantity is sold at the original retail price. The balance is reduced one-third in price, and only three-fifths of these reduced goods are sold at the first price reduction. The remaining stock is closed out at 50 percent off the original retail. What maintained markup is realized on the lot? Do you think that this example is typical of the pricing and sale of fashion merchandise?

10. How difficult is it to maintain correct records of markdowns taken:

(a) In amount?

(b) By causes or reasons?

part **III**

Inventory is the merchant's
major stock in trade. He must
(1) count it, (2) record it, (3)
value it, and (4) analyze his sales
and his profits relative to it.
The widely used retail method
of inventory, a merchandise
management tool involving the
first three of these activities,
receives detailed treatment in
this section. A special chapter
describes the profit return realized by management on the
merchandise investment and on
space occupied.

INVENTORY

9

PHYSICAL
INVENTORY

CHARACTERISTICS OF RETAIL INVENTORIES

In contrast to the inventories of goods carried by most other types of business concerns, inventories carried by retailers have certain marked characteristics. Their merchandise stocks constitute an exceptionally large part of total assets, frequently over 50 percent. They fluctuate seasonally a great deal, often varying 30 percent up and down from the year's average inventory. Their composition is continually changing as new items are added and old items dropped; in many stores, very few of the items carried five years ago are still being offered. Retail inventories are heterogeneous, consisting typically of thousands of different stockkeeping units.

Most retail inventories are perishable. Although this is particularly true of fashion stocks, even staples deteriorate or are soon replaced by new versions of the item. Thus, markdowns are a major consideration for the retailer.

Retail inventories are usually vulnerable to theft, both shoplifting and pilferage. They are generally stored and displayed in many locations and adequate physical safeguards are difficult to maintain.

In view of these differentiating characteristics, the problem of inventory planning and control is a major one for retailers.

REASONS FOR TAKING PHYSICAL INVENTORY

The counting and recording of the amount of stock on hand at a given time is an essential feature of retail merchandise management. A basic reason for taking a physical inventory is to determine the total value of the stock so that the balance sheet and departmental, storewide, and company-wide profit and loss statements may be prepared.

A second reason for taking a physical inventory is to familiarize the manager and salespeople with just what is in stock. Some articles may seldom be requested by customers and may remain unnoticed in stock indefinitely unless there is a formal, complete examination of all the stock at regular intervals. Taking of inventory brings these items to attention and leads not only to positive efforts to sell them but also to better service because salespeople become more fully aware of their entire stock assortment.

The third reason for taking a physical inventory is to enable management to analyze the stock in each department to control both buying and promotional activities. In the storewide inventory, the analysis is generally by classification, age (season letter), and sometimes price line, in order that the stock assortment may be better adjusted to customer demand and an accumulation of old stock may be avoided by positive efforts to realize a better stockturn. When frequent inventories are taken in a unit-control system, the inventory may be analyzed by characteristics such as style, color, and size. Such inventory analysis becomes the basis for merchandising, that is, for planning what to buy and what to promote.

REASONS FOR TAKING PHYSICAL INVENTORY

- Preparation of financial statements
- Familiarization of personnel with everything in stock
- Stock analysis for merchandising
- Sales determination and analysis by subgroups

A fourth reason is to calculate sales for groupings of merchandise for which it is impracticable to keep separate sales records. Sales records are kept for an entire store, for each department, and for each merchandise classification; but they may not be maintained for further subdivisions, for price lines, or for specific items. If physical inventories are taken by these breakdowns at regular intervals and purchase records are maintained for each, the sales may be derived. For example, when the stock was counted a month ago there might have been twenty-four of a certain article on hand. When counted today, eighteen may be in stock. Purchase records might reveal that thirty-six were received into stock during the month. The sales, then, may be derived by adding the purchases to the former inventory figure and subtracting the new inventory: $24 + 36 - 18 = 42$, the approximate sales. This use of inventories will be more fully discussed in subsequent chapters.

PHYSICAL INVENTORY AT COST AND RETAIL

Physical inventories may be counted at cost prices, at retail prices, or in units. For profit-figuring purposes, the value of the inventory is the important consideration. For planning specifically what to buy and what to promote, the units on hand are of major significance.

INVENTORY AT COST

Taking inventory at cost is still very common. The cost prices may be determined in one of two ways: the first is to indicate the cost price of each article in code on each price ticket attached to each item in stock; when merchandise is counted at the end of each control period, the cost prices are listed on the inventory sheet, and the total price is thus determined. The second way is to place on each item a number or other identification that refers to a separate record of cost, such as the invoice, the order, a cost book, or unit control record.

Cost codes. There are three types of codes in common use. The first is composed of a word or phrase of ten letters, each of which represents a consecutive digit. A well-known code is MAKE PROFIT. The cost $19.50 would be written MIPT. To avoid repeating the same letter another letter, such as X, may be used for the second of two identical numbers. For example, $22.00 may be written AXTX. There are innumerable codes of this sort. A few examples are MONEY TALKS, REPUBLICAN, and GOD HELP US, with X used for zero.

A second type of code is composed of symbols, one for each digit. Here is one:

1	2	3
4	5	6
7	8	9

$$0 = X$$

The price $19.50 is written ⌐ ⌐ □ X.

Symbol codes are easy to learn, but they take more time to write than letters or numbers.

A third type of code is a transformation of the cost digits by addition, subtraction, multiplication, or division. For example, the number 3 may be placed in front of the cost $19.50 and this amount added to each digit, dropping the tens. The code would appear as 34283. If the profix 6 is used, the same cost would appear as 67516. In other codes of this nature, the costs are multiplied or divided by 2. A simple plan is to put two meaningless numbers in front of the cost and two afterward, omitting the decimal point—$19.50 could be written 70195007. This might be regarded as a serial number by the uninitiated. The first two numbers could represent the year and the last two the month of purchase.

TYPES OF COST CODES

- Letter code:

      M E R C H A N T S X
      1 2 3 4 5 6 7 8 9 0
          ANH = $6.75

- Symbol code:
  A curved line (or) = 1, and a straight line slanted either right and left (╱ or ╲) = 3.

      < ⌠ ╱ = $6.75

- Number code:
  7167502 = $6.75 bought in the second month of the season, March, 1971

Buying and selling units. Many items are bought by the dozen or gross and sold by the piece. This raises the question as to whether cost prices on codes should be kept in terms of the buying unit or of the selling unit. For example, if of goods costing $22.75 a dozen and selling at $2.95 each, four are on hand in inventory, should the determination of unit cost be done at inventory time or in advance? The safer practice is to translate the cost per buying unit into the cost per selling unit when the goods are put into stock, otherwise there is danger of confusion and overstatement of the cost of the inventory. In the example, the cost might erroneously be computed as $91.00 (22.75 × 4) and the retail correctly as $11.80!

But to change cost per buying unit to cost per selling unit commonly involves uneven numbers. Thus, a cost of $22.75 a dozen is $1.892083 a unit. If this were rounded out to $1.90 for code purposes and a large quantity were involved, there would be a sizable cumulative error. As a rule of thumb, the cost per unit should be carried out to the nearest tenth of a cent, except in larger stores. This procedure is cumbersome and yet probably more satisfactory than attempting to make the adjustments by indicating the nature of the buying unit during the physical inventory and changing the cost to that of the selling unit after the count is taken.[1] This problem is eliminated when goods are inventoried at retail price only, as will be explained in the retail method of inventory.

Serial and reference numbers.   Instead of using codes, some stores primarily handling staple goods assign a serial number of each staple item carried and for each different item keep a control card that shows the manufacturer, description, cost price per unit, and quantities and dates of purchase. This serial number is placed on the price ticket or on the bins in which the merchandise is stored. As the inventory count is taken, the serial numbers and quantities of each are recorded and the office fills in the cost prices from its record. Since the goods are usually arranged by serial number, it is easy to find the corresponding cost records quickly. In some operations, the order is reversed; the office, from its records, draws up the sheets for physical inventory entering all the serial numbers carried and the cost of each. The inventory counters then simply fill in the quantities of each item on hand.[2] Although this method is satisfactory for staples, it requires considerable record keeping and would be unwieldy for items that are not carried in stock over a long period.

Instead of using serial numbers for each item, some stores record on the goods serial numbers assigned to each invoice. If a line number on the invoice is added, it is possible to refer to this original record to determine the cost. Instead of the invoice number, some use the serial number of the buyer's order, which, like the invoice, gives detailed cost information.

Still another plan is to put on the price ticket a code indicating

[1] Where units are usually sold by the set or by the dozen, it is permissible to record costs at the multiple unit rather than in individual pieces.

[2] A serial number may not be required for some standard merchandise because the very nature of the goods makes it easy to locate the cost record.

the manufacturer of the merchandise and also his style number. This allows reference to a unit-control record maintained for each style.

Except for the serial numbers for staples, these methods are better suited for reordering purposes than for determining cost value at inventory time. It takes a long time to look up the records and they may be unreliable.

INVENTORY AT RETAIL

In stores handling general merchandise it is a common practice to take the physical inventory at marked retail prices rather than at cost prices. Under the retail method of inventory, described in chapter 11, the aggregate retail value of the stock is then converted to cost. The taking of physical inventory is speeded up where goods are counted at plainly marked retail prices, and the inventory process is more accurate because no coding or decoding is required—nor is reference to other records required.

INVENTORY PROCEDURES

Large stores have developed elaborate and exact procedures to take physical inventory so as to avoid error, and many of these procedures apply to the small store as well.

TIMES OF INVENTORY

In many stores, it is the practice to take two inventories a year. In general merchandise and apparel stores, these inventories are usually taken at the end of January and at the end of July.[3] Some stores have only one, an annual inventory, and there are probably a few small stores that take no complete inventory, merely guessing the value of the stock on hand when making out their income tax reports.

In fashion departments and in some specialty stores, it is desirable to take frequent inventories—every three months, every month, or every week.[4] These frequent counts are primarily a phase

---

[3] January and July are the ends of selling seasons, and inventories are generally lower at the end of these months than at other times.

[4] Supermarkets commonly take inventories for reorder purposes very frequently, even daily.

of unit control to keep the stock balanced to sales and to discover shortages rather than to work out financial statements. They frequently do not require the detailed listing of every item. For example, a ready-to-wear department may arrange its stock by classification and price lines within each classification and count weekly the number of garments at each price line within each classification.

INVENTORY REQUIREMENTS

The two requirements for physical inventory are (1) accuracy in the listing and (2) thoroughness in counting all the stock regardless of its physical location. The assurance of an adequate physical count, then, depends primarily upon careful advance preparation.

In a small store it is important to go over the complete stock in advance, sorting it by price and type, attaching any price tickets that may be lacking, taking markdowns on slow-selling stock, and pulling out of dark corners and bins anything that has been stored away and is likely to be overlooked at the time of counting.

In a large store a more elaborate procedure is necessary because of the many people involved. The advance preparation involves five groups of activities:

1. Sorting the merchandise according to predetermined classifications
2. Preparing a layout chart of fixtures
3. Requisitioning and checking inventory forms and supplies
4. Instructing the sales force
5. Making sure that all merchandise is properly priced

In branch operations, the department manager rather than the buyer may perform these functions. Figure 9.1 shows an instruction sheet used for the guidance of department managers.

FORMS USED FOR COUNTING AND LISTING

There are three types of forms that may be used for the listing of stock: the inventory sheet, the inventory tag, and the punch card.

Inventory sheet. The inventory sheet (figure 9.2) allows the listing of a large number of items on one sheet. It carries spaces for the description of the merchandise, with the style or lot number, the season letter, the classification, the quantity, the unit of measure-

INVENTORY INSTRUCTIONS TO DEPARTMENT MANAGERS

Mr. ...., Dept. ....

To be of any value whatever, the inventory to be taken ....
(date) .... must be accurate. Listed below for your convenience
are some of the factors, in addition to correct listing of the stock in your department, that affect the accuracy of the final figures:

1. Merchandise out for repair, and so forth.

2. Merchandise in windows and on display in other departments.

3. Merchandise in advertising office and comparison bureau.

4. Merchandise returned by customers and held in adjustment bureau or at return desks.

5. Merchandise in your office or elsewhere that is included in your stock figures, but would not be otherwise included in the inventory.

6. Merchandise in marking room for which corresponding invoice has been passed on to the office for inclusion in the book inventory figure. These invoices are stamped "old stock."

7. Has reserve stock been inventoried? (See that there are no transfers between reserve and forward stock after reserve stock has been listed.)

8. Has stock in warehouse been inventoried? (Same precaution against transfer after listing.)

9. Go through your entire stock now, dislodge the pups and see that markdowns are put through and merchandise actually remarked before inventory. Don't wait until you discover it in the listing process, for then it must go over into the new year. No matter how willing the Controller may be to accommodate you, the income tax regulations absolutely prohibit any such adjustment. The merchandise must have been exposed for sale prior to inventory at the price at which it is listed in inventory.

10. See that you have cleaned up all claims, transportation claims, adjustments with customers, and approvals as far as they affect your stock or your figures.

11. If any of your stock must be listed prior to the actual closing hour, see that you have a supply of Temporary Inventory Tags, which may be obtained from the Controller's office. Never permit the use of scrap paper for this purpose. See that any sales made after listing are noted in the space provided on the tag.

12. Send to the Controller's office in plenty of time during the last day for your supply of inventory sheets and instruction sheets. Be sure the numbered sheets are distributed in numerical order. When the listing is completed and checked, mark the last sheet used, "Last Sheet," and sign it. Any sheets of an *earlier* serial number that are not used should be marked "Void." All numbered sheets received by you must be returned to insure accuracy in the tremendous task of checking and calculating which must be done by the Controller's office. Please keep this for reference.

Yours for accuracy,

(Signed) ....
Title.

FIGURE 9.1   Inventory Instructions to Department Managers

ment (yards, pieces, dozens, gross), the retail price per unit, and the extensions. When the count is made in advance of the inventory cut-off date and sales occur within a section in which the count has already been made, a special deduction sheet is made out. The form is the same as the regular inventory sheet but is clearly marked to differentiate it. Salespeople should carefully be instructed to make all such deductions as sales are made, otherwise there is danger of error and failure of the inventory figures to agree with the office records obtained from the previous inventory, purchases, sales, and mark-downs. If these records are to agree, the amount on the inventory sheets, as finally submitted, must indicate the goods on hand at the end of the inventory, that is, at the time that the book figure is computed.

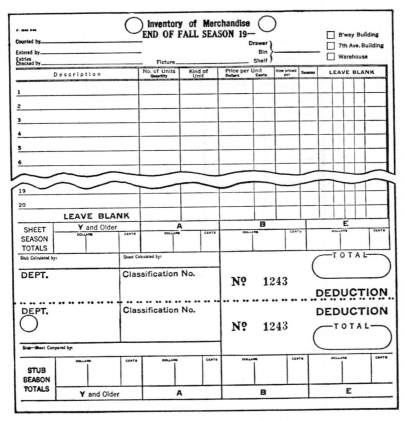

FIGURE 9.2   Inventory Sheet

Inventory tag. The second form is the inventory tag (figure 9.3). The information required is similar, but a separate tag is used for every different style or lot number and also for the same article if in different locations. These tags are entirely filled out in advance of the date the inventory is to be completed, and any sales or other deductions made between the time the tag has been filled out and

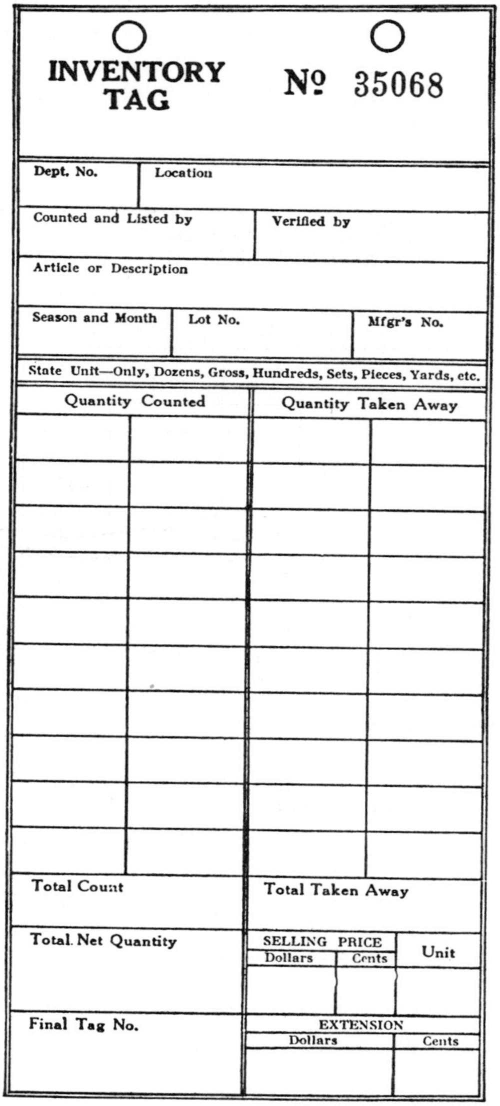
INVENTORY TAG
Nº 35068
Dept. No.
Location
Counted and Listed by
Verified by
Article or Description
Season and Month
Lot No.
Mfgr's No.
State Unit—Only, Dozens, Gross, Hundreds, Sets, Pieces, Yards, etc.
Quantity Counted
Quantity Taken Away
Total Count
Total Taken Away
Total Net Quantity
SELLING PRICE
Dollars
Cents
Unit
Final Tag No.
EXTENSION
Dollars
Cents

FIGURE 9.3 Inventory Tag

the inventory has been completed are recorded on the tag as such deductions are made. These tags are especially useful in connection with yard goods where it is convenient to measure goods in advance of the inventory date. Yardage sold after the count is entered at the time of each sale.

Both inventory sheets and tags have their advocates, and it is difficult to choose between them.

Punch cards.   With the expanding use of mechanical and electronic sorting and tabulating equipment, some stores now use punch cards or tape for taking inventory. A punching machine or electronic typewriter on wheels provides the original inventory record, eliminating the use of either the inventory sheet or the inventory tag. Two people work as a team: one calls off the description and quantity of each item in stock and the other operates the machine, punching a tabulating card for every different item called off.[5]

This method greatly facilitates processing and computing the data. It is easy to sort the inventory data by merchandise classification, season letter, vendor, and price line.

To simplify the process of counting, various devices may be used. A fixture may be devised to hold a predetermined quantity of a certain article or container. If a fixture is full, counting is unnecessary; if there is empty space in the fixture for a readily determinable number, this number may be subtracted from the number the fixture holds when full.

In some instances, it is quicker to weigh a quantity of small identical goods than to count them. For example, even though key chains may cost ten cents each, it may be easier to weigh the quantity in stock and divide by the average number of key chains to the pound, as determined from a sample. Measuring machines are helpful for yard goods, and a calibrating device is available which measures the width of a bolt and counts the number of folds to give the yardage.[6]

LISTING PERIOD

Some stores have succeeded in taking their complete forward stock, that is, the stock on the selling floor, in one evening, and thus

---

[5] In some instances, a sound-recording device is used to accumulate the inventory data.

[6] An inventory control device has recently been developed for yard goods. A bolt of cloth to be measured is fed between rollers. A control card that identifies the material by lot number is also inserted into the machine. This number and the exact yardage on the bolt are both fed into a computer. The system can be used both for inventory taking and for recording sales. (General Research Inc., Greenwich, Conn., as reported in the *New York Times*, September 5, 1970, p. 25.)

there is no difficulty in handling sales during inventory. Such rapid listing of forward stock is highly desirable and is possible where a reserve is carried and only a small quantity in each style or kind is carried on the selling floor. The warehouse and reserve-stock inventories may be taken in advance of the forward stock, but careful records are kept of everything sent to the selling floor or received from any source. Addition and deduction sheets should be used for this purpose, along with the regular listing forms. Thus, when the recorded additions and subtractions are made to the original inventory counts for warehouse and reserve, the quantities are those on hand at the time the forward-stock inventory is completed. If the selling department requisitions goods on inventory night, they should be held in reserve so as not to be included in the count and so that a deduction sheet will not have to be made for the reserve. Special groups of forms may be allotted to reserve and warehouse.

PROCEDURE WHEN COUNTS COMPLETED

When the counts are completed, reports are drawn up analyzing the inventory of each department by classification and season letter. If punch cards are used to take inventory, the sorting by classification, season letter, and price lines is automatic. If sheets or tags are used, a card may be punched for each item appearing on a line of the inventory sheet or on each tag. These cards are put through a sorting machine that arranges them as desired and then through a tabulating machine that issues a typed classified report.

The manager still has a few responsibilities in connection with the inventory even after the actual count is completed and the forms are turned in. He should submit a record of any price changes that had to be made just before inventory, and he should go over inventory sheets after the office has extended them to check errors.

The physical inventory figure is compared with the "book" figure to determine the stock shortages, as explained in chapter 10.

AGE ANALYSIS

Analysis of an inventory by age from the date of receipt into stock is of major importance as much merchandise either soon goes out of fashion or physically deteriorates. The count in the department illustrated in table 9.1 was made about two weeks before the official closing date at the end of January.

The managements of general merchandise stores, including

department stores, attempt to have 80 percent to 90 percent of their inventories consist of merchandise less than six months old. In departments such as candy and patterns, the ratio is commonly 100 percent. In some lines, 20 percent to 30 percent of the inventory value may be permitted to be over six months old—these include shoes, aprons, and pictures and frames. In a few lines, over 30 percent of the inventory is often over six months old—particularly men's clothing and summer and metal furniture. In grocery stores, analysis should not be in terms of six-month periods but rather in terms of months or weeks.[7]

Once the danger point in regard to age is determined, all inventory records are carefully scrutinized to spot the slow sellers. The control of this merchandise is discussed in the next section.

TABLE 9.1   Age of Inventory: Sportswear (Count Date: Jan. 15, 197–)

Class	Inventory[a] Dollars		Under 3 Months			3–6 Months			Over 6 Months		
	TY[b]	LY	TY $	TY%	LY%	TY $	TY%	LY%	TY $	TY%	LY%
Shifts	10.8	8.0	6.3	58	58	3.7	34	33	.8	8	9
Sweaters	19.2	18.7	15.0	78	80	3.1	16	15	1.1	6	5
Swimwear	27.7	30.8	18.4	66	63	7.8	28	30	1.5	6	7
Coordinates	19.1	13.7	13.1	69	65	5.3	28	31	.7	3	4
Pants	30.0	26.4	19.1	63	58	8.3	28	31	2.6	9	11
Blouses	11.2	9.3	6.2	55	60	4.1	37	33	.9	8	7
Total	118.0	106.9	78.1	66	64	32.3	27	29	7.6	7	7

[a] Dollar amounts given in thousands.
[b] TY: this year; LY: last year.

SLOW-SELLING MERCHANDISE

There are four distinct problems in regard to the control of slow-selling merchandise: (1) what to regard as slow-selling goods, (2)

[7] Although the date of merchandise receipt into the store is commonly entered on price tickets for stock control purposes, the notation may be in such a form as to make it incomprehensible to the customer. Currently, however, consumer groups, often backed by governmental authority, are demanding that the date of processing or the date the goods are to be removed from stock be included on labels of perishable goods in terms that the customer can readily understand to make it possible for her to select fresh goods. Such a requirement complicates the merchant's problem of disposing of the remnant of a former purchase after receipt of a new shipment. Nevertheless, national food chains, in certain of their geographic areas, are now providing code-dates that the customer can readily interpret.

how to locate these goods in stock, (3) how to dispose of them, and (4) how to avoid their accumulation.

What Is Slow Selling?

Slow-selling merchandise (sometimes called *prior stock*) may be defined as merchandise that has been in stock a longer period than experience indicates is desirable. The plan is to set a time limit for each department or classification. Although this is commonly six months, it may be shorter or longer. For example, any handbag that is in stock more than three months may be considered slow selling and in need of prompt disposal.

A second method used to determine what is slow selling is to set up a weekly rate of sale in units. Any items that fail to sell at the predetermined rate are considered slow selling. For example, for sport shoes, a rate of sale of two pairs a week may be set for every style. If a style fails to sell at this rate for two or four consecutive weeks, it may be adjudged slow selling. Here, attention is directed not to the length of time goods stay in stock but to the rate of sale.

This method is an excellent supplement to the time limit, for it makes it possible to identify an item that is likely to fail to sell before the time limit unless a special effort is made.

A third plan is to compute the rate of stockturn on individual items in stock. For example, over a two-month period, a shoe department may be maintaining an average stock of 60 pairs of shoes in a certain style, and the sales may be 5 pairs a week. On an annual basis, this is sales of 260 pairs (5×52), with an average stock of 60, and the turnover is 4.3. If 6 turns are planned for this classification of shoes, the style may be considered slow selling even though most of the goods may have been on hand less than two months.

This method is satisfactory only where stock is being kept up by reorders and therefore shows what styles should be taken off the reorder list and closed out. It is not satisfactory in determining the slow-selling items for fashion goods not commonly reordered. For example, fifty pieces may be put into stock at the beginning of a period and thirty left at the end of two months. It is incorrect to determine the turn by dividing the sales of twenty by an average stock of forty ($[50+30]/2$). This would give an erroneous one-half turn for the two months, or a projected three turns for the year. Actually, at the existing rate of sale of ten a month, it will take five months to sell out the supply. The average stock during the life of the item would only be twenty-five, a two-and-one-half month supply. On an annual basis, the turn is 4⅘ ($12 \div 2\frac{1}{2}$). An average of the stock during the early stages of the sales of a class of goods is not a true average indicative of its entire "life."

LOCATING SLOW-SELLING STOCK

The control of slow-selling stock is generally dependent upon periodic inventories.

In baked goods, for example, the day of delivery to the retailer is indicated on the wrapper by printing or perforation. A daily inventory by the grocer readily discloses the quantity of stale goods in stock.

For general merchandise, a common plan is to mark each price ticket to indicate the six-month season and often the date as well. *A* may represent the spring season, February 1971–July 1971, and *B* the fall season, August 1971–January 1972. February 1971 would be designated as *A1* and March as *A2*. October 1971 would be *B3*. Instead of season letters, some stores use a different colored pencil for each three-month period when they make notations on price tickets. Others change the color of the price tickets themselves. Some stores check over all stock each month or six-week period and make a list of all items bearing old season and month letters or colors in accordance with the time limits set.

A more common practice is to make lists every six months from the regular inventory sheets of all stock falling into various age categories. The items appearing on these lists are recounted every month, but additional items are not included until the next regular inventory six months later. A good system of this type used by a large store is briefly as follows:

> 1. Buyers or their assistants copy from the official six-month inventories all merchandise classified as slow selling. These items are listed by season and classification on slow-selling sheets.
>
> 2. Buyers budget the dollar amount of slow-selling merchandise they intend to have on hand on subsequent monthly inventory dates. For example, if at the beginning of the spring season there is $7,600 worth of merchandise over six months old, the buyer may plan to reduce this quantity to $2,000 by March 15 and to dispose of all but $100 worth before the next semiannual inventory, July 31.
>
> 3. The salesperson in charge of each section of stock in the department each month reports slow-selling merchandise by season, and the data for each classification and age group are summarized. See table 9.2 which ties in with the semiannual inventory, table 9.1.

  4. The monthly total on hand, by season, is checked against the slow-selling budget made at the beginning of the season. If the amount on hand is greater than the budgeted amount for that date, more drastic action is taken to bring the stock figure into line prior to the next monthly inventory.

  5. The next official six-month inventory is checked against the last monthly listing to make sure that salespeople did not neglect to list monthly all the slow-selling merchandise in their sections.

There is one objection to this plan as usually operated. Since items are added to the slow-selling list only every six months, some may be almost a year old before classed as slow-selling stock. For example, with six months as the limit, an unsold item bought in February, 1971 would not be put on the slow-selling list on August 1; according, it would not be listed as slow selling until February 1, 1972, when it would be almost a year old.

In some stores, to avoid difficulty, the entire stock (at least of certain departments) is checked over at frequent intervals, such as every six weeks. Every price ticket is inspected, and all goods that are older than the prescribed time limit are listed. This method takes longer than the usual one in that here all items must be inspected, whereas under the common plan only the items already listed on the slow-selling sheets are checked. But the periodic complete inspection allows a more exact control in that each item that has exceeded its time limit is promptly apprehended.

When detailed unit control records are kept, they may be used to reveal slow sellers. For example, one store keeps a purchase record of every dress and coat received, and each is assigned a serial number. Whenever a garment is sold, it is checked off against its purchase record. Since the purchase record is arranged according to date of receipt, it is possible at any time to determine how many of any day's receipts of merchandise are still on hand. For example, if any garment more than six weeks old is classified as slow selling, it is easy to locate the entries on the receipt six weeks ago and to spot the items that have not yet been checked out of stock.

In most control systems, serial numbers are not assigned to each item, but the system may nevertheless reveal slow sellers. For example, the record may show that twelve of a style were received on a certain date and that eight of these are still on hand three months later. If reorders had been received in the interim, however, it would not be possible to tell from the record whether the items remaining are three months old or not.

DISPOSAL OF SLOW-SELLING STOCK

The usual way to dispose of slow-selling stock is to take drastic markdowns, but sometimes the goods may be moved by less expensive but more intelligent methods.

One store has set up the following rules to assist in prompt disposal:

1. Every salesperson is required to keep a record of slow-selling merchandise sold daily. This record is tabulated for the general merchandise office.

2. Buyers are required to report to the general merchandise office in writing their day-by-day methods of clearing the slow-selling stock, that is, using drapery lengths to upholster furniture, and so forth.

3. Buyers are required to analyze "lumps" of slow-selling merchandise with the possibility of dramatizing them in newspapers and windows with some new slant in presentation or use.

The smart merchant considers alternate methods carefully, instead of assuming that the only method of disposal is to sell at cost or less. Actually, there are a surprising number of ways to dispose of slow sellers. Some may be used in lieu of markdowns and others in combination with smaller markdowns than would otherwise be required.

WAYS TO DISPOSE OF SLOW-SELLING MERCHANDISE

A. Price reductions
   1. Grant markdowns to customers
      a. As soon as slow sellers are spotted in stock
      b. At end-of-month clearance sales
      c. At end-of-season clearance sales
   2. Grant markdowns to employees, on small lots particularly
   3. Sell at reduced prices to jobbers who specialize in clearing out old stock
   4. Sell at reduced prices to other retailers who may be in a better position to find a market for the goods
   5. Donate, as a contribution to charity, with a tax allowance generally available

B. Price increases
   Raise the retail price when it is so low that customers question the quality

C. Promotions
   1. Display the goods effectively, usually inside the store rather than in the window

TABLE 9.2 Slow-Selling Summary: Sportswear (Count Date March 15, 197–)

Class	Under 3 Months			3-6 Months			Over 6 Months			Total		
	Beginning of Season[a]	$ On Hand	% Reduction	Beginning of Season	$ On Hand	% Reduction	Beginning of Season	$ On Hand	% Reduction	Beginning of Season	$ On Hand	% Reduction
Shifts	6.3	4.0	37	3.7	2.0	46	.8	.2	75	10.8	6.2	43
Sweaters	15.0	4.9	68	3.1	.8	74	1.1	.4	64	19.2	6.1	68
Swimwear	18.4	11.3	39	7.8	2.7	66	1.5	.6	60	27.7	14.6	47
Coordinates	13.1	2.6	80	5.3	—	100	.7	—	100	19.1	2.6	86
Pants	19.1	1.2	94	8.3	4.5	46	2.6	.6	77	30.0	6.3	79
Blouses	6.2	3.8	39	4.1	1.9	54	.9	.4	56	11.2	6.1	46
Total	78.1	27.8		32.3	11.9		7.6	2.2		118.0	41.9	

[a] Dollar amounts for beginning of season and on hand given in thousands.

    2. Advertise the goods in sale announcements, especially when large lots are to be cleared rather than individual pieces

    3. Stimulate the sales force to give special attention to the slow sellers

        a. By means of PMs, push money for selling specific items that are slow selling

        b. By means of contests with awards to those who sell the most merchandise designated as slow selling

        c. By department meetings and floor supervision where the importance of moving slow sellers is emphasized

D. Combination selling

    Package goods in sets, such as a slow-selling baseball glove with a bat and a ball

E. Reconditioning and remodeling

    1. Clean and repair goods if the cost is less than the markdown loss

    2. Remodel or repackage goods, such as changing the bow on a shoe

    3. Make new articles from slow-selling material, such as slow-selling tweed yardage made up into pillows

F. Transfers

    1. Move to another department in the store, to the basement perhaps

    2. Move to another store within the chain or branch system, often making possible an important sale of clearance merchandise

    3. Return to the vendor, provided he has a market elsewhere

G. Controversial methods

    1. Require that certain popular goods may be purchased by customers only if they buy a slow seller in addition (tie-in selling)

    2. Introduce slow sellers as new goods after holding them for a time in the reserve

    3. Take competing, more popular goods off sale to center attention on the slow sellers

    4. "Sweeten up" the lot of slow sellers by mixing them with new attractive goods in the hope that the old goods will be bought along with the new

Care should be taken to determine which method would be the best. This means incurring the least loss for disposal without injury to the store's reputation. The chief lesson to be learned is that markdowns should not be taken until other methods of disposal have been explored.

AVOIDING SLOW-SELLING STOCK

The chief concern of the merchant is not to dispose of slow-selling merchandise but to buy and control his stock in such a manner that it will be sold before it becomes slow selling. The primary advantage of unit control in this connection is that a balance may be maintained between purchases and sales that will result in most merchandise selling within a reasonable length of time after purchase.

One of the reasons for the accumulation of slow-selling merchandise is the fear of taking markdowns that will result in a lower gross margin and endanger the year's profits. This is sometimes the case where the buyer's contract with the store calls for a fixed minimum gross margin of profit if the buyer is to earn a bonus. Although a stockturn figure may also be set, this does not ensure an inventory consisting of fast-selling merchandise. To correct this difficulty, some stores find it the best policy simply to ask for a satisfactory showing. On such a basis bonuses have been paid for a cleaning up of stock inventories when the sales and profits actually fell behind.

Every time a change of buyers is made in some stores, the cost in markdowns on the old stock may be tremendous, and often far in excess of actual need. Every new buyer tends to feel that a predecessor's stock is poorly selected and wishes to clear it out before he shows what he can do with his own newly selected stock. Frequently, from the customer's viewpoint, the new assortment is little better than the old.

Without a careful system of control, slow-selling merchandise accumulates, clogs up the stock, and slows up the sales. As in an unweeded garden, the good stock is crowded out by the weeds, and the result is disastrous to all—the store, the buyer, and the salespeople.

From the customer's point of view, slow-selling merchandise is a serious obstacle to getting what is needed. Much lost time, energy, and dissatisfaction are charged to the stores on that account. Many customers are as well acquainted with stocks as are the store people. They have a bad reaction to seeing the same merchandise, unchanged, month after month, even year after year.

QUESTIONS FOR DISCUSSION

1. With careful planning, how quickly should the taking of physical inventory be completed in a large operation?
2. The same cost price may be coded in the following ways: 70325006; 69816;⌞⌴⌷X,1 and KAPT. See page 154 for form.
   (a) What is the cost?
   (b) Could the first code reveal any other information?
   (c) What may be the cost key for the fifth example?
3. For staple stocks do you recommend that in advance of the count

all the staples purchased and their prices be listed on the inventory sheets, with only the quantity columns left blank?

4. Do you recommend that inventories be taken at the same time in all departments and physical locations in a store?

5. Under what conditions would you recommend the use of each of the following physical inventory records: inventory sheet, inventory tag, punch card?

6. Should all goods belonging to a selling department be brought back, from wherever located, to the selling department's premises in advance of inventory?

7. Other than the determination of the value of an inventory for profit-figuring purposes, what merchandising decisions may be based on information that the inventory reveals?

8. (a) Do you think it justifiable to have over 30 percent of a men's clothing inventory over six months old?
   (b) In women's ready-to-wear, the figure is usually well under 10 percent. Should men's clothing do as well?

9. Should the customer have ready access to the age of merchandise in the inventory? Explain with reference both to foods and to general merchandise.

10. (a) To apprehend slow-selling stock would you depend primarily on seasonal and monthly inventory counts or would you maintain a perpetual unit control of these items?
    (b) Should slow-selling goods be checked more frequently or less frequently than once a month?

11. Under what circumstances are means, other than markdowns, used to move slow-selling goods likely to succeed?

12. What opportunities do computers offer to identify slow-selling goods as they provide data on sales and stocks?

10

BOOK INVENTORY AND STOCK SHORTAGE

Whether a store takes its physical inventories at cost or at retail prices, it is feasible to compute book inventories at more frequent intervals than the physical counts. The book inventory is a record of what ought to be on hand in view of what has been received and what has been sold. If a book inventory is calculated at regular intervals, such as every day, week, or month, it is called a *perpetual inventory*. Book inventories may be kept either in terms of dollar value or in terms of units of merchandise. In this chapter, attention will be centered upon perpetual inventories in dollars.

REASONS FOR DETERMINING A BOOK INVENTORY

- Makes possible the determination and control of stock shortages
- Aids in the control of purchases
- Allows the frequent calculation of profits
- Results in larger recovery on insurance if stock is destroyed

ADVANTAGES OF OBTAINING A BOOK INVENTORY

Stock shortage control. The calculation of book inventories makes possible the determination of merchandise shortage or shrinkage, that is, the excess of the book inventory over the physical inventory as of the same date. For example, if the book inventory is $10,000 and the physical inventory is $9,600, the stock shortage is $400.

A knowledge of the fact of loss by shortage is necessary if adequate steps to avoid the loss are to be taken. Those stores that fail to obtain a book inventory may continue for many years with no knowledge that large quantities of merchandise are being lost or stolen. Even when the loss is suspected, there is no way of attributing it to specific departments. Calculating a book inventory makes it possible to determine the shortage every time a physical inventory is taken. In those merchandise lines in which shortages are relatively large or in which they show a tendency to rise, prompt steps may be taken to trace the source of loss and take remedial action.

Purchase control. A book inventory, if calculated "perpetually," aids in the control of purchases. A record of stock on hand every week or month in every department is one of the most important guides to successful merchandising. Merchants attempt to maintain predetermined relationships between sales and stock, to have ample stock to meet customer demand, and at the same time to keep the investment as low as possible. A frequent determination from the records of the stock on hand is essential, without the expense of taking a physical inventory.

Profit control. Book inventories make it possible to estimate profits at any time, at least once a month. This is done by substituting the book figure for the physical inventory figure ordinarily used. Errors will be limited to stock shortages that will usually be relatively small. Before the use of perpetual inventories became common, merchants used to take their annual or semiannual inventories in fear and trembling, not knowing whether they would show a profit or loss. Today, the profits are known "perpetually" and there is time to change methods and even policies if an interim report reveals an unsatisfactory condition.

Insurance losses. Book inventories maximize collections from insurance companies in the case of fire loss. Without such a figure, less an adjustment for estimated stock shortages, the store has no way of determining the extent to which goods were destroyed in a fire except in rare instances where the fire occurs immediately after a physical inventory has been taken. The figure is a guess, and the insurance companies naturally accept a lower figure. When there is a perpetual inventory, the chief things to save from the fire are the stock ledger and sales records, for the inventories they represent as of the day of the fire are useful in determining the size of the loss.

CALCULATING BOOK INVENTORY

Book Inventory at Cost

Dollar book inventory, if calculated from cost rather than from retail data, requires that the cost of goods sold be subtracted from the sum of the opening inventory at cost and purchased at cost. Such a cost of sales figure may be obtained in one of two ways: (1) to *cost* the sales, which means to keep a running record of the sales not only at retail selling price but also at cost price or (2) to estimate the cost of the goods sold by applying the complement of the estimated maintained markup to the retail sales. The first method is cumbersome, requiring that cost codes be available on price tickets for transcription to sales records. It also makes no provision for depreciation in the value of the inventory which should be included in the cost of goods sold. This method is suitable only in lines where there are relatively few transactions of high unit value, such as major appliances.

The second method is guesswork. The actual maintained markup percentage cannot be found until the value of the closing inventory is known. To assume that last year's figure is applicable this year may lead to a large error in the inventory estimate.

CALCULATING LOSS DUE TO FIRE

A merchant who kept no formal perpetual inventory system suffered total loss of inventory by fire on March 10. His physical inventory at cost on February 1 was $20,000, and his invoices showed that $25,000 worth had been received subsequently. His sales had been $40,000 since February 1. Last year his maintained markup on sales was 30 percent. He figured his inventory at the time of the fire, as basis for a claim, as follows:

Opening inventory at cost		$20,000
Purchases at cost		25,000
Total merchandise handled		$45,000
Sales	$40,000	
Maintained markup	30 percent	
Cost of sales (70 percent of $40,000)		28,000
Book inventory at cost, March 10		$17,000

BOOK INVENTORY AT RETAIL

The retail method of calculating book inventory is much simpler than *costing* sales and far more accurate than estimating the maintained markup percentage.[1] It requires that the retail prices of all purchases be recorded as well as all price changes, but this is much less work than assembling and calculating the cost prices of all articles sold. The following example and figure 10.1 illustrate how the recording of purchases at retail price allows determination of book inventory to check against the actual physical inventory. The difference represents shortage.

	Cost	Retail	
Inventory at beginning	$20,000	$ 35,000	
Purchases (including adjustments)	70,000	110,000	
Total merchandise handled	$90,000	$145,000	
Net sales			$100,000
Net markdowns and discounts to customers and employees			4,000
Retail deductions (not including shortage)		104,000	
Book inventory at end		$ 41,000	
Physical inventory at end		40,250	
Shortage at retail		$ 750	

Shortage percent ($750 ÷ $100,000) = .75%

The corresponding retail values for inventory and purchase figures are easily obtained by marking on each invoice the retail price of each item. This allows the bookkeeper to determine the total retail as well as the total billed cost of each purchase. These two values are accumulated for the whole period for which profits are to be computed. Certain adjustments, to be explained in chapter 11, may be necessary in the cost and retail purchase figures for such items as transfers, transportation charges, and price changes.

[1] Calculating book inventories at retail is an integral part of the retail method of inventory, further explained in chapter 11.

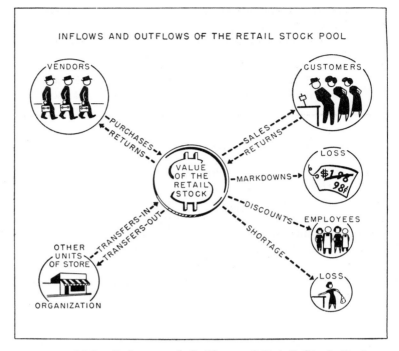

FIGURE 10.1   Inflows and Outflows of Retail Stock Pool

From the retail value ($145,000 in the example), deductions are continually being made. It is evident that net *sales* are not the only element of value reducing the total merchandise handled.[2] Markdowns (due to reduction of the retail value of stock on hand) have exactly the same effect on total merchandise handled at retail as do sales. Since all figures are expressed in terms of value rather than of physical merchandise, it is evident that markdowns reduce the total value of stock as much as do the sales. The same is true of discounts given to customers and employees—they reduce the retail stock. The amount of these discounts may be obtained from saleschecks. The amount of markdowns can readily be determined by filling out a form every time merchandise is reduced in price, giving the old price, the new price, and the number of items reduced. The difference in price, multiplied by the quantity, gives the total amount of markdown in each case.

[2] The net sales figure rather than the gross is used because returns from customers are put back in stock and allowances to customers are included in the markdowns.

When a reduction in price is originally made, it is known as a *gross markdown*. Any restoration of a markdown price to or toward the original retail is known as a *markdown cancellation*. The difference between the two is the *net markdown* figure, the amount of permanent markdown. For example, in preparation for a sale a buyer may reduce one thousand items retailing at $2.00 each to $1.50 each. The gross markdown is $500.00. At the end of the sale, two hundred of these items may remain unsold and be marked back to $2.00 each. The markdown cancellation is $100.00, and the net markdown $400.00.

In the example above, $100,000 of value is taken away from total retail merchandise handled in the form of sales, and $4,000 of value is taken away in the form of markdowns and discounts. If there were no shortage, the stock left on hand would be priced at $41,000 retail. This difference between total merchandise handled and the sum of sales and known reductions is called the *retail book inventory*. It represents the amount that should be on hand if there has been no stock shortage.

The actual count of stock on hand at retail prices may indicate the value as only $40,250, which is $750 less than the book inventory. This difference is the amount of retail shortage.

Shortage allowance.   In merchandise lines in which shortages are large, it is desirable, in computing the inventory for internal control purposes, to allow for estimated shortages based on past experience, as follows:

Total merchandise handled at retail		$145,000
Net sales	$100,000	
Markdowns and discounts to customers and employees	4,000	
Estimated shortage (2 percent of sales)	2,000	
Total retail deductions		106,000
Estimated physical inventory		$39,000

Were a count of stock to be made at this time, the actual would differ from this estimated figure only by the amount of error in estimating shortages. If the store has past records of shortages as a guide, such errors should be small.

Some stores always include an estimate of shortages in deriving inventories, no matter how small they may be. It should be recognized, however, that at the end of the fiscal year, the inventory valuation is based on an actual physical inventory and not on the estimated figure.[3]

A careful distinction should be made between *book inventory, physical inventory,* and *estimated physical inventory*. In the above illustrations, the book inventory is $41,000, the estimated physical inventory is $39,000, and the physical inventory is $40,250.

STOCK SHORTAGES AND OVERAGES

Merchandise shortage, as we have found, is the excess of the book inventory over the physical inventory. The figure has risen rapidly and has approached 3 percent of storewide net sales in department stores where it was less than 1 percent a few years before. The degree to which shortages are controlled seems to bear a close relationship to the degree of the concern of management. Where top management is active, shortages have usually been kept in check. The reasons for shortages are of two major types: (1) physical loss of goods and (2) clerical errors in the calculation of the book inventory or in the count of the physical inventory.

PHYSICAL SHORTAGES

Shortages may be caused by theft, by breakage, by disappearance, by physical shrinkage, and by giving the customer more goods than those paid for. There is no way to tell how much of the physical loss to attribute to each of these factors, but it would be erroneous to assume that theft either by outsiders or by employees accounts for all shortages. An occasional large shortage, however, will point to a plot in which a number of people have conspired to steal merchandise. It is estimated that today theft accounts for about half of the shortage figure.[4]

[3] Staggering the physical inventory: Although inventory is commonly taken at the end of January and July, under the retail method of inventory it is not necessary to wait until the last day of the fiscal year to take a physical inventory. The count may be made at any convenient date within a week or two of the end of the period, and the stock at the end of the year may be derived by means of a perpetual inventory. No allowance for estimated shortages during this interval is recognized by tax officials.

[4] Management Safeguards, Inc., a security and protection company, picked at random five hundred shoppers in a Manhattan department store and followed them from the moment they entered the store until they left. Of this number, forty-two, or one in twelve "lifted" something, stealing a total of three hundred dollars worth of merchandise. In Boston, one out of twenty shoppers followed stole, and in Philadelphia, one out of ten. Although most of the shoplifters are teen-agers, it is the adults that steal the expensive merchandise. (See *Business Week*, June 27, 1970, p. 72.)

Theft may be attributed to three groups: (1) professional thieves, (2) amateurs, young as well as old people, who think it is "smart" to steal or who have a compulsion to take merchandise without paying for it, and (3) employees, who often tend to regard pilferage as a "fringe benefit" to which they are entitled.

Physical shortage is not limited to theft. It occurs when something is broken or lost with no markdown taken. It also occurs in foods that lose water content while in stock and are sold by weight or in foods that are subject to spoilage. Shortage also results from selling goods at a lower price than that at which they are carried in stock. For example, because of improper marking a $100 watch may be sold for $10; thus, there is a shortage of $90. Such a practice is particularly common where measuring has to be done. For example, a customer may order three yards of woolen dress goods, but the salesperson may cut off an extra half inch or more. Such errors are more often in the customer's favor than in the store's favor because the salesperson knows that the customer is more likely to catch and report an undermeasurement than the store management is to catch an overmeasurement. Sometimes, of course, salespeople deliberately "sell" goods at fictitiously low prices to accomplices. This is a form of theft.

The flow of merchandise through a store may be likened to a pipeline with joints at which leakage develops. The points at which goods are transferred from one individual to another are the "joints" where shortages are most likely to occur. The most important of these is the point of sale.[5]

Control of physical shortages. Stores attempt to reduce physical shortages in a variety of ways, such as (1) physical safeguards, detection, checking at each transfer point and (2) care in employment and supervision of personnel.

Physical safeguards include ingress and egress control of receiving, marking, stock rooms, and fitting rooms; locks on merchandise trucks; fixture layouts on the sales floor so as not to obstruct vision; mirrors near the cash register and other strategic points which permit salespeople, security personnel, and supervisors to observe what is going on in every part of the store or department; and closed circuit television which makes it possible to watch the activity of customers—and thieves—from a central point. Use of cases with glass fronts and tops also tends to prevent customers from having direct access to the merchandise but limits freedom to inspect goods closely.

[5] Key-Rec has prepared a checklist of seventy-six ways to control retail shortages. Up to ten copies free on request. (Key-Rec Recommendation #30–66, Box 40, 2224 Benton Ave., Dayton, Ohio 45406.)

One or two stores have had some success with dogs roaming the premises at night to nose out thieves. Some stores have a checker at the entrance to the fitting room section, and all garments taken to the fitting rooms are checked off when returned. One store found that when it substituted curtains for doors on fitting rooms shortages declined sharply—shoplifters were deterred from concealing clothes on their persons when only a curtain rather than a door separated them from watchful eyes of salespeople. Another store found that the closing of a back exit from its men's department greatly reduced shortages. Another found shoplifting reduced by calling out executive personnel to surround a point in the store where a gang of youngsters were creating a disturbance as a cover-up for theft. The presence of a number of executives discouraged such attempts.

A novel and effective device is a permanent sensitized tag attached to merchandise.[6] It activates an alarm if a person attempts to carry out any item to which the tag is attached. Salespeople are instructed to remove the tag whenever a sale is made.

Detection includes the watchfulness of both employees and professional detectives, particularly plainclothesmen. Stores try to provide adequate personnel to cover the floor so as to discourage as well as apprehend shoplifters. Large stores hire detectives to watch suspicious customers and employees. Organizations such as the Willmark Service shop employees to make sure that they are following the store's system regulations exactly. If an employee fails to record a sale promptly or records it at less than the marked price, he becomes subject to suspicion.

Careful recounting of goods at all merchandise transfer points is a successful device to reduce shortages but may cost too much. A complete control of this kind is deemed too costly in most stores for the general run of goods but may be applied to expensive merchandise, such as real jewelry. One device that provides a check at minimum cost is the preparation by markers of the exact number of price tickets required according to the quantity information on the invoice. When the tickets are attached, if any are left over, it is clear that there has been a shortage between the time the goods were checked and the time they were marked. It is also advisable to make out written requisitions for all goods transferred from warehouse or reserve to forward stock and to check these requisitions against the quantity actually received.

In the area of personnel, great care must be taken to check references of potential employees who have access to stock. Lie detec-

---

[6] Sensormatic Electronic Corp., Akron, Ohio.

tors are sometimes used. Supervisors must learn to "run a tight ship," stressing good housekeeping and the observance of regulations. Salespeople and stock help must be warned repeatedly to handle goods carefully. All goods must be properly ticketed with the correct price so that there will be no excuse for selling at a lower, guessed price. To avoid mismeasurements, accurate scales and other devices should be available and should be used. The weight and measure should just as readily be observed by the customer as by the salesperson.

In nonselling jobs, functions that might be performed by one person could be divided between two, providing this makes dishonesty more difficult. For example, one person may handle orders and another receive the goods; one may authorize invoices for payment and another draw the check; and one person may put back returned goods into stock and another make the refund or issue the credit slip.

Much physical shortage is due to carelessness, to a lack of responsibility, and to a belief that pilferage is to be condoned. Some employees take the attitude that they have a right to supplement meager wages by helping themselves. Even more important than detectives and physical controls, then, is a plan for morale building that will make people interested in safeguarding the merchandise they handle. They must feel that their personal destiny is tied up with the interests of the store.

CLERICAL SHORTAGES

There may be a discrepancy between book and physical inventories even though no physical shortage has occurred. There may have been an error in calculating the book inventory figure or in counting the physical inventory. The most common errors in deriving the book inventory are the failure to report all markdowns, marking goods at a price lower than that appearing on invoices, and charging purchases to wrong departments. The department that is charged for merchandise it did not receive shows too large a book inventory and a shortage, whereas the department that received the goods but was not charged for them shows too small a book inventory and an overage. In connection with markdowns, it should be noted that any price reduction not reported to the office will overstate the book inventory calculated at retail and show up as a shortage.

Control of clerical shortages. To eliminate clerical reasons for shortages, stores have introduced systems that make it very difficult for an employee to put a price on the goods different from that

17 RULES FOR EFFECTIVE PILFERAGE CONTROL

Pilferage of merchandise is reported to be steadily increasing. Here's of list of DO's and DON'T's which will help you control your pilferage problem.

DO

- Remember that the best safeguard against pilferage is alertness on the part of all employees.
- Reduce temptation to the minimum. Make shoplifting difficult, and losses will drop.
- Arrange displays and placement of employees so that all parts of the store are under supervision.
- Have all parts of your store well-lighted.
- Keep small, expensive items where they will have constant supervision.
- Post signs in prominent spots to say in effect—"We reserve the right to inspect all packages."
- Be most watchful for shoplifting during rush periods.
- Watch suspected shoplifters on their return trips to the store.
- Watch people who wear loose, baggy clothing.
- Watch people who keep returning to a certain spot, or who linger without reason.
- If shoplifter will sign a confession, with a witness present, it will lessen the danger of lawsuits.

DON'T

- Don't make displays higher than eye level, if possible.
- Don't accuse anyone of stealing unless you are certain of the fact.
- Don't confront shoplifters inside the store. Allow person to leave store, then follow. Request them politely, but firmly, to re-enter.
- Don't use force or threats.
- Don't let anyone but the store manager or supervisor handle suspected cases of theft.
- Don't prevent anyone from leaving store. Barring the way may be considered the same as arrest and can lead to a damage suit.

Courtesy, Lever Brothers

on the invoice or on the buyer's order and for managers to change any price, up or down, without reporting the change to the office. Similarly, they have systematic methods of taking physical inventory to eliminate errors in counting.[7] Great care is exercised in the office to

[7] These methods were described in chapter 9.

make sure that figures upon which the book inventory is based are correctly compiled. A particularly difficult problem is that of timing, to be sure that every last-minute change in the physical inventory is reflected in the records, particularly that every invoice representing goods that have been moved into stock is included in the calculation and that invoices representing goods not yet in stock are excluded.

Excessive Shortages

Established stores, on the basis of past experience, set up a measure of tolerance for shortages. For example, a shortage not exceeding 1 percent of sales of a particular line of merchandise may be deemed reasonable and the physical inventory may be accepted as sufficiently accurate for the calculation of profit and loss. On the other hand, if the shortage exceeds the limit set, an attempt will be made to reconcile more nearly the book and the physical inventories. [The calculation of the book inventory will be rechecked. If a large discrepancy still exists, a recount of the physical stock will be ordered. There have been instances where a stock has been recounted three times because the management feared that errors had been made. If after considerable rechecking, a large shortage still exists, the physical inventory must be accepted and profits calculated on this basis.

Overages

Although shortages are normally expected, it is not logical to have on hand in the physical inventory more than the book figure indicates. Goods are stolen, but they are not donated to a store. Overages are therefore largely due to errors in record keeping. The most common errors causing overage are as follows:

1. Charging purchase invoices to the wrong department
2. Improper charging to selling departments of goods manufactured in the store
3. Crediting and recording sales to the wrong department
4. Taking markdowns on the records without actually reducing prices on price tickets
5. Overstating the physical inventory
6. Including in the physical inventory goods that have not yet been charged in as purchases

The overage increases the profits of the period somewhat as shortages decrease them, but the recognition of the overage is really a recognition of an error that tended to understate profits. Such recognition may be deferred for several seasons because it sometimes happens that an overage in one period is offset by an unusually large shortage in the next.

QUESTIONS FOR DISCUSSION

1.   Is it sometimes easier to take a physical inventory weekly than to maintain a book inventory at weekly intervals? If so, give an example.
2.   If a store were on the cost method of inventory, would it be feasible to estimate the retail value of the total merchandise handled and to subtract sales from this total to obtain a reasonably close estimate of the closing inventory at retail? Explain.
3.   In calculating the book inventory at retail in a nondepartmentized specialty shop, what is probably the most common error made?
4.   Which of the following measures of stock shortage is the most useful: (a) percentage of sales, (b) percentage of the cost inventory, or (c) percentage of the retail inventory?
5.   Explain why the following practices tend to cover up stock shortages: (a) retailing invoices at a lower price than those placed on the merchandise, (b) reporting markdowns that are not actually taken on the stock, and (c) restoring marked-down goods to their original retail prices without reporting the markdown cancellations.
6.   Relate an example of collusion among customers and/or employees in perpetrating a theft of merchandise. What preventive steps should be taken by management to guard against such occurrences?
7.   A trucker in league with a store's receiving clerk brought to the store's receiving dock more cases of merchandise than he actually delivered. The clerk signed for the entire shipment and made out the receiving record accordingly. Typically, 20 percent of the cases received were not delivered; instead, they were sold to a fence and the proceeds divided between the trucker and the clerk. By what procedures could management largely eliminate thefts of this sort?
8.   What are the transfer points between the point of merchandise receipt and the point of delivery to the customer at which physical loss may occur?
9.   Appraise the practicality of the sensitized tag that triggers an alarm when merchandise to which it is attached is removed from the premises.
10.   Is there such a thing as a physical overage? If so, give an example.
11.   How much could retail prices be reduced if retail stock shortages could be eliminated?
12.   How does the younger generation view the question of merchandise theft from retail establishments? How can management use such information in coping with the shortage problem?

11

INVENTORY
VALUATION
AND
THE RETAIL
METHOD

Valuation of the inventory on hand is a vital consideration in merchandise management decision-making, since the interpretation of the elements involved in the determination of current value has a decided effect on the profit result. Valuation involves much more than the determination of either the purchase price of the goods in the inventory or their retail price.

EFFECT OF VALUATION ON PROFIT

The value placed on the inventory is important because of the effect of the inventory figure on profit. If the closing cost inventory is overvalued, the cost of merchandise sold will be too small and the gross margin and the profit overstated. This can be noted in table 11.1 where an evaluation of $10,000, on a closing inventory worth only $8,000, makes the cost of merchandise sold $40,000 rather than the correct $42,000. This in turn leads to a gross margin of $20,000 rather than $18,000. Since the expenses are not affected, the profit is overstated $2,000, by the same amount that the closing inventory was overvalued.

Conversely, an underevaluation of the closing inventory will overstate the cost of merchandise sold and understate gross margin and profits.

Merchants are more anxious to avoid overstatement of profits than understatement. Overstatement results in unnecessarily larger income tax payments and endangers future operations in that an attempt may be made to spend or distribute profits that are actually nothing but increases in the alleged value of stock on hand. Underevaluation acts as a hidden reserve of profits and may curb expenditures.

TABLE 11.1   Effect of Inventory Value on Profit

	Inventories Correctly Evaluated	Overstated Closing Inventory, First Year	Overstated Closing Inventory, Both Years
Opening inventory, first year	$10,000	$10,000	$10,000
Purchases	40,000	40,000	40,000
Total	$50,000	$50,000	$50,000
Closing inventory, first year	8,000	10,000	10,000
Cost of merchandise sold	$42,000	$40,000	$40,000
Sales	60,000	60,000	60,000
Gross margin	$18,000	$20,000	$20,000
Opening inventory, second year	8,000	10,000	10,000
Purchases	42,000	42,000	42,000
Total	$50,000	$52,000	$52,000
Closing inventory, second year	9,000	9,000	11,000
Cost of merchandise sold	$41,000	$43,000	$41,000
Sales, second year	60,000	60,000	60,000
Gross margin, second year	$19,000	$17,000	$19,000
Gross margin, two years	37,000	37,000	39,000

Hired department managers, on the other hand, tend in the opposite direction. Where they are paid bonuses on their profits, there is danger that they may attempt to put too high a valuation on their stocks. Goods may be counted at the original cost or even above, when the current market value may be considerably less. To avoid such manipulation, close supervision by top management is necessary, and sometimes the counting and evaluating of the stock are done by outside unbiased authorities.

It must be recognized, however, that overevaluation of a closing stock of one period means overevaluation of the opening stock of the next period. An overevaluated opening stock tends to overstate cost of merchandise sold and understate profits. The overstated profit of the first year may thus be offset by the understated profit of the following year, provided that the inventory is correctly valued the second year.

From the figures in table 11.1, it is evident that where the overstatement occurs only once, the profits for the two years combined are accurate. When inventories are consistently overstated, the first year of this practice shows an overstatement that is not wholly corrected, but the profit figures of later years will nearly be correct. They would be correct should opening and closing inventories be overstated by the same amount. This would seldom occur in practice, however.

The tendency for errors in inventory valuation to offset one another over a period of years should not move merchants to minimize the importance of correct valuation. A hired manager may overevaluate his stocks one year, show a handsome profit, and then resign, leaving his successor to show a loss the following year.

METHODS OF INVENTORY VALUATION

There are many different approaches to the problem of valuing an inventory. Those of most importance to the retailer are:

The original-cost method
The first-in, first-out method, called the *FIFO* method
The last-in, first-out method, called the *LIFO* method
The cost-or-market-whichever-is-lower method
The retail method, which approximates the cost-or-market method

ORIGINAL-COST METHOD

For merchandise that is staple and that depreciates negligibly, the original-cost method is satisfactory. The merchandise at inventory time might be worth approximately what was originally paid for it. But for fashion merchandise and staples that may have depreciated in value, the method defers losses due to depreciation to the period in which the goods are sold rather than take them in the period in which losses became apparent. Thus, if goods are valued at a $10,000 original cost figure when they can be replaced today for $8,000, the profits will not be reduced by the depreciation of $2,000 that has taken place. When the goods are ultimately sold at a reduced retail price, however, the loss will then be registered in the form of low sales at a relatively high cost. Were tax rates stable and the personnel constant, it might not make much difference when losses were recognized, but tax rates tend to change year by year and managers also. Again, inventory (real property) taxes and insurance premiums are based on the value of the inventory, and a large profit showing may lead to large dividends or drawings by owners. Losses, accordingly, should be recognized as soon as possible and should not be disregarded until the goods are sold at distress prices.

FIRST-IN, FIRST-OUT METHOD

Where items in an inventory are identified neither by cost codes on price tickets nor by reference numbers and where different portions of a stock have been purchased at different prices, the assumption usually made is that the goods bought first are sold first and that the more recent purchases are still in stock. This is called the FIFO (first-in, first-out) method. For example, on January 31, there may be on hand five hundred of a staple item. Reference to invoices may reveal the following facts:

January 1	last year purchased 400 at	$1.10	
September 1	last year purchased 100 at	1.14	
October 1	last year purchased 250 at	1.12	
December 1	last year purchased 200 at	1.18	

Because five hundred are still on hand, it is assumed that all of the December and October purchases are still in stock and fifty of the September purchases. Thus, the cost value is as follows:

December 1	quantity 200 at	$1.18 =	$236
October 1	quantity 250 at	1.12 =	280
September 1	quantity 50 at	1.14 =	57
Total	500		$573

Accordingly, the first-in, first-out method approximates the cost method.

THE LAST-IN, FIRST-OUT METHOD

The last-in, first-out method of inventory valuation—called LIFO—is based on the assumption that a retailer needs a basic stock assortment to conduct business and that this may be evaluated at a fixed cost, even though the items comprising the assortment actually cost the store more (or less) due largely to inflationary (or deflationary) forces. To give some semblance of reality to this concept, it is assumed that the customer who purchases an article in stock is buying an identical article that costs not what the store paid for it but the current replacement cost. In theory, the item delivered to the customer is borrowed from the fixed stock to avoid making the customer wait for the replacement. When the replacement does arrive, it finds its way into the fixed stock at the basic price, since the item that was delivered has already been sold at a retail that reflects the replacement price. Thus, the goods ordered at current cost prices (the last ins) are assumed to be the items sold (the first outs).

In periods of inflation, this theory values the basic assortment at less than the actual current price of the inventory and thus increases the cost of goods sold and keeps down the gross margin figure and also taxable profits.

On a declining market, when replacements costs less than the fixed value of the basic stock, LIFO evaluates the inventory above cost and thus undervalues the cost of goods sold and overvalues the profit figure. Thus, its advantage to the merchant is primarily during periods of inflation so as to avoid heavy taxes and also the pressures to pay out seemingly large profits that are actually tied up in inventory.

The method is primarily used for income tax purposes and not as a management tool for the determination and appraisal of departmental profit and loss.

COST-OR-MARKET METHOD

Many stores in the field of general merchandise value their inventories at original cost or current market value, *whichever is lower*. This means that if an article that cost $1.00 has a market or replacement cost of $1.10 at the store, it will be valued at $1.00 because the appreciation of $0.10 would erroneously be recognizing a paper profit of this amount—a real profit is not earned until the goods are actually sold. If it has a replacement value of $0.90, it will be valued at $0.90. By using the lower of the two figures, profits are stated at a minimum. The rule may be justified on the basis that experience shows that most goods that can be replaced for less than the original cost have to be marked down to sell, whereas most goods that will have to be replaced at higher than cost cannot, or may not practically, be marked up to sell at a price higher than the one originally intended.

AN EXAMPLE OF COST-OR-MARKET METHOD

	Original Cost	Market Value
Coat inventory	$8,000	$8,500
Dress inventory	$6,000	$5,000
Inventory valuation:		
Coats at cost		$ 8,000
Dresses at market		5,000
Total		$13,000

Most merchants of general merchandise increase prices only when replacements are actually made at higher costs and not when they hear that replacements will cost more in the future. Even when present stock is marked up in anticipation of a higher replacement cost, there is still a question as to whether the goods will sell at this new price, but when goods are marked down, there is virtually no hope of selling them eventually at the original retail price. Thus, cost-or-market is conservative, recognizing paper losses but not paper profits.

Quotation method.   If the store takes physical inventory at original cost prices, the market price as distinct from the original cost price may be determined by one of four methods. A widely accepted method is to compare current price quotations on the wholesale market. These may be obtained from vendors' catalogs and price lists, from market quotations in periodicals, or by direct inquiry. Allowance should be made for deterioration if the goods in the inventory are in imperfect condition.

The difficulty of obtaining market quotations for thousands of different items in the inventory makes the quotation method impracticable for all but staple commodities handled in considerable quantity.

Markdown method.   A satisfactory method of determining depreciated market value for fashion merchandise is to keep a record

AN EXAMPLE OF THE MARKDOWN METHOD
OF DETERMINING DEPRECIATION ON VALUE

Price Ticket

XYZ STORE

Dept. 25

$16.95

$12.50

7110754*

*Cost code for $10.75

Original markup: $\dfrac{\$16.95 - \$10.75}{\$16.95} = 36.6\%$

Derived market value: $\$12.50 \times (100\% - 36.6\%) =$
$\$12.50 \times 63.4\% = \$7.93$

Depreciation: $\$10.75 - \$7.93 = \$2.82$

on price tickets of original retail prices as well as current retail prices. A markup figure may then be determined from each original cost and *original* retail price to apply to the *current* retail price. For example, a price ticket may indicate that an article that cost $0.60 has a current retail price of $0.80 but that it was originally marked to sell at $1.00. The buyer was planning a markup of 40 percent. Since he has found it necessary to reduce his price 20 percent, it is logical to assume that the cost has also depreciated 20 percent to $0.48. This market value may also be obtained readily by multiplying the present retail price, $0.80, by the complement of the original markup, 60 percent, yielding $0.48. This represents what the merchant would be willing to pay in view of the current retail price and the markup percentage he originally applied in pricing the goods.

The chief objection to this plan is the amount of calculation it entails. All price tickets must carry original retail prices; separate markup percentages must be computed for each item in the inventory that is now reduced in price; and the present retail price of each of these items must be converted to market value.

Aging method. Another way to determine depreciation and market value from actual cost figures is to set up a depreciation schedule on the basis of time limits. For example, past experience may show that nearly all merchandise in a department less than three month is salable without markdowns and is worth about what was paid for it. But goods three to six months old may require such heavy markdowns to sell as to indicate that they are worth only 75 percent of their cost. Goods between six months and a year old may be valued at 50 percent of their cost; goods from one year to two years at 25 percent, and goods more than two years at zero percent. The inventory, then, may be analyzed by age and market value determined as the following example shows:

INVENTORY AT END OF PERIOD

Age	Actual Cost	Rate of Depreciation	Market Value
Less than 3 months	$30,000	0%	$30,000
3–6 months	12,000	25	9,000
6–12 months	4,000	50	2,000
12–24 months	3,000	75	750
Over 24 months	1,000	100	000
	$50,000		$41,750

Although this plan eliminates individual judgment as long as the depreciation rates and age brackets remain unchanged, it is arbitrary and assumes a relation between value and age that only partially exists. Of course, the rates of depreciation should vary with the importance of style in the merchandise under consideration. In some staple lines, goods a year old may still have full value.

Appraisal method. Another possible method of finding market value is the appraisal method. An expert in the line who is in close touch with current market values takes an inventory, judging the value of each item. Thus market value is obtained directly without making use of records of original cost. This method is ordinarily used when a stock is being sold to another dealer, but it is not so common for periodic inventory valuation.

ALLOWANCE FOR TRANSPORTATION IN THE INVENTORY

Regardless of the method or methods described to determine a depreciated value for the inventory, a portion of the transportation charges paid or incurred on incoming purchases should be included in the inventory value.[1] In chapter 3, it was explained that transportation on merchandise purchases is treated as an addition to the purchase price, not as an operating expense. It follows that a portion of this figure should be allocated to the closing inventory rather than be permitted to enter totally into the current cost of merchandise sold. Such allocation is automatically made under the retail method of inventory, as will be explained. If the store is using one of the other methods of valuation, management should determine the ratio of all transportation costs to total cost purchases for the period and apply this ratio to the cost of the closing inventory, preferably before depreciation is provided for. In theory, it is possible to allocate transportation to each unit of merchandise as received, adjusting unit cost prices accordingly. But this would be a most costly and cumbersome procedure, involving fractions of a cent. It is much more feasible to determine the proportion of total transportation paid that should be added to the cost value of the total inventory at the end of a period.

THE RETAIL METHOD OF INVENTORY

MAJOR CONSIDERATIONS

The retail method of inventory is a method of approximating for each group of related merchandise the "cost-or-market value, whichever is lower" without the bother of determining market value of individual items. Although it is based on the same principle as the markdown method sometimes used in connection with cost-or-market valuation, it is simpler to apply. It frequently proves to be a more satisfactory system than those described above.

It involves (1) taking physical inventory for each group at current retail selling prices only, by listing and totaling the prices appearing on price tickets, or estimating physical inventory by methods described in chapter 10; (2) determining the markup percentage on the total merchandise handled; and (3) deriving the cost or market value of the inventory from the retail by means of this markup percentage. The total retail value of the stock on hand is reduced to a cost or market value by the one operation of multiplying the retail total by the complement of this markup percentage.

---

[1] Many small stores operating on the cost or cost-or-market method do not make the adjustment for transportation charges. Many of them treat transportation as an expense of doing business, not as a part of the purchase price of the goods. Where most of the transportation cost is borne by wholesale suppliers, there is little objection to this practice.

This eliminates the whole system of cost codes and similar records to determine what was actually paid for each item in stock, and also the separate determination of a market value for each item. Although the retail method of inventory had its inception in the department store field, its popularity has spread to many other kinds of stores.

It should be observed that the retail method is much more than counting goods at retail prices. A store might take periodic inventories at retail prices for the purpose of guiding buying but might depend upon cost data to determine inventory value for profit-figuring purposes. It would then not be on the retail method of inventory. To warrant the use of this term, the cost price must be determined from the aggregate retail value of the group of goods by means of the markup percentage.

DEPARTMENTIZING NECESSARY

It should also be observed that the groups of merchandise to which the retail method is applied must be homogeneous. The method is essentially a system of departmental control. It is not applicable to an aggregate stock comprising many different types of goods. Since markups vary greatly by merchandise type, a separate markup must be determined for each department.[2]

DERIVING COST FROM RETAIL

A shoe merchant took his inventory at retail prices only at the end of the year and found a stock of $40,000 on hand. This was his first year of operation and his invoices, reflecting his purchases, totaled $75,000 at cost. Since he had calculated the retail value of each invoice and made a note of it on the invoice at the time the goods were received, he was also able to total his invoices at retail and found they totaled $125,000. He then calculated the cost value of inventory as follows:

$$\frac{\$50,000}{\$125,000} = 40 \text{ percent, markup percent}$$

$40,000 × 60% (complements of the markup)
= $24,000, the cost value of the closing inventory

---

[2] For the principles involved in establishing groups or departments, see chapter 14.

APPLYING THE MARKUP PERCENTAGE

The markup percentage used to find cost from the retail is the markup on the total merchandise handled in an appropriate merchandise grouping—that is, the markup on the sum of opening inventory plus purchases.[3] This difference between the cost and the retail of the total merchandise handled divided by the retail is called *initial markup percentage*.[4]

The complement of the markup percentage is 100 percent minus the markup percentage. It can also be obtained directly by dividing the total merchandise handled at cost by the equivalent retail figure. The following example shows the calculation:

	Cost	Retail	Markup	
Inventory at beginning	$20,000	$ 35,000	$15,000	
Purchases	70,000	110,000	40,000	
Total merchandise handled	$90,000	$145,000	$55,000	37.931%
Complement of markup percent				
(100% − 37.931%)				62.069
				100.000%
Retail inventory at end		40,250		
Cost inventory at end				
($40,250 × 62.069%)	24,983			
Gross cost of merchandise sold	$65,017			

The initial markup of $55,000 is expressed as a percentage of $145,000, giving 37.931 percent. For accurate results, if figures are large, it is desirable to carry this figure out to three or four places beyond the decimal point, although for rough calculation for practice purposes one decimal place is sufficient. The complement of the markup percentage is 100 percent minus 37.931 percent, or 62.069 percent. This figure can also be obtained by dividing $90,000 by $145,000.[5]

Derivation of cost inventory. Of the total merchandise handled, $145,000 at retail, there is left on hand at the end of the

---

[3] When the term *cost* is used in connection with inventory valuation under the retail method of inventory, *cost or market, whichever is lower* is understood.

[4] *Initial markup* is perhaps the best term to use in describing this concept. Other terms sometimes used as synonyms are *cumulative markup, cumulative initial markup, markon, initial markon,* and *cumulative markon.*

[5] It should be noted that the markup percentage is not found by an unweighted average of the markup percentages on opening inventory and on purchases but by dividing the aggregate dollar markup by the total merchandise handled.

period, $40,250. The retail method is based on the assumption that the markup on the part remaining ($40,250) is the same as the markup on the total ($145,000). This would always be true were each article purchased given the same markup percentage. Even when some of the total purchases may have been marked up as high as 50 percent and others as low as 25 percent, it still is approximately true that both high and low markup goods are proportionately represented in the closing inventory. The markup of 37.931 percent on the total is taken to represent fairly the markup on that portion of the total that is left on hand.

Because the closing stock is retailed at $40,250 and has a markup of 37.931 percent, the cost of the stock is readily found by multiplying $40,250 by 62.069 percent, the complement. This gives a derived cost inventory of $24,983, which is accepted as the correct cost valuation of the stock on hand.

It sometimes happens that purchases having a low markup sell more rapidly than purchases having a high markup. In this case the closing inventory may largely be composed of high markup goods, even though the markup has been reduced by the low markup goods handled but already sold. When this happens, the retail method overstates the cost inventory by understating the markup.[6]

DETERMINATION OF TOTAL MERCHANDISE HANDLED

The markup percentage used in inventory valuation has been explained as the difference between the cost and the retail values of the total merchandise handled divided by the retail. The total merchandise handled, in turn, is the sum of opening inventory plus purchases, but the purchase figure used is really a composite of a number of items. "Returns and Allowances" from manufacturers are subtracted from the gross purchase figure at both cost and retail values of the goods returned.

---

[6] If this happens regularly due to a policy of special sales at low markups, the two types of goods may be separated into different departments or merchandise classifications for the purpose of applying the retail method. Thus, a separate markup would be calculated for the sale of goods, and in taking inventory the leftovers of the sale goods would have to be treated as a separate inventory. Another answer to the problem of errors in inventory valuation caused by one class of goods selling faster than another is that the errors in opening and closing inventories will tend to compensate for one another and give an approximately correct profit figure. Even though low markup goods do probably sell faster than high markup goods and closing inventories are probably overstated somewhat, the opening cost inventory will also be overstated if a similar situation existed the year before. Uniformity in overstating inventories will yield approximately correct profit figures. Errors will be encountered only when merchandising policies are changed. Nevertheless, it should be observed that overvalued inventories might increase merchandise taxes and insurance costs.

Transfers. Receipts of merchandise into one department or unit of an organization from another unit are called *transfers in* for the receiving department, and the transaction is a *transfer out* for the unit disposing of the goods. Transfers in are added at both cost and retail to the purchases, and transfers out are subtracted. Transfers out are not to be confused with sales since no income is involved. Whenever a merchandise transfer is made between two departments, the cost prices for the department transferring goods *out* and for the one transferring goods *in* should be the same, but the retail prices may differ, depending upon the independent decisions of the two department managers involved.[7]

Transportation charges. Transportation charges on incoming goods are added to the cost purchase figure, as explained in chapter 3. Because the retail figure is not increased (except possibly indirectly by an increase in the retail price), the cost increment increases the total merchandise at cost only and thus reduces the initial markup percentage somewhat. When the complement of this lowered markup is applied to the closing retail inventory, the derived cost inventory figure is increased by the transportation cost attributable to the inventory still on hand. In the example given on page 195, suppose that the total merchandise handled figure of $90,000 includes $1,500 transportation cost. Had the transportation been omitted in the markup calculation, the markup on the total merchandise handled would have been $56,500 and the markup percentage 38.97 percent. Were the complement of this applied to the closing retail inventory of $40,250, the cost would be $24,565. The difference between this and the $24,983, as calculated in the example, is $418, which represents the portion of transportation cost automatically included in the closing inventory.

ADDITIONAL MARKUP AND REVISION OF RETAIL DOWNWARD

Additional markups represent additions to the retail price of goods already in stock. They increase the retail value of the total

[7] A problem arises when goods are transferred for clearance purposes. For example, the buyer for a clearance department, A, may agree to pay $900 for a lot of goods that cost department B $1,125. He may plan to price the goods at a retail of $1,200 even though they are now in B's stock at $1,800 retail. The buyer for B must bring his cost down to $900 to effect the transfer. He does this by dividing $900 by the complement of his cumulative markup percentage, which may be 37½ percent. This calculation gives him a transfer retail of $1,440. He then takes a markdown of $360 from his present retail of $1,800. This procedure avoids distorting the markup in the B department because the markup applied to the transfer out is the same as the markup on the total merchandise handled before the transfer.

merchandise handled without increasing the cost value. Thus, they tend to increase the initial markup and to prevent the cost price of the closing inventory from increasing during periods in which additional markups are being taken. Additional markups do not include the marking of marked down goods back to or toward their original retail prices. These markdown cancellations are instead subtracted from the gross markdown figure and accordingly have no effect on the initial markup percentage.

There are occasional price reductions that are subtracted from the total retail merchandise handled rather than being treated as markdowns. Thus, they tend to reduce the markup percentage. These "revisions of retail downward" largely represent downward corrections of errors made in original pricing but also include cancellations of additional markups taken earlier and the retail equivalent of cost rebates received from vendors. For example, goods costing $600 may be introduced into stock at $1,000, a 40 percent markup. The vendor may subsequently grant the retailer a $60 cost rebate (10 percent). If competitors are also getting a similar rebate, the buyer may reduce the retail price of the goods 10 percent to $900. The $100 reduction is a revision of retail downward, not a markdown. To treat it as a markdown would result in a markup higher than 40 percent, a markup that has not been realized since the price reduction resulted from the rebate. Following is a summary of how to handle the various types of price changes.

TYPES OF PRICE CHANGES

- Price reductions

    Markdowns. Not to be subtracted in arriving at the total merchandise handled at retail and accordingly do not affect the markup.[8] Added to sales in the calculation of total retail deductions.

    Revisions of retail downward. Deducted from the retail purchase figure and reduce the markup percentage. Include: cancellations of additional markups, correction of clerical errors and price reductions accompanying cost rebates from vendors.

- Price increases

    Additional markups. Added to the retail purchase figure already recorded; increase the markup percentage.

---

[8] Discounts to customers and employees are price changes but are generally deducted on the point-of-sale records and thus require no separate recording for purposes of the retail method.

Markdown cancellations. Subtracted from gross markdowns; not added to the total merchandise handled
at retail. Do not affect the markup percentage.

The example below indicates in detail how the total merchandise handled is computed. It is important that the complement of
the markup applied to the closing retail inventory be calculated
exactly as indicated here. If certain items are omitted or others
added, the derived cost value of the inventory will be distorted.

	Cost		Retail		Markup Percent
Inventory at beginning		$20,000		$ 35,000	
Gross purchases from vendors	$72,000		$115,000		
Less returns and allowances	3,000		4,700		
Net purchases from vendors		69,000		$110,300	
Transfers in	$ 1,000		$ 1,600		
Less transfers out	1,500		2,400		
Net transfers out		−500		−800	
Transportation inward		1,500			
Additional markups				700	
Revisions of retail downward (not markdowns)				−200	
Total merchandise handled		$90,000		$145,000	37.931
Retail inventory at end				$40,250	
Cost inventory at end ($40,250 × 62.069%)		$24,983			

The length of the accumulation period. The length of the
period of time over which the total merchandise handled is accumulated is normally six months, but for fast-turning goods it might be
shorter, perhaps three months, and for slow-turning goods longer,
perhaps a year. As for fashions, little if any of the goods in the opening inventory will be on hand at the end of six months. If the markup
on the opening inventory differed materially from the markup on the
more recent purchases, the use of a six-months aggregate would distort the markup properly applicable to the closing inventory. With
a three-month period of accumulation, however, some of the opening
stock would still be in the closing inventory.[9]

[9] While book inventories at retail may be calculated weekly or monthly,
the accumulation of purchases covers the entire three- or six-month period. The
interim inventory figures do not enter into cumulative totals.

Applying the retail method between physical inventory dates. The retail method of inventory may be used for book or estimated physical inventories calculated between physical inventory dates. It is a common practice to prepare monthly profit and loss statements based upon estimated physical inventories, even though physical inventories are taken only semiannually or annually.

By such means, it is possible to estimate at any time closing cost inventory and profits without taking a physical inventory. The error will be limited to error in estimating shortages.

Book Inventories Essential

Even though a merchant may not be interested in interim profit and loss reports, it is nevertheless important that he calculate a book inventory to compare with his physical inventory. This is necessary to determine actual stock shortages. Also, the federal tax authorities insist that stores using the retail method maintain retail purchase and price change records so as to determine book inventories.[10]

	Cost	Retail	Markup Percent
Total merchandise handled for season	$90,000	$145,000	37.931
Retail deductions for season			
Net sales		100,000	
Net markdowns		3,500	
Discounts to employees and customers		500	
Total		$104,000	
Closing book inventory		$ 41,000	
Closing physical inventory		40,250	
Merchandise shortage		$ 750	0.75 of net sales
Closing cost inventory ($40,250 × 62.069%)	$24,983		
Gross cost of merchandising sold	$65,017		
Maintained markup ($100,000 − $65,017)	$34,983[11]		

---

[10] This is done so as to apprehend stores that try to establish fictitious markups by charging purchases into stock records at exorbitant markups and by marking the physical stock less. For example, goods costing $6,000 might be entered on the records at $12,000 retail, a markup of 50 percent. The actual goods may be marked $10,000. With the fictitious markup, the derived cost value is only $5,000. The result is to understate the closing inventory $1,000 and profits by the same amount. A perpetual inventory system acts as a check on such manipulation.

[11] By adding cash discounts and subtracting alteration costs, the gross margin may be arrived at.

Accordingly, a complete statement of the retail method is not limited to the application of the complement of the markup to the closing physical inventory at retail but also includes the calculation of a closing book (or estimated physical) inventory. This is illustrated on page 200 by continuing with the figures on page 199.

Since the shortage in the above example is a retail, not a cost figure, the loss of $750 worth of retail stock should not be assumed to mean a corresponding loss in profits. The real loss to the store is the cost of the goods that had a $750 retail value. Since the markup on total merchandise handled is about 37.9 percent ($145,000 − $90,000)/($145,000), the cost of the merchandise lost must have been about $466 (62.1 percent of $750). In practice it is not necessary to calculate this figure, since the multiplication of the physical retail inventory by the complement of the markup gives a cost inventory that reflects the cost of the shortage—this cost inventory is $24,983 in the example.

The calculations described above can be greatly facilitated where a computer is employed. It may be programmed to perform what is otherwise an arduous operation and to print out the calculation for each department, including the gross margin, at any time interval desired.

DEPRECIATION BY THE RETAIL METHOD

One of the major features of the retail method is that it automatically gives an inventory valued at cost or market, whichever is lower. Thus, it automatically allows for depreciation because the *current* retail value is reduced to cost by the complement of the markup. When the current retail value is less than the original retail, the application of the complement of the markup reduces the cost value correspondingly. The following example shows how the cost value is reduced by markdowns.

	Cost	Retail	Markup Percent
Inventory at beginning	$ 6,000	$10,000	
Purchases—net	24,000	40,000	
Total merchandise handled	$30,000	$50,000	40
Original value of closing inventory	6,000	10,000	
Markdown taken on inventory		1,000	
Present value of closing inventory	5,400	$ 9,000	
Depreciation resulting from markdowns	$ 600		

Here there is a markup of 40 percent, and of the $50,000 total merchandise handled at retail, $9,000 at present value is still in stock. But these goods were originally priced at $10,000, before markdowns of $1,000 were taken on them. Since the markup averages 40 percent, goods that were first retailed at $10,000 actually cost $6,000; but under the retail method, the *present* retail value of $9,000 is reduced to market cost by means of the complement of the markup. Sixty percent of $9,000 is $5,400, the market value. The stock that cost the store $6,000 is now valued at $5,400. The markdown of $1,000 on the retail stock reduces the cost inventory $600. The cost of merchandise sold is thus increased $600, and profits are decreased $600. As a general statement, then, the immediate effect of a retail markdown is to reduce profits by the *cost of the markdown*, which is the retail markdown multiplied by the complement of the markup. The effect of a markdown may also be stated as reducing the cost value of the inventory in the same proportion as the retail is reduced. See figure 11.1. In the example above the retail value is reduced from $10,000 to $9,000, or 10 percent. The original cost value of $6,000 is also reduced 10 percent to $5,400.

EFFECT OF MARKDOWNS ON INVENTORY VALUE

It should be noted particularly that markdowns do not reduce the markup percentage, since they are not subtracted from the retail purchase figure used in the computation of the markup.[12] Were markdowns to be subtracted from the retail in computing the total merchandise handled, the markup would be reduced and the closing inventory would be overvalued. In the example, were the $1,000 markdowns to be deducted in finding total merchandise handled, the total merchandise handled would be $49,000 rather than $50,000, and the markup, 38.77 percent. If this were applied to the closing retail inventory of $9,000, the derived cost would be $5,511 rather than $5,400. The cost would not be reduced in proportion to the decline in the retail value.

To avoid any challenge by tax authorities to cost inventory values arrived at by means of the retail method, it is imperative that the retail prices entering into the retail purchase records are those at which the goods are actually offered for sale and that all merchan-

---

[12] Nevertheless, in some stores markdowns are subtracted from the total merchandise handled before the initial markup is calculated rather than added to the sales as a part of the total retail deductions. This practice is not generally recommended for it lowers the initial markup and thus increases the closing cost inventory.

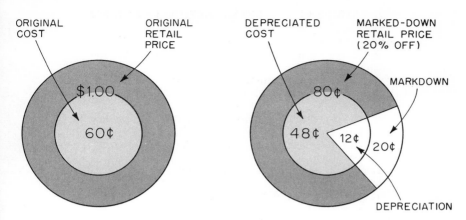

FIGURE 11.1   Effect of Markdowns on Cost Price

dise price changes are reflected in the records used in calculating the markup and the book inventory.

PROS AND CONS OF THE RETAIL METHOD

The following list gives the major benefits and limitations of the retail method. For merchants handling general merchandise, the benefits preponderate.

BENEFITS OF THE RETAIL METHOD OF INVENTORY

- Simplifies and makes more accurate the taking of physical inventory and the preparation of budgets.
- Provides a perpetual book inventory figure. Useful in merchandise control for planning purchases and obtaining desired stockturn.
- Allows the determination of shortages and thus checks on dishonesty.
- Allows profit calculation between inventory dates.
- Determines the stock on hand for insurance purposes in connection with fire and similar losses.
- Automatically includes transportation in the closing inventory, since the transportation charge added to purchases reduces the initial markup and thus increases the cost of the closing inventory.
- Evaluates the cost on a basis approximating *cost or market, whichever is lower.*

LIMITATIONS OF THE RETAIL METHOD OF INVENTORY

- Additional records are required.
  All invoices must be marked with the retail price of each item.
  All price changes must be recorded.
- Unless there is careful supervision, the system may be manipulated.
  Fictitious markups may overvaluate or undervaluate cost inventories.
  Fictitious markdowns may undervaluate cost inventories.
  Deferred markdowns may overvaluate cost inventories.
- The store must be departmentized, unless only a narrow line is carried.
- Where goods at different markups are handled in the department and the high and low markup goods are not sold in the same proportion as that in which they were bought, the closing cost inventory may be either over-stated or understated—generally it is overstated.
- The retail method is not adaptable to all lines, especially to such departments as fresh produce with much spoil-age, or to cases where the closing inventory is not repre-sentative of the total merchandise handled or when price changes are very frequently made.

QUESTIONS FOR DISCUSSION

1. (a) To what extent do tax considerations enter into decisions in inventory valuation?
   (b) If an inventory is overvalued $600 at the beginning of a year and undervalued $500 at the end of the year, what is the effect on the year's profit showing?
   (c) If an inventory is undervalued $200 at the beginning of a year and undervalued $300 at the end of the year, but at the end of the *next* year it is overvalued $500, what is the effect on profits this year? Next year? For the two years combined?
2. Since overvaluation of an opening inventory tends to offset over-valuation of the closing inventory, why should an attempt be made to recognize depreciation in the inventory valuation? Will such recognition make any substantial difference in the profit showing?
3. What are the difficulties in using the market quotation method of valuation? The appraisal method?
4. Is the FIFO method of inventory valuation the same as the cost-or-market method? Explain.
5. In connection with the example of the markdown method in the box on page 191 suppose that the item now in stock at a retail

price of $12.50 has a relatively poor chance of selling at that price and may have to be reduced ultimately to $10.00.

(a) At what figure would you value the item for profit-figuring purposes?

(b) Would your answer be different if taxes were involved rather than merchandise management?

6. Is it sound to base the market value of an inventory on its age or should other factors be given equal attention?

7. Since the last-in goods are seldom the first-out (sold) goods, is there a sound basis for the premise on which the LIFO method is based: that the first-in goods remain as a fixed investment at a fixed cost?

8. Is it better merchandising strategy to include a portion of transportation costs on incoming goods as an element in the closing inventory or to omit transportation in the inventory valuation, even though it is included in the cost purchase figure?

9. The retail method is based on the assumption that the markup on the closing inventory is representative of the markup on the total merchandise handled. Is this assumption justified?

10. (a) If virtually all the stock on hand at the end of a six-month period is less than three months old, does the cumulative markup for the period give too much or too little weight to the markup on the opening inventory?

(b) If the markup on the opening inventory six months before was less than the markup on the subsequent purchases, in what direction would the closing inventory be distorted?

11. If a garment costing $10 and retailing at $20 is to be transferred to a clearance selling unit at a cost of $6, what markdown should be taken in advance of the transfer so as not to distort the mark-up of the department transferring the goods out?

12. (a) A closing inventory consists of goods currently in stock at a retail value of $25,000, but this merchandise costs $18,000 and was originally priced at $30,000. What is the market value and how much are profits reduced by the depreciation reflected in this figure?

(b) If the goods referred to above are marked down to $25,000 just before the end of a period with no intention of selling them at the reduced price and if at the start of the next period the inventory is marked up back to its original retail price by means of an additional markup, would the profit figures for both periods be distorted and, if so, to what extent?

13. Try to demonstrate how the handling of additional markups under the retail method tends to evaluate the inventory at the end of the period at original cost rather than at a higher market value.

14. Suggest how the information required for the retail method of inventory could be prepared so as to be fed into a computer.

15. (a) How would you explain to a merchant who is unfamiliar with the retail method the importance of distinguishing among the four different kinds of price change and of reporting these changes to his bookkeeper?

(b) A merchant purchases one thousand items at $0.60 each and marks half of them at a regular price of $1.00 and the other half at $0.89 for a special sale. But before the sale takes place, he marks the $0.89 goods up to $1.00, the regular price, and sells them at this price without reporting the price increase as an additional markup. What will be the effect of this handling on the merchandise shortage figure? The initial markup? The closing cost inventory? The gross margin?

16. What advice would you give to a small retailer in regard to the introduction of the retail method were he a dress shop operator? An independent grocer?

12

STOCKTURN

The inventory that the typical store carries represents the major portion of its net working capital[1] and the largest single element in its total assets. The sale of goods from this inventory is the merchant's chief source of operating profit. Thus, the way in which this merchandise investment is put to work is of utmost importance in achieving a profitable operation.

A specialty store owner may carry an average inventory at retail of $200,000 and in the course of the year produce sales of $600,000 and a profit of $60,000. Another merchant, more astute perhaps, may take that same merchandise inventory and produce sales of $800,000 and a profit of $80,000. Each shows the same 10 percent profit on sales. But the second merchant has $20,000 more profit because he turned his stock investment four times instead of merely three. Thus, it can be seen that a higher stockturn tends to lead to a higher profit, an essential goal of the merchant.[2]

---

[1] The excess of current assets over current liabilities.

[2] In the next chapter we shall discuss the profit return relative to investment and to space occupied. Here the relationship of the merchandise investment to sales is considered.

THE STOCKTURN CONCEPT

To understand the significance of the relationship between sales and stocks, it is first necessary to know exactly what stockturn means and how it is computed. Stockturn may be defined as the sales during a period divided by the average stock. The sales and stock figures may be expressed either in dollars or in units. If in dollars, either retail or cost values may be used. The retail basis is the usual one:

$$\frac{\text{Net sales } \$10,000}{\text{Average retail stock } \$2,000} = 5, \text{ the stockturn at retail}$$

If stockturn is computed at cost, the gross cost of merchandise sold is divided by the average cost stock. This plan results in a slightly higher turnover than stockturn at retail because the markup on the cost of merchandise sold expressed as a percentage of sales is generally less than the markup on stock. The difference between cost and retail stock represents the initial or attempted markup. The difference between gross cost of merchandise sold and sales is the maintained or realized markup. This is the markup after markdowns and shortage losses have been included in the gross cost of merchandise sold. For example, in the above illustration the maintained markup may be only 35 percent when the markon or initial markup is 40 percent. The turnover at cost could then be computed as follows:

$$\frac{\$10,000 \times .65}{\$2,000 \times .60} = \frac{6,500}{1,200} = 5.4$$

In order to insure comparability of figures, it is desirable to use one base or the other as the standard of practice. The retail basis is to be preferred for two reasons: First, stores operating under the retail method of inventory have information continually available in regard to sales and retail stocks, whereas the corresponding cost figures require a computation that is entered into only when profits are computed. Second, the retail basis gives the smaller or more conservative figure.

Stock turnover may be computed in units or pieces of merchandise also. Thus, if one thousand hats are sold during a period with an average stock on hand of one hundred hats, the turnover for the period is ten.

For comparative purposes, it is desirable that the period of time be standard. This is generally one year, and the term *rate of stock turn* should be limited to references to this period.

Where monthly turnovers are computed, the annual *rate* may be found by multiplying by twelve. For example, the sales in August may be $3,000 with average retail stock of $6,000. The monthly turnover is one-half, which is at a rate of six ($\frac{1}{2} \times 12$). Cumulative turnover figures may be determined. For example, September sales may be $4,000, and average retail stock for August and September combined, $7,000. The two-month cumulative turnover is

$$\frac{\$3,000 + \$4,000}{\$7,000} = \frac{\$7,000}{\$7,000} = 1$$

The annual rate is again six.

Seasonal Stockturn

It is to be observed that the actual stockturn achieved in a month tends to vary considerably from one-twelfth of the annual

---

THREE WAYS TO EXPRESS STOCKTURN

In a rug store, sales were $80,000 during the year. *This represented 1,000 rugs.* The average stock was $20,000 at retail and $12,000 at cost. This represented 225 rugs. The cost of goods sold was $50,000 for the year. The merchant then computed his stockturn in three ways:

A. Sales ÷ Average retail stock
   $80,000 ÷ $20,000 = 4
B. Cost of goods sold ÷ Average cost stock
   $50,000 ÷ 12,000 = $4\frac{1}{6}$
C. Unit sales ÷ Average unit stock
   1,000 ÷ 225 = 4.4

---

turnover. For example, a store with six stockturns may have net sales of $120,000 a year; its average stock is $20,000 at retail; its average monthly sales are $10,000; and its average monthly stockturn is one-half. In December, it may sell $15,000, 50 percent more than average, but it will probably not need to increase its stock 50 percent to provide for the Christmas rush; a 25 percent increase from $20,000 to $25,000 may be sufficient. Thus, December stockturn will be $15,000 divided by $25,000, or three-fifths, a figure higher than the average of one-half.

Likewise, in July, sales may fall from an average of $10,000 a month to $5,000, but to maintain basic assortments of merchandise a 25 percent reduction in stock from $20,000 to $15,000 may be all that is desirable. The July stockturn, then, is $5,000 divided by $15,000, or one-third; this is considerably less than the average monthly stockturn of one-half.

Since most merchants have to maintain basic assortments throughout the year, it follows that stockturn is generally higher in the months of greatest seasonal sales demand and less than average in the dull months.

APPLYING THE STOCKTURN RATIO

Since stock turnover, by definition, is sales divided by average stock, it follows that sales and average stock may be expressed in terms of the turnover: Let T = stockturn; S = sales; and A = average stock:

$$\text{Since } T = \frac{S}{A}, \ S = T \times A \text{ and } A = \frac{S}{T}$$

These relationships are helpful in planning. For example, a new store may have $3,000 to invest in merchandise that can be retailed for $5,000. If the usual rate of stockturn in this line is six, a reasonable sales expectancy for the year will be six times $5,000, or $30,000. This assumes that the merchant does not expect to increase his stock during the year.

Again, an established store or department may forecast sales for the coming year of $50,000 and the turnover standard may be five. Since the average retail stock may be found by dividing the sales by the stockturn, an average stock of $10,000 can be planned as a guide for purchase control. But the stock carried at the beginning of the year might properly be considerably less.

TRIPLE RELATIONSHIPS

$$\text{Stockturn} = \frac{\text{Sales}}{\text{Average stock}}$$

$$\text{Sales} = \text{Stockturn} \times \text{Average stock}$$

$$\text{Average stock} = \frac{\text{Sales}}{\text{Stockturn}}$$

FINDING AVERAGE STOCKS

The chief problem in computing stockturn is to determine the average stock carried during the period.

Chief methods. There are several methods commonly used.

1. The stocks at the beginning and at the end of the year are averaged. For example, if the stock on February 1, the beginning of the fiscal year, is $2,100 at retail, and on February 1 next, the end of the fiscal year, it is $1,900, the average is $2,000. The objection to this practice is that the stock at one time is not an accurate reflection of the average of the stock carried throughout the year. Stocks on February 1 may be 15 to 25 percent below the true yearly average because the winter merchandise has largely been disposed of through clearance sales and the spring goods have not yet been added to the stock. The derived turnover is accordingly, too high. This method cannot be recommended for control purposes within a store, although it may have to be used by an outside analyst who has only the annual stock figures available.

2. The stocks at the beginning, middle, and end of the year are averaged by dividing the sum of these figures by three. For example, stock on February 1 may be $2,100; on August 1, $2,150; and on February 1 next, $1,900. The average is $2,050. This plan is only a little better than the first method because stocks at the middle of the year are frequently at a very low point, too. Summer merchandise is cleared in July, and few fall goods have been stocked. The heavy stocks carried during the important spring and fall seasons have been wholly disregarded in the average, which is consequently too small—and the resultant stockturn too large.

3. The stocks on the first of each month are averaged by dividing the sum of the stock figures by their number. If the fiscal year is from February 1 of one year to February 1 of the next, thirteen stock figures are required, for the twelfth represents January 1; an average based upon twelve figures would disregard the stock carried at the end of the twelfth month. This plan is the one most commonly used in stores operating under the retail method of inventory. February 1, July 31, and January 31 inventories are likely to be physical inventories, and the other ten estimated physical inventories. This approach is open to the objection that heavy or low stocks carried during the month, but not at hand at the beginning or end, have no influence on the computed stockturn figure. Some buyers tend to allow their stocks to get low at the end of each month and to bring in large purchases early in each succeeding month. If this is the practice, the stockturn figures on a basis of monthly stocks will be higher than the facts warrant.

4. Another plan for averaging stocks is to use weekly stock figures. This requires fifty-three figures in order to include the end of the final week in the year. These may be averaged as in the monthly plan by summating the fifty-three figures and dividing by fifty-three. This method makes allowance for stock fluctuations during a month. The use of weekly figures gives a highly accurate average but is cumbersome to compute. A daily average is possible but not often practicable. In practice, the weekly plan is most common in the large department store field. Since uniformity of calculation is more important than statistical accuracy, either the third or the fourth plan may be recommended.

What stockturn is not. While stockturn is the ratio of sales to average stock, it is not, as has often been stated, the number of times a physical stock of goods is bought and sold during a period. For example, a merchant may purchase a staple article in units of three months' supply and not restock until the old stock is completely sold out. During the year, four purchases are made and four lots are sold, but the stockturn is not four. The average stock is about a month and a half's supply, since three months' supply is on hand only at the start of each quarter and virtually none is on hand at the end of each quarter. Thus, the average stock is about half the amount received every quarter. This results in a stockturn of two for a three-month period, or eight per year.

AVERAGING STOCKTURN

After the stockturn has been computed for the various departments of a store or for the various classifications within a department, it might be desirable, for comparison purposes, to compute the overall turnover. This could be done, of course, by using the totals of the sales and stock figures involved, but it may also be calculated from the stockturn figures themselves, provided the relative sales volume in each category was known. In the following example, the percentage of sales made by each department is indicated. Then, by letting $100 equal total sales:

Department	Stockturn	Percentage of Sales	Sales in Dollars	Average Stock at Retail
A	10	50%	$50	$5
B	7	35	35	5
C	5	15	15	3
Total		100%	$100	$13

$100 ÷ $13 = 7.7, the aggregate stockturn for the store

The sales must be divided by the stockturn to give the stocks. The sum of these stocks divided into the total sales of $100 gives the aggregate stockturn.[3]

PLANNING STOCKTURN

The averaging method just described may prove useful in deciding what turn to aim at in one department or subdivision when an overall goal has been established. Thus, in the above case, an aggregate stockturn of eight may be set. It may also be felt that no increase in the stockturn in either A or B is possible without sacrificing sales but that the turn in C can be increased somewhat. The averaging method may be used to determine what turnover in C will yield the aggregate desired:

Department	Stockturn	Percentage of Sales	Sales in Dollars	Average Stock at Retail
A	10	50%	$50	$5.00
B	7	35	35	5.00
C	?	15	15	(2.50)
Total	8	100%	$100	$12.50

$100 ÷ 8 = $12.50, the aggregate average stock to carry. Since a stock of $10.00 is required in A and B combined, there is only a stock of $2.50 left for C. With sales of $15.00, the turnover must be six. Whether the turnover in C can be increased from five to six cannot be determined by mathematics. It would be necessary to study the stock assortment carefully to see whether necessary assortments can be maintained at the lower level.[4]

AVERAGING STOCKTURN

A merchant has two departments (A and B) and wants a stockturn of 5 for his store as a whole. He does 70 percent of his business in department A and 30 percent in B. He is sure he can obtain only 4 turns in A. He calculates the turnover to aim at for B as follows by assuming total sales of $100:

---

[3] It should be noted that stockturn figures must not be weighted by sales to derive an average, but rather by average stocks.

[4] It should be borne in mind that changing the stock investment in any one category may change the relative sales that can be achieved and require a new calculation of overall stockturn.

Department	Percentage of Sales	Sales in Dollars	Stockturn	Average Stock at Retail
A	70%	$70	4	$17.50
B	30	30	?	(2.50)
Total	100%	$100	5	$20.00

$$\text{Turnover for B} = \frac{\$30.00}{\$\ 2.50} = 12$$

CAPITAL-TURN

The term *capital-turn* is generally used to designate the relationship between net sales at retail and average stock at cost. It differs from stockturn in that the denominator is on a cost basis but the numerator is at retail. In stockturn, both are at retail or both are at cost. For example, sales may be $10,000, average stock at retail $2,000, and average stock at cost $1,200. The capital-turn is $10,000 ÷ $1,200, or eight and one-third, whereas the stockturn at retail is five ($10,000 ÷ $2,000). Capital-turn is always higher than stockturn.[5] Capital-turn is frequently used in financial circles, but retail merchants usually prefer to use the concept of stockturn. Capital-turn is a useful measure of efficiency in the hands of outside observers, however, who have sales and cost inventory figures available from published corporate statements but do not have access to the retail stock figures.

STOCK-SALES RATIOS

A third important relationship between stock and sales is the stock-sales ratio.[6]

Monthly Ratios

There are two chief varieties of monthly ratios: (1) the B.O.M. stock-sales ratio is the retail stock at the beginning of the month divided by the sales for the month. For example, the retail

---

[5] Since the numerator for both stockturn and capital-turn are the same and since the difference in the denominators is caused by the markup element, the following relationships can be readily established:

Stockturn = Capital-turn × Complement of the Markup

and

$$\text{Capital-turn} = \frac{\text{Stockturn}}{\text{Complement of the Markup}}$$

[6] See chapter 16 for application of the stock-sales ratios to planning.

stock on February 1 may be $10,000, and the sales for February, $5,000. The February stock-sales ratio (as of the first of the month) is two. (2) The E.O.M. stock-sales ratio is the retail stock at the end of the month divided by the sales for the month. If stock at the end of February is $15,000, the February stock-sales ratio (as of the end of the month) will be three. Of the two, the beginning of the month ratio is the more useful, since there is a causal relationship between beginning stocks and sales for a month. The stock of $10,000 on February 1 is on hand to make possible the February sales of $5,000. At the end of February, however, the stock of $15,000 has no direct relation to February sales but is on hand to make March sales possible.

Stock-sales ratios differ from stockturn in three ways: numerators and denominators are reversed; the period covered for a stock-sales ratio is commonly a month, whereas stockturn can be for any period that proves useful, such as a month, season, or year; and the stock figure in the stock-sales ratio represents the stock at a specific time, whereas in stockturn the stock is the average maintained over a period of time. Accordingly, the stock-sales ratio cannot be defined as the reciprocal of the turnover ratio. In the above example, the stockturn for February is

$$\frac{\$5,000}{1/2 \ (\$10,000 + \$15,000)} = \frac{\$5,000}{\$12,500} = .4,$$

but the first of month stock-sales ratio is

$$\frac{\$10,000}{\$5,000}, \text{ or } 2,$$

not

$$\frac{\$12,500}{\$5,000}, \text{ or } 2.5.$$

STOCK-SALES RELATIONSHIPS

Stockturn:
(a) At retail—Net sales ÷ Average retail stock
(b) At cost—Cost of sales ÷ Average cost stock
(c) In units—Unit sales ÷ Average stock in units
Capital-turn: Net sales ÷ Average cost stock
Stock-sales ratio:
(a) B.O.M. stock-sales ratio—
    Stock at retail B.O.M. ÷ Sales for month
(b) E.O.M. stock-sales ratio—
    Stock at retail E.O.M. ÷ Sales for month
Weeks' supply: Stock on hand at a given date expressed as
    equal to the sales for a subsequent number of weeks

It is evident that a reduction in stock, in relation to sales, decreases the stock-sales ratio. Thus, increased stockturn is equivalent to a lower stock-sales ratio each month, and decreased stockturn to a higher stock-sales ratio.

Comparing the stock-sales ratio with stockturn. It is easy to convert stock-sales ratios into stockturn if ratios are available for both the beginning and the end of a period: Thus, the B.O.M. stock-sales ratio for December may be four and the E.O.M. ratio for December two:

$$
\begin{aligned}
\text{Let December sales} \quad &= \$1 \\
\text{December } 1 \text{ stock } (\$1 \times 4) &= \$4 \\
\text{December } 31 \text{ stock } (\$1 \times 2) &= \$2 \\
\text{Average stock} \quad &= \$3 \\
\text{December stockturn} \quad &= 1/3 \\
\text{Annual rate of turn } (1/3 \times 12) &= 4
\end{aligned}
$$

When beginning of the month stock-sales ratios only are available, ratios for the first of two consecutive months may not be averaged to obtain the turnover for the first month, since the two are based on different amounts of sales. The sales for each of the months must be known. Thus:

$$
\begin{aligned}
&\text{B.O.M. stock-sales ratio, December} = 4 \quad \text{Sales } \$100{,}000 \\
&\text{B.O.M. stock-sales ratio, January} \;= 5 \quad \text{Sales } \$\;60{,}000 \\
&\text{December } 1 \text{ stock } (4 \times \$100{,}000) \quad \$400{,}000 \\
&\text{January } 1 \text{ stock } \;(5 \times \$\;60{,}000) \quad \underline{\;\;300{,}000} \\
&\text{Average December stock} \qquad\qquad\quad \$350{,}000 \\
&\text{December turn: } \frac{\$100{,}000}{\$350{,}000} = 0.29
\end{aligned}
$$

WEEKLY RATIOS

For fast-turning lines, stock-sales ratios are sometimes compiled from weekly rather than monthly data. Thus, stock on August 1 in a dress store may be eight hundred units and sales may be averaging two hundred a week. The first-of-week stock-sales ratio, then, is four. This signifies that there is a four weeks' supply on hand. In many ready-to-wear operations, it is the practice to plan ahead the number of weeks' supply to have on hand and to adjust purchases accordingly.

ADVANTAGES OF STOCK-SALES RATIOS

The chief advantage of the stock-sales ratio as compared with stockturn is that it gives a basis for planning stocks that should be on hand at a given time rather than for planning average stocks. For example, comparison with past experience and with other stores may indicate that an annual turnover of six is desirable for a merchandise line with a sales volume of $60,000. The average retail stock to be carried, then, is $10,000, but this does not indicate how much stock should be on hand at any given time. From a control point of view, an average stock figure for a season is of limited value; the important considerations are the stock at the beginning of the season, at the end the of the season, and at specific dates during the season.

Such planning is facilitated by determining stock-sales ratios for each month or week based on both past experience and comparison with other stores of similar size and with a similar clientele. It may be found, for example, that a desirable B.O.M. stock-sales ratio in February for a certain hosiery shop with an annual sales volume of $60,000 is two and one-fourth. If February sales are planned at $4,000, the figure for the stock on the first of the month would be $9,000. In summary, then, the B.O.M. stock-sales ratio planned for a month or a week may be multiplied by the planned sales for the period to find the stock for the first of the period.

There are a number of groups of stores that exchange information in regard to the sales and stocks of each department, and the MOR annual reports of the NRMA now include stock-sales ratios. These figures make it possible to work out average ratios that can be used as a guide by each store to help correct an overstocked condition or to plan stocks next year, on a basis of planned monthly sales.

In addition, there are several major retail trade associations that include B.O.M. stock-sales ratios for many categories of merchandise.

WEEKS' SUPPLY COMPARISONS

Another method of comparing sales and stocks, similar to the weekly stock-sales ratio, is used by some merchants in the practical application of day-to-day merchandising. This is the weeks' supply method, whereby the stock level at any point in time is related to a standard number of future weeks of anticipated sales.

For example, a dress department with a stockturn goal of six and one-half may be assigned a standard of eight weeks' supply of anticipated sales. On February 1, the buyer anticipates sales of

$4,000 for four weeks in February and $6,000 for four weeks in March, or a total of $10,000 sales for those eight weeks. Accordingly, the stock level for February 1 would be set at $10,000.

In practice, the number of weeks' supply should not be held constant throughout the year, since to maintain assortments it is generally necessary to carry a larger number of current weeks' supply in dull periods than in peak periods. This means that a higher turn can generally be obtained in the peak periods. For example, if the sales for an eight-week period near the peak of the fall season are estimated at $20,000, a stock of this magnitude will probably be too large; it would not need to be twice the stock carried early in the season. A stock at the peak of seven weeks' supply, or about $17,500, might be adequate.

A variation of this method takes into account merchandise that is on order. For example, if the normal delivery time is four weeks, including a cushion for delay, then four weeks' supply is added to the weeks' supply coverage requirement. This coverage requirement is expressed as a "total commitment," or combination of stock on hand plus on order. Thus, in the example above this figure might cover twelve weeks' supply.

If the twelve weeks of anticipated sales were $15,000 (February 1 to late in April) and stock on hand were $9,000 and on order $4,000, the buyer would know he should order an additional $2,000 to maintain the planned relationship.

For each line of goods a decision is made as to how far ahead commitments should be made, and every month or week the actual commitments are checked against this projection. To be committed too far ahead makes for inflexibility in adjusting to unexpected demand; to commit for too short a period leads to delays in getting delivery and to lost sales. This matter will receive further attention in chapters 19 and 20, in connection with unit control.

IMPORTANCE OF RAPID STOCKTURN

The ability to realize a large volume of sales on a small investment in merchandise has received varying emphasis depending upon the stage of the business cycle. During a period of declining prices, large stocks have caused heavy markdowns, and high stockturn has been regarded as of the utmost importance. The merchant with the small, clean stock has suffered smaller losses. On a rising market, however, stockturn receives less emphasis, for the stock is less likely to depreciate and may appreciate in value. An item bought in a depression at $1.00 to sell at $1.50 may be in stock six months later when similar articles are selling in the wholesale market at $1.15. The old stock may thus prove salable at $1.75, yielding a handsome profit. In such cases, there is an element of speculation that is quite distinct from merchandising with its attempt to sell goods as quickly as possible at a price that will yield a profit over cost. The speculator, on the other hand, attempts to hold goods until their market value rises. While every merchant probably speculates at times, his major attention is devoted to merchandising. In fact, finished consumer goods are less likely to appreciate than raw materials.

ADVANTAGES OF RAPID STOCKTURN

- Reduces markdowns
- Reduces certain expenses
    Interest
    Insurance
    Merchandise taxes
    Space charge
- Increases sales due to rapid flow of fresh new merchandise
- Increases return on the merchandise investment

On a comparatively constant price level, rapid turnover is desirable, although it is not the only major consideration. Speedy obsolescence owing to fashion change necessitates the prompt sale of merchandise if a profitable price is to be realized.

Fast stockturn reduces markdowns.   There seems to be a fairly close relationship between markdowns and turnover. For example, recent figures for department and specialty stores show that stores with $1 million to $2 million sales had markdowns of 8.2 percent, whereas stores with volume over $50 million had markdowns of 6.05 percent.[7] The stockturn in the first group was 2.6 and in the second 3.6. The probabilities are that the lower markdowns in the large stores are partly caused by the high stockturn they enjoy.[8] Since markdowns are a function of time, there is logic in such a relationship. Thus, with three turns the stock is equal to a four months' supply; with four turns the stock is equal to a three months'

---

[7] Report for 1968, Controllers' Congress, National Retail Merchants Association.
[8] The likelihood of better-trained buyers in the large stores is an additional explanation of the lower markdowns.

supply. Obsolescence, if distributed equally over time, would be only three-fourths as much in three months as in four. Of course, all markdowns are not caused by obsolescence; some are caused by buying unsalable goods in the first place. Thus, the planner would hardly expect markdowns to be reduced in direct ratio to the increase in stockturn.

Fast stockturn reduces expense and costs.   Another advantake of rapid turnover is that it reduces certain items of expense. If funds have been borrowed and reinvested in stock, a reduction in the stock will make it possible to pay back the loan and to reduce interest payments.

Increased stockturn also reduces insurance charges and taxes on the merchandise inventory. For example, an increase in stockturn from two to three on a constant sales volume reduces the dollar stock one-third and accordingly may reduce insurance, merchandise tax, and perhaps interest in the same proportion. Should the increased turn come about from a sales increase of 50 percent, these dollar expenses would remain the same but would be reduced one-third in percentage of sales.

Increased stockturn may sometimes reduce storage or rent charges. This is particularly true in the case of selling departments in a departmentized store. If a simplification of the stock assortment allows the same volume to be realized on one-fifth less stock, it may be possible to reduce the storage space considerably as well as the selling space allotted to the department. The released space may be given to a department that is expanding in volume. For the store as a whole, there is no such direct relationship between stockturn and rent. A reduction in space needed to store goods does not directly reduce rents paid or, in owned properties, interest on the investment in building. However, reduced stocks do allow business expansion without the necessity of building or leasing additional space; they allow liberated space to be devoted to profitable uses.

Fast stockturn increases sales.   Indirectly, improved stockturn often increases sales volume. An effort to increase stockturn is generally a part of a broader objective, the balancing of stocks to customer demand. More adequate assortments, coupled with the frequent receipt of new merchandise, create customer interest and engender enthusiasm of salespeople for their goods. Faster stockturn means a faster flow of merchandise through the store, thus attracting customers who always find something new. On the other hand, a low stockturn may impair sales volume because customers find it hard to choose from a static assortment with too many similar styles.

Fast stockturn increases the return on the investment. Rapid stockturn is also of advantage from the standpoint of profit return on both the investment in merchandise and the total investment (net worth). This will be discussed in the next chapter.

LIMITATIONS OF RAPID STOCKTURN

Danger of lost sales. As a general rule, it may be stated that stockturn gained at the expense of sales volume is not profitable. Stock reductions that do not deplete desirable stock assortments offered to the customer are worth making, but reductions that interfere with sales are not. For example, a store may be realizing sales of $100,000 on a $25,000 stock, a turn of four. If a reduction in stock to $20,000 should curtail volume to $90,000, the turnover would be four and one-half but the situation much less satisfactory than before because a loss of $10,000 in sales volume more than offsets the possible savings attributable to the higher turn.

While most stores and departments have not reached the limit at which rapid stockturn ceases to be profitable, this limit should be recognized. A store cannot afford to lose sales by being "out." It has frequently been estimated that many stores lose 10 percent of their possible sales volume by not having the goods they intend to carry in stock. However, these stores are generally suffering, not from too high a stockturn on total stock, but from having too much old stock and too little new, desirable stock.

LIMITATIONS OF RAPID STOCKTURN

- Presents the danger of lost sales due to an out-of-stock condition
- Increases merchandise costs
    Transportation on purchases
    Lost quantity discounts
- Increases certain expenses
    Correspondence
    Handling of merchandise
    Clerical

Increase in merchandise costs. Another limitation of high stockturn is that it increases certain merchandise costs, particularly transportation and the net cost of purchases through the loss of quantity discounts. An example of hand-to-mouth buying is as follows: An item selling at the rate of 10 a week has been ordered in quantities of 130 at a time, or once a quarter, with a low unit cost of transportation. If 10 are now ordered every week, the transportation per unit will be higher and orders of 10 a week may not qualify for a discount that may have been available on the larger orders.

Increase in certain expenses.   Furthermore, a very high turn leads to an increase in certain expenses, particularly correspondence, clerical, and handling costs. Thirteen weekly reorders in a three-month period will cost thirteen times as much as one reorder in the quarter. Again, if thirteen separate payments have to be made, the cost will be in proportion. Furthermore, the cost of receiving, checking, and marking thirteen small shipments is much more than that of processing one shipment thirteen times as large.

For fashion merchandise, these costs and expense factors may not outweigh the advantages of rapid turn, but for staples, the cost of frequent orders may easily offset the advantages. It is probably seldom wise to order less than one week's supply at a time, except merchandise that customers replenish almost daily, such as perishable foodstuffs.

In general, the lines in which customers repurchase frequently and in which a small assortment is demanded at the time of selection have the highest stockturn. On the other hand, those goods that are bought only once in many years but require a large assortment to satisfy customers turn the most slowly. Fresh fruits and vegetables are an example of the first, and furniture of the second. In between are found the great majority of commodities. The merchant's constant effort is to keep stocks large enough to meet demand but also small enough to minimize the risk of obsolescence and undue expense of merchandise charges.

INCREASING STOCKTURN

From an inspection of the basic stockturn relationship, it is clear that there are three ways to increase stockturn:

1. Increase sales without increasing the average stock assortment proportionately
2. Decrease stocks without interfering with sales
3. Increase sales and at the same time reduce stock

For example, present sales may be $100,000 and the average retail stock $25,000, yielding 4 turns. A 10 percent increase in sales to $110,000 with the same inventory gives 4.4 turns. Reducing the stock to about $22,700 with the same sales also gives 4.4 turns. Or reducing stocks 5 percent to $23,750 and increasing sales to $104,500 would also give 4.4 turns.

The approach used depends on the circumstances. Since the planner has greater control over his stocks than over his sales, first attention should probably be given to reducing stocks without interfering with sales.

Probably the surest way to increase stockturn over a period of time, however, is to increase sales volume. For once a basic stock is provided for, increases in sales do not usually require proportionate increases in stocks. Table 12.1 showing performance in department stores reveals that the larger the sales volume, the higher the stockturn tends to be. Chapter 13 will explore the opportunity to reduce inventories without adversely affecting sales.

TABLE 12.1   Relationship between Sales Volume and Annual Stockturn

Volume Code[a]	Total Store	Dresses[b]	Sports- wear Women's	Shoes[c]	Furnishings	Personal Needs and Small Wares	House Furnish- ings[d]
1	2.41	3.4	3.1	2.0	1.9	1.9	2.1
2	2.97	4.4	4.0	2.7	2.4	2.3	2.5
3	3.10	5.1	3.9	2.0	3.1	2.9	2.2
4	3.24	5.6	4.4	—	2.8	3.0	2.0
5	3.15	4.7	4.3	2.4	3.2	3.2	2.3
6	3.33	5.8	5.4	—	3.5	3.5	2.6

Source: Merchandise and Operating Results of 1968, Controllers' Congress, National Retail Merchants Association, New York.

[a] Each merchandise line is broken down into sales volume groupings in ascending order. For the department store as a whole, the volume groupings are $1–$2 million, $2–$5 million, $5–$10 million, $10–$20 million, $20–$50 million, and over $50 million. In dresses, code 1 represents dress departments in department and specialty stores with sales volume up to $130,000, code 6 volume of $350,000 and more. The various volume intervals for each merchandise line vary.
[b] Women's, Misses' and Juniors'.
[c] Women's and Children's.
[d] Includes furniture.

QUESTIONS FOR DISCUSSION

1. If the stockturn in a merchandise line is six times a year, does that mean that the physical stock has been replaced six times? Why?

2. If the stockturn is figured in terms of units of merchandise rather than in dollar value, would the resultant figure be the same as it would be in dollars?

3. Would you expect stockturn based on weekly inventory averages to differ much from that based on monthly averages? Which is likely to give somewhat higher results?

4. If there are only two departments in a store and sales in department A are 72 percent of the total and in department B 28 percent and if the stockturn in A is six and in B only two, what is the store's stockturn?

5. (a) Is there any practical value in calculating capital-turn? Explain.

(b) Since stockturn equals sales divided by average retail stock and capital-turn equals sales divided by average cost stock and since average cost stock equals average retail stock times the complement of the initial markup, calculate the derivation of the following relationship: Stockturn = Capital-turn × Complement of the initial markup.

6. If the B.O.M. stock-sales ratio for June is 2.6 and for July 3.0 and if July sales are 20 percent less than June sales, what is the stockturn for June? What is the annual rate? Which is the more meaningful figure: the B.O.M. stock-sales ratio for June or the stockturn for June?

7. If you plan to keep inventory equal to the sales for the eight weeks just ahead, what stockturn are you aiming at? Should the number of weeks' supply differ at different times during the year?

8. (a) In your opinion, what is the chief advantage of increasing stockturn?

(b) The chief disadvantage?

9. Do you think that many stores or departments have achieved an optimum stockturn figure?

10. Would it make for good managerial control to charge each selling department with interest on its average cost investment in inventory (perhaps at 6 percent) even though the store has not had to borrow money to provide the inventory? Such a charge would reduce the department's profit showing without reducing the storewide profit figure.

13

RETURN
ON INVESTMENT
IN MERCHANDISE
AND
IN SPACE

Without sufficient capital to invest in merchandise and space, even the leading store in a community can quickly fall back to second or third place or be forced out of business, as some have. To attract the necessary investment, retailing competes with every other business in the money market. If money is tight and interest rates are high, competition for those dollars necessitates an adequate return on investment.

There was a time when this concern with return on the investment was not as critical as it has become. The traditional criterion for a successful operation was adequate net profit expressed as a percentage of sales. Interest rates were low and business was moderately steady, with only a few branch stores needing financing. Retailers now require additional capital as they develop large-scale operations. Millions of dollars are necessary for additional investment even to maintain their share of the market. Many companies have gone public, owned by stockholders who demand an attractive profit return on invested capital.

Thus, modern retailing management is scrutinizing profit productivity as it relates to investment in merchandise and space. This chapter will discuss the importance of these factors and the techniques of evaluating and optimizing their profitability.

PROFITABILITY OF THE MERCHANDISE INVESTMENT

The merchandising executive generally has little control over fixed assets and accounts receivable, but he does control the investment in merchandise. It is therefore important to evaluate his profit performance not in relation to the entire assets (or to the net worth) but rather in relation to the merchandise investment. There are different levels of profit performance, each suited to the operation to be evaluated. The levels frequently used are the gross margin level, the contribution level, and the operating profit level.[1] If a department buyer has no control over selling expenses, he is best evaluated on the gross margin level; but if he controls the direct expenses of his department as well as the inventory investment to a degree, he is properly evaluated on the contribution profit level. If indirect expenses are allocated to each department equitably, the operating profit level may be a suitable one against which to evaluate inventory investment data.

Since methods of distributing operating expenses differ, the National Retail Merchants Association, in its annual merchandising and operating reports, presents data for each selling department comparing gross margin with average cost inventory. By dividing the annual gross margin for each department by the average cost inventory, "the gross margin return per dollar of inventory at cost" is determined. While the return varies greatly by department and size of store, most of the figures in a recent year range between one and four dollars. The candy department was an exception on the upside, earning a gross margin of about six dollars for every dollar of inventory investment. On the downside, the piano department earned about sixty cents.

Merchants usually press for a reduction in merchandise investment in certain categories, and a consequent increase in the rate of return, not for the purpose of removing funds from the business but for utilizing investment dollars to expand operations, thus earning additional profit. They may add new merchandise lines, promote the store more effective, modernize the premises, or open branches.

LIMITATIONS OF A HIGH RETURN ON THE INVESTMENT

It should not be concluded that the goal of every merchant is only to increase the percentage return on his investment. If this

---

[1] From the point of view of general management, the level of profit studied may be the net profit rather than the operating profit.

were the case, some stores would remain small. The real goal is dollar profits. Business is often expanded with a decreasing ratio of profit to both sales and investment because dollar profits grow. A small store owner may make 50 percent profit on a $20,000 investment, but this is only $10,000. He may increase his investment to $200,000 over a period of time, even though his return on investment falls to 15 percent or less. But at 15 percent, the dollar profit is $30,000, and the merchant is netting three times as much as he did before. Nevertheless, to attract outside capital today, a substantial return must be earned relative to the investment.

CALCULATING RETURN ON MERCHANDISE INVESTMENT

Given: sales $100,000; stockturn at retail 5; markup 40% ; gross margin 36% of sales.

Gross margin in dollars: 36% of $100,000 = $36,000

Average retail stock: $\dfrac{\$100,000}{5} = \$20,000$

Average cost stock: 60% of $20,000 = $12,000

Gross margin % on cost stock: $\dfrac{\$36,000}{\$12,000} = 300\%$

Gross margin return per dollar of inventory at cost: $3

THE INDEX OF RETURN ON THE INVESTMENT

The profit return on the investment can be calculated not only at various profit levels but also in one of two ways. (1) In the example in the box, it is calculated at the gross margin level by *dividing the year's dollar gross margin by the average inventory at cost.* (2) It may also be calculated by *multiplying the profit margin on sales by the capital-turn.*[2] In the example, the gross margin is 36 percent of sales and the stockturn is five. As observed in the last chapter,

[2] Why it is that the product of the capital-turn and the profit on sales yields the profit on the investment may be demonstrated from the meanings of these terms:

$$\text{Capital-turn} = \frac{\$\,\text{Sales}}{\$\,\text{Average stock at cost}}$$

$$\text{and Profit on sales} = \frac{\$\,\text{Profit}}{\$\,\text{Sales}}$$

Therefore, Capital-turn × Profit on sales =

$$\frac{\$\,\text{Sales}}{\text{Average stock at cost}} \times \frac{\$\,\text{Profit}}{\$\,\text{Sales}} = \frac{\$\,\text{Profit}}{\$\,\text{Average stock at cost}}$$

the capital-turn can be found by dividing the stockturn by the complement of the markup percent. Thus, 5 divided by 60% equals 8 1/3, the capital-turn; and 36% × 8 1/3 = 300%, the gross margin as a percentage of the merchandise investment. As a formula, the return on the investment may be stated as follows:

$$\text{Profit return on investment} = \frac{\text{Stockturn}}{\text{Complement of markup \%}} \times \text{Profit on sales}$$

The above relationship makes the factors that result in a high return on investment stand out in relief. One is the ability to sell merchandise for more than the sum of its cost and its expenses, and the other is the ability to obtain a high stockturn. Even if a merchant sees no opportunity to increase his markup or to cut his expenses relative to sales, he may still earn a greater return on his investment if he increases his stockturn.

There is then a triple relationship among (1) gross margin on sales, (2) profit return, and (3) capital-turn. If two are given (either as goals or as the result of past experience), the third can be found.

COMPARISON OF RETURN ON INVESTMENT WITH RETURN ON SALES

It has been suggested that the return on the investment in merchandise is a good measure of merchandising performance; but, alone, it may be misleading. On a declining sales volume, for example, a merchant might increase his markup and cut his stock drastically. Thus, he might show a higher return than before but would be in a much worse condition with smaller dollar profits and loss of goodwill caused by inadequate stocks. For most merchants, it is more desirable to increase sales and resultant dollar profits than to aim at a maximum return on a static investment.

Nevertheless, the common practice of judging the value of classes of goods in a store by comparing their profits as a percentage of sales is also misleading. One class may show a very high profit on sales but have a low stockturn and thus only an average return on the merchandise investment. Another may show a low profit on sales but a high turn and be earning as much or more on its investment. For example, the corset department has often been singled out as one of the most profitable in the department store because of its very high gross margin on sales, but many other departments earn more on their merchandise investments because of their higher stockturns.

The return on the investment is not the only measure of overall success. A healthy operation exhibits an increasing volume of sales, a satisfactory margin of profit, and a relatively high stock-turn. These three factors mean increased dollar profits, without a proportionate increase in the merchandise investment.

An analysis of two of the ways of comparing profits—as a percentage of sales and as a percentage of the merchandise investment—leads to this conclusion: If the merchant is faced with the choice of spending one hundred dollars to promote either one of two classes of goods and the anticipated increase in sales in both instances is the same, he should promote the class that can earn the larger profit on the sales. On the other hand, if he is faced with the choice of investing one hundred dollars in either of two classes of goods, he should choose the class that can achieve the higher return on the merchandise investment.

TRENDS IN PROFIT RATIOS

Table 13.1 compares the profit figures for department stores over a six-year period. Net profit before federal income tax is expressed both as a percentage of net sales and as a percentage of net worth (capital and surplus).

The comparison reveals that profits relative to net worth are about three times as large as their relationship to sales. This indicates that sales are about three times the size of net worth in this

TABLE 13.1   Profit Relative to Investment and to Sales in Department Stores

| | Pre-Tax Earnings | | Gross Margin | | |
| | % of Capital Stock and Surplus | | Return per Dollar of Average Cost | % of Sales of Owned | |
Year	(Net worth)	% of Sales	Inventory	Departments	Stockturn
1968	16.91	5.53	2.13	38.38	3.27
1967	17.07	4.77	2.25	37.94	3.48
1966	17.01	5.50	2.11	37.42	3.35
1965	17.24	6.17	2.14	37.17	3.47
1964	15.05	5.31	2.13	36.85	3.50
1963	14.68	4.61	2.05	36.46	3.41

Source: Financial and Operating Results of Department and Specialty Store (FOR) 1968, National Retail Merchants Association, New York. (Figures based on data from 179 stores.)

type of retail operation. The return on the net worth seems to be stabilizing around 17 percent, but with no clear-cut trend in the profit to sales ratio.

In making comparisons with the merchandise investment, the gross margin is a more meaningful figure than net profit, since there is a much closer relationship between gross margin and inventory than between net profit and inventory. As the table indicates, gross margin of 38.38 percent relative to sales in 1968 resulted in a return per dollar of average cost inventory of $2.13.

Even though gross margins have increased relative to sales, along with the rising expense ratios, department stores have not succeeded in increasing their stockturns (or their capital-turns). Thus, the return on the merchandise investment has exhibited no upward trend. The sagging stockturn, in spite of increased attention to stock control, may be attributed to several factors.

Branch store operations, virtually unknown in 1953, now account for over half the sales volume of department stores. Relatively larger stocks are required to do business in different locations. For example, in a costume jewelry operation, an average stock assortment of $7,500 may be adequate to reap $30,000 of sales if concentrated in one location; but if this volume is spread over three selling units averaging $10,000 in each, a stock of $2,500 in each location will be inadequate to provide a good assortment; a stock of $3,330 may be required in each, or a total stock of $10,000. Thus, stockturn may drop from four to three.

A second influence tending to lower stockturn is the growing affluence in the economy, even though affected by cyclical changes. As customers become more affluent they become more exacting in their demands and are quicker to switch from established items to novelties. This calls for relatively broader assortments, with heavier stocks, even though there is some limitation in depth.

A third and closely related factor is the ever-increasing demand for fashion elements in lines of merchandise that were formerly considered basic in nature, such as bed sheets and men's white shirts. The assortment in sheets has greatly been expanded with a profusion of patterns in numerous colors. And white shirts that at one time accounted for 90 percent of the sales volume have more recently represented only 20 percent or even less.

REDUCING THE MERCHANDISE INVESTMENT WITHOUT SACRIFICING SALES VOLUME

An examination of the expenses and costs involved in carrying an inventory for resale indicates that they are much higher than commonly supposed. They include:

1. The rental value of the space in which the inventory is housed.
2. Maintenance costs, such as heat, light, and housekeeping.
3. Interest, insurance, and property taxes on the inventory.
4. Depreciation of the value of the inventory and fixtures.

The size of these costs and expenses in carrying an inventory (sometimes referred to as *inventory holding costs*) for staple stocks has recently been explored by Donald Edwards of Louisiana Polytechnic Institute.[3] His analysis of fourteen staple items distributed over two department stores indicated holding costs varying from 11.5 percent to 33.3 percent of the *retail* value of the average inventory, with an average of about 18 percent. He did not report the stockturn on the items, but if the average approximated six times, the holding costs would average about 3 percent of the sales of the items. On fashion goods, where obsolescence is much higher than on staples, inventory carrying costs would doubtless be considerably higher.

While most merchants are well aware of the high cost of markdowns, few realize how much it costs simply to maintain a merchandise inventory. Accordingly, a great deal of attention should be devoted to keeping the inventory as low as practicable.[4]

STRATEGIES TO REDUCE INVENTORY LEVELS

To increase the return on the merchandise investment and to keep inventory costs low, the merchant must investigate every opportunity to lower his inventory without jeopardizing sales volume or at least to increase his inventory more slowly than sales and gross margin increase. The major means to achieve this are discussed below.

Reduce the number of price lines carried. Many stores carry more price lines than are necessary to satisfy customer demand. Prices a few cents apart not only increase the stock investment but also confuse the customer. If, for example, there were six price lines of nylon hosiery between $0.79 and $2.49 and three would be sufficient, the assortment at these three price lines could be expanded while cutting the total stock investment perhaps as much as 25 percent.

---

[3] Donald E. Edwards, "Is Your Sales Dollar Being Consumed by Inventory Holding Costs?", Journal of Retailing, 45, Fall 1969, 55.
[4] The expenses of merchandise handling are also surprisingly high. Receiving, marking, internal handling, wrapping, and delivery expenses total nearly 3 percent of sales in department stores—and this does not include transportation on incoming goods, which is included in merchandise costs. The whole study of merchandise logistics is an important one but is not covered in this book.

Just how many price lines to carry is a question that cannot be answered categorically.[5] In general, three major price lines are desirable—a low, a medium, and a high. Intermediate prices are frequently needed to satisfy customer groups who differ in their willingness to pay. One women's dress chain tried selling at a single retail price but found that not enough women would buy at this one price to allow it to operate economically. A range of prices was found to be necessary.

Concentrate on key items. Many chains and discount houses achieve high return on their merchandise investments by limiting their assortments to the most popular item. They do not cater to the person looking for something different but rather to the one who follows mass demand. While stores catering to a discriminating clientele cannot follow this policy completely, they may employ the technique late in each selling season. In many localities there is some demand for summer goods as late as August, but to attempt to maintain full assortments for the latecomers means heavy inventories of summer goods at a time when fall stock is being introduced. This leads to massive markdowns a short time later. The best plan seems to be to maintain complete stocks of only the items that have proven most popular during the season. All others are not replaced when they sell down earlier in the summer season.

Reduce size or color assortments. In some cases, size and/or color assortments may be restricted without significant loss of sales. In the home furnishings field particularly, manufacturers, in their attempt to cater to many tastes in many localities, commonly offer more sizes and colors than any one store needs to carry. Yet there is a tendency for the merchant to think he should buy the entire line. But items of home furnishings seldom have to fit exactly. For example, one large store that had carried drain mats in twelve sizes found that it could satisfy virtually all customers with an assortment of five sizes. Again, a limitation of colors to the evidently popular ones may assure nearly all the business available, even though other colors sell if stocked.

In the clothing field, a reduction in color and size assortments is more risky. Recently, however, the manufacturers themselves have been simplifying size assortments by making some articles of clothing in three rather than six or more sizes, such as in shorts, undershirts, sport shirts, and raincoats. Such simplification has enabled stores to reduce greatly the assortment necessary to support a given volume of trade.

[5] See chapter 6 for a fuller discussion.

Again, end sizes may account for such a slight portion of the business as not to warrant the investment. Figure 13.1 indicates the area of active volume in shoes as determined by one store. The heavy-shaded portion is known as the *heart stock* and the light-shaded portion as the *fringe stock*. Since it is not possible to forecast demand exactly, it is better to err in the direction of overbuying on the heart stock and of underbuying on the fringe stock. This rule applies not only to sizes and widths but also to colors and brands.

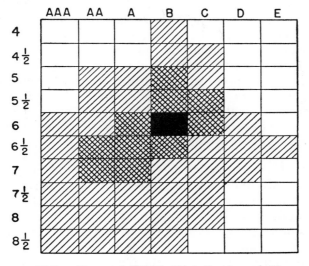

FIGURE 13.1   Size and Width Distribution of Women's Shoes in One Store

As for colors, the variety necessary depends upon the store's clientele. In general, groups with no special feeling for color are satisfied with a limited assortment of popular colors, whereas a more discriminating clientele demands a larger assortment, including in-between colors, shades, and tints.

It does not necessarily follow, however, that all stores will find it wise to reduce size and color assortments. Some stores create a personality for themselves by carrying unusual sizes and colors and draw a steady, repeat patronage from the stout, the small, or those who seek the uncommon.

In connection with size and color requirements, it should be noted that a detailed analysis of past sales alone will not provide the answer. If a pot is carried in six sizes, all may sell fairly well even though 99 percent of the customers probably would have bought had only four sizes been available. It is necessary to supplement sales analysis with imagination based upon an understanding of customer psychology.

Avoid duplicating styles and brands.   Another common practice interfering unduly with both stockturn and return on investment
is to carry a number of different styles that resemble one another so
closely that any one of them would satisfy the great majority of
customers. Items bought from different resources, often under different brand names, may be very similar. It is true that customer
demand for certain brand names may make some duplication unavoid-
able, but the practice should be kept to a minimum. One chinaware
buyer had a good system: He kept in his office a rack of the bread-
and-butter plates of every pattern he had in stock. Whenever a new
pattern was offered him, he compared it with those on the rack. If
the new pattern was very nearly the same as one he already had, he
would pass it up, even though it might have good sales potentialities.
It would simply compete with a pattern already on hand.

Manufacturers, as well as retailers, have found it possible to
reduce assortments without losing business. For example, a confec-
tionery company that once made 286 separate items reduced the number to 65 with no loss in volume.

Plan heterogeneous SKUs.   As already defined, an SKU is a
stockkeeping unit, the unit to control buying and selling. Where a
customer is not likely to accept a substitute, the SKU may be homogeneous, a specific style in a particular color and size. Where the
demand is simply for an assortment within a broader heterogeneous
category, the category may be the SKU. For example, customers
might demand an assortment of gilt pins to wear on dresses or coats
at about five dollars each but would not insist on any one of many
variations that might be stocked. Suppose, for example, that the
buyer believes he should provide about fifteen different pins to assure
the customer a nice selection. Where he to try to maintain a stock of
each pin, he might have to provide six of each to avoid running out
of a particular style before a reorder could be obtained. This would
mean an inventory of ninety pieces. Instead he regards the five-dollar
pins as the SKU and keeps perhaps forty-five in stock, filling in
assorted styles every week but not trying to keep any particular style
in stock. The customer always finds a variety from which to choose,
and the inventory is kept low.

There are many such cases where rigidity of demand does
not exist and where depth can be sacrificed to provide breadth with
a modest investment. Of course, very often the customer will not
accept a substitute for something she has in mind; here depth is
essential and it may be possible to sacrifice breadth by deleting other
items less in demand.

Keep stocks balanced to sales.   Another method of keeping stocks at a minimum is to work out a model stock and buying plan based upon sales expectations. A department may include ten subdivisions or classifications of merchandise with 25 percent of its sales volume in dollars in the largest classification and only 2 percent in the smallest. But a stock analysis may reveal that it is carrying 10 percent of its stock investment in each. In all probability, more stock could profitably be carried in the leading classification and considerably less in the least important one. By planning the stock with sales volume and customer needs in mind, a better balance can be achieved; and the reductions of stock planned in certain classifications will probably not be completely offset by increases at others. Even if the total stock were no smaller, the improved assortment might lead to an increase in sales and profits.

Buy more frequently.   When merchandise is reordered, one of the best ways to reduce stock is to reorder more frequently but in small quantities each time. This results in a small average inventory. There are some extra expenses in buying frequently and a quantity discount may be available only on large purchases, but it is possible to weight the gains against the cost.

Reduce reserve.   The extra or reserve stocks carried for many staples are sometimes larger than necessary. For example, a merchant may find that sales of a certain item are very regular at twelve a week and that he has never had to draw on more than eight pieces from his reserve of two dozen. Obviously, this reserve is much larger than necessary; one dozen is clearly enough. By cutting down such excessively high reserve stocks, it may be possible to reduce the stock investment without in any way limiting the customer in his choice of merchandise.[6]

Eliminate slow-selling merchandise.   Perhaps the most obvious way to reduce stocks without interfering with sales is to weed out slow-selling merchandise. Odds and ends tend to accumulate in every stock; a promotional sale may be held and the leftovers from the sale must be cleared out by drastic measures. When items are discontinued, broken assortments may be left on the shelves. Clearly, this merchandise is contributing very little to the current sales volume and even less in attraction value. Yet it clogs the stock and holds down the rate of return on the inventory investment. Methods of disposing of such merchandise were discussed in chapter 9.

[6] See chapter 19 for an analysis of the reserve.

SOME WAYS TO REDUCE INVENTORY WITHOUT
INTERFERING WITH SALES VOLUME

- Reduce number of price lines.
- Concentrate on key items.
- Concentrate on best-selling sizes and colors.
- Avoid duplicating items.
- Plan heterogeneous SKUs.
- Keep stocks balanced to sales in each classification.
- Buy more frequently in smaller quantities.
- Reduce unnecessarily large reserve stocks in staples.
- Eliminate slow-selling merchandise.

RETURN ON SPACE OCCUPIED

At the beginning of this chapter, it was suggested that investments in merchandise and space are the two scarce resources to be prudently used in merchandising. We have discussed the inventory investment and its costs in considerable depth. Now some attention must be given to space.

PRODUCTIVITY OF SPACE

Efficiency in the use of space may be determined by comparing the amount of space used with the sales and with the margin or markup it generates.

Sales per unit of space. Sales are customarily related to the number of square feet of selling space used to generate the sales.[7] The department store with $8 million in annual sales and one hundred thousand square feet of selling space would have sales per square foot of selling space of eighty dollars. Due to departmental differences in the sales volume, in the size of the average unit of sale, and in the variety of goods carried in the stock to satisfy customer demand, the annual sales per square foot vary greatly by selling department.

---

[7] Selling space includes space assigned to forward stock and to departmental displays, customer contacts, and sales recording. Window display space and interior display space that is rotated among different departments are not included in determining sales per square foot in selling departments, but a charge for the space is customarily made to the departments using the space. Space on the selling floors adjacent to elevators, escalators, and stairs is not usually included in selling space.

In a small china and glassware department they may be as low as twenty-five dollars per square foot a year. Higher productivity in excess of four hundred dollars per square foot is not unusual in departments such as drugs and fine jewelry.

With current recognition of the importance of making maximum use of vertical as well as horizontal space, some stores are now calculating sales per cubic foot of selling space. While the ratios are much lower than those per square foot, the cubic foot ratio tends to emphasize the importance of making use of as much vertical space as practicable for stock and display.

Sales may also be compared with the number or total square (or cubic) feet of total space occupied by the store as a whole (both selling and nonselling). But it is probably wiser to compare the ratio of selling space to total space and to attempt to keep as large a portion as possible in the selling category.[8] Traditional department stores devote about half their total space to selling, and some selling units of discount houses and supermarkets as much as 90 percent. In lines where fast stockturn is possible, the store should not be conceived as a storage place but rather as a funnel through which goods flow from producer to consumer. The policy in many stores is to have as much merchandise as possible flow from the receiving and marking area directly to the selling floor. Bulky goods such as furniture and major appliances are exceptions. They are stored in a warehouse in a location where rental values are low; accordingly, the selling area is made highly productive because the selling is done from samples.

Margin per unit of space. While in the past most analyses of the productivity of space have been limited to sales results, there is now an increasing use of the concept of the annual margin per square (or cubic) foot. Two classifications in the same department may enjoy sales of one hundred dollars a year per square foot, but the margin in the first may be 42 percent and in the second 33 percent. The first contributes forty-two dollars a square foot to expenses and profits, and the second only thirty-three dollars. Since the low markup in the second classification is likely to be due to direct competition on virtually identical items in other stores, it may be decided to move this class to space in the department where there is less public exposure, replacing it with a classification that has a higher margin and would benefit from the greater customer traffic.

---

[8] In multi-unit operations, the total nonselling space may include warehouses and administrative offices as well as the "back rooms" in the selling units. One supermarket chain reports that for every square foot of space the customer sees, it occupies almost another square foot (0.9367 sq.ft.) in space that the customer does not see.

Staple items, as well as an entire classification or department, may be located with reference to their margins relative to space. One stockkeeping unit may occupy half a square foot of shelf space and contribute annual sales of sixty dollars at a margin of 33 1/3 percent. On a square foot basis, the margin is forty dollars. Another SKU may occupy a square foot of shelf space having greater exposure and have annual sales of ninety dollars and a margin of twenty-seven dollars (30 percent). The location of the two SKUs may be reversed with extra space available in the better location for still another SKU with high margin and sales per square foot potential.

Food chains experiment in making adjustments in the amount of display space allotted to different categories within a department to determine if a reallocation of the space to the various classifications will increase the total gross margin realized in the department. For example, in one chain the standard arrangement of the dairy case and sales margin results in one unit were as follows:[9]

	Space Allotted (sq. ft.)	Sales Distribution	Weekly Margin (per sq. ft.)
Milk and cream	19	29%	$2.37
Butter	7	24	4.09
Oleomargarine	20	13	1.70
Cheese	65	29	1.25
Miscellaneous	33	5	.53
Total or average	144	100%	$1.43

The superior gross margin results on milk and butter suggest that the number of square feet devoted to these products be increased, with a corresponding reduction in the space allotted to the other products. It is generally true that an increase in display space allotted to a product increases its sales and a decrease reduces them. The problem, however, is to attain a space distribution that will bring an average margin above $1.43 a week and thus make the dairy case as a whole more productive. Controlled experiments with various allocations are the only sure way to determine a better allocation.

[9] See "Space Allocation in Dairy Cases of Retail Food Stores," a survey published by the Marketing Research Department of the American Dairy Association. Data presented reproduced with the permission of the American Dairy Association, but the authors have combined the data for various kinds of cheeses. (Original study out of print but has been included in *Retail Management Cases* by Thompson and Dalrymple, The Free Press, New York, 1969.)

There are statistical techniques where the probable results with various allocations can be simulated. Without actually conducting experiments, however, it is hard to estimate the effect on margin per square foot if space is changed. For example, to double the space allotted to milk from nineteen feet to thirty-eight feet would increase sales, but the margin for each of the thirty-eight feet is likely to be much lower than the present $2.37 realized for each of the nineteen square feet.

MAKING MAXIMUM USE OF SELLING SPACE

Below are shown major ways of increasing the productivity of space. The underlying concept is to make the entire selling area an efficient organization designed and arranged for a specific purpose: to produce a maximum of sales and margin. The third point below needs explanation. A manager may fail to put low-priced convenience items adjacent to the cash register or check-out desk. Sometimes carts and tables can be placed in wide aisles or goods can be placed on display ledges in corners that do not seriously interfere with passing traffic.

The concept of moving goods out of a location if a sales goal is not realized has long been employed by merchants in connection with aisle tables. The normal sales return on different days of the week and in different seasons can be determined for an aisle table occupying a specific location. New goods placed on the table are watched hourly. If sales fail to achieve the anticipated hourly rate, the goods are promptly removed and are replaced with something that will hopefully sell at the higher rate.

While a great deal of analysis is required, it is quite possible to set such standards of performance for different counters and shelf space and to move goods about if they fail through their sales and margin results to deserve the space to which they have been assigned.

WAYS TO MAXIMIZE THE USE OF SPACE

- Devote as much of the total space as possible to selling activities rather than to storage and nonselling functions.
- In prime shopping areas, consider assigning nonselling activities to other locations where the rental costs are much lower.
- In the space assigned to selling, eliminate unused space and space unnecessarily assigned to clerical activities within the area.

- Make use of vertical as well as horizontal space for stock and display, within the dictates of the desired store image.
- Replace outmoded ineffective fixtures with those that will produce more sales. Good fixtures expose a larger proportion of the total stock and make it less necessary to depend on salespeople to perform the entire selling job.
- Analyze sales and margins per square foot of space and relocate departments, classifications, and SKUs to realize maximum sales and dollar margins. Some ways to accomplish this are:
  a. Make seasonal changes where appropriate. For example, the normal coat department has an extremely high sales peak between November and January and is entitled to space usually devoted to other lines. Conversely, in the April-through-July period, this department would give up some of the space it normally occupies, perhaps to the swimwear department.
  b. Add new departments and classifications and drop unprofitable ones. New selling opportunities, such as car rental and travel bureau, may be in urgent need of space that may be taken from merchandise classifications that are losing customer acceptance.
  c. Set a minimum acceptable rate of sale or of dollar margin per square foot for each of the various selling locations within the store or department and move classifications and SKUs out of space where they fail to achieve an acceptable rate. Conversely, move units with a sales or margin return well in excess of the rates set for the fixtures they occupy into space to which a higher rate of return is assigned.

SPACE ALLOCATION FOR A NEW STORE

Proper allocation of space to nonselling activities and to the merchandise lines is a vital factor in every store's success, but the need for systematic planning has only recently been recognized with the proliferation of store units. With skilled study and planning the store can produce to its maximum. If a branch store is to be opened, much of the required data on which to base space allocation decisions are available from other stores already open. A completely new store may use trade association figures or other industry statistics.

The following is a procedure that may be followed in planning space for a new store:

A. *Market Survey of the Trading Area*
    Determine the demographic characteristics of the market, including analyses of the following factors:

Population—present and projected
Income
Age
Ethnic background
Occupational background
Family—size, age of children
Housing—single family or multiple
Education

B. *Survey of Competition*
   1. List stores by type and estimated volume.
   2. Estimate the total sales potential of the consumer market for the types of goods the new store is to carry.
   3. Set a share-of-market goal for the new store.

C. *Merchandising Strategy*
   1. Estimate the particular needs of the customers in the area.
   2. Determine which merchandise lines should be emphasized, de-emphasized, or omitted. (For example: If this is a young, family-oriented suburban community, the children's lines may be assigned more space than usual.)

D. *Space Allocation Analysis*
   1. Based on the merchandising strategy, predict the sales of each line as a percentage of the store's total sales. While the actual performance of other stores in the group will be used as a guide, this new store's sales distribution is made in accordance with particular characteristics of its consumer market.
   2. Predict total store sales based on the share-of-market goal, taking into account existing and projected competition.
   3. Calculate each department's sales by applying its estimated percentage of store sales to the predicted dollar sales of the store as a whole.
   4. Set productivity standards. Based on other stores' sales per square foot, each department is given a standard of productivity. (For example: The store's total may be set at $75 per square foot of selling space and main floor sportswear at $100.)
   5. Now divide the productivity goal into the planned dollar sales for the department to calculate the preliminary space allocation. (Example: If sales for main floor sportswear are estimated at 3 percent of the store's total of $8 million, or $240,000, and if productivity is set at $100 per square foot, the space allocation would be 2,400 square feet. (Some adjustment may be necessary to accommodate all the departments to be located on one floor.)
   6. Adding up the total department space allocations will *not* equal the store's total selling space available. It should be close, however, and the reconciliation of the figures to the fixed total is a matter of mathematics or judgment. (For example: If all departments totaled 127,000 square feet and only 120,000 were available for selling, a simple proportionate reduction of about 5 percent would bring the departments into line.) Where a

new facility is being built, the space planner may be able to adjust his plans to provide for all the selling space desirable and also to provide for necessary nonselling operations.

QUESTIONS FOR DISCUSSION

1. Is a retail operation healthy if the profit on net worth is increasing while the profit as a percentage of sales is decreasing?

2. If the merchandise inventory is half of total assets and is then reduced 10 percent, with no change in the dollar profits, what is the change in the return on the total assets?

3. In determining the ratio of profit to merchandise investment, which profit figure is most useful: (1) maintained markup, (2) gross margin, (3) contribution profit, (4) operating profit, (5) net profit before federal taxes, or (6) net profit after taxes? Why?

4. Since the return on the merchandise investment, calculated at the gross margin level, equals the capital-turn times the gross margin percentage (on sales),
   (a) Find the capital-turn in terms of the return on the merchandise investment and the gross margin percentage.
   (b) Find the gross margin percentage in terms of the capital-turn and the return on the investment.
   (c) How might the relationships found in *a* and *b* above be used in planning?

5. What reasons can you suggest to explain why small department stores (under $1 million) have sometimes shown larger profits relative to net worth than have large stores?

6. Suggest specific ways of reducing the cost of maintaining retail inventory without reducing the size or value of the inventory itself.

7. Of the various ways suggested of reducing inventory without interfering with sales opportunity, which are the more practical?

8. What kinds of stores should concentrate on key items in the assortment? Why?

9. Are the opportunities of reducing size variations in the assortment increasing or decreasing? Defend your answer.

10. Give examples of merchandise categories in which the SKUs should represent heterogeneous components.

11. How might the coordination of colors in related merchandise be effective in increasing the return on the merchandise investment?

12. In determining departmental selling space, how should the following areas be handled: aisles between departments, space in front of elevators and escalators, platforms and display fixtures rotated among different departments, aisle tables in main traffic corridors that feature different lines?

13. Is the productivity of space a responsibility of the buyer, the department manager, or the operating superintendent?

14. What merchandise characteristics result in high sales and high gross margin per square foot of selling space occupied?

Since a major aim of retail merchandising is to maintain proper merchandise assortment —the balance between sales and stocks that will contribute to both profit and growth—planning and control are essential. Planning sets the objectives for sales, inventories, purchases, and other profit factors; and control ensures that the plans are followed or adjusted in view of the unfolding situation. To be a viable, valid tool, the merchandise plan must be dynamic, continuously reflecting the current trends and developments.

On the store and department levels, planning and control are expressed in dollars and cover the major elements entering into profit: sales, markups, markdowns, inventories, purchases, and expenses. On the merchandise classification level, planning is often limited to sales, stocks, and purchases in dollars, but in some stores markups and markdowns by classification are also planned and controlled.

On the price line and SKU levels, the planning is done in units or pieces of merchandise and is generally limited to sales and stocks. Merchandise classifications may also be planned in units as well as in dollars.

Part IV deals with dollar planning and control on the store, department, and classification levels, whereas Part V deals with unit planning and control, largely on price line and other SKU levels.

part IV

MERCHANDISE

PLANNING

AND

CONTROL

IN DOLLARS

243

14

MERCHANDISE
ANALYSIS
BY
DEPARTMENT
AND
CLASSIFICATION

Dollar sales and stocks may be analyzed and controlled (1) for the store as a whole, (2) for separate departments, and (3) for separate merchandise classifications, sometimes called categories.

Where the merchandising is performed by buyers or department managers rather than by the merchant himself, departmental and also classification sales and stock records become important as a guide, especially in view of the large volume and complexity of the merchandise carried. But even in a small store, control by classification is being increasingly depended upon to maintain balanced stocks.

DEPARTMENTIZING

Many stores that are not commonly called department stores are, nevertheless, departmentized. A small drug store, for example, may have separate departments for prescriptions, soda fountain, and drug sundries.

Store and departmental records of sales and stock are readily obtained by the retail method of inventory. The value of the sales is totaled daily from sales registers that may be tied into a computer and from saleschecks, and book stock figures are available as frequently as desired, since a perpetual inventory must be maintained in connection with the retail method. It is also necessary to keep records of orders placed. This is done by keeping duplicate copies of orders in a file and moving to a closed file orders that have been filled. Some stores also maintain an order register on which all orders are entered and totaled as they are placed. Stores not on the retail method analyze cost rather than retail inventory records; but, as explained in chapter 10, it is harder to maintain accurate perpetual inventory records at cost.

Departments are set up to manage buying, pricing, and selling activities more precisely and to attract customers more effectively. The groupings must be small enough to insure that a single executive (buyer or department manager) is responsible for the group, and they must be large enough to enable merchandise managers to avoid the necessity of studying a great many detailed figures and yet to spot weak points in the operation readily.

DEPARTMENTIZING AND THE INITIAL MARKUP

In addition to the problem of having a department small and yet large enough to insure efficient management, the retail method of inventory sets up a control requirement. The markup of the different items in the department should not vary greatly, or there should be good reason to believe that both high markup and low markup merchandise represented in the closing inventory are in proportion to their representation in the total merchandise handled. If the difference in the markup on the merchandise in the closing inventory varies considerably from the markup on the merchandise handled, the closing cost inventory will be either understated or overstated and profits distorted (see chapter 11).

SALES DEVELOPMENT

Better management and control are not the only reasons for departmentizing and for setting up classifications. The effect on sales is of equal or even greater importance. The physical concentration of related stock makes it easier for customers to purchase. Furthermore, departmentizing focuses attention on a particular class of goods. Today, target selling is receiving a great deal of attention. Instead of appealing to everyone, offerings are aimed at a particular segment of customers. For instance, by establishing a riding-habit department, a store can attract patronage more readily than it could if this merchandise were included in the suit department; it aims directly at those who ride.

The opening of a teen-age department for girls who feel themselves no longer children but who are hardly "misses" is a great force in attracting their patronage; they have shied away from the children's department, but they do not feel at home in the misses' department, where much of the merchandise is unsuitable. Many stores have had great success with their "sub-deb" shops. If there are many customers interested in sports, it may be desirable to open a sportswear department carrying dresses, coats, sweaters, hosiery, shoes, and other accessories. The ensemble idea can be expressed, and conflicting appeals or suggestions of other departments, each carrying only one of these lines, can be eliminated.

The establishment of the boutique is a newer version of market segmentation. Certain customers want to browse through a selection of early American antiques; others want to inspect Italian handicraft; and still others Mexican *objets d'art*. Style shops are also set up to cater to those interested in certain fashion characteristics, such as the mod look, the tailored look, or the Edwardian look. These categories and many others are set up as selling departments to focus the attention of particular segments of the public and to create for them an interesting atmosphere.

Sometimes it is desirable, even necessary, to establish seasonal departments. For example, a gift shop may be opened about the middle of October and carried as a separate department only through December. One store runs a department for party favors through the fall and winter months.

Budget departments.   Two long-established examples of departmentizing in order to appeal to different customer groups are the budget floor departments and the deluxe departments. The budget departments cater to a lower-income group than that attracted to the regular departments. Should the latter introduce lower price ranges to cater to this price conscious trade, they would run the risk of losing their more quality- and service-minded clientele.

Some budget operations feature job lots, but the tendency is in the direction of carrying regular lines. Thus, the budget floor becomes a distinct store, often with different service standards, aiming at its own distinct clientele.

Deluxe departments.   Deluxe departments, on the other hand, have been established in many stores to cater to a more discriminating and higher-income group than that reached by the regular departments. Many patrons of specialty shops will not patronize the regular departments of stores because of the fear that the merchandise will become popularized too quickly. They prefer to deal directly with the manager of a shop and not with salespeople. Deluxe departments, each with a separate buyer and entirely divorced from the regular departments, attract them. Such a department realizes sales from a class of customers that could not be reached otherwise and affords a good talking point for publicity. It provides a high markup and often yields large profits. It acts as a proving ground for acceptance by the fashion leaders, making it possible for the buyers of the regular departments to forecast more accurately.

The difficulty with such a deluxe department is to fit it into the store system. Some store rules should not apply to it because it should be on the footing of a specialty shop and have a buyer-manager who has a high level of taste and creativity. This type should not be unduly curbed by a store system that may be desirable in the regular departments.

In conclusion, in determining whether or not to departmentize on a basis of sales possibilities, the management should first consider the availability of a suitable manager, of a suitable location, and of sufficient capital. It should also avoid undue duplication of existing departments. There should be a good reason for duplication, whenever it is attempted, such as convenience to the customer and greater volume growing out of a specialized appeal or out of an appeal to a special class of customers. Most importantly, it should consider the potential demand on the part of a substantial group of customers for a distinct selling unit in the store that features the class of merchandise in question.

THE DEPARTMENT VERSUS THE MERCHANDISE CLASSIFICATION

A merchandise classification is a major subdivision of a merchandise department for which separate dollar sales records, and commonly cost of sales records, are maintained but to which expenses are not charged. Thus, classification planning and control normally end at the gross margin level rather than at the operating profit or department contribution levels.

Now that the computer is available to facilitate the preparation of detailed records, the classification is taking the place of the department for the analysis and planning of sales, inventories, purchases, and pricing. By manual methods, it was formerly arduous to analyze merchandising data by merchandise categories within each department, but with the computer each department can readily be broken down into many subclasses, averaging five or more per department. However, it is usually not feasible, even with the computer, to eliminate departments in favor of classifications. It is difficult to allocate direct expenses to classifications because salespeople commonly sell in all or a number of different classifications and because buyers and department managers supervise entire departments, not single classifications. Also, buyers may need latitude in making shifts in purchases among the classifications under their jurisdiction.

As the number of classifications is increased, each should become increasingly homogeneous, with the goods in each tending to be substitutable for one another in satisfying customer demand. But when this point is actually reached, the breakdowns are so narrow that they can be controlled more effectively in units rather than in terms of dollar value.

Dollar control by departments and classifications as contrasted with unit control is important not only to the department manager (or buyer) but also to the merchandise manager who supervises a group of departments. The department manager is guided in his day-to-day operations chiefly by unit plans and records, but he is expected to show the results of his buying and selling activities in terms of his success in reaching dollar objectives. Thus, he must have a hand in the planning of these objectives and maintain the proper dollar balance among his many purchases. His supervisor, the merchandise manager, is primarily interested in the dollar plans and results. He has neither the time nor the expertise to determine whether each purchase decision, involving a host of variations in items, is a good one, but he wants to make sure that the dollar sales realized, the markdowns taken, the dollar purchases made, the dollar inventories carried, the overall markup percentage achieved, and the direct expenses incurred are all in line with the plans to assure a profitable balance among these factors.

Thus, dollar control is a tool for both the merchandise manager and the department manager or buyer, whereas unit control is chiefly a tool for the department manager or buyer.

ESTABLISHING CLASSIFICATIONS

The nature of the inventory assortment comprising a merchandise classification in one store may be identical with goods comprising a department within another. As volume in a general class

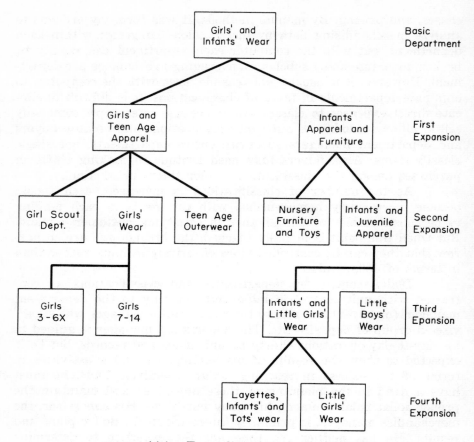

FIGURE 14.1   Expanding a Basic Department

of goods grows, groups of goods that were formerly classifications become separate departments. Thus, a dress department with a single buyer may have the following classifications: (1) women's and misses' dresses, (2) budget dresses, (3) junior dresses, (4) bridals and formals, and (5) maternity shop. As the operation grows, these may become separate departments, each with its own buyer. Figure 14.1 depicts this fanning out process. Whether to call the subdivisions departments or classifications depends upon the degree of sales development and the physical separation possible. If salespeople sell in all or in a number of them, if one department manager supervises a number or all of them, and if advertisements feature merchandise in more than one grouping, the categories are being treated as classifications. When a manager and a group of salespeople devote all of their attention to a single category and when direct expenses at least are charged to that category, the grouping is being treated as a department.

STANDARDIZED MERCHANDISE CLASSIFICATIONS

To permit accurate comparisons with other stores, there must be standardization as to what merchandise to include in a department and in each of its merchandise classifications. If one store carries only costume jewelry in its jewelry department and another carries both costume jewelry and fine jewelry including watches, comparisons are almost meaningless. Stores—even small ones—are making increasing use of computer centers for an analysis of departmental and classification data. Reporting by such centers is greatly facilitated if all the stores serviced make use of the same departmental and classification groupings.

To provide such standards for general merchandise, a committee of the National Retail Merchants Association has developed a *Merchandise Classification Manual* that has received wide acceptance. In making decisions as to what specific lines to include in each class, the committee gave attention to substitutability in "end use" and to homogeneity. The goods in a classification, except for size variations, should be limited so far as practicable to those items of merchandise that an undecided customer might be interested in comparing before making a buying decision. Thus, a customer looking for a dining room table might be interested in dining tables at different prices, styles, and finishes but would not be interested in bedroom furniture or occasional pieces. Again, a customer interested in a high quality drapery fabric would not be interested in inexpensive materials. Thus, higher price lines may well be set up as the better drapery classification. Or if there is a new fashion demand for bulky knit sweaters, they should be set up as a special classification in the sweater department, so long as the active demand lasts. Brand may sometimes be a suitable basis for classification, if certain brands have a loyal following of customers who would not consider buying another brand. The store's own private brand may also be made a separate classification.

In addition to trying to limit the goods in a classification so that they are homogeneous from the point of view of the customer, the goods included should have certain other similarities: in markup, in markdown risk, in stockturn, in seasonal activity, in their use as leaders, and in their need for alterations. If the units comprising the classification differ materially in the above respects, it will be difficult to analyze the data to determine what the real problems are. For example, a stock with a retail value of $6,000 may seem adequate in a certain classification in midsummer. But if it consists of $4,000 worth of goods that are in demand primarily in the spring and only $2,000 worth that are in demand in the summer and early fall, it is clear that the data revealed by the hybrid classification is of little value.

METHODS OF COMPILING CLASSIFICATION DATA

There are two distinct methods of obtaining sales and stock information by classification: perpetual inventory and periodic physical inventory.

PERPETUAL INVENTORY METHOD

By the perpetual inventory method, information is derived from sales and purchase records rather than from an actual count of the physical inventory. A complete retail method of inventory may be operated for each classification, as explained in chapter 11, or the procedure may stop short with an analysis of sales and inventories but not of markup. Classification numbers or letters are marked on price tickets, and the information is transferred to cash registers or to sales checks. Invoices are similarly marked with classification numbers (preferably a separate invoice is required for each classification), and markdowns are also classified. Thus a separate initial markup and a separate gross margin may be determined for each classification. From the standpoint of records, such a classification would differ from a separate department only in the fact that expenses would not be allocated to it.

A simpler variation of this plan is to classify sales records, markdown records, and invoices and to maintain a running record by classification of stock on hand as above, but to compute no separate markup for each classification. Under this method the classification records are for the purpose of analyzing sales and stocks and not of determining gross margin by these divisions. If a merchant decides to use the perpetual inventory method of classification control, it would seem desirable to apply the retail method of inventory to each classification because of the additional information regarding profits that can be had at very little additional expense.

Computer operation. As sales are recorded on the cash register by classification, a tape is automatically prepared that can be read by the computer and can provide sales analysis by classification. Data for analysis, such as purchases, transfers, inventory, and price change information are recorded by classification not at the point of sale but in a back room and fed into the computer by similar means.

Former manual methods of recording sales by class, such as having salespeople write the classification numbers on price ticket stubs or maintain a tally near the cash register, are becoming obsolete as the newer sales registers come into use. These handle not only cash-take sales but all other types as well, with saleschecks being inserted into the machine. Thus, all sales data clears through the register.

Data processing centers. The National Retail Merchants Association has been instrumental in setting up two electronic processing centers primarily to provide member stores with classification data.[1] Stores send in their sales, purchase, inventory, and markdown data by standardized classification numbers. The center then sends the stores a variety of reports. A major one, usually issued every month, is reproduced in figure 14.2. The exhibit covers ten classifications within a departmental grouping. These are called *codes* on the chart. Sales, purchases (additions to inventory), and inventories are reported in both dollars and in units of merchandise sold, received, and on hand.[2] The opening inventory figures in each classification are reported semiannually or annually by the stores, and the inventory data for the intervening months represent estimated physical inventory figures calculated by the computer. The inventory adjustments represent estimated shortages primarily. The columns headed "additions to inventory" include purchase adjustments, and in the retail column, additional markups less additional markup cancellations.

The comparison of the sales distribution by classification compared with the present inventory distribution is particularly significant for merchandising control. Note, for example, that only 13.8 percent of the department's season sales to date were in classification 438 but that 30.1 percent of the ending retail inventory is invested at that point. This classification would seem to be overstocked. Note the other points spotlighted on the chart to indicate weak spots.

---

[1] Retail Electronic Systems, 100 Park Avenue, Staten Island, N.Y. 10302. This organization also has a California office.

[2] The units approximate the number of items, but multiple units may be recorded with a single entry on the records.

RES Reports Tell The Whole Story . .

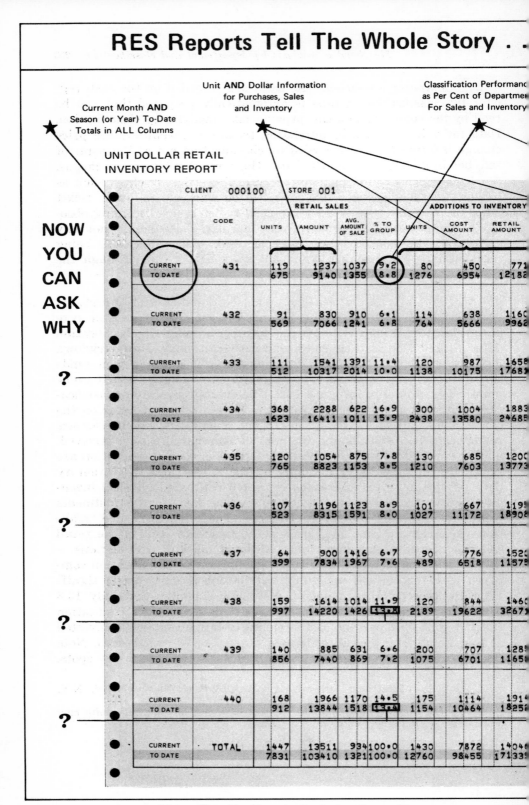

Unit **AND** Dollar Information
for Purchases, Sales
and Inventory

Classification Performance
as Per Cent of Department
For Sales and Inventory

Current Month **AND**
Season (or Year) To-Date
Totals in ALL Columns

UNIT DOLLAR RETAIL
INVENTORY REPORT

CLIENT 000100   STORE 001

NOW
YOU
CAN
ASK
WHY

? ? ? ?

	CODE	RETAIL SALES				ADDITIONS TO INVENTORY		
		UNITS	AMOUNT	AVG. AMOUNT OF SALE	% TO GROUP	UNITS	COST AMOUNT	RETAIL AMOUNT
CURRENT	431	119	1237	1037	9·2	80	450	771
TO DATE		675	9140	1355	8·8	1276	6954	12182
CURRENT	432	91	830	910	6·1	114	638	1160
TO DATE		569	7066	1241	6·8	764	5666	9962
CURRENT	433	111	1541	1391	11·4	120	987	1658
TO DATE		512	10317	2014	10·0	1138	10175	17689
CURRENT	434	368	2288	622	16·9	300	1004	1883
TO DATE		1623	16411	1011	15·9	2438	13580	24685
CURRENT	435	120	1054	875	7·8	130	685	1200
TO DATE		765	8823	1153	8·5	1210	7603	13773
CURRENT	436	107	1196	1123	8·9	101	667	1198
TO DATE		523	8315	1591	8·0	1027	11172	18908
CURRENT	437	64	900	1416	6·7	90	776	1520
TO DATE		399	7834	1967	7·6	489	6518	11575
CURRENT	438	159	1614	1014	11·9	120	844	1460
TO DATE		997	14220	1426	13·8	2189	19622	32673
CURRENT	439	140	885	631	6·6	200	707	1288
TO DATE		856	7440	869	7·2	1075	6701	11650
CURRENT	440	168	1966	1170	14·5	175	1114	1914
TO DATE		912	13844	1518	13·4	1154	10464	18252
CURRENT	TOTAL	1447	13511	934	100·0	1430	7872	14046
TO DATE		7831	103410	1321	100·0	12760	98455	171339

FIGURE 14.2   Classification Analysis by Computer

. Compare These Five Star Features!

Adjustments To Inventory
Exposed - Not Buried
In Sales or Purchases

Months On Hand
(Stock-Sales Ratio)
For Each Classification

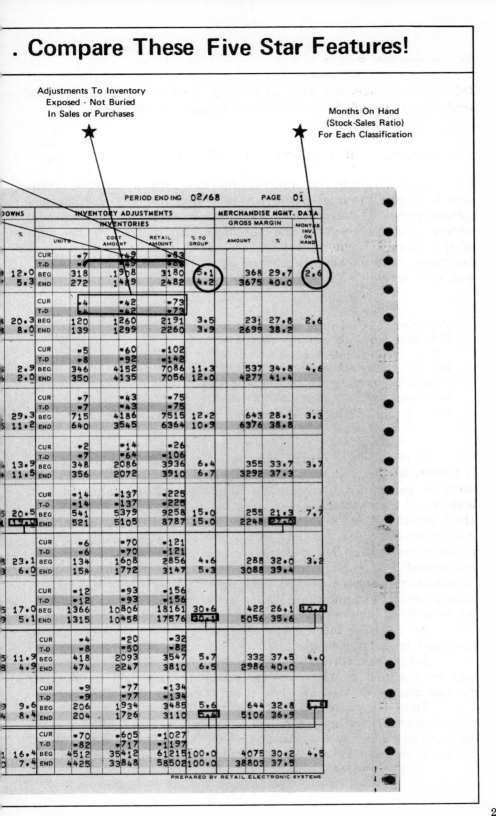

Other associations are also sponsoring similar central processing centers; an example is the Menswear Retailers of America.

PERIODIC PHYSICAL INVENTORY METHOD

In contrast to the perpetual inventory method, where inventory is derived from sales and purchase data, the periodic physical inventory method derives sales from inventory and purchase data by adding opening inventory and purchases and subtracting the sum of the closing inventory and markdowns. Retail inventories, retail purchases, and markdowns may be analyzed for each classification, and sales derived, as follows:

February 1, retail stock on hand in a classification	$ 5,000
February 1 to July 1, retail purchases	10,000
Total merchandise handled	$15,000
July 1, retail stock on hand	6,000
February 1 to July 1, sales and reductions	$ 9,000
February 1 to July 1, markdowns	1,000
Derived sales (including shortages)	$ 8,000

If the average rate of shortages for the store or department is known, the derived sales may be divided by 100 percent plus the shortage percentage to determine the estimated net sales. In this instance, if the shortages determined for the department as a whole are 2 percent of net sales, $8,000 may be divided by 102 percent to give estimated sales of $7,843 on the theory that the shortages are probably evenly distributed over all the classifications. In practice, an adjustment for shortages is not necessary in computing sales by classification since the derived sales figures of all would include the same percentage of shortage. Where gross margin is to be calculated for each class, however, shortages should be considered.

An analysis for a men's furnishings store that disregards shortages appears in figure 14.3.

Retail inventories, cost and retail purchases, and markdowns may be analyzed by classification, and both sales and maintained markup may be derived for each classification, as shown below.

Thus, except for a possible error in the shortage estimate, the maintained markup figure for each classification may be found without analyzing sales by classification. Once the system is in operation, the stock on hand at cost at the beginning of the period is found

	Cost	Retail	Percentage
February 1, stock on hand	$3,000	$ 5,000	
February 1 to July 31, purchases	6,000	10,000	
Total stock	$9,000	$15,000	40.0
July 31, retail stock on hand		6,000	
July 31, cost stock on hand ($6,000 × 60%)	3,600		
February 1 to July 31, sales and reductions		$ 9,000	
February 1 to July 31, markdowns		1,000	
Sales and shortages		$ 8,000	102.0
Estimated sales ($8,000 ÷ 1.02)		7,843	100.0
Gross cost of merchandise sold	5,400		
Maintained markup	$ 2,443		31.1

from the retail by applying the initial markup for the preceding period then ending. When the system is being first introduced into a store or department already on the retail method, the cost may be determined from a study of invoices on hand or (for internal control purposes solely as distinct from official income tax reports) by assuming that the initial markup of the store or department as a whole applies to each classification. The actual differences in markup will come to light as the purchases are accumulated at both cost and retail.

It will be noted that the classification data based on periodic inventories require that only three records by classification be kept: (1) inventories, (2) purchases (including returns and transfers), and (3) markdowns. Physical inventories should be taken whether or not a classification control is kept. Classifying the goods, and listing each classification on a separate group of sheets, add little to the cost of inventory taking. In the case of purchases, it does require slightly more clerical work to extend invoice amounts charged to each department to classification columns, however, and it may require a larger number of invoices from vendors if it is decided to require vendors to make out separate invoices for each classification. As for markdowns, all that is required is that the buyer indicate the classification number, as well as the department number, on each markdown requisition and that the markdowns be totaled by these divisions.

COMPARISON OF PERPETUAL AND PERIODIC METHODS

A comparison of the two fundamental methods of obtaining merchandise statistics by classification indicates that the perpetual inventory control method has the following advantages:

FIGURE 14.3   Classification Analysis at Retail

Men's Furnishings—Period: July 1 to July 31

| | Total | | Classifications | | | | | | | | |
		1	2	3	4	5	6	7	8	9
Inventory July 1	$5,000	$500	$350	$1,150	$750	$250	$1,000	$500	$100	$400
Purchases and transfers in	2,000	100	200	300	100	500	100	100	500	100
	$7,000	$600	$550	$1,450	$850	$750	$1,100	$600	$600	$500
Less inventory July 31	4,000	400	250	1,200	600	220	700	430	100	100
Sales and markdowns	$3,000	$200	$300	$250	$250	$530	$400	$170	$500	$400
Markdowns	300	50	40	....	20	30	100	25	....	35
Sales	$2,700	$150	$260	$250	$230	$500	$300	$145	$500	$365
Sales % of total	100%	5.5%	9.6%	9.3%	8.5%	18.5%	11.1%	5.4%	18.5%	13.6%
Average inventory % of total	100%	10.0%	6.7%	26.1%	15.0%	5.2%	18.8%	10.4%	2.2%	5.6%

1. It readily provides a daily or weekly, and cumulative, record of sales by classification.
2. It provides stock figures by classification as often as they are desired without taking a physical inventory.
3. By providing continual information about sales and stocks, it makes it possible to take action as soon as a maladjustment develops rather than at the end of a season or of a month, when it may be too late to remedy the situation.

Until recently, the perpetual inventory system had the disadvantage of requiring arduous and error-prone sales analysis by class. With the general use of the newer registers and of the computer, these objections have largely been overcome.

In conclusion, it would seem that when a computer is available—perhaps at a processing center—a perpetual inventory method based on current sales analysis can be maintained accurately and at a low cost. When the cost is high and the equipment is not available, the periodic method may be used. Either one represents a decided advance over the general practice of mere departmental control.

QUESTIONS FOR DISCUSSION

1. Name some merchandise departments in which an apparently satisfactory markup and balance between sales and stocks would be very misleading because of great differences in the nature of the merchandise classifications included in the department.
2. Do you agree with the following statement: Unit control is primarily a tool to assist the buyer in maintaining an assortment balanced to customer demand, whereas dollar control is primarily a tool to assist the merchandise manager in supervising the operations of the buyers under him?
3. (a) Is market segmentation becoming more or less important to retailers? Defend your position.
   (b) Give examples of new departments or classifications that have been set up to appeal to comparatively narrow target groups of customers. Include a number of seasonal shops.
4. Chart the fanning out process in connection with a basic blouse and sportswear department or any other department of your choice.
5. Similarity of end use by a particular group of customers has been suggested as the chief basis for setting up merchandise classifications. Manually operated and electric can openers both have the same end use and range in price from twenty-five cents to nearly twenty dollars. Would you include them all in one classification? Can you think of other examples where the question of substitutability is not in itself a sufficient basis for setting up classifications?
6. (a) Under what conditions would you recommend that a store or

department make use of the periodic inventory method of classification analysis and control?

(b) If the only records kept for each classification are inventories every six months, purchases, and markdowns, what facts and important relationships can be determined semiannually?

(c) Are there circumstances that would justify the use of both the perpetual and the periodic inventory methods concurrently in the same classification?

7. What do you think will be the future developments in communicating sales and other merchandising data by classification to processing centers?

8. Does classification control simply raise questions or does it also provide answers? (Refer to figure 14.2.)

15

SALES
PLANNING

The most critical merchandising decision that a merchant must make is the forecasting of his sales. Every other element of the business, such as capital investment, number of employees, and quantity of merchandise, is always planned in relation to sales.

When a company is faced with a choice to build or not to build a new branch or other selling facility, it must be able to predict the sales and the ultimate profit that the new store will yield on its capital investment. If the sales actually realized are considerably below plan, the company may find itself in a precarious financial situation.

Similarly, the manager of a toy store or department must order most of his toy stock at least six months ahead of his Christmas season's needs. If the predicted sales on which his purchases are based are not realized, he may not be able to pay his bills and he may find himself out of business.

LONG- AND SHORT-RANGE SALES PLANNING

LONG-RANGE PLANNING

The sales forecast is the key element in planning, whether for a good many years ahead or for the coming season. Long-range planning involves looking ahead at least five years and setting policies and objectives—matters already discussed in chapter 2.

In looking ahead, it is important to recognize where the organization is currently located in its life history. The life history of a business concern from a sales standpoint resembles that depicted in figure 15.1. After a period of uncertainty in early infancy is survived (*a*), sales are likely to increase for a time at about the same *rate* each year (*b*), they flatten out into an upward straightline trend (*c*), they just hold their own for some years (*d*), there is a decline (*e*), this will lead to abandonment of the business (*f*), unless there

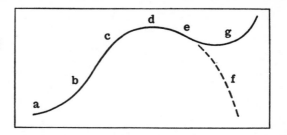

FIGURE 15.1   Life History of a Business

is a radical revision in policies, a complete reorganization that will allow a revival of business, and the beginning of a new cycle of business life (*g*). Cyclical fluctuations, not depicted, will of course also occur, caused by changes in the price level and by recurring periods of depression and prosperity. The secular trend depicted covers a number of complete cycles. It represents the underlying long-time tendency (represented by the *b*, *c*, *d*, and *e* sections in figure 15.1) to grow or decline. It is independent of the short-time tendencies of expansion and recession.

Many retail businesses today are in the *e* stage, especially if sales are measured in transactions. Radical changes in policies and procedures are increasingly demanded for survival and renewed growth.

An orderly procedure for long-range planning involves the following steps:

1. Making a decision—on the part of management—to adapt its policies, methods, and preconceived beliefs promptly to keep pace with the rapid changes taking place in its environment.

2. Undertaking a self-study to determine objectively the true characteristics of the organization at present and how it arrived where it is today. This will include a review of policies and procedures, store image as seen by various customer groups, and perti-

nent figure relationships, particularly those that measure sales, margins, expenses and productivity of investment, space occupied, and people.

3. Projecting the probable characteristics of the store's evolving trading area looking five to ten years ahead. The findings and projections of outside agencies, such as community planning groups, may be drawn upon at this point. The entire country may be a national chain's trading area, but plans will be made for each city and its environs in which the chain now functions or in which it may function in the future.

4. In view of its philosophy and expertise, management envisioning itself in this trading area of the future, deciding how and where it should expand, what policies and practices it should change, and what adjustments it should make in its merchandise mix. This is the most difficult step in the planning process.

5. Making a sales forecast and setting related performance goals, such as gross margin ratio, stockturn, and sales per square foot. On a long-range basis these are generally set for the organization as a whole rather than for individual selling departments. In looking five to ten years ahead, it is helpful to make use of statistical methods in determining the trend of sales over a similar length of time in the past.[1] But probable changes in both outside and inside conditions must be given even greater weight. While a reasonable degree of accuracy in planning is necessary in order to make commitments for expanded space and for the employment of executive personnel, exact sales forecasts need not be attempted.

In a branch or chain store system, forecasts will be made for each branch or unit on a long-range basis as indicated in table 15.1. Note that the increases planned for the various branches differ considerably from the overall expectations.

6. Selling the plans made for the evolving organization to middle management, with each department head responsible for suggesting and implementing the immediate steps that should be taken within his area of responsibility so that goals may be achieved on

---

[1] Since these methods of forecasting are covered in courses and texts on statistics, they are not presented in this book. Useful references include: William Copulsky, *Practical Sales Forecasting*, American Management Association, Inc., 1970, 109 pages (especially chapters on "A Survey of Product Demand Forecasting Methods," "Simple Numerical Techniques," "Forecasting the Economy," and "Example of Simple Model Forecasting"); also *Time Series Forecasting; A New Computer Technique for Company Sales Forecasting*, American Marketing Association, 1962, 72 pages; and *Forecasting Sales*, National Industrial Conference Board, New York, 1963, 109 pages.

target. Managers should be assured of a personal reward if they cooperate in achieving the goals. It should be observed that no plan has any merit unless it calls for some immediate steps towards an ultimate goal.

TABLE 15.1   Sales Projections: Company Y

Store Location	Sales in Millions of Dollars				Percentage Increase 1970–80
	1965[a]	1970[a]	1975[b]	1980[b]	
Downtown	18.2	20.2	21.0	23.0	14
Eastport	10.0	16.1	19.5	22.0	37
Southport	8.5	14.1	16.0	18.0	28
Westport	8.0	10.2	12.5	14.0	37
Northport	—	7.1	9.0	12.0	70
Midland (new)	—	—	6.0	9.0	50 (Over '75)
Company Total	44.7	67.7	84.0	98.0	45

[a] Actual
[b] Projected

7. Reviewing—at least annually—the results of the plans made and of the steps already taken toward the goals set. This analysis may lead to changes in the plan itself and determine the steps to be taken toward revising the plan for the coming year. Five or ten years from now the organization may reach a point quite different from the one originally envisioned, but it will be in a much stronger position than it would have been in if had it simply drifted along. Such frequent revisions of long-range planning may be thought of as *intermediate* plans, falling between the long-range plans and the short-range plans discussed below.

SHORT-RANGE PLANNING

Short-range plans may be made for one or two selling seasons ahead or simply for a few days or weeks. The seasonal plans are generally made on a departmental or merchandise classification basis and then checked against storewide estimates. Failure to look ahead at least for a number of months leads to improvised sales effort and to unbalanced stocks.

Seasonal forecasts in dollars. The seasonal plan in dollars is closely related in point of time to the placing of orders in the wholesale markets; it is prepared far enough ahead to allow ample time to shop the market, place orders, and receive the goods into stock as needed. Since few categories of merchandise are ordered more than six months ahead and since many items purchased for the fall and winter season differ materially from those for the spring and summer season, the six-month planning period has become the standard for many stores.[2]

Forecasts in units of merchandise.   Forecasts in units are made a few days to a few months ahead depending upon the time required for delivery to the store and the frequency of reorder considered desirable. The purpose of unit forecasting is to calculate the correct quantity of each item to order.[3]

In the rest of this chapter we shall examine the forecasting of dollar sales for a season to a year ahead. We shall first consider the established store and then the new store.

PLANNING SALES FOR THE GOING STORE OR DEPARTMENT

TOP-DOWN PLANNING

The forecasting of sales in connection with merchandise planning for a coming season or year may be approached from the top down or the bottom up. Top-down planning means that top management sets overall sales goals based on trends, changes in policies, and appraisal of outside conditions. These are broken down into plans for each department and, if a chain or branch system, into sales for each store and for each department in each store. If there is central buying, departmental sales plans include the sales in all the selling units. Buyers and department managers have their goals set for them by higher authority and can only make suggestions for possible adjustment in the figures presented to them.

Although annual sales plans made by the top-down approach based on statistical and economic analysis may often prove to be very close to the actual sales volume for the store as a whole, they are frequently inaccurate for individual departments. Top management is not usually close enough to the forces that influence the sale of various merchandise lines to make intelligent distinctions among departments regarding their ability to increase sales volume. Thus, management may erroneously assume that each department's percentage of sales increase should be the same as that of the store as a whole. In a group of large department stores, for example, the

---

[2] Certain variations from this period are discussed in chapter 17.
[3] This matter is discussed in chapters 19 and 20.

planned total sales increase of 2 percent was achieved, but only four of sixty-two different departments realized the average 2 percent increase. Eight departmental lines had a decline in sales; piano and musical instruments suffered a 26 percent decrease. On the other hand, six departments showed an increase of over 10 percent, with the pattern department 21 percent ahead. Arbitrary departmental sales plans lead to unrealistic stock plans which result in a store's failure to optimize profits.

BOTTOM-UP PLANNING

With bottom-up planning, each buyer plans the sales for his department, whether it be located in one store or in many selling outlets. Similarly, department managers in selling units make their own forecasts which are totaled and checked against the buyers' forecasts and those of branch or unit store managers. Thus, the initial planning is done by those directly concerned with implementing the plan, and the storewide plans are largely built up from the plans of each department and of each selling unit. This is the generally favored approach in stores, but consultation and flexibility are required in the checking of departmental plans. For example, after the buyer has made his initial plan, he will confer with his merchandise manager who is aware of objectives developed by top management for the organization as a whole and for each major merchandise division. If the sum of his buyers' plans fall short of overall objectives, a good deal of probing is done to find departments that could increase their sales goals. The final decision is likely to be a compromise if there is a major difference of opinion.

A conscientious sales planner is always pulled in two directions. His optimistic nature wishes to plan sales as high as their potential, insuring enough merchandise and sales help to get the job done, and to spur an all-out effort to achieve it. His conservative nature is motivated to control expenses and keep stock levels low to minimize markdown risk.

The best approach, of course, is a *realistic* one, where sales are forecast as close to actual results as possible. This insures the proper stock level, minimum markdowns, adequate sales force coverage, controlled expenses, and therefore optimum sales and profit.

BACKGROUND FOR PLANNING

In making his sales plans for a coming season, the buyer in an ongoing store considers each merchandise classification in his department separately in developing his departmental plan, for opportunities vary greatly by class. For example, the housewares section in department stores in a recent year showed a sales increase of 7 percent but the small electrical appliance classification went ahead only 2 percent, whereas kitchen utensils enjoyed an 11 percent increase.

Before he starts his planning, the buyer is provided, by the control division of the store, with data on his last year's sales broken down usually into classifications. Many stores find it helpful to assemble the sales records of the past three or four years to determine a trend. Management also provides the buyer with a general economic forecast and information on plans that are being put into effect, such as the opening of a new branch, the introduction of a new credit policy, or the elimination of low-end merchandise that is making no contribution to profit.

APPRAISING OUTSIDE CONDITIONS

Conditions outside the store have to be given considerable weight in making sales projections. These include general and local business conditions, changes in the competitive situation, fashion changes, and even the weather. Long-range weather forecasting is still in the experimental stage, but the weather bureau already provides fairly reliable monthly forecasts, reporting expected variations from the average temperature and humidity.

In studying business conditions, the retailer is particularly concerned with the trend in employment and wages in his community. If a factory that was one of the mainstays of the town is about to close and throw many customers out of work, a past favorable trend may be reversed. If the retailer caters to upper-income groups, changes in dividend payments and stock market prices will also have a major influence on customers' ability and willingness to spend. While the average merchant is not in a position to undertake the research to appraise business conditions statistically, his personal contact with customers and others businessmen provides him with a reasonably good picture. He also has access to the predictions of economic analysts that are reported in the press or are available through a business service.[4]

Broad fashion trends. In individual lines of goods or selling departments, fashion trends are frequently more important than busi-

---

[4] A useful source of information on organizations that prepare economic forecasts is *Business Trends and Forecasting Information Sources*, edited by J. B. Woy and published by Gale Research Company, Book Tower, Detroit, Michigan 48226.

ness conditions in their influence on sales. The introduction of panty hose in 1968 and 1969 led to a big increase in hosiery volume, largely by increasing the average sale. And also in 1970, the "peacock" flair in men's fashions brought back the wide tie and inflated the prices of men's ties, leading to a dramatic sales increase.

In planning, then, it is particularly important to forecast those fashions that influence an entire line, for these may alter trends materially.

APPRAISING INSIDE CONDITIONS

Conditions within the store or department, as well as those outside, have a marked influence on possible sales. Changes in store policy, changes of personnel, changes in promotion plans and the advertising budget, changes in merchandising technique, changes in department location, merchandise layout, and area of space occupied —all are important factors in determining sales possibilities. These are the factors largely within control, which the store must manipulate to offset adverse outside factors or to augment the returns from favorable outside conditions.

Since outside conditions face all competitors alike, adequate sales volume in the long run depends upon these inside conditions, that is, upon the efficiency of management. There is danger, however, that the sales forecaster will give too much immediate weight to a favorable change in inside conditions. It sometimes takes a year or two to reap benefits from improved policies and techniques.

Presented below is a checklist of the various approaches a buyer or department manager may take to increase his sales. He should select from the list one or more of these possibilities—those that at any given point of time seem to have the best chance of success.

WAYS TO INCREASE DOLLAR SALES

Since dollar sales are the product of the number of transactions and the size of average sale, with adjustment for customer returns, dollar sales may be increased by one or a combination of the following:

* Increase the number of transactions by:

Carrying better, more balanced stock assortments.

Improving advertising and publicity methods to get more people into the store.

Improving point-of-sale selling efforts to prevail upon customers in the store to purchase. These include layout and display, as well as personal salesmanship.

- Increase the size of average sale by:
    Promoting and selling higher-priced goods.
    Paradoxically, lowering the price of expensive goods
      may accomplish this result by increasing the volume
      of sales at prices still above the average unit of sale
      in the store.
    Prevailing upon customers to buy more goods at one
      time by suggestion selling and multiple pricing. The
      latter practice involves marking a number of articles
      at a lower price than the sum of their individual
      prices, such as thirty-five cents each, three for one
      dollar.
- Reduce returns from customers by:
    Stocking goods free of defects.
    Training salespeople to help customers make final deci-
      sions while in the store.
    Eliminating service faults.
    Setting, publicizing, and following reasonable rules in
      regard to returns.

PLANNING IN DOLLARS

Armed with this background material, the planner may proceed as follows: He may observe that, in one of his classifications,
sales last year were $8,000 ahead of the previous year and that this
year sales are $12,000 ahead of last year, an average increase for the
two years of $10,000.[5] He will next check his current sales and eco-
nomic reports to see whether the increase is likely to continue at
about the same pace. He will further consider the probable impact of
new merchandise that is being added to his stock and changes that he
may be making in his promotional and service policies. Thus, he will
come to a judgment as to what further increase seems probable for
the coming year or season. Referring to the figures above, if he feels
confident of a minimum increase of $7,000 but believes that an in-
crease of $12,000 is a reasonable possibility, he will probably plan an
increase of $9,500, halfway between.

THE TRANSACTIONS APPROACH TO SALES PLANNING

A more scientific approach to sales planning is to recognize
that dollar sales are a composite of two elements that may not move
in the same direction—the number of transactions and the size of the

[5] It is desirable to consider the percentage increases as well as the
dollar increases from the previous year.

average sale. To study the probable change in each of these factors and then to bring them together is likely to provide a more accurate forecast than to treat sales as a single component.

As a formula:[6]

$$\text{Dollar sales} = \text{Number of transactions} \times \text{Value of the average sale}$$

This method of planning provides for separate detailed consideration of the factors that are likely to affect each of the two variables. The number of transactions are usually much more regular in their changes than are dollar sales which are affected by forces of inflation and deflation. Therefore, it is easier to project transactions accurately than it is to project dollar sales. For example:

	$ Sales	Number of Transactions	Average Sale
Fall season—3 years ago	$180,000	90,000	$2.00
Fall season—2 years ago	191,000	91,000	2.10
Fall season—last year	200,000	93,000	2.15

If the planner feels that the increase of two thousand transactions last year was abnormally large, he may plan an increase of fifteen hundred transactions. If the average sale is likely to stabilize, dollar sales would be estimated at 94,500 × $2.15, or $203,175. Concentration on the dollar sales alone would have given a projection to about $210,000.

Size of the average sale.   The most difficult step in the above procedure is to forecast the size of the average sale. Consideration should be given to all of the following factors:

1. Price changes.
   a. Supply of money and credit in relation to business activity—more credit, higher prices.
   b. Supply of goods of a specific type in relation to demand—restricted supply, higher prices.
2. Changes in the physical quantity of merchandise in an average transaction. Changes in consumer habits and suggestion selling methods must be considered.
3. Changes in markup percentage. A reduction in the markup per-

---

[6] If the data available represent the number of *gross* transactions—before customer returns—and the *gross* average sale, the product will represent *gross* sales. To find net sales, then, customer returns and allowances would have to be subtracted.

centage may reduce the average sale with no change in the general price level or physical quantity of goods purchased at one time.

4. Changes in the quality of merchandise desired and purchased. A demand for better quality may increase the average sale with no change in the other factors.

5. Changes in the relative demand for different goods at different prices. If, in men's furnishings, for every ten transactions of ties at $2.00, there are ten transactions of shirts at $6.00, the average sale is $4.00. But if the demand shifts to twelve transactions of ties at $2.00 to eight of shirts at $6.00, the average transaction is $3.60, even though prices have not changed.

Transaction and average sale relationships. Since dollar sales are the product of the number of transactions and the average sale, the following two relationships can be established:

$$\text{Average dollar sale} = \frac{\text{Dollar sales}}{\text{Number of transactions}}$$

and

$$\text{Number of transactions} = \frac{\text{Dollar sales}}{\text{Average dollar sale}}$$

These relationships are of value in cases such as the following: Sales last year were $800,000, and this year, $720,000, a decrease of 10 percent. Transactions last year were 450,000, and this year, 436,500, a decrease of 3 percent. This means a 7.2 percent decline in the average sale, derived as follows from the percentage changes:

$$\text{Average dollar sale} = \frac{100\% - 10\%}{100\% - 3\%} = \frac{90\%}{97\%} = 92.8\%,$$

indicating the decline of 7.2 percent stated above.

Again, if dollar sales are expected to increase 5 percent while the average sale rises 2 percent:

$$\text{Transactions} = \frac{100\% + 5\%}{100\% + 2\%} = \frac{105\%}{102\%} = 102.94\%,$$

indicating a rise in transactions of 2.94 percent.

BREAKDOWN OF SEASON PLAN INTO MONTHS

After the sales for a store or department have been planned on a basis of the above factors for a year or a six-month season, they must be planned for each month. This may be done by calculating the normal seasonal variation that the store or department has experienced in the past. For example, monthly sales over a five-year period may be totaled as follows:

	Five-Year Sales of Hosiery	
August	$67,000	12.3%
September	78,000	14.4
October	85,000	15.7
November	85,000	15.7
December	173,000	31.9
January	54,000	10.0
Season total	$542,000	100.0%

If the planned sales for the coming fall and winter season are $120,000, August sales may be planned at 12.3 percent of this, or $14,760, January sales at 10 percent, or $12,000, and other months may be planned in the same way.

In practice, adjustments will still have to be made for such factors as the following:

1. An upward or downward trend in sales. If sales are increasing rapidly as compared with the past five years, a larger percentage of the season total may be expected late in the season and a smaller percentage early. The August figure might be cut down to $14,400, for example, and the January figure increased from $12,000 to $12,250.

2. Special sale plans. A decision to hold in October a sale formerly held in September will considerably change the relative importance of the two months.

3. Changes in customer buying habits. There may be a tendency to buy relatively more in November and less in December than formerly.

4. In the case of fashion merchandise in the spring season, changes in the date of Easter. Since Easter varies from late in March to late in April, the relative business to be obtained in the two months varies a great deal, but other months are not affected. A good scheme is to combine the two months for planning purposes. For example, 36.6 percent of the spring hosiery business may be done in March and April combined. If the season total is $100,000, $36,600 may be planned for the two months. If the year before, with Easter on April 1, 55 percent of the two-months' business was done

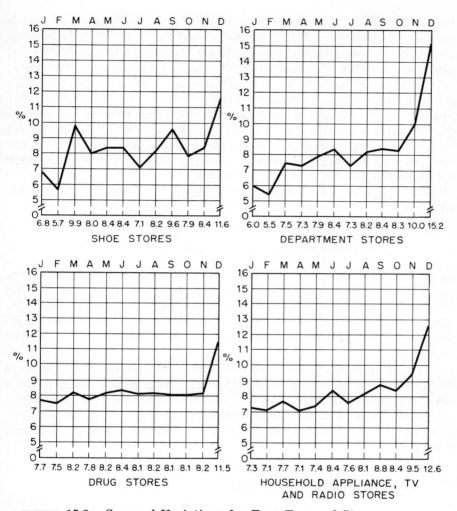

FIGURE 15.2   Seasonal Variations for Four Types of Store
Based on *Monthly Trade Statistics*, U.S. Dept. of
Commerce, and Compiled by the Controllers' Congress,
NRMA.

in March and 45 percent in April, this year, with Easter on April 21,
the business will probably be more evenly divided between the two
months. The probable distribution may be judged by comparing the
records of an earlier year when Easter was also late in April.

5. Number of selling days. It would be desirable to have each
month represent four or five full weeks rather than periods varying

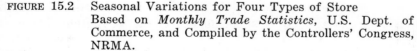

both in number of selling days and number of Saturdays.[7] Each month may be regarded as a four-week period, with thirteen periods a year, or two months of each season may represent five-week periods, and four months, four-week periods. Some stores break down their season plans directly to weeks rather than months. If such periods are not set, an adjustment in monthly plans has to be made for changes in the number of selling days and peak days in the month. For example, a preliminary August sale figure of $14,760 may be set on a basis of an average of twenty-seven selling days in the past, but this year there may be twenty-six selling days; the plan then may be multiplied by 26/27, giving $14,213.

Figure 15.2 shows the typical seasonal variation in four types of store.

FORECASTING SALES FOR THE NEW STORE

It is difficult to forecast the sales for a new store with any degree of accuracy. There is no "history" on which to base a prediction. Nor is any new store identical to another in all of several key variables such as location, competition, composition of the consumer market, total income in the trading area, and merchandising sense of the manager.

The predicted first-year sales for a new store must therefore be a calculated guess, based on the study and use of the pertinent data available. In this section, we shall explore the techniques employed by a unit of a convenience goods chain such as a supermarket, by a shopping center, and by a department store planning a branch.

NEW UNIT OF A CONVENIENCE GOODS CHAIN

A chain can predict sales of a new unit within reasonable limits. For example, if a supermarket chain is contemplating the

---

[7] A more sophisticated plan of adjustment is to set a weighting for each selling day of the week, such as

Monday	1.1
Tuesday	0.9
Wednesday	1.0
Thursday	0.8
Friday	0.7
Saturday	1.5
Total	6.0

If the weightings for the average month of about four and one-third weeks total 26 and the weighting for February only 24, the original sales plan based on the average month would be reduced by the ratio of 24/26.

opening of a new store in a town with a population of fifty thousand, it will have for comparison established stores of similar size and frontage in other cities of similar size and character. There are also certain factors that serve as good guidelines in predicting sales—traffic counts, stockturn, sales per square foot, and rent.

Traffic counts. Studies of other units in the chain may reveal the following typical experience: Twenty percent of the passing traffic enters the store, 80 percent of those who enter purchase, and the average value of purchases is $6. It is then possible to estimate the sales probabilities by means of a traffic count. Spot checks may indicate that 2,000 people pass the proposed location each day on the average during the hours that the store will be open. In this case, 400 people will probably enter, of whom 320 are likely to purchase $1,920 worth of goods a day. If the store is to be open 306 days a year, it would seem to have a sales possibility of about $588,000 a year.

For the independent merchant, it is difficult to obtain reliable ratios for such a calculation; but if he has been in business before or has friends with stores similar to his, he may find the above method of some value.

Stockturn. Another valid guideline for prediction is the stockturn goal. The merchant can obtain from the experience of his other stores, or from his trade association or trade journal, fairly reliable standards of stockturn for his line. For example, should the stockturn for self-service grocery stores of his type be thirty a year, he can apply this to his planned merchandise inventory. If this is $15,000 at retail, his sales would be $450,000. Since typical stockturn performance represents going stores, the figure of $450,000 is likely to prove too optimistic at the start.

Sales per square foot. Another approach to the problem is to use a typical figure of sales per square foot of either total space or of selling space. His contemplated store may have ninety-two hundred square feet of selling space and the typical ratio may be fifty dollars a square foot. From this approach, sales possibilities would seem to be sales of $460,000.

Rent. Rent should also be considered, or a rent equivalency if land and building are to be owned. Rent in similar stores may average 3 percent of sales. If the rent in the proposed location is $12,000 a year, the merchant should sell $400,000 to keep his rent in a desirable relation to his sales.

As suggested above, the merchant should approach his initial sales forecast from a number of different points of view. When different approaches give considerably different results, the merchant would be well advised to plan a figure closer to the lower estimates than the higher ones.

STORES IN A NEW SHOPPING CENTER

The problem is more difficult when a new shopping center is being created in an open suburban area. The promoter makes studies of the population and purchasing power in the area from which he believes the center will draw repeat traffic. He then estimates how many people are likely to be attracted to the center, largely in the light of what has happened in other developments and the distance from nearby residential areas to other shopping centers.

One technique is to divide the entire area from which the center is likely to draw trade into octants radiating from the center. See figure 15.3.

The planner can determine from census data and related studies the number of families in each octant, their typical family income, and the total income of all the families in each octant. Then by a careful study of the center's accessibility from each octant with special attention to time distance and competing shopping opportunities, he can estimate the percentage of customers in each segment who are likely to buy their convenience goods in each center and the percentage likely to buy their shopping goods there. Customers residing in segments near and accessible to the center will buy a large proportion of their convenience goods needs there, particularly in supermarkets. The proportion of customers in each segment who are likely to buy their shopping goods in the center will be smaller, but shopping goods business will be attracted from more distant segments. Thus, the total shopping goods potential of a regional center may be even larger than that for convenience goods purchased in the supermarkets planned.

In each segment the incomes of that portion of the families who are expected to buy convenience goods in the center and the incomes of those who are expected to buy shopping goods there are determined and totaled. For example, it may be concluded that 80 percent of the families within a two-mile radius are likely to buy their convenience goods regularly in the center and that the incomes within these inner segments total $50 million. Foodstuffs are the chief item in this category. If studies of consumer expenditures in the income bracket typical of the entire community report 24 percent

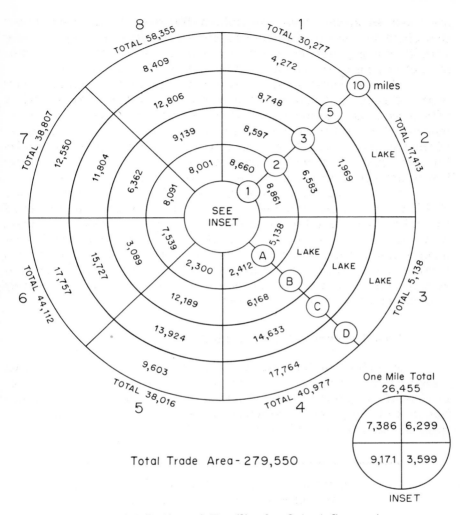

FIGURE 15.3 Distribution of Families by Octant Segments
From *The Selection of Retail Locations*, F. W. Dodge.
Copyright 1958, McGraw-Hill Book Company. Used
with permission of McGraw-Hill Book Company.

of family income for food and closely related items, it will be concluded that food store purchases from these segments should be
about $12 million. Of this, 80 percent, or $9.6 million, would seem
destined for the center. In addition, some convenience goods buying
will be done by shopping goods customers who come from a greater
distance. It may be estimated that these outlying customers who will
shop at the center have incomes of about $42 million and that they

are likely to spend about $10 million for food. It has been found that about 10 percent of this, or $1 million, is likely to be spent along with shopping goods purchases at the center. Thus, the total supermarket buying at the center may be estimated at $10.6 million.

If supermarkets can be expected to sell two hundred dollars worth of goods per square foot of space, they will require a total of fifty-three thousand square feet. If two supermarkets are to be accommodated, the total space allotted should be close to the derived figure. If the two stores plan larger facilities, they are not likely to realize the per square foot goal of two hundred dollars and will probably fail to achieve sales goals they may have set for themselves.

In planning for a shopping goods store in the center, many customers would be attracted from a distance greatly in excess of two miles, but the total income of these shopping goods customers would also be spread over retail facilities elsewhere. Thus, the department stores acting as a magnet for the center will capture only a portion of the total income destined for shopping goods. The amount destined for the center may be estimated with considerable accuracy if each octant is studied separately.[8]

NEW DEPARTMENT STORE BRANCH

A method of forecasting sales for a new branch is based on a prediction of the share of the market that the store should produce in view of the present share of the market obtained by the organization and of the special characteristics of the new trading area. The steps in the process are below.

FORECASTING SALES FOR A NEW BRANCH
OF A GENERAL MERCHANDISE STORE

• Estimated population of the trading area in which the new branch is to operate	200,000
• Estimated total income of the population within the area	$500,000,000
• Estimated potential sales of general merchandise stores of this type within the area (12 percent of income)	$ 60,000,000
• Estimated current annual sales of competitors within the area	$ 40,000,000
• Estimated annual sales of competitors projected to opening year	$ 45,000,000

[8] For a detailed analysis of this technique see R. L. Nelson, *The Selection of Retail Locations*, especially chapters 17, 18, and 19. F. W. Dodge Corporation, New York, 1958.

- Share of market goal (10 percent of potential sales of general merchandise stores) $ 6,000,000
- Sales estimate for the coming year after downward adjustment of 10 percent.[9] $ 5,400,000

THE LEVERAGE FACTOR

If a store or a selling department has few fixed expenses and most of its expenses vary with the amount of business done, it is clear that increases in volume will not greatly increase profits, since expenses will increase almost as fast. However, fixed expenses may be a large portion of the total expense. Accordingly, increases in volume would increase the gross margin faster than they increase the expenses, and profits would rise rapidly.

To exemplify this principle, direct expenses may be classified into three groups: (1) fixed, (2) variable with dollar sales, and (3) variable with transactions.

A specific department may show the results indicated for last year and be able to approximate this year's planned results, assuming inflationary forces do not affect fixed expenses:

	Last Year	Plan This Year
Sales	$1,000,000	$1,100,000 (up 10%)
Number of transactions	$ 500,000	$ 525,000 (up 5%)
Gross margin (35%)	$ 350,000	$ 385,000 (up 10%)
Fixed expenses	$ 20,000	$ 20,000 (no change)
Expenses varying with $ sales	$ 50,000	$ 55,000 (up 10%)
Expenses varying with transactions	$ 80,000	$ 84,000 (up 5%)
Total direct expenses	$ 150,000	$ 159,000 (up 6%)
Department contribution (Gross margin less direct expenses)	$ 200,000	$ 226,000 (up 13%)

THE BREAK-EVEN POINT

The fact that dollar expenses generally change more slowly than do dollar sales has led to the concept of the break-even point.

[9] Such downward adjustments are often necessary because of limits to capital available for investment, the below average nature of the available location, or the need to allow a year or two for the branch to hit its stride. Note that the sales estimate determines the space requirement for the new facility. This can be found by dividing the share of market goal by the typical sales per square foot of total space.

This is the minimum sales volume required at current margin and expense relationships to avoid an operating loss. The usual way to determine this point is (1) to classify expenses into groups, fixed and variable; (2) to determine the percentage of the variable expenses to the sales; (3) to determine the current gross margin ratio; (4) to subtract the variable expense percentage from the gross margin percentage; and (5) to divide the remainder into the fixed expenses.

For example, with sales of $1,000,000, fixed expenses may be $140,000 and expenses that vary directly with dollar sales volume, $160,000. These variable expenses are then 16 percent of sales. The gross margin may be 36 percent. The break-even point is the volume level at which the gross margin of 36 percent will just equal the fixed expenses plus the variable expenses. It is assumed that the variable expenses will continue to be 16 percent of sales. Since the gross margin is 36 percent of sales, only 20 percent of sales is left for the fixed expenses of $140,000. The break-even sales, then, are $140,000 divided by 20 percent, or $700,000. Thus, a decline of 30 percent in volume from the current $1,000,000 level will reach the theoretical break-even point.[10]

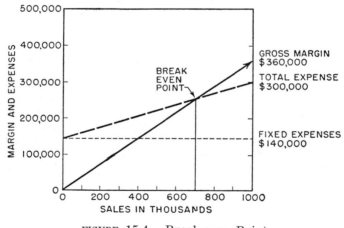

FIGURE 15.4   Break-even Point

The break-even point may also be calculated graphically by drawing a chart similar to figure 15.4. Sales are plotted along the x-axis and expenses along the y-axis. A straight line is drawn from

[10] Algebraically: Let x = sales at break-even point
and $.36\,x = \$140,000 + .16\,x$
$.20\,x = \$140,000$
$x = \$700,000$

0 to the point on the chart where the current sales volume and current gross margin intersect. A second straight line is drawn from the point on the y-axis that measures the fixed expense to the point where the current sales volume and current total expenses intersect. This point is the break-even point.

Application to departments. While the above example has been worked out for a store as a whole rather than for a single selling department or a unit of a multi-unit organization, the method of analysis is applicable to the department if fixed expense is replaced with a figure representing the *sum* of fixed department expenses and the minimum contribution that management feels the department should make to store overhead and overall profit.

Limitations of break-even analysis. Break-even analysis, as presented above, makes some assumptions that may not be true. First, it assumes that currently fixed expenses stay fixed; they may not. Second, it assumes that variable expenses move in direct ratio to changes in sales. In practice, some such expenses may increase more rapidly than sales or they may decrease more rapidly, depending upon the point at which an additional salesperson is employed or the point at which the marginal one is separated. And as indicated, some expenses may be influenced more by transaction changes than by dollar sale changes. Thus, expenses may not take the form of a straight line on the chart. The gross margin also may not remain constant as a fixed percentage of sales. While a mathematical model could be developed to allow for expected variables of these types, the crude analysis presented is probably sufficiently accurate to suggest either sales increases necessary to change a losing operation into a break-even one or sales decreases that can be countenanced without incurring a loss.

QUESTIONS FOR DISCUSSION

1. Since changes in sales volume from one year to the next are generally less than 10 percent, why not plan for the coming year or season the same sales as last year, and as the new period progresses increase or decrease purchases as the sales differences from last year become apparent?
2. For a chain of appliance stores, which is likely to be the better plan: a top-down determination of the sales goals for each store or bottom-up planning done by each store manager? Why?
3. Which do you think will provide greater motivation to managers: a sales goal that will be very difficult to reach or one that can be exceeded by a comfortable margin? Why?

4. Do you think that a department manager will do a better job of sales planning if he thinks in terms of number of transactions, value of the average sales, and customer returns than if he concentrates on the dollar net sales figure without considering its components separately? Why?

5. In attempting to increase dollar sales, which is likely to provide the greatest opportunity at present: to increase transactions, to increase the average sale, or to reduce customer returns? Defend your stand.

6. Of the methods presented to increase the value of the average sale, which could a manager apply most effectively? Why?

7. If the average sale next year is expected to be 5 percent higher than it is this year (due to inflation) but the number of transactions is expected to drop 5 percent, what changes, if any, would you expect in the dollar sales?

8. What categories of merchandise might seriously be affected in their sales potential due to sudden change in customer acceptance?

9. In what types of stores or departments is December *not* the month of largest sales volume?

10. A certain residential segment of a trading area is one to two miles away from a planned large new shopping center; there is a small supermarket between the center and the segment; and there is another large shopping center three miles away from the segment in another direction. Under these circumstances, is it possible to forecast with any degree of accuracy the proportion of families living in the segment that will patronize the new center?

11. In an inflationary period, when expenses as well as sales are affected, are increases in sales likely to increase the percentage of profit? Explain.

12. (a) Is the break-even point analysis of practical value to the merchant in forecasting his sales?

   (b) What is the chief value of the break-even point analysis?

16

PLANNING
STOCKS
IN
DOLLARS

IMPORTANCE OF STOCK PLANNING

The inventory problem in retail stores is closely linked to booms and recessions in the national economy. Retailers tend to overstock when prospects of sales increases are good and to understock when prospects are bad. Thus, a relatively small increase in sales often leads to excessive buying and excessive production. The resultant oversupply may lead to sharp markdowns and to a cessation of buying that virtually shuts down production and throws people out of work.

A great need in merchandising is to maintain steadier stocks that provide adequate assortments when sales are low and are not excessively built up when sales pick up.

There seem to be three major reasons why retailers overbuy in boom periods:

1. A fear of shortage—a fear that goods will not be available unless bought now in quantity.
2. An expectation of price increase. By purchasing to "beat the rise" the buyer may hope to increase his markup, but more often he hopes to increase his sales by being able to offer submarket prices.

3. An expectation of increased sales. The buyer's optimism often exceeds realities. Even should a 20 percent sales increase material-ize, it is not necessary to increase stocks in the same proportion in order to maintain adequate assortments.

Conversely, the main causes for sharply curtailed buying are:

1. Inventories are found to be increasing more rapidly than sales, and a quick halt is called.
2. Sales actually turn down and buyers cut purchases even more.
3. A price decline is feared, and merchants cut purchases in the hope of selling out inventories before sharp markdowns are necessary or in the expectation that stock replacements will cost less if pur-chases are delayed.

While these reasons are understandable, they do not justify the sharp inventory extremes that could be avoided by regularizing buying operations, that is, by setting up controls to keep inventory fluctuations less extreme than sales fluctuations.

CONSIDERATIONS IN STOCK PLANNING

After sales and reductions have been planned month by month, the stocks necessary to realize the volume goals may be deter-mined.

Dollar stocks may be planned in terms of either cost value or retail value. If the store operates under the retail method of inven-tory and/or regularly counts its stock at retail prices, it will logically plan stock at retail. But many small stores take physical inventory and keep inventory records at cost only. They plan their stocks at cost prices.

It is a good practice to plan stock for the beginning of each month rather than for the end, even though the planned beginning stock for one month is the same as the planned ending stock for the month before. In planning, however, the stocks must be related to the expected sales of the month just ahead, not to the sales of the month past.

In setting the stocks for the first of each month, there are two major considerations. The first is to have an adequate assortment and a quantity of each item necessary to meet customer demand in the volume anticipated. This involves the planning of classifications, price lines, types, materials, styles, colors, sizes, and quantities in each. The second consideration is to achieve a desired *stockturn* rela-tionship so that markdowns may be minimized and an adequate return on the merchandise investment may be realized.

Here then is the merchant's universal challenge: to have enough of the right merchandise so that no sale opportunity is lost, yet to keep merchandise investment as low as feasible.

It is the buyer who strives to maximize the breadth and depth of the merchandise assortment, and it is the merchandise manager or controller who serves as a brake to limit investment dollars. The true merchant strikes a delicate balance between the two, since a well-conceived stock plan should achieve both aims.

In practice, many stores depend upon the buyer to assess his own department's sales potential and to determine the detailed breakdown of the merchandise investment that will support the planned sales. If his total sales and stock estimates are in line with stockturn goals, the plan is generally accepted by management.

THE BUYER'S APPROACH TO STOCK PLANNING

Let us first examine the approach a buyer usually takes in stock planning and then the financial approach that applies stockturn goals.

The buyer plans in terms of the specific items of merchandise that he believes he should present to the customer throughout the season as components of his total assortment and translates his unit plans into dollars.

BASIC ASSORTMENT

While each department will vary in detail, assortments found in stores carrying general merchandise are usually broken down into the many components listed above with a minimum quantity of each component planned. For example, in a women's sportswear department, one SKU in the basic assortment would be a women's sweater in the bulky cardigan category from vendor X, in wool at fifteen dollars, in blue, size thirty-four, and perhaps with a minimum quantity of two pieces.

In a volatile fashion department, however, such as junior dresses, the SKUs may consist only of the major classifications and price ranges, such as junior cocktail dresses in the forty-to-fifty-dollar range. Other components within the classifications and price ranges would not be determined until the time of merchandise selection in the wholesale market.

Quantities of each item in the assortment plan are generally listed at the level below which the stock should not fall at any time during the season. When the value of this minimum stock is totaled, it should be considerably less than the amount of stock dollars that are planned for the first of each month.

ADDITIONS TO THE BASIC STOCK

In planning for the stock to carry at the first of each month, the buyer must add to the basic stock provision for the following requirements that vary from month to month: (1) the *clearance* goods that are likely to be carried over to the first of each month— these are not a part of the regular basic stock; (2) the specially priced promotional merchandise to be made available at about the first of each month for special sales that are planned for that month; (3) prestige merchandise, usually high-priced special items, that are not a part of the regular assortment but are to be brought in for publicity purposes; (4) added breadth to the basic stock to meet the wide demands of customers shopping at important seasonal periods; and (5) increased depth in the items carried in the basic assortment to avoid lost sales during periods of peak buying.

For example, at the beginning of the fall season on August 1, the stock would consist of the basic assortment plus some summer clearance goods, plus perhaps some goods for special August sales. Both breadth and depth will be expanded as the season progresses. Late in December, even before Christmas, the stock may be cut back toward the basic assortment, but there may also be a great deal of clearance goods and by January 1 some new goods may be on hand for the January special sales.[1]

MONTHLY STOCK FLUCTUATIONS

An important principle of monthly stock planning is to plan percentage fluctuations in the value of the stock smaller than the fluctuations in the sales. For example, if a $10,000 retail stock is necessary on February 1 to allow February sales of $5,000, a stock of $15,000 should not be necessary for March 1 if March sales of $7,500 are expected. Usually, in the busy months, monthly turnover should be higher than the average for the season and lower in the dull months, since once basic assortments are provided, monthly variations in sales do not require proportionate variations in stock. Some stores handling staple lines can keep their stocks nearly constant even though the sales fluctuate seasonally. This means, of course, that the turnover in peak months is higher than it is in dull months.

---

[1] Planning of unit stocks will be considered in much more detail in Part V.

THE FINANCIAL APPROACH TO STOCK PLANNING

Merchandise managers and store controllers who must set limits on the investment that buyers are permitted to make are generally not in a position to determine whether the basic stocks and additional styles that the buyer plans to purchase are the most desirable. They require formulas based on stockturn goals that they believe to be appropriate, against which to check the buyer's built-up plans. When the buyer's plan for the first of a particular month differs materially from the mathematical stockturn-oriented plan, the buyer's plan is not summarily rejected, but he must defend it. Without such a financial control, the buyer in his zeal to carry a large stock to satisfy every conceivable demand is likely to be faced with very heavy markdowns late in the season. Furthermore, the extra investment in stock may contribute very little in the form of additional sales and thus make the investment unproductive.

There are four well-known formal or financial methods of balancing stocks to sales.

FINANCIAL STOCK-PLANNING METHODS

Know

- Basic stock method
   Planned sales for each month added to a basic stock to obtain the stock on the first of each month.
- Percentage variation method
   Stock increased or decreased from the average stock desired by one-half the percentage variation in sales from average monthly sales.
- Weeks' supply method
   Based on planned turnover, the number of weeks' supply to be carried is determined and sales estimated for this number of weeks ahead.
- Stock-sales ratio method
   A planned ratio between the stock on the first of any given month and the sales for that month. This ratio is multiplied by the planned sales for that month.

BASIC STOCK METHOD

This method gives special recognition to the need to have a basic stock on hand at all times. It is expressed by the following equation:

Retail stock at the first of a month = Sales for the month + (Average stock for the season − Average monthly sales).

For example, during a fall-winter season of six months with season sales of $60,000, a stockturn of three may be planned. Sales for October may be estimated at $13,000, and for November at $15,000. The average monthly stock is $60,000 ÷ 3, or $20,000, and the average monthly sales $60,000 ÷ 6, or $10,000. Applying the formula:

$$\text{Stock, October } 1 = \$13,000 + (\$20,000 - \$10,000)$$
$$= \$13,000 + \$10,000 = \$23,000$$
$$\text{Stock, November } 1 = \$15,000 + \$10,000 = \$25,000$$

This plan increases and decreases stock at the first of each month in the same dollar amount as sales increase or decrease. In the example, November's sales are $2,000 higher than October's, and stocks are $2,000 higher, too. The plan also provides for a *basic* stock, which term may be interpreted here as the difference between the average stock and the average monthly sales (the $10,000 in the example.)[2] This basic stock is constant through the season; thus stocks for the first of any month may be found by adding the sales for that month to the basic stock. If sales for some month were to drop temporarily to zero, the formula would still provide for the basic stock. See figure 16.1 where the stock each month exceeds the sales by the same margin, which margin represents the basic stock.[3]

So long as stockturn is less than twelve a year—that is, so

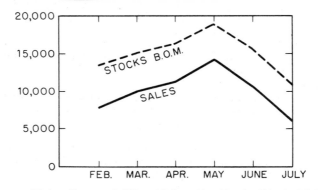

FIGURE 16.1   Seasonal Plan Using the Basic Stock Method

[2] The term *basic* as used here should not be confused with the term *model* stock.

[3] A comparison of monthly sales and stocks in department stores in 1967, as reported in the *Survey of Current Business*, shows that the basic formula, when applied to the sales, yields monthly stocks that are very close to the reported stocks, except in December when the reported stocks do not increase as much as the calculated stocks.

long as the average monthly sales are less than the average monthly stock—this formula provides for a fixed basic stock and thus yields a higher turn in busy months than in dull months. When stockturn is over twelve times a year, the basic stock will become a *negative* figure and the equation will fail to give satisfactory results. In fact, this equation is not recommended for use when stockturn is more than six times a year. For high stockturns, however, there is modification of the equation:

Stock at retail first of month = Average weekly sales for the month + (Average stock for season − Average weekly sales for season).

For example, season sales, $260,000; planned turnover for season, 5; sales for December (4 1/3 weeks), $65,000, or $15,000 a week.

$$\text{Stock December 1} = \$15,000 + \left(\frac{\$260,000}{5} - \frac{\$260,000}{26}\right)$$
$$= \$15,000 + (\$52,000 - \$10,000)$$
$$= \$15,000 + \$42,000 = \$57,000$$

PERCENTAGE VARIATION METHOD

A second method of stock planning is based on the premise that the percentage fluctuations in monthly stock from average stocks should be half as great as the percentage fluctuations in monthly sales from average sales. This method is suitable for stockturn of six times a year or more.[4]

For example, if sales in one month are 20 percent above the average monthly sales, the stock for the first of the month would be increased 10 percent above the average monthly stocks. Again, referring to the example on page 288, with October sales of $13,000, average sales of $10,000, and average monthly stocks of $20,000, sales are 30 percent above average. Stocks, then, are increased 15 percent above $20,000 and become $23,000. This is the same figure as that calculated by means of the first method; in fact, the two methods give the same result when a turn of six is planned for the year or three for the season. When higher turns are planned, the

---

[4] The "half-as-great" relationship is arbitrary. There is no doubt that the percentage seasonal fluctuation in stocks should generally be less than that of sales (see page 286); 50 percent of the sales rate rather than some other percentage is used as an approximation.

percentage method gives stocks that fluctuate less than those found by the first method with the use of monthly (not weekly) sales data. Were the percentage method to be used for stockturn of less than three times a season, it would yield stocks that fluctuate more than those derived by the first method. Which to use depends upon whether the nature of the goods calls for a large basic stock that needs to vary only a little as sales change. If this is the case, plan one (monthly basis) may be recommended for stockturns of less than six times a year (three a season) and plan two for turns of more than six a year.

This percentage method may be expressed as a formula, as follows:

$$\text{Retail stock, 1st of month} = \text{Average stock} \times 1/2$$
$$\left(1 + \frac{\text{Sales for month}}{\text{Average monthly sales}}\right)$$

For example, the planned sales for the year may be \$48,000; the planned sales for July, \$2,500; and the planned yearly turnover, 8:

$$\text{Retail Stock July 1} = \frac{\$48,000}{8} \times 1/2 \left(1 + \frac{\$2,500}{\$48,000 \div 12}\right)$$
$$= \$6,000 \times 1/2 \left(1 + \frac{\$2,500}{\$4,000}\right)$$
$$= \$6,000 \times \frac{1.625}{2} = \$6,000 \times .8125 = \$4,875$$

In other words, July sales are 37.5 percent less than the sales in the average month and this equation reduces stocks from average by one-half this percentage, or 18.75 percent. Six thousand dollars times the complement of 18.75 percent, or 81.25 percent, gives \$4,875.

Adjustments for monthly differences in selling days.   There is one caution that should be observed in connection with either of the two methods presented thus far. The monthly sales used in calculating B.O.M. stocks for succeeding months should represent the same number of selling days. For example, October, with twenty-seven selling days, might have planned sales of \$27,000, and November, with twenty-five selling days, might have planned sales of \$25,000. If the difference in selling days were disregarded, November 1 stocks would be planned lower than the October 1 stocks even though the daily rate of sale is just the same and there is need for as much stock in November as in October. To avoid increasing or decreasing planned stocks simply because of changes in the number of selling days in a period, a good rule would be to express the sales for each month in the season in terms of a normal twenty-six selling days, before either of the two stock-planning formulas are applied. This suggestion is not to be construed as calling for an adjustment in the monthly planned sales entered in the merchandise plan but simply in the monthly planned sales figures to be used in a stock-planning formula.[5]

WEEKS' SUPPLY METHOD

A third method of stock planning is to plan sales ahead on a weekly basis and to set stocks equal to a predetermined number of weeks' supply, depending upon the stockturn desired.[6] For example, if about ten turns a year are desired, the stock should equal about five weeks' supply (52/10 = 5.2), that is, enough to cover the estimated sales for about five weeks ahead.

This method has the shortcoming of varying stocks in direct proportion to the changes in sales. If the rate of sale doubles, the stocks double and vice versa. Thus, the turnover is the same throughout the year, a situation that is not generally desirable because it is likely to mean carrying too much stock at the peak of the season and not enough in dull periods. This method does not provide for a minimum basic stock to be carried no matter how low sales may drop. It also causes a stock increase or decrease some weeks ahead of anticipated changes in sales. It is probably more frequently used for the unit control of some staple items than for storewide or departmental dollar stock planning.[7]

---

[5] Another way to adjust for differences in days is to determine the average sales for a period equal to the number of days in the month for which stocks are being planned. For example, the sales for a six-month season may be $60,000; planned sales for February (a four-week period) may be $7,000; and the stockturn desired may be three. The average sales for a four-week period will not be one-sixth of the season's sales of $60,000 because there are six and one-half four-week periods in the season of twenty-six weeks. So, $60,000 is divided by 6.5, yielding $9,231 as the average sales for a four-week period. Formula 1 might then be applied as follows:
Sales February + (Average stock − Average 4 weeks' sales) = Stock February 1
$7,000 + ($20,000 − $9,231) = $17,769
Were the "month" five weeks, the sales for the season would be divided by 5.2.

[6] With low stockturns, stocks may be kept equal to a predetermined number of *months'* supply rather than *weeks'* supply.

[7] This *weeks' supply* method may be adjusted to make it more suitable for dollar stock planning by setting a smaller number of weeks' supply than average for peak periods and a larger number of weeks' supply than average for dull periods. With such an adjustment, the plan may give excellent results, but it is difficult to plan how much to deviate from normal in peaks and valleys. Only judgment can determine how many fewer weeks' supply to carry in busy seasons and how many more to carry in dull seasons.

STOCK-SALES RATIO METHOD

Some planners are making increased use of monthly stock-sales ratios as the basis for stock planning.[8] For example, it may be found upon investigation that the February 1 stock-sales ratio for a medium-sized hosiery operation is four—meaning that the stocks on the first of February are usually four times the February sales. Thus, if the store forecasts sales of $10,000 for February, it may multiply this figure by the stock-sales ratio of four to find planned stocks of $40,000 for February 1. Were sales planned at $15,000, the planned stock would be $60,000.

Stores may develop their own stock-sales ratios for each month, based on their own past experience, or they may make use of ratios calculated for a group of stores of which they are members.

The interest shown by store management in this approach has led the Controllers Congress of the NRMA to include stock-sales ratios for each month in its annual MOR reports. Medians for key departments are grouped according to store size (see table 16.1). In general, stock-sales ratios, as is to be expected, are largest when sales are lowest in January and February. Stock-sales ratios tend to decline as sales volume increases.

TABLE 16.1   B.O.M. Stock-Sales Ratios[a]

Annual Sales	Up to $40,000	$40,000 to $100,000	$100,000 to $190,000	$190,000 to $450,000	Over $450,000
January	6.2	5.8	4.6	3.4	2.6
February	4.8	4.6	3.7	3.1	2.5
March	4.4	2.6	2.0	1.8	1.9
April	4.4	2.6	2.1	2.1	1.5
May	3.4	2.6	1.9	1.6	1.4
June	4.1	2.2	2.3	1.9	1.5
July	3.4	2.3	2.3	2.0	2.2
August	3.9	2.4	2.2	2.4	1.8
September	4.1	2.3	1.9	2.2	1.7
October	4.3	2.5	2.5	3.1	1.8
November	5.8	3.0	2.8	3.8	2.5
December	3.9	2.0	2.4	2.3	1.9

Source: Merchandising and Operating Results for 1968, Vol. I, National Retail Merchants Association.
[a] By annual sales volume of daytime dresses in department stores.

[8] See chapter 12 for a definition and analysis of stock-sales ratios.

When a group of stores exchanges monthly sales and stock information for purposes of calculating typical or average stock-sales ratios, it should be noted that a median or mean figure for the entire group would not be suitable if there were a considerable difference in the sales volume of the different stores included and in the seasonal variation. When monthly sales are large, stock-sales ratios are relatively small, and when monthly sales are small, stock-sales ratios are relatively large. For example, a small hosiery department selling $1,000 worth of hosiery a month may need a stock of $5,000 on the first of the month—a stock-sales ratio of five. But a large store selling $100,000 a month will not need stock 100 times as great, or $500,000 —assortments do not have to be increased in direct proportion to the increase in sales. It may be possible to operate with a stock of $300,000—sixty times as great as that of the small operation—and to achieve a stock-sales ratio of three. Accordingly, stores should be grouped into sales volume classifications as the NRMA is doing, and separate stock-sales ratios should be calculated for each sales volume group.

Another difficulty with stock-sales ratios obtained from a group of stores is that differences in seasonal variation in different stores in the group tend to distort the average ratios computed. The stock-sales ratio concentrates all attention on the relationships between stock on the first of the month and sales for the on-coming month, whereas the stock on the first of a month is also influenced by the sales expected for the season as a whole.

After the best available ratios have been determined, the monthly stocks arrived at by means of the ratios should be averaged for the year or season and the resultant stockturn determined. This should be compared with the stockturn goal planned, and adjustments should be made in the ratios to bring the resultant turn into line with plan. For example, if the stock-sales ratios produce a turn of four, where the plan calls for five, the monthly ratios may all be reduced by 20 percent.

PLANNING IN UNITS OF SALE

An important consideration with each of these formal methods so far discussed is that an allowance may have to be made for variations each month in the price of the average item sold and in stock. For example, referring to formulas 1 or 2, if in any two months of the season dollar sales are the same, the dollar stocks will be the same. But in February, the first month of the season, sales may be

$10,000 and February stocks $38,000, with an average unit value of $10. Thus, in terms of units, sales are one thousand and stocks thirty-eight hundred. In July, the last month of the season, sales may also be $10,000 and stocks also $38,000, but the average unit value at this time may be $5. Thus sales in units are two thousand and stocks in units seventy-six hundred. A comparison of the sales units reveals that they have doubled from February to July and that stocks have also doubled. But it has already been observed that stocks should fluctuate less than sales: if thirty-eight hundred units in stock are adequate for February with one thousand sales units, it should not be necessary to carry as many as seventy-six hundred units in July to provide for sales of two thousand units. It may be concluded that where the average price per unit declines as the season progresses, the formulas will tend to provide too little stock early in the season and too much stock late in the season.

To avoid this difficulty, sales planning by months or weeks may be done in terms of units and stocks for the first of each period calculated in terms of units. These figures may be converted into dollars by applying the estimated average unit price at that time.

Referring to the example above depicting February and July, the total dollar sales for the six-month period may be $84,000 and the average unit of sale $7, yielding twelve thousand sales units. A stockturn of two may be planned for the season, giving an average unit stock of six thousand. The average monthly sales are two thousand units. With February unit sales of one thousand, the stock for February 1 is:

$$1,000 + (6,000 - 2,000) = 5,000 \text{ units}$$

With July sales of two thousand units, the stock for July 1 is:

$$2,000 + (6,000 - 2,000) = 6,000 \text{ units}$$

In dollars, February 1 stock is 5,000 × $10, or $50,000, and July 1 stock is 6,000 × $5, or $30,000. These figures compare with stocks of $38,000 for both February 1 and July 1, obtained from dollar figures alone.

LIMITATIONS OF THE FINANCIAL APPROACH

Any one of the methods discussed above tends to center attention on stockturn goals and on variation in monthly sales and gives no weight to other factors that may have considerable bearing in determining what a desirable stock should be.

Accordingly, any stock plan arrived at mathematically must

be revised in view of the requirements not only to provide an adequate physical assortment but also to allow for any necessary advance buying or for the carry-over of nonseasonable or slow-selling goods that cannot economically be disposed of at once. It would be unwise to allow a predetermined stockturn figure to dominate the monthly stock plans. The merchandise manager who supervises boys' clothing, for example, may estimate seasonal sales of $36,000 and October sales of $8,000 and planned seasonal turn of three. Apply the first of the formulas:

$$\text{Stock October } 1 = \$8,000 + \left(\frac{\$36,000}{3} - \frac{\$36,000}{6}\right)$$
$$= \$8,000 + (\$12,000 - \$6,000) = \$14,000$$

But the buyer will give careful consideration to his merchandise requirements in each classification and price line. He may conclude that he should have on hand on October 1 at least $15,000 worth of current seasonable merchandise and that there will also still be in stock $1,000 worth of old merchandise carried over from the previous season.

With such an analysis, a stock of $16,000 may be planned for October 1, even though this is $2,000 in excess of the stock figure arrived at mathematically. But the availability of the figure arrived at by formula acts as a check upon the buyer's detailed plans to avoid too great a deviation from stockturn goals.

QUESTIONS FOR DISCUSSION

1. Is there a tendency currently for retailers to overstock or to understock? Why?
2. Should the buyer give any consideration to a stockturn goal as he plans his stock requirements in units?
3. Which of the four financial methods of stock planning would seem most suitable for most stores handling general merchandise? Why?
4. Would the percentage variation method of stock planning be of value in planning stocks for a supermarket? Why?
5. Compare the percentage variation method with the basic stock method modified to make use of the average weekly sales each month rather than the monthly sales. At twelve turns a year, which gives the steadier stocks? Why?
6. If you aim at six turns a year in a department that does 12 percent of its volume in November and 18 percent in December, about how many weeks' supply would you plan to have on hand on November 1? Explain.
7. Since published stock-sales ratios are based either on aggregate

figures or on medians, are they likely to be of much value in setting goals for a specific store? Defend your answer.

8. The following B.O.M. stock-sales ratios are available for a specific
department in large specialty stores: for November, three, and
for December, two. One store that is considering using these
ratios plans department sales of $10,000 in November and $30,000
in December. The same department in another store in the same
size classification expects sales of $13,000 in November and
$26,000 in December. For which of the two departments are the
available stock-sales ratios more suitable?

9. If the average unit price in a department gets smaller as the
season progresses, will formulas based on dollar sales tend to
overstate or understate inventories late in the season? Early in
the season? Explain.

10. Under what conditions would you select each of the financial
stock-planning methods to check against the buyer's dollar plans
that are built up from his unit plans?

11. If the buyers reporting to a merchandise manager make good
defenses for their dollar stock plans developed from unit plans
but the aggregate stocks are 20 percent higher than management
feels it can afford to invest in inventory, should the buyers be
forced to cut their inventories approximately 20 percent? Why?

17

THE SEASONAL
MERCHANDISE
PLAN
AND
OPEN-TO-BUY

The stores that have been successful for many years are those that
have set for themselves definite goals of achievement. These goals
receive tangible expression in the merchandise plan. Planning maps
out future business; it provides executives with a yardstick against
which to check actual operations, and it assists in coordinating all
branches of the business so that all can play their appointed roles
in the realization of sales and profit goals.

It is true that a store management may, without planning,
sell all it can each day; it may obtain as high a markup as seems
possible, and it may attempt to keep stocks and purchases balanced
to actual sales. But if it has no objective for each of these profit
factors, it will have difficulty in keeping them all in balance, and
the lack of definite goals is a psychological disadvantage that hinders
the management from doing its best. Again, since purchases must be
made and stock quantities must be set in view of future sales, any
control that considers sales to date alone cannot possibly result in
scientific buying and adjustment of stocks.

THE SEASONAL MERCHANDISE PLAN

The merchandise plan, the basis for dollar control (see figures 17.1
and 17.2), is generally made out for each department or classifica-

tion of goods or for the store as a whole if the store is small. The plan covers a six-month period and is broken down into monthly or weekly subdivisions. For apparel, the spring season period ordinarily runs from February 1 to July 31, and the fall season from August 1 to January 31 next. February 1 and August 1 are better dividing points than January 1 and July 1 because stocks are generally lower at these times and because the transitions from winter to spring goods and from summer to fall goods take place on February 1 and August 1.

Some merchandising experts are critical of plans that cover the traditional six-month period of time. They point out that the classic planning period of six months is unrealistic for many lines of merchandise; they recommend that proper planning periods be determined independently for each kind of merchandise. For one type of goods, the ideal planning period may be one month, while for another it may be two, three, six, or eight months. Some merchandisers also condemn the use of the orthodox fixed time period as opposed to a moving period. A fixed six-month plan, for example, could begin on February 1 and end on July 31 to be followed by the next plan beginning August 1 and ending January 31. A moving six-month plan is one that moves forward month by month, in six-month blocks. The six-month plan starting February 1 would end July 31; then on March 1, the six-month plan would be redefined so as to start on March 1 and end on August 31; and on April 1, the plan would encompass the period from April 1 to September 30, and so on. The dynamic character of a moving plan appeals to an increasing number of merchants. This discussion will be illustrated with an example of the six-month plan. It can readily be modified as a moving plan or can be used for shorter or longer periods.

ELEMENTS INCLUDED

Although there are minor variations in the forms in use, virtually all provide for three entries in connection with every item: last year's actual performance (labeled LY in figures 17.1 and 17.2) ; the plan for this year (labeled PL) ; and the actual results for this year filled in at the end of each period as a feedback (labeled TY).

Both last year's and this year's figures are provided by the store's controller or accountant. The planned figures are generally supplied by the buyers or department managers in conjunction with the merchandise manager, and they are reviewed by top management.

There are two essential items to be included for each month or week: sales and stocks. The forecasting of sales for each season

A.   Key Elements in Dollars

DEPARTMENT: *#43 - Blouses & Sportswear*

Spring 19 Fall 19		Feb. Aug.	March Sept.	April Oct.	May Nov.	June Dec.	July Jan.	Total Total	% of Change
Net sales in $1000	LY PL TY	45 48 –	55 60 –	53 58 –	60 65 –	97 106 –	40 41 –	350 378 –	+8.0
Markdowns in $1000	LY PL TY	5. 6. –	4. 4. –	4. 5. –	4. 6. –	9 10 –	18. 14. –	44 45 –	+2.3
Retail stocks B.O.M. in $1000	LY PL TY	157 155 –	172 170 –	176 178 –	184 185 –	208 212 –	166 165 –	EOM 162 160 –	
Retail purchases in $1000	LY PL TY	66.5 69 –	62 72 –	65 70 –	90 98 –	68 69 –	56 50 –	407.5 428 –	+5.0
Direct expenses in $1000	LY PL TY	7. 7. –	8. 8. –	8. 8.4 –	8. 9. –	10. 11. –	6. 7. –	47. 50. –	+6.6

FIGURE 17.1   Season Merchandise Plan—Key Elements

and month has already been considered in detail in chapter 15, and the planning of stocks for the first of each month to support the sales has been treated in chapter 16.

Planning forms usually provide for a *planned purchase* figure in addition to planned sales and stocks. This represents the purchases planned for *delivery* to the store during each planning period, usually a month in length. Purchases are not planned independently; rather they are derived by means of the formula: Planned purchases at retail = Planned retail stock at the end of the period + Planned sales − Retail stock at the beginning of the period.[1] Planned pur-

---

[1] If a store is on the cost method, the merchandise plan is very similar except that the sales plan is replaced by an estimated cost of sales (planned sales times the complement of the estimated maintained markup percentage). Planned purchases will then be computed at cost by means of the formula:
   Planned purchases at cost = Planned stock at cost at end of the period + Planned cost of sales − Stock at cost at the beginning of the period.

B. Seasonal Goals

Cumulative Results

		Total for Season	Feb. Aug.	March Sept.	April Oct.	May Nov.	June Dec.	July Jan.
Initial	LY	42						
markup %	PL	43	X	X	X	X	X	X
	TY							
Markdowns	LY	12.5						
%	PL	12	X	X	X	X	X	X
	TY							
Shortages	LY	2.5						
%	PL	2	X	X	X	X	X	X
	TY							
Cash disc.	LY	5						
% to sales	PL	5	X	X	X	X	X	X
	TY							
Alteration	LY	0.2						
costs %	PL	0.2	X	X	X	X	X	X
	TY							
Gross	LY	38.1						
margin %	PL	39.8	X	X	X	X	X	X
	TY							
Direct	LY	13.4						
expense %	PL	13.2	X	X	X	X	X	X
	TY							
Stock-	LY	2.0						
turn	PL	2.2	X	X	X	X	X	X
times	TY							
Customer	LY	10.5						
returns %	PL	10.0	X	X	X	X	X	X
of gross sales	TY							
Transportation	LY	1.5						
% of cost	PL	1.5	X	X	X	X	X	X
purchases	TY							

APPROVED: _____ _____ _____ _____

Buyer　　　　　　Date　　　　Merchandise Manager　　　　Date

FIGURE 17.2　Season Merchandise Plan (cont'd)—Season Goals

chases should not be equated with the open-to-buy discussed later in this chapter.

PLANNING MARKDOWNS

In stores where markdowns are significant, it is desirable to estimate them and to include them in the derivation of the planned purchase figure. The purchase formula, illustrated in figure 17.3, then reads:

Planned purchases at retail = Planned stock at the end of the period + Planned sales + Estimated markdowns − Retail stock at the beginning of the period.

Some stores transpose this to read:

Planned purchases at retail = Planned sales + Estimated

FIGURE 17.3   Balance of Input to Output

markdowns + Increase in retail stock during the period or − Decrease in retail stock during the period.

For example, sales of $50,000 and markdowns of $2,000 may be planned for December. The retail stock planned for December 1 may be $100,000 and for January 1 next $80,000, a decrease of $20,000. The planned retail purchases, then, are:

$$\$50,000 + \$2,000 - \$20,000 = \$32,000$$

Planned markdowns are included because they reduce the value of the retail stock, even as sales do. Since the stock plans are made in terms of dollar value rather than of units of merchandise, retail purchases are necessary to restore value of stock lost by both sales and markdowns. From an angle of physical stock requirements, too, it should be noted that markdowns reduce the assortment of fresh merchandise at original retail prices and that such assortments must be kept up. Were markdowns to be omitted in the planning of purchases, actual retail stocks would be smaller than planned at the end of each monthly or weekly control period.

Some merchants prefer to omit markdowns from the merchandise plan, fearing that the setting of a specific figure will influence buyers or department managers to hold off taking needed markdowns because the planned figure has already been reached, or to take unneeded markdowns because the markdowns to date are below plan. Since the actual retail stock at the beginning of the next month is reduced by the markdowns of the preceding month, however, the planned purchases for the next month are automatically increased. Thus, actual markdowns taken in one month increase the planned purchases for the following month.[2]

Stock shortages may also be included in the plan, but there is a difference of opinion as to whether to do so. If omitted, the actual or estimated shortages recognized each month do reduce the inventory figure for the end of the month and thus increase the planned purchase figure for the following month. However, with the alarming increase in shortages, prompt recognition is becoming most important. It is necessary to replace not only what is sold but also what is stolen. If planned shortages are included in the plan, they may be set for each month at a fixed percentage of the planned sales. But the December percentage may be set somewhat higher, since more thievery tends to occur in a crowded environment.

---

[2] If markdowns are omitted from the merchandise plan, the planned purchases for each month do not provide for markdowns that are likely to be taken each month. Thus, the buyer is not able to make new commitments in the market to replace the value of goods to be marked down in advance of the actual markdowns, and probably not until the next month. This time lag may result in undue delay in maintaining desired assortments of fresh merchandise.

Estimating the markdown percentage.   Whether or not markdowns are actually included in the seasonal merchandise plan, it is important that an estimate of the markdown as a percentage of net sales be made to control the stock position and the gross margin result. In setting this percentage, outside standards as well as past experience are usually considered. For lines subject to much obsolescence, standards developed by trade groups are available. There is some danger of following such standards slavishly, perhaps planning larger markdowns than are required simply because the typical reported figure is high. Even more important than the standard is the distribution of the store's own merchandise by age. For example, last year 25 percent of the stock may have been six months old and older at the beginning of the fall season, whereas this year only 20 percent of the stock is that old. This improvement would tend to justify planning a smaller markdown ratio than that realized last year. But other considerations may pull in the opposite direction— sharp price competition, growing out of accumulated surpluses in the wholesale markets, may be predictable and may make a reduction in markdown plans only wishful thinking.

The chief factors to consider in setting the season's markdown percentage may be summarized as follows:

1. Past experience.
2. Appraisal of economic conditions insofar as they affect customer ability and willingness to buy.
3. Trends in wholesale prices. Tendency to increase during periods of dropping wholesale prices and to decrease when wholesale prices are rising.
4. Comparative figures of similar stores.
5. Percentage of old stock on hand at the beginning of the season compared with former years.
6. Changes in merchandising policies, methods, and personnel.

Distributing the season's markdown allotment.   It does not follow that the allotment for each month's plan would be 7 percent of the month's sales if that is the percentage plan for the season. Early months in the season would probably require markdowns in smaller proportion than the average. The bulk of the markdowns might take place in the last two months; however, some markdowns should be taken earlier in the season.

In distributing the season's appropriation to months, the considerations are:

The dates in the season at which changes occur in the style and type of goods wanted by customers.

The store's policy in regard to the timing of markdowns.[3]

The amount of old stock on hand at the beginning of the season.

The merchandising plan (figure 17.2) shows last year's markdowns as 12½ percent for the season with a plan of 12 percent for this year. This percentage is applied to the planned dollar sales of $378,000, and the resultant markdowns of about $45,000 are distributed to the months roughly in proportion to last year's distribution.

SETTING SEASONAL GOALS

While sales, markdowns, stocks, and purchases are the only merchandising items that usually require monthly or weekly planning, certain seasonal standards should be set and actual performance to date should be entered on the plan at the end of each monthly or weekly period.

The most important of these is the initial markup percentage. In chapter 4 we discussed how this figure might be arrived at, as a season's goal. The actual cumulative markup to date should be recorded on the form monthly or weekly to see how closely the plan is being followed. It is sometimes desirable to set a separate markup goal for each month, but most stores find the season's goal sufficient because markup percentages do not generally vary seasonally unless the department has a policy of special sales at low markups.

Other seasonal goals that may advantageously be set and compared with actual cumulative figures are markdowns, shortages, cash discounts earned both as a percentage of cost purchases and of sales, net alteration and workroom costs, returns from customers, and transportation costs as a percentage of cost purchases. The season's stockturn goal should also be recorded even though it bears a mathematical relationship to the planned season sales and the average of the inventories planned for each month or week.

Other merchandising ratios that may be planned ahead are sales per square foot, number of transactions, the average sale, returns to vendors, and foreign purchases as distinguished from domestic purchases. While these relationships are recognized as important for analysis, most stores do not find it necessary to set specific planned figures. Instead they determine the actual figures periodically and compare them with previous performance or outside standards available to see where improvement can be made.

---

[3] See chapter 8 for a discussion of this policy.

IMPROVING THE GROSS MARGIN RATIO

In setting seasonal goals, the aim of the department planner is usually to achieve as high a gross margin ratio to sales as possible without interfering with sales growth. If he also controls direct expenses, he attempts to keep them at a point consistent with growth in sales and goodwill but also free from waste.

To increase the gross margin, the planner must appraise the four types of opportunity presented in the box below. The first two are usually of major importance. But all four should be carefully considered whenever the merchandise plan is prepared, for the opportunities that are likely to prove most fruitful differ with changing circumstances.

WAYS TO INCREASE THE GROSS MARGIN RATIO

- Increase the initial markup

    By buying for less through
    1. Wider market coverage and intensive negotiation
    2. Quantity purchases, including merchandise for special sales
    3. Specifications for private brands that can be sold at a high markup
    4. Reduced transportation costs
    By selling for more through
    1. Acquisition of exclusive and confined goods
    2. Elimination of odd prices
    By selling a larger proportion of the higher markup goods already stocked by extra emphasis on advertising, selling, and display

- Reduce the reductions
    By reducing markdown losses, including allowances to customers
    By reducing merchandise shortages
    By reducing or eliminating discounts to preferred customer groups, including employees
- Increase cash discounts on purchases
    By paying invoices on time
    By negotiating
- Reduce alteration and workroom costs
    By increasing workroom productivity
    By increasing charges to customers

PLANNING SELLING PAYROLL AND DIRECT ADVERTISING

Frequently, the merchandise plan contains space for certain expense items that are particularly controllable by the department head and that bear a close relation to the planned sales of the department. The most important of these are selling payroll and direct advertising. It is common practice not only to set seasonal goals for these items but also to plan them by month and/or week.

Selling payroll. Although the details of direct expense planning are beyond the scope of this book, it should be observed that the monthly selling payroll is commonly planned by first determining the size and cost of a basic sales force required at all times and then making an estimate of the number of additional full- and part-time salespeople needed each month to handle the additional transaction load expected. The sales force required each month can be calculated on a clerk-hour basis for both regulars and part-timers and then translated into dollars.

Advertising. In setting the advertising figure, a plan may be made for each month in terms of media to be used and amount of linage and broadcast time necessary to make the desired impact on customers. The cost of this space is determined and expressed as a percentage of planned sales which is compared with a predetermined ratio for the season as a whole. It is not generally wise to hold the advertising percentage for each month constant. For the store as a whole, if not for all departments, the percentage should generally be higher in dull months and lower in peak months even though the dollar advertising allowances are smallest in the dull months and largest in the peak months. Such planning provides for a basic advertising appropriation even in the dullest months of the year; this is similar to the concept of a basic sales force. Additional advertising in other months need not be increased in direct proportion to the additional sales volume in order to provide adequate exposure to the public in the more active months. For example, a department store group recently reported that December accounted for 17 percent of its annual sales but that only 11.5 percent of the year's expenditures for newspaper space was expended in December. Conversely, February accounted for only 5.7 percent of annual sales, but this month was allotted 6.6 percent of the year's appropriation for newspaper space.

There is a tendency to refrain from allotting to each department head a certain amount each month to spend on advertising because an allotment has frequently led to careless spending of the appropriation. Some leading stores are finding it wise to allot each month a certain amount for advertising to each merchandise division or group of related departments. This is then used in the promotion of whatever merchandise seems to offer the best opportunity for large sales volume at a reasonable markup. Thus, no department manager is placed in the position of having money to spend before he knows what he wants to promote. Instead he must—in advance of each month—request funds for the promotion of specific goods that he believes will yield successful results. The advertising appropriation is thus used where it will do the most good, and buyers are forced to plan promotions before they are allotted funds.

Relative Importance of Profit Factors

An attempt was recently made to determine the relative importance of the factors entering into profits in conjunction with a Los Angeles area department store chain and to see if a model could be developed that would so combine the profit factors as to maximize profits.[4] While the study did not succeed in developing a satisfactory merchandising decision model, it did arrive at some interesting conclusions:

Sales volume, not unexpectedly, was found to be the major factor in the production of profits. Increases and decreases in sales both seasonally and over a period of years showed a very high correlation with profits. A calculation of ten variable regressions on profit suggested that each additional dollar of sales contributed twenty-six cents to profit.

Markdowns were found to be the second variable most closely related to profit, increasing as profit declined.

Changes in initial markup also showed significant correlation with profits, particularly in clothing departments where customers were not in a position to make valid price comparisons. It seemed to be negatively related to profits in departments such as toys where exact price comparisons were made.

Other profit factors of considerable effect on the final results were change in the average stock carried and in the amount of space occupied.

[4] D. J. Dalrymple, *Merchandising Decision Models for Department Stores*, Division of Research, Michigan State University, East Lansing, Michigan, 1966.

THE OPEN-TO-BUY

In chapter 1, it was pointed out that merchandising includes the functions of planning and control. The seasonal merchandise plan is the prime *planning* tool. The open-to-buy is the *control* tool. It is prepared weekly or monthly, allowing a check on the validity of the plan and providing a method of allocating purchases so that planned stock levels may be met. Open-to-buy may be defined as the amount of merchandise that may be bought for delivery during the balance of a control period if a planned closing stock is to be achieved. It may be calculated either in dollars or in units. In this chapter attention is centered on dollar open-to-buy. Unit OTB is considered in chapters 19 and 20.

How Calculated

The basic imput of data used in the open-to-buy report comes from the seasonal merchandise plan. The two most important elements are planned monthly sales and planned stock levels. All other data are recorded from the results of the current operation, that is, actual stock on hand and merchandise on order.

The relationship is a fairly simple one, as can be seen from the following example:

	End of month (or period) planned retail stock	$28,000
PLUS	Planned sales for the month or period	15,000
EQUALS	Total	$43,000
MINUS	Stock on hand at retail	30,000
EQUALS	Planned purchases at retail	$13,000
MINUS	Commitments at retail for current delivery	5,000
EQUALS	Open-to-buy at retail	$8,000

At the beginning of a period, the commitments are limited to the outstanding orders for delivery during the current month including any back orders that are now expected during the current month.[5] When the open-to-buy is calculated during the month, the commitments include the purchases that have so far been received dur-

---

[5] Some stores include another figure in commitments, called *goods in transit*. This represents shipments on their way to the store or selling department but not yet officially entered as receipts. Nor are they outstanding orders, since the invoices have been received and subtracted from the outstanding order record.

ing the month plus the outstanding orders at the time of calculation. In some stores, planned markdowns are included along with the planned sales figure.

ORDER AND PURCHASE CONTROL

To calculate open-to-buy requires a careful control over all orders placed. No goods may be ordered without an official order made out on the store order form. One copy of this form, with notations if possible as to the planned retail price of each item ordered, is submitted to an order department at the time the original is sent to the vendor. Here it is filed under the department or classification and month of delivery. In some stores, these orders are kept in two files only: (1) *current*, for orders that call for delivery during the current month, and (2) *future*, for all orders for later delivery. At the end of each month, orders for the coming month must be sorted out of the future file and put into the current file.

As invoices are received, they are checked against the corresponding orders. If an invoice completes an order, the order is removed from the outstanding file. If there is a balance still outstanding, the items received are checked off and the balance outstanding is written on the order, which is then returned to the outstanding order file. The amount of outstanding orders and balances in the current and future files are totaled every week or ten days to provide the outstanding order figures to use in the open-to-buy calculation.

Where it is not feasible to demand that buyers put retail prices on the store's orders in advance of merchandise receipt, orders outstanding may be totaled at cost rather than at retail. In this case, the planned retail purchase figure for each period is reduced to cost by applying to it the complement of the planned season's markup percentage. The cost of the commitments is then subtracted from the planned purchases at cost to give an open-to-buy at cost.

MULTIPLE OPEN-TO-BUYS

It should be observed that the OTB system of purchase control outlined above may require more than one open-to-buy figure at all times. Major emphasis may be placed on the open-to-buy for the current month, but if much advance ordering is necessary, open-to-buys for the following months in which delivery is expected are also necessary. In many lines, virtually all the open-to-buy for any month is used up before the month begins and all orders placed that month apply against open-to-buys for later months.

To obviate the need to maintain such a series of open-to-buys, some stores are now using an *open-to-order* control, which will be explained later in this chapter.

ADJUSTING THE OPEN-TO-BUY

The open-to-buy may be recalculated or adjusted at any time during the month, usually every week. While this may be done in a number of ways, a good plan is to determine the book inventory at the present time and calculate the open-to-buy for the balance of the period. Using the same monthly data appearing in the calculation on page 308, the book inventory at retail on the eighth of the month may be calculated as follows:

Inventory, first of month at retail		$30,000
Purchases (receipts), first week		3,000
Total merchandise handled to date		$33,000
Sales, first week	$3,300	
Markdowns, first week	200	3,500
Book inventory at retail, eighth of month		$29,500

The open-to-buy at retail on the eighth of the month may then be determined:

Planned inventory, end of month	$28,000[6]
Planned sales, balance of month	10,700[7]
Total	$38,700
Inventory, eighth of month	29,500
Planned purchases, balance of month	$ 9,200
On order, for delivery balance of month	6,000
Open-to-buy, balance of month	$ 3,200

In large stores, it is a common practice for the buyer to meet with his merchandise manager every week to set or adjust the open-

---

[6] The closing stock may be adjusted if the originally set planned figure now seems too small or too large.

[7] Sales for the month adjusted downward from $15,000 to $14,000. Markdowns for the balance of the month may also be estimated and included in the calculation.

to-buy for the balance of the month.[8] The chief items of information needed are the following:

1. Estimated sales and perhaps estimated markdowns.
2. Planned stock at end of month.
3. Actual stock on hand.
4. Outstanding orders for delivery during the balance of the month.
5. Markup desired for the month if OTB is to be figured at cost.

By repeating this control process weekly, the merchant will realize at the end of each month a stock very close to the planned figure. When larger stocks occur, they are deliberately allowed rather than suddenly found to exist.

A weekly open-to-buy report. Figure 17.4 is an OTB report that permits weekly adjustments. It is prepared in the controller's office for the use of the buyer. A similar report that includes all departments within the merchandising division is also prepared weekly for the merchandise manager.

Line 2 on the form shown refers to planned sales for the entire month, adjusted if need be. Since the OTB is being figured on October 12, the actual sales from the beginning of the month to date have to be added to the stock on hand and outstanding on October 12. Of the $45,000 stock required for the month, $9,520 has already been sold, $23,600 is still on hand, and $7,840 is on order. So, $4,040 more is needed. The same results could be achieved by including in line 2 only the planned sales for the balance of the month. Line 4 could then be omitted.

INCREASING THE OPEN-TO-BUY

Frequently, the orders placed for delivery during a month are so large in relation to the planned purchases for that month as to deter the purchasing of necessary or desirable merchandise. In fact, stores are frequently *overbought*, that is, the outstanding orders exceed the planned purchases for the balance of the period.

To correct an overbought condition or to increase an inadequate open-to-buy, there are the following possibilities:

1. Increase the planned sales figure for the month or balance of the month. This should never be the result of wishful thinking

---

[8] In some stores, stocks are planned for the end of each week rather than simply for the end of each month. In this case the procedure is the same, except that the calculation at the first of each week involves planned sales for the week only and not for the balance of the month.

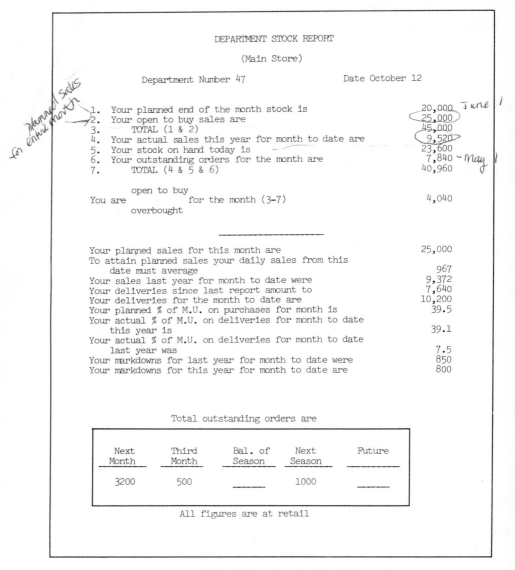

DEPARTMENT STOCK REPORT

(Main Store)

Department Number 47   Date October 12

for planned sales for entire month

1. Your planned end of the month stock is .... 20,000 *June*
2. Your open to buy sales are 25,000
3.   TOTAL (1 & 2) 45,000
4. Your actual sales this year for month to date are 9,520
5. Your stock on hand today is 23,600
6. Your outstanding orders for the month are .... 7,840 ~ *May*
7.   TOTAL (4 & 5 & 6) 40,960

You are   open to buy   for the month (3-7)   4,040
           overbought

Your planned sales for this month are   25,000
To attain planned sales your daily sales from this
    date must average   967
Your sales last year for month to date were   9,372
Your deliveries since last report amount to   7,640
Your deliveries for the month to date are   10,200
Your planned % of M.U. on purchases for month is   39.5
Your actual % of M.U. on deliveries for month to date
    this year is   39.1
Your actual % of M.U. on deliveries for month to date
    last year was   7.5
Your markdowns for last year for month to date were   850
Your markdowns for this year for month to date are   800

Total outstanding orders are

Next Month	Third Month	Bal. of Season	Next Season	Future
3200	500	_____	1000	_____

All figures are at retail

FIGURE 17.4   Department Stock Report

but should reflect favorable conditions not anticipated when the original sales plans were made.

2. Take more markdowns in the immediate future than were originally planned. This is a satisfactory method if the markdowns are really needed to move the goods but otherwise will be a most costly way to obtain an open-to-buy.

3. Reduce the stock on hand by returning goods to vendors or transferring them to another unit of the store organization. The former is often unethical, but the vendor may have a ready market for an oversupply of goods he has sold the store. The transfer device is a good one if the goods in question are really needed in a branch or other department. If the goods to be transferred will have to be sold at a lower price in a budget department, it will be necessary to take a markdown before the transfer is made.

4. Postpone outstanding orders for delivery to a later month. This would reduce the outstanding orders for the current month and make it possible to place new orders for current delivery. Vendors will frequently consent to such postponement.

5. Cancel outstanding orders. If they are overdue, this is a legitimate practice but may be unethical otherwise. However, a vendor who has not yet made up goods may be able to substitute sizes and colors, and possibly styles, if the items outstanding are not just what the store currently needs, or he may be glad to accept a cancellation if he is having difficulty filling the order.

6. Revise the planned closing stock upward. This is something of a last resort but will be justified if the original stock plan has been carelessly made, if the sales for the succeeding month are probably going to be more than originally estimated, or if the immediate need for certain specific merchandise is deemed more important than keeping stocks under rigid control. This possibility is elaborated on in the following paragraphs.

WAYS TO INCREASE OPEN-TO-BUY

- Increase planned sales.
- Increase planned markdowns.
- Reduce stock on hand by return or transfer.
- Postpone outstanding orders to a later month.
- Cancel outstanding orders.
- Increase planned closing stock.

Fractional distillation of the OTB. This is essentially a phase of the method whereby planned closing stock are revised upward by planning separate open-to-buy figures for subdivisions of the operation. This procedure is likely to reveal points where additional buying is imperative even though there is an overstock at other points. For example, a store's or department's overall plans may be broken down as follows, with three classifications involved (markdowns are omitted in the interest of simplicity):

	Store or Department as a Whole	Class A	Class B	Class C
Planned closing stock	$40,000	$20,000	$12,000	$8,000
Planned sales	20,000	8,000	6,000	6,000
Total stock required	$60,000	$28,000	$18,000	$14,000
Opening stock on hand	45,000	15,000	16,000	14,000
Planned purchases	$15,000	$13,000	$ 2,000	0
Outstanding orders	15,000	11,000	2,000	2,000
OTB	0	$ 2,000	0	−$2,000

If sales and closing stocks have been carefully planned for each classification, it is clear that there is an OTB of $2,000 in Class A in spite of the fact that the operation as a whole shows none. The overbought condition in C should not normally prevent needed buying in A.

Similarly in class B, with no OTB, a breakdown by subclasses such as price lines is likely to uncover some.

	Class B	$5 Price	$10 Price
Planned closing stock	$12,000	$5,000	$ 7,000
Planned sales	6,000	2,000	4,000
Total stock required	$18,000	$7,000	$11,000
Opening stock on hand	16,000	6,000	10,000
Planned purchases	$ 2,000	$1,000	$1,000
Outstanding orders	2,000	1,500	500
OTB	0	−$500	$ 500

Thus, in class B with no apparent OTB there is room for the purchase of $500 worth of $10 merchandise.

A breakdown of the $5 price, with an overbought condition, would probably reveal some OTB in certain sizes, colors, or styles.

The above analysis reveals a possible weakness in planning for a multi-unit operation where the OTB is worked out for the merchandise lines in the organization as a whole, without regard to the situation in the individual stores, and where resultant purchases are distributed to the store units. Since some stores may be overbought, the company-wide OTB is likely to be smaller than the sum of the legitimate requirements of the stores that do have open-to-buy. Thus, overstocked conditions in some stores of the organization hold down the amounts available for distribution to the other units. It might be wiser to compute the company-wide OTB by adding together the open-to-buys of the individual stores without subtracting the overbought figures of overstocked units in the group.

OPEN-TO-BUY BY CLASSIFICATION

With a computer in use, it is not difficult to assemble the data necessary to prepare plans for each classification and also to compute open-to-buys for each. However, some managers feel that an open-to-buy should also be calculated for the entire department under their control, even though classification data are available. In fashion lines especially, sudden shifts occur in customer acceptance of goods in the various classifications. The buyer must be in a position to redirect his purchase plans quickly as such shifts in demand are first observed by him. If he is given a separate open-to-buy for each classification, he may need to get permission from his superior to transfer an open-to-buy from one classification to another. The buyer may feel that the decision should be his and not subject to the discretion of someone not close to the situation. It is argued, and probably correctly, that the buyer should be judged on his overall performance rather than on his achievment of predetermined objectives for each classification. This conclusion, however, does not deny the need for classification data as guides to the buyer and also as signals to the merchandise manager whenever the relationship between sales and stocks in a classification get out of balance.

For his own guidance, the buyer is well advised to distribute his departmental planned purchases to classifications by drawing up a form similar to figure 17.5. Planned season purchases are calculated for each classification, and these figures are broken down to months in accordance with the buyer's knowledge of probable need. The open-to-buy for any classification in any month is determined by subtracting the outstanding orders from the planned purchases. Thus, with planned purchases for Class B in February of $5,640, the outstanding orders in that classification for February delivery may be $4,000 at retail on the first of the month; the OTB then is $1,640.

OPEN-TO-ORDER CONTROL

The open-to-buy controls the amount of merchandise that may be ordered for *delivery* each month, but it does not control the *timing of orders*. In many lines, orders should be placed many weeks or months ahead to assure good quality and receipt when needed. For the men's clothing buyer, for example, to know that he has a certain open-to-buy for March does not give a guide as to *when* the goods for March delivery should be ordered. Accordingly, it may be desirable to make an open-to-order plan indicating how much should be *ordered* each month, regardless of the time of delivery. This requires the planning of total outstanding orders at the end of each month.

					Purchase Plan by Classification							
Department: ___X___						Febuary 1 – July 31						
						Planned Purchases by Months						
Classification	Planned Season Sales	Planned Stock Feb. 1	Planned Stock July 31	Total Planned Purchases	Feb.	March	April	May	June	July
A	$15,200	$10,000	$11,160	$16,360	00	00	5,730	5,730	2,450	2,450
B	18,900	13,000	13,560	19,460	5,640	3,890	5,640	3,890	200	200
C	21,600	15,000	10,930	17,530	7,890	3,860	4,380	880	350	170
D	600	650	630	580	400	60	60	60	00	00
E	400	500	490	390	270	40	40	40	00	00
F	200	350	150	00	00	00	00	00	00	00
G	5,100	4,000	1,820	2,920	00	00	1,750	1,170	00	00
H	1,400	1,500	1,260	1,160	820	120	110	110	00	00
Total	63,400	45,000	40,000	58,400	15,020	7,970	17,710	11,880	3,000	2,820

FIGURE 17.5   Purchase Plan by Classification

Planning Outstanding Orders

This planned figure is based on an estimate of how far ahead orders should be placed in view of the time required by the manufacturer for production and delivery. It represents the planned purchases for this period of time ahead. This method is particularly suited to situations such as ready-to-wear where delivery takes from two to eight weeks rather than for lines that are largely bought far ahead on a seasonal basis. Here is an example:

Planned stock, June 1	$15,000
Planned sales and markdowns, May	8,000
Stock, May 1	17,000
Planned outstanding orders, June 1	10,000
Outstanding orders, May 1	9,000
(both May and future delivery)	

Open-to-order = Planned closing stock + Planned outstanding orders at close + Planned Sales and Markdowns — (Stock on hand + Outstanding orders)

Filling in the figures:

Open-to-order = $15,000 + 10,000 + 8,000 − (17,000 + 9,000)
= $7,000

This means that the buyer may order $7,000 in May. Some may be for May delivery and some for June and possibly July delivery. For example, if, of the $9,000 outstanding on May 1, $5,000 are for May delivery, the open-to-buy for May would be only $1,000: $15,000 closing stock + $8,000 sales and markdowns − $17,000 opening stock − $5,000 outstanding for May. Accordingly, the buyer is expected to order $1,000 for May delivery and $6,000 for later delivery. On June 1 his outstanding orders of $10,000 would consist of $4,000 worth placed before May 1 and $6,000 worth ordered in May.

Maximum Supply Method of Order Control

Where delivery of reorders can be obtained quickly and regularly, another method of controlling orders, as distinct from receipts, is sometimes used. A decision is made as to how many weeks' or months' supply to carry in stock, and also the length of the delivery period and the length of the reorder period. The sum of these figures, expressed in months (or weeks), represents the number of months' supply to plan to have on hand and on order. This method is generally more appropriate for unit than for dollar control and is discussed in chapter 19 in connection with staple stock control.

QUESTION FOR DISCUSSION

1. (a) How much freedom would you give a department buyer to make his own merchandise plan?
    (b) Would you give him great freedom but hold him responsible for carrying out his own plan?
    (c) Where merchandise plans are developed separately for each classification, should the buyer who purchases for a number of classifications be free to switch his open-to-buys from one classification to another, depending on his appraisal of his immediate merchandise requirements? Why?
    (d) Should the merchandise manager and the controller be expected to work out merchandise plans for the various departments independently in order to have a set of planned figures to check against each buyer's plans?
2. If the fall-and-winter season starts on August 1, when should the merchandise plans for that season be completed? Defend your answer.
3. What elements in the merchandise plan, if any, are likely to be upset by the activity of competitors?
4. (a) If planned markdowns for each month are not included in the merchandise plan, how would the actual closing stock for each month compare with the planned stock?
    (b) How would the planned purchases for the following month be affected?
    (c) Should planned purchases be increased in anticipation of markdowns or only after markdowns have been taken? Explain.
5. Can you suggest any seasonal goals that may be planned in addition to those suggested in this chapter?
6. Of the ways listed to increase the gross margin ratio, which is likely to have the best potential today in most stores? Why?
7. What are the most practical ways to increase the OTB?
8. Is there any danger that OTB calculations will be based on original sales and inventory plans and fail to reflect changing conditions that may call for increasing or decreasing the OTB?
9. Might the use of the fractional distillation technique lead to too much emphasis to buy in the categories where more stock is needed and not enough emphasis to dispose of overstocks in other categories? Defend your position.
10. (a) Distinguish between OTB and OTO.
    (b) What useful purpose is achieved in the calculation of the OTO?
    (c) Should the concept of open-to-order generally replace that of open-to-buy?

part

PLANNING

AND

CONTROL

IN UNITS

While dollar relationships are the major concern of the merchant in controlling his investment in merchandise, the major concern of his customers is to find exactly what they want. Accordingly, the merchant must maintain the proper unit relationships, that is, the right assortments in adequate depth. This requires unit planning and control.

Comprehensive yet readily operated systems are required to collect the needed information about the pieces of merchandise that are purchased, sold, and on hand at frequent check points. Armed with the pertinent data on sales to date and the present stock situation, as well as on the outstanding purchase orders, the merchant is in a position to place future orders so as to meet all reasonable sales expectations and yet avoid excess inventories with their heavy carrying costs.

UNIT
CONTROL
METHODS

NATURE OF UNIT CONTROL

Unit control is an organized method of determining, analyzing, and controlling sales and stocks in terms of units. The records are kept by pieces of merchandise, as distinct from dollar values. Other unit data that are commonly analyzed are purchases, outstanding orders, and price changes. All unit control involves the following steps: (1) determination of the type of system for each classification of merchandise; (2) daily or periodic recording of the facts; (3) daily, weekly, and monthly summaries arranged for convenient analysis; (4) analysis by the merchant; and (5) control of operations in the light of the analysis.

The purposes of unit control are (1) to control buying so that units will be stocked in proportion to sales and (2) to control selling so that the proper promotional emphasis may be given to each type of item in the light of its rate of sale and quantity on hand. This includes the repricing of the merchandise and the clearance of slow sellers.

Unit control summaries by classification and price lines are readily translated into dollar amounts; thus unit control may provide the information for dollar control, and plans made in dollars may be checked against actual operations in units. Sometimes unit control replaces dollar control; but usually the latter is used by merchandise managers and controllers to regulate the activities of buyers, whereas unit control is used by the buyers and departmental managers themselves to keep their stock assortments balanced to sale opportunities.

It must not be concluded that unit control is the all-inclusive technique for maintaining a stock assortment balanced to customer requirements. Unit control is concerned only with purchase orders, inventories, and sales. It does not reveal expressed or latent demand for goods that have not been included in the stock assortment. Accordingly, it must be supplemented by other means of investigation, such as the use of want slips, market reports, reports regarding competitor activity, and consumer research studies.[1]

PHYSICAL INVENTORY SYSTEMS OF UNIT CONTROL

There are two main classes of systems used in connection with unit control: the physical inventory system and the sales analysis system, which often includes a perpetual inventory.

Under the *physical inventory system*, the stock is counted at intervals and the sales are derived by the formula:

Former physical inventory + Subsequent net receipts of merchandise − New physical inventory = Derived net sales.

Net receipts normally consist only of the purchases received from the vendor less returns to him, but they may also include transfers in and out of a selling department. When the unit of control is a price line rather than a specific article, the net merchandise receipts figure also includes goods marked down into a price line from a higher price less goods marked down out of the price line to lower prices.

The derived sales figure represents net sales, since returns from customers are reflected in the closing inventory.[2]

The inventory counts are usually taken at periodic intervals, such as every four weeks, but in some systems counts are recorded only when a visual inspection of the stock indicates that a danger point has been reached. To accomplish this, a suitable quantity of the item may physically be segregated from the rest of the stock by

---

[1] These are discussed in a companion book, Wingate and Friedlander, *The Management of Retail Buying* (Englewood Cliffs, N.J.: Prentice-Hall, Inc., 1963).

[2] Technically, the sales figure derived is sales plus merchandise shortages but is close enough for inventory control purposes, since shortages as well as sales have to be replaced when reorders are placed.

a divider or a banding device. When it becomes necessary to break into this reserve quantity, a control ticket that was attached to this reserve is relayed to the buyer for action. In many small stores, merchants or salespeople simply make a notation of a reorder need at any time that they happen to observe that the supply of an item is low or depleted. This is called *visual*, or *eyeball*, control.

The task of counting inventory at periodic intervals is usually assigned to the sales force in the case of the forward stock and to stockmen in the case of reserve and warehouse stocks. To avoid the pressure of counting everything on the same day, the counts are commonly spread over a four-week cycle so that a portion of the stock is inventoried every day. Care is taken to include on the list for any specific day all the items purchased from a single resource. See figure 18.1, which shows a form provided by a manufacturer for the monthly counting of his merchandise in a store's inventory.

While most items in the staple assortment may be included on only one day's list in the four-week cycle, some items may be

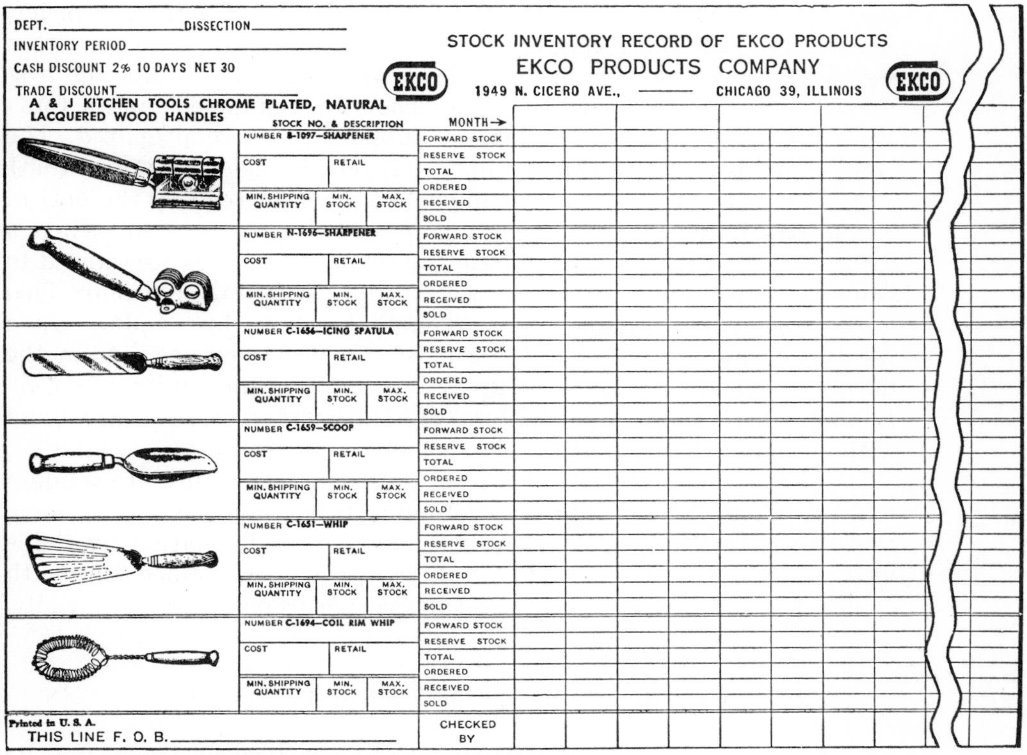

DEPT.________ DISSECTION________
INVENTORY PERIOD________
CASH DISCOUNT 2% 10 DAYS NET 30
TRADE DISCOUNT________

EKCO

STOCK INVENTORY RECORD OF EKCO PRODUCTS
EKCO PRODUCTS COMPANY
1949 N. CICERO AVE., CHICAGO 39, ILLINOIS

EKCO

A & J KITCHEN TOOLS CHROME PLATED, NATURAL LACQUERED WOOD HANDLES

STOCK NO. & DESCRIPTION			MONTH→
NUMBER B-1097—SHARPENER			FORWARD STOCK
COST	RETAIL		RESERVE STOCK
			TOTAL
			ORDERED
MIN. SHIPPING QUANTITY	MIN. STOCK	MAX. STOCK	RECEIVED
			SOLD
NUMBER N-1696—SHARPENER			FORWARD STOCK
COST	RETAIL		RESERVE STOCK
			TOTAL
			ORDERED
MIN. SHIPPING QUANTITY	MIN. STOCK	MAX. STOCK	RECEIVED
			SOLD
NUMBER C-1656—ICING SPATULA			FORWARD STOCK
COST	RETAIL		RESERVE STOCK
			TOTAL
			ORDERED
MIN. SHIPPING QUANTITY	MIN. STOCK	MAX. STOCK	RECEIVED
			SOLD
NUMBER C-1659—SCOOP			FORWARD STOCK
COST	RETAIL		RESERVE STOCK
			TOTAL
			ORDERED
MIN. SHIPPING QUANTITY	MIN. STOCK	MAX. STOCK	RECEIVED
			SOLD
NUMBER C-1651—WHIP			FORWARD STOCK
COST	RETAIL		RESERVE STOCK
			TOTAL
			ORDERED
MIN. SHIPPING QUANTITY	MIN. STOCK	MAX. STOCK	RECEIVED
			SOLD
NUMBER C-1694—COIL RIM WHIP			FORWARD STOCK
COST	RETAIL		RESERVE STOCK
			TOTAL
			ORDERED
MIN. SHIPPING QUANTITY	MIN. STOCK	MAX. STOCK	RECEIVED
			SOLD
			CHECKED BY

Printed in U. S. A.
THIS LINE F. O. B.________

FIGURE 18.1 Stock Inventory Record

included on two or even four lists so that they will be counted two or four times during the four-week cycle. The list of the items to be counted each day are kept in a tickler file, so arranged that the list for any given day works up to the front of the file on that day. Where such a file is maintained, the system is sometimes called a *tickler control*.

COMPUTER APPLICATION

Today, computers are being used in many large stores to facilitate the counting procedure. The computer issues a list of all items to be counted on any given day, and salespeople simply fill in the quantity of each of the listed items actually on hand. They record the quantity on hand in what is called *optical front style*, which permits the counts to be fed into the computer by means of an optical reader (see figure 18.2).

In a similar fashion, receipts are fed into the computer (see figure 18.3). The original of this form serves as a purchase order, and a copy as the receiving record. Purchase orders are written weekly after any buyer adjustments have been entered into the system. A standard two-part purchase order for vendor use and a four-part scannable purchase order for internal use are prepared. The right-hand portion of the scannable purchase order (Figure 18.3) serves as a receiving document to be subsequently read by the optical reader after the receipt quantities have been hand printed. When a store receives the four-part purchase order, one copy is forwarded to store purchase order control clerks and the remaining copies are filed in the department open-order file, alphabetically by vendor. Upon receipt of the merchandise, the purchase order is removed from the file and the quantities received are handprinted in the "units received" column. The is footed and the total is hand printed on the form along with the date the merchandise was entered in stock.

Other data needed to calculate sales, such as returns to vendors and transfers, are fed into the computer from what are called *exception sheets*. With the inventory and purchase information available in the computer's memory, the net sales of each item, for each month or other control period, can be calculated and reported electronically.

SALES ANALYSIS AND PERPETUAL INVENTORY SYSTEMS

Under the *sales analysis system*, sales are classified and tabulated by units each day. Records are kept of each day's sales in units, and

COUNT SHEET

DATE COUNT TO BE TAKEN WEDNESDAY 04-28-60

COUNT BY CASES AND UNITS

ALL ITEMS ON THIS PAGE TO BE COUNTED ON SAME DAY, PRIOR TO ANY RECEIVING

PAGE NO. 4310

STORE 24 | DEPT 57 | PAGE NO. 1316 | CODE |

015   074   4310   2

CASES   UNITS   SELLING PRICE CHANGE

DESCRIPTION	COUNT INSTRUCTIONS	SELL PRICE	WORK AREA	EDP CODE
LAVORIS ORAL SPRAY CLASS 1111 ITEM NO 502220	CASE-PK IS 24	.69		01
VICKS THRIFT PACK CGH DRPS REG CLASS 1201 ITEM NO 502120	CASE-PK IS 24	.23		02
VICKS THRIFT PK CGH DRP CHERRY CLASS 1201 ITEM NO 502130	CASE-PK IS 24	.23		03
VICKS THRIFT PK CGH DRPS LEMON CLASS 1201 ITEM NO 502140	CASE-PK IS 24	.23		04
VICKS VAPORUB 11/20Z CLASS 1202 ITEM NO 50210	CASE-PK IS 36	.69		05
VICKS FORMULA 44 DISCS CLASS 1202 ITEM NO 502100	CASE-PK IS 12	.79		06
VICKS VAPOSTEAM 3 OZ CLASS 1202 ITEM NO 502110	CASE-PK IS 12	.89		07
VICKS VAPORUB 3L/P OZ CLASS 1202 ITEM NO 502220	CASE-PK IS 36	.89		08
VICKS FORM. 44 8 1/2 OZ CLASS 1202 ITEM NO 502240	CASE-PK IS 12	1.59		09
VICKS VAPORUB 5L/P OZ CLASS 1202 ITEM NO 502230	CASE-PK IS 12	1.69		10
VICKS VATRONOL 1 OZ CLASS 1202 ITEM NO 50240	CASE-PK IS 12	1.69		11
VICKS SINEX SPRAY 15CC CLASS 1202 ITEM NO 50250	CASE-PK IS 22	1.09		12
VICKS INHALER WINDOW CLASS 1202 ITEM NO 50260	CASE-PK IS 72	.49		13
VICKS COUGH SYRJP 6 OZ CLASS 1202 ITEM NO 50270	CASE-PK IS 12	1.09		14
VICKS FORMULA 44 3 OZ CLASS 1202 ITEM NO 50280	CASE-PK IS 36	.99		15
VICKS FORMULA 44 6 OZ CLASS 1202 ITEM NO 50290	CASE-PK IS 12	1.39		16
CLEARASIL SOAP 3L/4 OZ CLASS 1521 ITEM NO 502170	CASE-PK IS 12	.29		17
CLEARASIL STICK 4L/2 OZ CLASS 1722 ITEM NO 502180	CASE-PK IS 12	.84		18
CLEARASIL LOTION 1.8 3Z CLASS 1722 ITEM NO 502190	CASE-PK IS 12	1.09		19

TOTALS
6/23
7/80

HANDWRITING GUIDE   1 2 3 4 5 6 7 8 9 0

INSTRUCTIONS

EDP CODE
01
02
03
04
05
06
07
08
09
10
11
12
13
14
15
16
17
18
19

8-12

COUNTED BY (PRINT NAME)   DATE COUNTED

FIGURE 18.2   Inventory Sheet for Computer Input

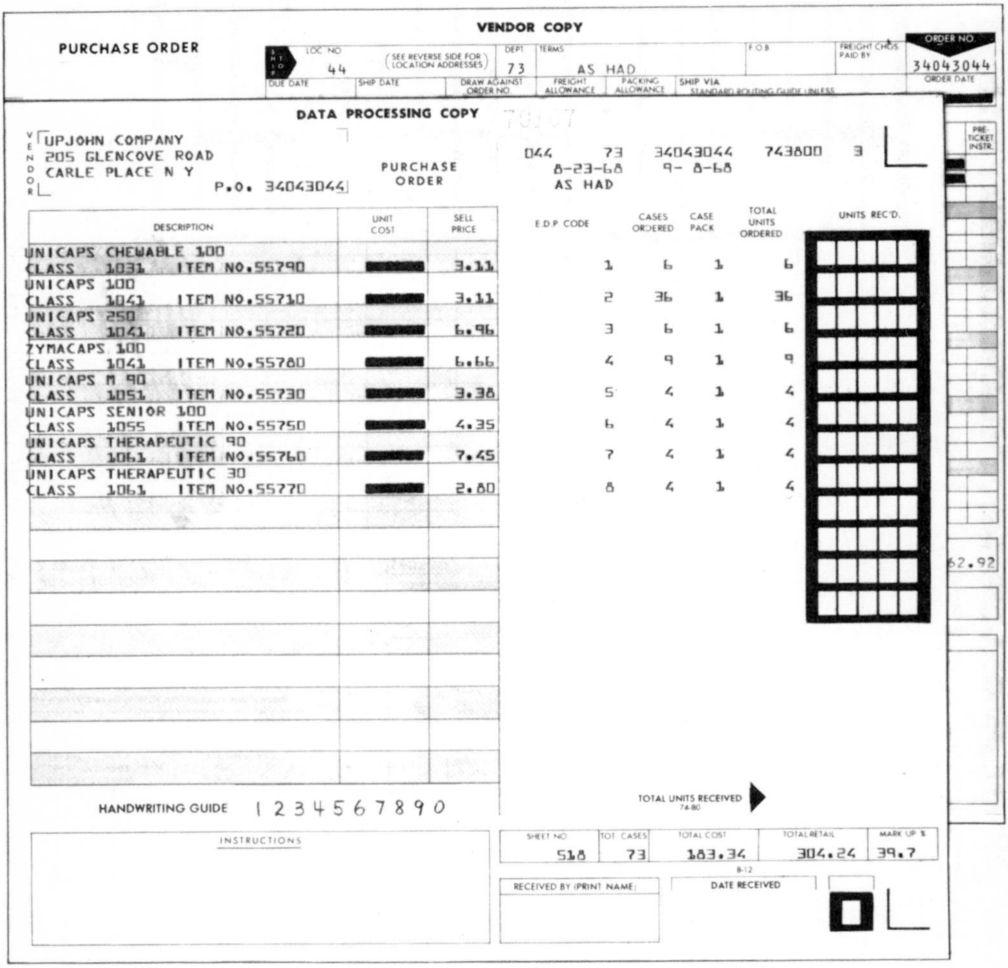

FIGURE 18.3 Receipt of Merchandise Form for Computer Input

these are sorted and tabulated by such factors as classification, price line, resource, color, size, and style number, as shown in figure 18.4. Frequently, a perpetual unit inventory is maintained—that is, the daily sales of each unit are subtracted from the record of the previous amount on hand to indicate the current book inventory. The formula used for this purpose is:

Former book inventory + Subsequent merchandise receipts — Net sales = New book inventory.

DAILY SALES REPORT											
DEPT. _____								DATE _____			
Class	Price	Season	Resource	Style	Color	Size	Sales	Credits	Sales to Date	On Hand	On Order

FIGURE 18.4   Daily Sales Report

RETRIEVING SALES INFORMATION

The desired sales information can be obtained in any one of a large variety of ways. The most common of these are as follows:

1. Copy of the salescheck. The necessary factors about each item are recorded on the salescheck by the salesperson. The store's copies of the checks are sorted and counted, and the information is transcribed to a permanent record.

2. Stub or section of the price ticket (see figure 18.5). When price tickets are prepared and attached to the goods, they contain a stub that duplicates the information on the body. This is removed at the time of sale, sometimes by automatically cutting it off and depositing it in a locked box. These stubs are sorted and counted daily, and the data are transcribed to permanent records.

3. Stub of cash register receipt. When the sale is recorded on the register, the salesperson removes the stub from the customer's receipt and jots down on it information about the item, such as style number and size, as the merchant may direct. These are then handled in a way similar to that of price ticket stubs.

4. Floor tally kept by cashier. Where a central cashier records sales on a register for a department or group of classifications, she

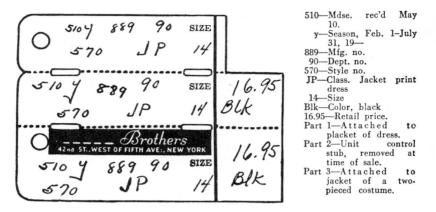

510—Mdse. rec'd **May** 10.
  y—Season, Feb. 1–July 31, 19—
889—Mfg. no.
90—Dept. no.
570—Style no.
JP—Class. Jacket **print** dress
14—Size
Blk—Color, black
16.95—Retail price.
Part 1—Attached to placket of dress.
Part 2—Unit control stub, removed at time of sale.
Part 3—Attached to jacket of a two-pieced costume.

FIGURE 18.5   Ready-to-Wear Tag

may be required to maintain a tally of all items sold, checking each item by classification, price, color, size, or other factor desired. These tallies are turned in at the end of each day, and the sales of each item are totaled.

5. The requisition from reserve stocks. A requisition form may be used to transfer goods from the reserve to the forward stock. Where a small forward stock is carried, one that is replenished daily from the reserve, the fill-ins from the reserve give an approximation of the sales to customers, which is sufficiently accurate for control purposes.

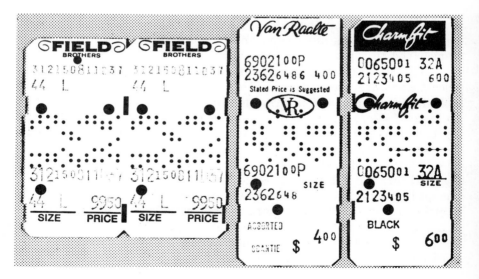

FIGURE 18.6   Punched Price Tickets

AUTOMATIC DATA PROCESSING

Stores that still use ADP (automatic punch-card data processing) as distinct from EDP (electronic data processing) have made some use of the technique for unit control, depending primarily on the price ticket for sales information. A standard tabulating card is punched from the information on the stub or other portion of the price ticket which is removed from the goods at the time of sale. These punch cards are sorted in any way desired for analysis, usually by merchandise classification, price line, vendor, and style number. Other data such as size and color may also be included. After sorting, the cards are fed into a tabulator that totals the number of each SKU sold and prints out a report.

Punch cards are also prepared for customer returns, making it possible to prepare current gross and net sales reports.

To maintain a perpetual book inventory for each item, some stores prepare punch cards for merchandise receipts and beginning inventories as well as for sales. The purchase data are available from the records used in the preparation of the price tickets. The necessary additions and subtractions may be made automatically to obtain the book inventory.

To assure speed and accuracy in the transfer of data from price tickets to punch cards, marking machines have been devised that in a single operation print the control data on each price ticket and also punch tiny holes in code.[3] See figure 18.6. These punched tickets are fed into a machine that prepares standard punch cards that correspond to each ticket.

THE COMPUTER: ELECTRONIC DATA PROCESSING

With the advent of the computer, new methods of capturing, storing, sorting, and tabulating sales information are coming into wide use especially in the larger stores, chains, and branch systems.[4] Unit sales information is fed into the sales register (imput recorder) at the time of sale in a form that the computer can read. There are

---

[3] It is possible to use a sensitized magnetic code on the tickets rather than punch holes.

[4] Selecting the right computer is a major problem for the large retailer. There are at least five manufacturers of computers for on-premise use by small businesses: IBM, Honeywell, Sperry-Rand, General Electric, and National Cash Register. Several other companies specialize in the manufacture of mini-computers, which are portable and have a limited capacity for information storage. To reduce cost, many stores today subscribe for the services of a data processing center—of which there are over seven hundred—which prepares reports for each store based on sales, purchases, and inventory data submitted. Some stores subscribe to a time-sharing service that maintains a large computer that can be hooked into a store for use during a certain number of hours each day or week.

a number of ways to do this. A common way is to use price ticket stubs or duplicate portions that are punched in advance, when prepared for marking, with the control information desired by the merchant. These tickets are removed and inserted into a point-of-sale imput recorder which automatically transcribes the data in code to optical font or punched paper journal tape.[5] These tapes are removed daily and sent to the computer center for processing.

A punched tag reader is available (Kimball) that transmits tag data at speeds of twelve hundred a minute directly to the computer, eliminating the intermediate steps of preparing punched tape or cards.

A slower way to feed the information into the register is to punch keys on the sales register to record the style number of the item and other pertinent features of the article, such as size, color, material, and trim—and/or other features deemed to be important for analysis. The recording follows the usual ringing up of the sale that lists classification, price, and salesperson's number.

Another method, recently devised, makes use of an optical scanning device that can be held over a price ticket attached to goods moving over a check-out counter. The device may feed the information on the ticket directly to a computer or onto tape for later processing.

The National Cash Register Company has recently perfected an electronic point-of-sale register of this type. An optic light wand held by hand "reads" special price tickets at a check-out point, and the register is then automatically operated. The wand looks like a penlight extended from a cable, making it unnecessary to remove the price ticket from the merchandise. Sales slips are issued by the register automatically for both cash and credit transactions. Charge sales can be handled and even authorized, since the wand scans color-coded bars on customers' credit cards.

The wand reader transmits the data to a magnetic tape recorder, and the tape prepared can be taken after business hours to a central computer for processing. Thus, this new system makes possible the automatic preparation of sales data by department, classification, style number, size, color, charge customer, and salesperson, with little chance of error.

Maintaining Cumulative Unit Records

Style control cards. Unless a computer is available, the daily sales information is transferred to style control cards. Ordinarily, a

---

[5] Optical font involves forming numbers and letters so that the computer can read them directly. See the examples in figures 18.2 and 18.3.

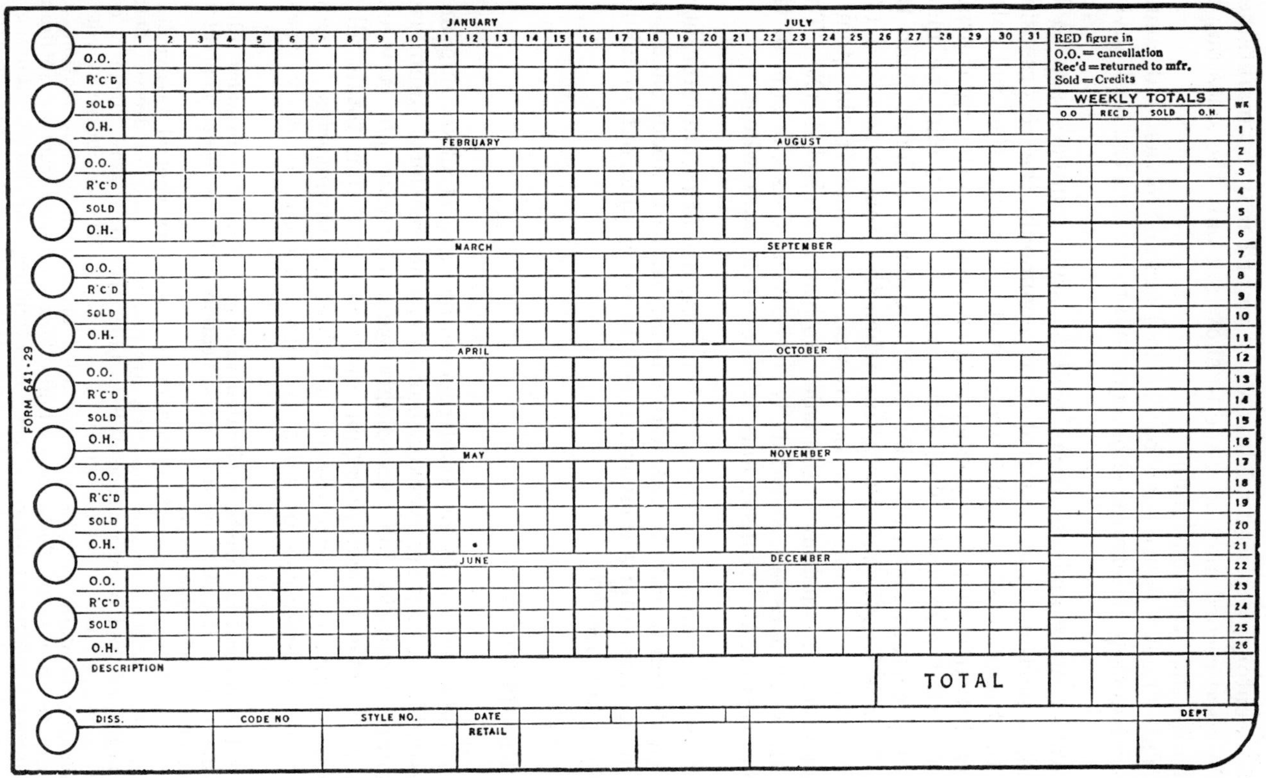

FIGURE 18.7 Perpetual Inventory Control Card

RED figure in
O.O. = cancellation
Rec'd = returned to mfr.
Sold = Credits

WEEKLY TOTALS

O.O.   REC'D   SOLD   O.H.

JANUARY   FEBRUARY   MARCH   APRIL   MAY   JUNE   JULY   AUGUST   SEPTEMBER   OCTOBER   NOVEMBER   DECEMBER

O.O.   R'C'D   SOLD   O.H.

DESCRIPTION   DISS.   CODE NO   STYLE NO.   DATE   RETAIL   DEPT

TOTAL

FORM 641-29

control card (see figure 18.7) is kept for each style number.[6] By subtracting sales from purchases or from the sum of purchases and the last inventory, a perpetual inventory record may be maintained. Thus, the card record may be made to show not only the sales day by day but also the stock on hand.

This "book" figure may be checked against occasional counts of physical stock to determine shortages and to correct the book inventory.

When sizes and colors as well as style numbers are to be analyzed, a portion of the control card, commonly the reverse side, is used for the purpose. Squares are provided for each size and color, and as each transaction is reported it is entered into the appropriate square for that size and color. For example, a dot may be made whenever a certain size and color combination is ordered from the vendor. This is lengthened into a line when the item is received (/). When it is sold, the line may be crossed (X); and if the item is returned from the customer, the sales notation is circled (X̄). This side of the card does not reveal daily activity as does the side of the card that reports the transactions for the style as a whole.

Computer memory record.[7]   With the use of a computer, style control cards can be eliminated, with the information about each style stored in the computer's memory, ready to be printed out in tabular form whenever needed.

RECAPITULATION

In addition to the detailed reports on each stockkeeping unit, it is desirable to prepare weekly, monthly, and seasonal summaries. The computer can do this exceedingly well. For example, a weekly summary of sales by classification and price line that totals all of the styles involved is most useful in balancing inventories to sales. These weekly summaries of sales are often accompanied by weekly

---

[6] The control is sometimes limited to a grouping that includes all the style numbers in a classification or subclassification, with no record kept of the movement of the individual styles.

[7] A study of the use of computers for inventory control in five large department store systems reveals that they are primarily used for dresses, better blouses, negligees, and women's shoes, all fashion lines that were formerly controlled by a manual perpetual inventory of each style. The computer speeds up the availability of data, permits more detailed breakdown of information, and assures greater accuracy. These advantages lead to better control of branch stocks, quicker spotting of styles in need of attention, and better planning of assortments. (David McConaughy, "An Appraisal of Computers in Department Store Inventory Management," *Journal of Retailing*, 46, No. 1, Spring 1970.)

inventory data by classification and price line. Other periodic reports, important in fashion goods analysis, are presented in chapter 20.

PERPETUAL INVENTORY CONTROL FOR CENTRAL MERCHANDISING

Unit control systems are frequently maintained in a central buying office rather than in the individual store.[8] Particularly for dresses, millinery, shoes, and men's clothing, chains and branch systems maintain central records of each store's stock and make shipments to the stores according to the information these records reveal. Groups of independent stores, largely through the facilities of their resident buying offices, have emulated the chains and operate unit control systems for fashion merchandise.

Most of these systems are of the sales analysis type with a perpetual inventory. Stores report unit sales of each style daily to the central office. The sorting of sales checks or price ticket stubs may be done in the stores and a daily sales report, or the sales checks themselves, mailed in. If a central computer is used, the sales in each store may be recorded on tape that is sent in daily to headquarters. Direct wire connections are also being perfected so that sales in the store units may be fed directly into the central computer. Daily reports of unit merchandise receipts (purchases) are also prepared and submitted to the central office. These daily reports are commonly supplemented by weekly inventory reports of the stock by classification, type, price line, color, and size. The weekly sales in each category may also be entered on this form from the daily sales reports. Instead of depending upon weekly inventory and daily sales reports from the stores, some chains maintain perpetual inventories centrally for each classification and price line in each store, obtaining the information from the daily sales reports and from records of daily shipments to the stores. Again, the computer may be used to accumulate and arrange this information.

Store managers also submit weekly letters emphasizing special needs and explaining local conditions that have had their influence on the sales, merchandise receipts, and inventory figures.

Even though many other analyses may be made, the style report and the weekly inventory and sales report are essential. The style control record indicates (1) to the buyer what styles and how many of a style to reorder for the group as a whole and (2) to the

[8] For a detailed account of central merchandising organization and methods, see Wingate and Friedlander, *The Management of Retail Buying* (Englewood Cliffs, N.J.: Prentice-Hall, Inc., 1963).

distributor how many of the style to ship to each store when the reorder is ready for delivery.[9] It also reveals when to transfer a style from one store to another and when to mark it down. By analyzign styles by type, the records reveal the most popular types in which new styles may safely be purchased.

The weekly inventory and sales reports are commonly made by classification, price line, color, material, and sometimes size. They indicate unbalanced conditions in each store's stock so that the distributor can ship styles in the classifications, price lines, and colors that need more stock to satisfy demand.

COMPARISON OF BASIC CONTROL METHODS

The physical inventory control systems described early in this chapter are adapted to the control of staples, or "never-out merchandise." This is merchandise that is regularly reordered during a season. Goods of low unit value are also so controlled. This system is inexpensive to operate but does not provide day-by-day information, nor does it reveal shortages.

In retail stores that have introduced the computer, it is possible to use the sales analysis system for staples, feeding in sales data as sales occur and purchase data as items are received. Without the computer, the continual recording of sales for each staple stockkeeping unit is likely to be arduous and inaccurate.

The sales analysis systems are adapted to the control of fashion merchandise where it is important to keep a daily watch on sales trends, where the average unit sale is large enough to warrant the expenses, and where shortages must be checked by comparing book with actual inventory figures. The system may not be desirable where the average sale is very small and the number of sales very large.

There is danger in a departmentized store in allowing every buyer to follow his own whims in regard to unit control. Under the pressure of other duties, buyers may fail to keep records that would be helpful and they may depend on memory, which is often faulty; and if they do introduce a system, they are likely to "lift" it from

---

[9] Where goods are received at a central distribution point for checking, marking, and distribution to the stores in a multi-unit system, the responsibility for proper distribution is usually assigned to *distributors* rather than to buyers. In some organizations, even though the goods are ordered centrally, most shipments are made directly from the manufacturers to the store units. The use of a central distribution point permits better inspection and an allotment of incoming goods to the stores in view of their immediate requirements, whereas direct distributions have to be planned well in advance, when orders are placed.

elsewhere. Accordingly, many large stores find it desirable to have a unit control manager to work with each buyer to develop the most suitable system and sometimes to assume the responsibility for the clerical work of record keeping involved. A degree of standardization is also required if a central computer is being used to keep the records for a group of stores. In the interests of economy and accuracy, all stores in the group agree on how to analyze the data for each merchandise line.

QUESTIONS FOR DISCUSSION

1. Why may returns from customers be disregarded in deriving net sales by means of physical inventory control?
2. (a) Is it generally practical to use the minimum control variation of physical inventory control? Why?
   (b) Can salespeople and stock help be depended upon to report when the minimum set for each stockkeeping unit is reached? Why?
3. In a small store without access to a computer, what method would you largely depend upon to accumulate unit sales data? Defend your answer.
4. (a) What would you suggest as the best method for accumulating unit data about merchandise receipts?
   (b) About outstanding orders?
5. What advantages does EDP have over ADP in retail inventory control?
6. What would seem to be the advantage of using optical printed (font) journal tape rather than punched paper tape?
7. Should there be a substantial reduction in clerical help when records of the movement of each style are kept by a computer rather than by hand on style control cards? Defend your answer.
8. Do you think that in the future most staple stocks will flow through a reserve stockroom, making reserve requisition control desirable, or will they flow directly from the receiving room to the selling floor?
9. (a) What information must be transmitted from store units to the central buying office for purposes of stock control and buying?
   (b) How would you get it there?
   (c) What data should flow back to the store units?
10. (a) Should the introduction and operation of unit control be centralized in a store that is departmentized or should each buyer introduce and supervise his own unit control operation?
    (b) What plan of organization and operation of unit control activities would you suggest to maximize the advantages to be gained from unit control?

19

THE PLANNING
AND
CONTROL
OF STAPLE
STOCKS

CHARACTERISTICS OF STAPLE MERCHANDISE

The goal of stock planning—to repeat—is an adequate assortment (breadth) in sufficient quantities (depth) to minimize customer walk-outs and to obtain an adequate return on the merchandise investment; in short, to keep the investment as low as possible without losing sales.

An IBM survey,[1] based on three hundred telephone responses from department-store-type customers, revealed that merchandise inadequacies accounted for twenty-five times as many lost sales as did poor salesmanship and that for every one hundred dollars spent by customers, an additional ninety dollars would have been spent if the stores had been able to meet their merchandise requirements. At least half of this loss of sales was attributed to out-of-stock conditions.

The results of this survey bolster the belief that in the great majority of stores, the *level of service*, that is, the ratio of sales completed to expressed customer demand, is low, averaging perhaps be-

[1] *Retail Impact Inventory Management and Application Program*, 1967, p. 1. IBM Technical Publications Department, White Plains, N.Y. 10601. This report is an excellent source of information on the subject explored in this chapter.

tween 50 and 75 percent. Yet, merchants generally agree it should be well over 90 percent. The controls in most stores have been inadequate, but now the computer is making a higher level of customer service easier to obtain. The key to success is still the proper system, properly supervised, whether that system be manual or computerized.

The methods of planning and control have to be different for each of the two major classes of consumer goods: staple and fashion. This chapter is concerned with staple goods (except for big-ticket items and seasonal commitments which will be discussed briefly in chapter 20).

Goods classified as staples (1) have a relatively long life with infrequent changes in the features of the goods, (2) have sales that can be predicted with reasonable accuracy, (3) have a relatively short delivery period, since vendors maintain stocks for quick delivery, and (4) are subject to frequent reorder, usually on a regular schedule. A large part of the merchandise carried in the following lines is staple: food products, undergarments, cosmetics, drugs, stationery, housewares and garden supplies, domestics, floor coverings, jewelry and silverware, sporting goods, toys, and books.

The general merchandise business is characterized by the need to have a very large number of stockkeeping units (SKUs) in both staples and fashions to meet demand; big department stores have many thousands—it is estimated that 90 percent of them have sales of less than one a week. But in the staple goods category, higher weekly sales per item can be expected, since the varieties in any classification do not have to be large.

Nonseasonal and Seasonal Staples

It is clear that any items in the staple category that the merchant decides to stock should be available either at all times or at least during recurring seasons of demand. Some staples may be subject to fairly regular demand through a long period such as a number of years and may not be affected materially by seasonal variations. This is true of some foodstuffs, hardware items, and toiletries. But most staples tend to be seasonal, with sales varying throughout the year or season in a predictable manner. And some, such as Christmas decorations, may be staple for only six weeks a year.

Homogeneous and Heterogeneous Staples

A staple may be homogeneous or heterogeneous. The former is a stockkeeping unit (SKU) in which all items are identical. All are the same style, material, color, and size. A heterogeneous staple unit consists of a group of items that are similar but not identical. The group then comprises the SKU. For example, a mail-order house may treat each different color in a style or design as an SKU but may not provide for a record of each different size within a color. Thus, sales are not reported by size, but orders are placed according to a predetermined ratio of size demand. The size scale is, however, analyzed periodically, and changes are made in it.

TERMS USED IN THE PLANNING OF STAPLE STOCKS

1. Delivery period: A liberal estimate of the interval between the time a reorder is deemed desirable and the time the resultant reorder is in stock, ready for sale. The delivery period *quantity* is the expected sales volume during the delivery period.
2. Reorder period: The time interval at which reorders should normally be placed. The reorder period *quantity* is the expected sales volume during the reorder period.
3. Review period: The interval at which the inventory is to be checked. It may be the same as the reorder period or shorter. For example, with the normal reorder period of four weeks, the inventory may be checked every two weeks.
4. Lead time: Usually synonymous with delivery period, as defined above, but may be regarded as the sum of the delivery and review periods.
5. Reserve (safety stock, or safety factor): A stock allowance for chance (random) variations in sales from the expected norm during the delivery and the review periods.
6. Minimum (order point): The stock level (on hand and on order) at which a reorder should be placed. If the system makes it possible to "flag" this level whenever the stock on hand (and on order, if any) reaches this point, the minimum is equal to the delivery period quantity plus the reserve. (See page 349 for a variation where no reorder is placed until the minimum is reached.)
7. Maximum (order-up-to level): The commitment level to which the inventory on hand and on order should be built up by a reorder. It is the expected sales during the normal reorder and delivery periods plus a reserve. It may also be defined as the minimum plus the normal reorder quantity.
8. Unit open-to-buy (reorder quantity): The maximum minus the stock actually on hand and on order at a reorder date. It may also be calculated as the quantity to be reordered when the minimum is reached or broken into.
9. Unit rate of stockturn: The annual sales expectancy (which may be expressed as fifty-two times the average weekly rate of sale) divided by the sum of the reserve plus one-half the normal reorder period quantity. (In some systems, half the review period quantity is also added to the denominator.)

10. Customer service level: Two definitions—(1) the percentage of delivery plus reorder periods[2] in which stock will probably be sufficient to avoid running out before the next receipt; (2) unit sales over a season or year divided by the number of units demanded by customers. The number of units demanded by customers may be calculated by adding to the unit sales an estimate of lost unit sales.

THE FORMULA FOR STAPLE STOCK CONTROL

With literally thousands of staple items reordered periodically, it is essential to develop a formal and systematic way to control reorders. For this purpose, a formula has been developed that lends itself to both manual and computer use.

DATA NEEDED

The data needed for the control of each stockkeeping unit are (1) the delivery period, (2) the reorder period, (3) the normal sales expectancy during the delivery and reorder periods, (4) a reserve or safety factor to take care of random fluctuations in expected sales, (5) the stock currently on hand, and (6) the merchandise currently on order. If the stock level is checked between the normal reorder dates, the length of this review period must also be known. The unit for measuring sales, stocks, and orders is usually the number of pieces but may be expressed in terms of dozen or of cases where the volume is large.

APPLICATION OF THE MAXIMUM SYSTEM

How this data is applied to determine reorder quantities is best explained by means of an example: A staple unit may normally require two weeks for *delivery* and the *reorder period* may be set at every four weeks, with no review of the inventory between reorder dates.[2] Once an order has been placed, there will be no opportunity to adjust the actual level of stock further until six weeks have passed; the next order will not be placed for four weeks, and it will take two weeks for it to arrive and be ready for sale. When a reorder is placed, it is necessary to have not only enough stock to meet the requirements

---

[2] Review period rather than reorder period if reviews are more frequent.

of the delivery and reorder periods but also an additional amount to provide against running out of stock should sales exceed expectations. The latter is called the *reserve,* or *safety factor.*[3]

Sales for the coming weeks may be estimated as averaging six a week, or thirty-six for the six weeks required for delivery and reorder. A study of likely variations from norm may suggest that the sales in the delivery and reorder periods might occasionally be as high as forty-eight, even though only thirty-six are expected. Accordingly, twelve extra units are set as the reserve, or safety factor. Provision must be made for the six weeks' normal supply of thirty-six units plus an additional twelve, giving a total of forty-eight. This is called the *maximum,* or *order-up-to point.*

The normal reorder point is the delivery period quantity (twelve) plus the reserve (twelve), or twenty-four. This is called the *minimum.* It is the point at which a reorder should be placed to avoid the danger of running out of stock before the reorder arrives. At the planned reorder date, the stock on hand (and on order, if any) should be close to the minimum if the sales forecast used in setting the minimum and in placing the last reorder has been reasonably accurate.

The unit open-to-buy is found by subtracting the stock on hand and on order from the maximum. If the stock on hand (and on order) is exactly at the minimum (twenty-four in the example) the OTB will be twenty-four, just four weeks' supply (48 − 24). If the stock is somewhat less than the minimum, say twenty, the OTB will be twenty-eight (48 − 20) to adjust for the depleted stock. If the stock is somewhat above the minimum, say twenty-six, the OTB will be twenty-two, less than four weeks' supply.[4]

The derivation of the unit open-to-buy may be stated as a formula, with all figures in units:

Open-to-buy = Planned sales during delivery and reorder periods + Reserve − (Stock on hand and on order).

SETTING THE REORDER PERIOD

The reorder period is usually set by the buyer not for each staple separately but rather for all the items bought from a single

---

[3] Definitions of *delivery period, reorder period,* and *reserve* are given in the list of terms used in planning staple stocks.
[4] While in this example the reorder period is longer than the delivery period, the method of calculation is equally applicable when the reorder period is shorter than the delivery period, with a reorder outstanding when a new reorder is placed. This outstanding order is added to the "on hand" in the OTB calculation.

source. The length of this period is generally based on three considerations:

1. The vendor's minimum shipping quantity. If an SKU in the seller's line sells at the rate of three a week, the reorder period will not be set shorter than four weeks if the order unit is twelve.

2. The cost and inconvenience of placing and receiving into stock frequent small reorders. This cost should be in reasonable ratio to the size of the order. Orders for different items from the same vendor may be combined, however, to justify ordering at one time a very small quantity of a single item.

3. The cost of carrying an inventory (see chapter 13). Frequent small reorders reduce the average stock level and therefore reduce the inventory carrying costs but increase the reorder costs. While there are mathematical ways of computing the reorder quantity at which the combined costs to reorder and to carry stocks are at a minimum, most buyers arrive at their reorder periods by weighing mentally all the considerations referred to above.

Once the appropriate reorder period for each item has been determined, the items will be grouped accordingly. Most general merchandise of a staple nature may be placed on a four-week schedule, with separate lists of what is to be inventoried on each day of the cycle. Thus, the task of checking the entire inventory may be spread out over the period so as to avoid interference with other activities. Fast-selling items may be listed for inventory weekly or even daily. Dry groceries are commonly checked weekly.

When a computer is used, instead of determining sales information by means of a periodic analysis of the inventory, it becomes feasible to feed information from price tickets into the computer as sales are made. It may then be found economical to reorder most of the staples every two weeks rather than every four weeks. If the maximum is unchanged, the computer can automatically prepare reorders equal to the sales of the previous two week period. This practice will materially reduce the size of the average inventory carried, and increase the stockturn realized on the items. However, this change requires price tags of a rather sophisticated nature. It may prove more practical to depend on regular inventories rather than to pick up sales information on many thousands of staple sales units.

SETTING THE RESERVE

In addition to providing for sufficient stock commitments to equal expected sales during the delivery and reorder periods combined, it is necessary to provide a reserve, or safety factor, to allow for the possibility of sales exceeding expectations, with a resultant out-of-stock condition. This reserve may be set by observing the random sales variations that have occurred in the past, as suggested on page 340. If these variations from the norm seem to have been caused by chance and not by seasonal factors or special promotional events, the reserve might be set equal to the maximum variation.

But sales information about each item covering a number of delivery and reorder periods is often not available, and changes in the rate of sale of the item may make past relationships an unreliable guide.[5] In such cases, it is desirable to apply a table of probability distributions that measure chance variations from a series of norms. These reveal that the reserve necessary for large sales volume is relatively less than the reserve required for small sales volume. A statistical probability distribution that seems to be well suited to the measurement of the variations of unit retail sales of staple stocks is called the *Poisson distribution*. It may be used where the average sales expectancy can be forecast with reasonable accuracy. This distribution makes it possible to develop formulas for varying degrees of protection against running out of stock. If a merchant wants to create an image of not being out of stock on staples, he may set a goal for the reserve that is intended to avoid depletion in ninety-nine out of one hundred delivery-reorder periods. It reads approximately as follows:[6]

$$\text{Reserve} = 2.3 \times \sqrt{\text{Normal sales expectancy during delivery and reorder periods}}$$

Thus, if sales are estimated at six a week with a two-week delivery period and a four-week reorder period, the reserve is:

$$2.3 \times \sqrt{6\ (2+4)}, \text{ or } 14.$$

This means that while sales of thirty-six are to be expected in the next six weeks, there is only one chance in one hundred that they may exceed fifty units $(36 + 14)$.

Many management may not wish to set a goal as high as this.

---

[5] The review and reorder periods are likely to be identical, but some operators check the stock between normal reorder periods to catch an unforeseen increase or decrease in the rate of sale. For example, even though reorders are placed regularly every four weeks, the stock may be reviewed every two weeks. When the review period is shorter than the reorder period, the reserve need provide protection only for the delivery and review periods, not for the delivery and reorder periods.

[6] For evidence of such relationships see the tables on the Poisson distribution appearing in various collections of statistical tables, such as Burlington and Macy's *Handbook of Probability and Statistics* (New York: McGraw-Hill Book Company, 1953).

If 95 percent protection is deemed adequate (one lost sale in twenty periods), the reserve needs to be only:

$$1.6 \times \sqrt{\text{Normal sales during delivery plus reorder periods}}$$

As applied to the example above, this formula for 95 percent protection results in a reserve of 1.6 × 6, or approximately 10, instead of 14. If management is willing to take an even greater risk, a reserve set at simply the square root of the normal sales expectancy would provide more than 80 percent protection.

It should be observed that the reserve increases at a much slower rate than the increase in sales. Thus, the higher the sales, the lower the reserve in relation to sales, resulting in a higher stockturn on staples that sell in volume.

This phenomenon can be illustrated as follows: A small lunchroom manager, on a basis of past experience, may expect nine customers during the lunch hour and find that if he provides seven extra seats—a total of sixteen—he nearly always has enough. Were he to average four times as many customers, or thirty-six, he would not have to provide four times as many extra seats, or twenty-eight. He would probably find that he very seldom had more than fifty customers coming in during this period, so he would increase his reserve only to fourteen, which is only twice the reserve required for a normal expectancy of nine customers.

Charting the Stock Fluctuations

Figure 19.1 shows the stock fluctuations that may occur in operating the maximum system. In the example, sales are planned at 6 a week, but the actual sales during part of the twenty-week period depicted vary by *chance* from the norm, as indicated on the chart.

It is expected that the stock actually on hand at each reorder date will be close to the minimum of 18 (the delivery period quantity of 6 plus the reserve of 12). At this reorder date, an order will be placed to bring the commitments up to the maximum of 42 (the minimum plus the normal reorder of 24).

The chart indicates that through the eighth week sales materialize as planned, but during the ninth through the twelfth weeks they reach 7 a week, or 28 for the four-week period. At the end of the twelfth week, the stock is 4 below the planned minimum, and 28 rather than 24 are ordered to bring the commitments back to the maximum of 42.

During the thirteenth through sixteenth weeks, there is a chance decline in the rate of sale to 5 a week, so that at the reorder

Actual sales:

Delivery Period 1 week, Reorder Period 4 weeks, Reserve 12 units

weeks 1 – 8, 6 per week;   weeks 9 – 12, 7 per week; weeks 13 – 16, 5 per week; weeks 17 – 20, 6 per week;

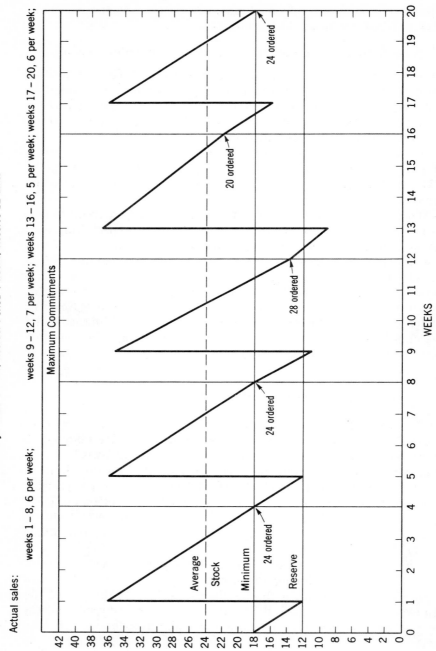

FIGURE 19.1   Staple Stock Fluctuations with a Fixed Maximum

date at the end of the sixteenth week 22 are on hand rather than the planned minimum of 18. Accordingly, 20 rather than 24 are ordered.[7]

During the eighteenth and following weeks, sales return to normal (6). Thus, the stock is at the planned minimum at the reorder date at the end of the twentieth week. What this system does is to reorder at reorder date the amount sold in the previous reorder period, so long as the maximum is not changed.

Stockturn.   So long as the rate of sale over the period averages out to the norm expected (in the example, 6 a week), the average stock is half way between the reserve on the low side and the sum of the reserve and the reorder quantity on the high side. In the example, the stock tends to fluctuate between 12 and 36, an average of 24.[8]

COMPUTER APPLICATION

For staples exhibiting a steady sales movement with fluctuations limited to chance, the computer may be programmed to write orders at the end of each period for the amount sold in the previous period. This is the same as bringing the stock commitments up to the

```
ABC DRUG COMPANY             FOB PHILADELPHIA, PA.              THE NATIONAL STORES, INC.    PAGE
721 SUNRISE AVENUE                                        TO   MAIN STORE                       1
NEW YORK, NEW YORK  10078     VIA CONSOLIDATED                 123 CENTRAL AVENUE
                                                              DAYTON, OHIO
DT OF ORD DT TO SHIP  DT TO CANCEL     ORDER NUMBER  TERMS      R/C  DIV  DEPT NO. VEND NO. ST.  DATE  REF
  6-10-6X  AT ONCE      6-28-6X        123-61123410  2/10 NET 30      1        123      234   1

ORDER QUANTITY    DESCRIPTION               SIZE     COLOR  CL  COST        EXT. COST  ITEM NO. UNITS OTY/RETAIL

20              D2  EASY FLO HAIR RINSE     6 OZ.   WHITE  101  5.00 D2      100.00*   24083  240   2/ 1.48

15    6/12      D2  EASY FLO HAIR RINSE    10 OZ.   WHITE  101  8.70 D2      134.85    24166  186   1/ 1.25

12              D2  EASY FLO SHAMPOO       MED             101  5.25 D2       63.00    38125  144   1/  .75

4     6/12      D2  EASY FLO SHAMPOO       KING            101  6.80 D2       30.60    38364   54   1/ 1.00

                                                          TOTAL COST    328.45     TOTAL RETAIL 572.10

                                                          TOTAL DISC      9.85           MU %   44.3

                                                          NET AMOUNT    318.60
```

FIGURE 19.2   Purchase Order Calculated and Issued by the Computer

[7] In practice, the mathematical reorder quantity will have to be rounded out to coincide with the vendor's shipping unit. In the example above, if the reorder unit is 3, the large sales would trigger a reorder of 27 and the low sales one of 21.

[8] The average may also be determined by adding to the reserve one-half of the normal reorder quantity. In the example, 12 plus ½ of 24 equals 24, the average.

planned maximum. However, the maximum may be adjusted either up or down at any reorder period, depending upon anticipated changes in the rate of sale. Computers may be programmed to make changes in the maximum, applying the basic formula to a differing rate of sale. They can then prepare buyers' orders automatically for the appropriate open-to-buy. (See figure 19.2.) When a system such as that exemplified by Figure 19.2 is in use, purchase orders are automatically issued at review time. The purchase order shows the department identification, applicable terms, and details of items ordered. It also shows dollar totals and markup percentages by class, cost and retail prices by item, quantity discount, and net amount of the order. Before such an order is delivered to the vendor it should be closely scrutinized by the buyer, because pertinent data may not have been fed into the computer, or some mechanical error may have occurred.

Stockturn Resulting from the Application of the Maximum Formula

In figure 19.1, it was observed that the stock on hand normally tends to fluctuate between the reserve on the low side and the reserve plus the normal reorder quantity on the high side. The sales of the item under control may then be projected for a year, and the rate of stockturn may be derived by dividing the annual unit sales by the average unit stock. In figure 19.1, the sales of 6 a week can be projected to 312 a year. The average stock is 24 units, as indicated. Thus, the annual rate of stockturn on this item is thirteen. This projection is actually realized only if the sales continue to average 6 a week and if the reserve and the maximum remain unchanged.

It should be noted that the stockturn realizable on homogeneous staples is relatively high. They are commonly recorded frequently and do not require that assortments be maintained. The reserve for individual staple items does not have to provide for a variety of goods, although as we shall see later in this chapter, the formula for control may be adjusted to provide for heterogeneous staples; then the stockturn tends to be lower.

Comparison with Dollar Control

Basically, the planning the maximum stocks, as discussed so far, is nearly the same as the calculation of dollar open-to-buy for a department or classification. In chapter 17 the following was established:

Dollar open-to-buy = Planned sales[9] + Planned closing stock − (Stock on hand and stock on order), with the control period usually one month.

In unit planning, the control period depends upon the delivery and normal reorder periods. The *planned sales* are those for the delivery and reorder periods combined, and the reserve is the planned closing stock, the point at which a reorder is due to arrive. Since in staple stock control the merchant is dealing with a homogeneous unit, the stock at the end of the period does not need to be large enough to provide a basic assortment at all times. Rather, it needs to be only large enough to protect against depletion.

ORDER-UP-TO TABLES

To facilitate the use of the maximum, or *order-up-to* formula (where a computer is not used), it is desirable to make use of a series of tables that give various delivery periods, reorder periods, and weekly rates of sale. An example of this is shown in table 19.1. The reserves used have been calculated by the Poisson formula for 99 percent protection. (This guards against running out of stock in ninety-nine out of one hundred delivery plus reorder periods, which is about once in twelve years if the delivery-reorder cycle is six weeks.)

If an item with a four-week reorder period and a two-week delivery period sells at the rate of 4 a week, the buyer will note from table 19.1 that the maximum is 36. At a reorder period he will order the difference between 36 and the stock then on hand, plus stock on order if any. He can also use the chart for rates of sale that vary seasonally. With a four-week reorder period and a two-week delivery, suppose he expects to sell 10 in the coming three weeks and 14 in the following three weeks. This is 24 in the six-week period, or an average of 4 a week. So he will locate the maximum opposite the weekly rate of 4 on the chart.[10] The stockturn figures included are calculated as explained earlier in this chapter.

---

[9] Markdowns are omitted in planning unit stocks because they affect value, not the number of items in stock.

[10] The Controllers Congress of the National Retail Merchants Association has recently published a series of "order-up-to" tables, similar to table 19.1. Different tables are provided for different reorder periods and for 95 percent protection as well as for 99 percent protection. Weekly rates of sale are given from 1 to 40.

TABLE 19.1   Section of a Table of Maximum (Order-up-to) Points[a]

Rate of sale (weeks)	Delivery Periods in Weeks							
	One		Two		Three		Four	
	Max.	ST[b]	Max.	ST	Max.	ST	Max.	ST
½	7	5	7	5	8	4	9	4
1	11	7	12	6	13	6	14	6
2	18	9	20	9	23	8	26	7
3	24	10	28	10	32	9	36	9
4	31	11	36	10	41	10	46	9
5	37	12	43	11	49	11	55	10
6	43	12	50	12	57	12	64	11

[a] For a four-week reorder period, with 99 percent protection.
[b] Stockturn.

CONTROL OF HETEROGENEOUS UNITS

The discussion thus far has had to do with homogeneous SKUs (stockkeeping units) where the function of the reserve is simply to avoid running entirely out of stock. With one adjustment, however, the maximum plan of control can be applied to heterogeneous SKUs, such as a collection of different sizes and colors within a style or a collection of different style within a price line.

For the heterogeneous SKU, the reserve must not only assure against stock depletion, it must also provide enough additional units to permit as assortment of the variants within the group. For example, an SKU may consist of three sizes and two colors and sell at the rate of six a week. With a two-week delivery period and a four-week reorder period, the appropriate reserve to avoid running out of stock would be fourteen pieces, as calculated on page 342. In addition, however, there are six variants; an assortment reserve of twelve pieces, an average of two of each variant, may give reasonable assurance that each size and color will be in stock just before a reorder is due to arrive. This extra reserve of twelve should be added to the normal reserve of fourteen, making the maximum sixty-two rather than fifty.[11]

THE MINIMUM-MAXIMUM SYSTEM

A variation of the maximum system is the minimum-maximum (mini-max) system where a reorder is placed whenever the stock on

[11] Maximum for a heterogeneous item: sales expected during the delivery plus reorder period plus the normal depletion reserve plus a basic assortment reserve.

hand (and on order if any) falls to the minimum point or below, instead of reordering only at predetermined reorder dates. Should actual sales exceed plan, the minimum would be reached sooner than expected and a reorder would be placed at once. On the other hand, if actual sales are below plan, it will take longer for the stock to reach the minimum and reorders will be postponed accordingly.

To determine the moment when the stock reaches its minimum in the course of selling, it is possible to segregate a minimum quantity of every item under control whenever a reorder is received. A reorder is triggered whenever salespeople or stock clerks find it necessary to draw upon the minimum supply. Thus, there is no set reorder period. This system is cumbersome and subject to neglect.

The determination of whether the minimum has been reached or not is more expeditiously achieved at periodic review dates, but to trigger the reorder the minimum has to be set somewhat higher than the quantity needed to cover the delivery period plus the reserve for chance variations in sales. This is necessary to avoid deferring a reorder until the stock is dangerously low. For example, with sales of four a week, with a two-week delivery period and with a reserve of eight, a minimum of sixteen would normally be appropriate. But at a biweekly review period, seventeen might be on hand and no reorder placed. But two weeks hence at the next review, the stock may be down to nine or less with the likelihood of an out-of-stock condition before the reorder can arrive. Accordingly, the minimum may be set at twenty, not sixteen, an extra week's supply. A reorder would then be called for at any review date at which the stock falls to or below that point.

This procedure is not practicable where it is economical to reorder at one time all the items to be procured from a single vendor. It would be wasteful to place a separate order for each item when its minimum quantity is reached. Rather, a single reorder date will be set for all the items in the group, with some being ordered before their minima are reached and others after the minima have been pierced. On this predetermined date, each item will be built up to its planned maximum.

THE RATE OF SALE

The predicting of the rate of sale is probably the most difficult part of the control process. While a few items may sell at a predetermined rate with weekly variations due mostly to chance factors, most items exhibit seasonal variation of sales which are greatly influenced by special promotional activities, particularly special sales at reduced prices. They are also affected by changes in customer preference which may sometimes be rapid. Thus, the planning of sales for the delivery and reorder periods requires a good deal of judgment.

The technique for unit sales forecasting that seems to be best suited for fast-moving staple stocks requires a knowledge of past sales of the item by weeks or months over at least a two-year period.[12] These sales may be charted with the weeks (or months) along one axis and the units sold along the other. By inspection of the points plotted, it can be determined whether the weekly or monthly variations are due to chance or whether they exhibit some regularity in movement. They may indicate an upward or a downward trend over the period, a distinct seasonal variation, or a combination of both trend and seasonal variation. If a trend seems to exist, its slope may be approximated by inspection or by calculation using a standard statistical technique and projecting ahead.

If the sales variations seem to show only random variations, with no upward or downward trend, the average rate of sale during the period can be used in planning.

SEASONAL PATTERNS

Many staples will reveal a pattern of seasonal variation. Here it is necessary to superimpose on the sales points plotted a model that shows the general tendency, without taking in all those points on the chart that look like chance variations or that may be caused by a known abnormal factor such as a newspaper strike one month, a special sale another, or a known out-of-stock condition that distorted the trend.

There are statistical methods of smoothing the data to determine the general tendency. These are being fed into computers that are controlling stocks in some stores already, but the approximate trend can be drawn by inspection and projected ahead. Figure 19.3 is an example of such a chart. Sales appear along the x-axis, horizontally, and the months are presented vertically. Guided by the points on the chart for the first two years, the model or trend line is fitted and then extended through the third or coming year. In this example, a computer did the work. The report provides space to compare the actual sales each month with the forecast. If a considerable error between the monthly forecast and the actual should appear, a correction will promptly be made in the forecast.

---

[12] When the identical item has not been stocked this long, the sales of its previous counterpart may be used.

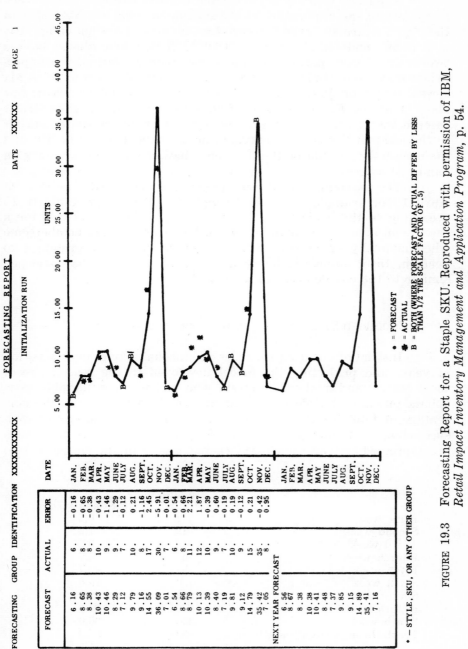

FIGURE 19.3   Forecasting Report for a Staple SKU. Reproduced with permission of IBM,
Retail Impact Inventory Management and Application Program, p. 54.

The sales forecast derived from a chart like this can be used as follows in the application of the maximum formula. Note that in the chart, figure 19.3, the forecast for January of the planning year is 7 (6.56) and for February, 9 (8.67). If this item should have a two-week delivery period and four-week reorder period, the appropriate maximum would equal six weeks' supply plus a reserve. A six weeks' supply on January 1 consists of 7 units (January sales) plus about 4 of the February sales of 9, a total of 11. An appropriate reserve for 11 sales is 8, according to the formula presented earlier in this chapter. Thus, the maximum on January 1 would be 19; and the open-to-buy would be the difference between 19 and the stock on hand and on reorder on January 1.

The maximum is subject to change every reorder period. On April 1, for example, six weeks' supply would be approximately 15 according to the projections in figure 19.3, which would call for a reserve of 9 and a maximum of 24. Such calculations are cumbersome when manually performed, but a computer can be programmed to perform them automatically or a reference table can be developed similar to the one depicted in table 19.1.

MODIFIED SEASONAL PLAN OF FORECASTING

Instead of charting the sales of seasonal staples over a period of years and projecting the model developed to the season ahead, some central and mail-order buyers who realize a considerable sales volume on each SKU develop a cumulative chart that shows the percentage of total season's sales last year achieved at the end of each succeeding week during the season. See figure 19.4 where the weeks are expressed as fractional parts (percentages) of the entire season.

	Cumulative Units	% of Season's Total
First week	2	0.2
Second week	12	1.2
Third week	32	3.2
Fourth week	57	5.7
Fifth week	97	9.7
Sixth week	150	15.0
Seventh week	200	20.0
Eighth week	270	27.0
Ninth week	350	35.0
Tenth through twenty-sixth week	650	65.0
TOTAL	1,000	100.0

If the sales during a six-month period last year were 1,000, the sales during the first week of the season may have been only 2, with sales of 10 the second week, 20 the third week, 25 the fourth, 40 the fifth, 53 the sixth, 50 the seventh, 70 the eighth, 80 the ninth, and so on. The cumulative weekly sales are tabulated as shown.

During the first three weeks of the current season, the sales of this item may be 40. This is set at 3.2 percent of the total season's sales for this year: $40 \div 3.2\% = 1,250$, the projected sales for this season compared with 1,000 last year. Again, suppose that the delivery and reorder periods for this item are four weeks. At the end of the third week, then, they extend through the seventh week during which 20 percent of the season's sales are expected. Subtracting from this the 3.2 percent of season's sales that are normal for the first

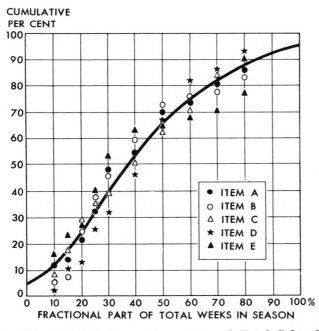

FIGURE 19.4   Cumulative Sales as Percentage of Total Sales for Season: Line and Individual Items. Typical dispersion of items around line average, computed from sales records of past seasons. From *Forecasting Sales* (Studies in Business Policy No. 106). Courtesy National Industrial Conference Board, New York, 1964.

three weeks gives 16.8 percent for the four weeks ahead—16.8 percent of the estimated season's sales of 1,250 is 210, the estimated sales for the coming four weeks. This figure would be the one used in calculating the maximum and the reorder at the end of the third week.

This calculation may be repeated at weekly or at reorder intervals. For example, at the end of the fifth week the actual sales may be 125. This is set equal to 9.7 percent, which gives a revised sales estimate for the season of 1,300. The sales expected for the coming four weeks are 25.3 percent of the season's total (35% − 9.7%). Since 25.3 percent of 1,300 is 329, it is the forecast sales figure for the control period ahead.

To avoid chance irregularities in the weekly variations, it is possible to plot the sales of a group of similar items on a chart and to determine a composite curve for the group rather than for each item separately. This is what has been done in figure 19.4.

This method is frequently used by mail-order houses who do a large volume on identical items. Its use is not strictly limited to staples; it is applicable to new styles and models that are similar to those carried the year before. Where the same pattern of seasonal variations occurs from one year to the next, the cumulative percentages are found to be an excellent guide for prediction, and the system provides for increases and/or decreases in the season's total estimate of sales as the season progresses. But where the seasonal variation is erratic, especially during the early weeks of the season when sales may be abnormally large or small, the forecasts may be far from correct. Rather than base the season cumulative percentages entirely on the corresponding season the year before, former seasons may well be considered and also changes in promotion plans and in variable key dates that are likely to change last year's seasonal pattern. Mail-order merchants have found that the initial sales forecast, even before the selling season starts, is greatly influenced by the position of the item in the new catalog and by the illustrations and copy.

Unless a computer is used for unit control purposes, many stores find it cumbersome to keep weekly sales records for each unit. In such instances, weekly data may be replaced by monthly (four-week) records based on physical inventory analysis, with the seasonal chart based on four-week rather than weekly intervals.

As already indicated, judgment should be exercised where a special promotion of the item is planned, one that is not reflected in last year's seasonal chart or where a delay in delivery is to be expected. If a computer is used, such special information must either be fed into it or brought into the picture by the merchant as he analyzes the reorder quantities that the computer spews forth.

QUESTIONS FOR DISCUSSION

1. Why is it not feasible to base all staple stock control on homogeneous units, that is, on each separate size and color instead of setting up heterogeneous SKUs?

2. (a) Demonstrate how an SKU with large weekly sales can achieve a higher stockturn than one with low weekly sales even though delivery and reorder periods are constant.
   (b) Are delivery and/or reorder periods likely to be shortened as sales volume of a unit increases?

3. (a) Why are markdowns, which are included in dollar planning, omitted in unit planning?
   (b) Would unit control by price line be an exception?

4. How would you allow for delays in delivery in applying the formula for unit stock control?

5. (a) Is a reserve that protects against loss of sales during 99 percent of the delivery and reorder periods generally too large for most operations?
   (b) What degree of protection do you recommend? Why?

6. Instead of applying a generalized rule for setting the reserve, such as the formula based on the Poisson distribution, would it be wiser to develop the reserve for each staple item (or group of related items) by analyzing the actual sales variations in the past from the norm and selecting for the reserve the largest variation that seems to have been due to chance? Defend your position.

7. (a) Explain the reasoning behind the following statement: If the control system makes it possible to determine the moment at which the *minimum* is reached and if reorders are then placed immediately, the *reserve* would need to protect for random sales variations during the delivery period only rather than during the delivery and reorder periods.
   (b) Would such a system improve stockturn materially?

8. What degree of protection would you recommend in planning shelf space allotted to an item, that is, should the reserve carried on the selling floor be the same as that set for reordering?

9. Is it generally feasible to check inventories between planned reorder periods so as to act promptly if sales of an SKU should be subject to a sudden and unforeseen increase?

10. (a) How would you forecast the sales of a staple carried in your stock for which past sales information is not available?
    (b) How would you forecast the sales of a staple item that you are now adding to stock for the first time?
    (c) How would you attempt to forecast the sales of an item that sells intermittently and spasmodically, showing no sales activity from time to time? Should you feel that forecasting is not feasible for such an item, how would you control it?

11. (a) If the sales of a staple item averaged two per week two years ago and three per week last year, what rate would you project for the coming year?
    (b) If the first quarter of the year (thirteen weeks) normally

accounts for a third of the year's sales of the above item, what weekly rate of sale would you plan for the first quarter?

12. Are seasonal variations regular enough to make the forecasting of sales on the basis of cumulative sales ratios generally practical?

13. To chart the weekly or monthly sales for hundreds, even thousands, of SKUs under a single buyer's jurisdiction and to determine the pattern of demand for each as well as to forecast the sales for each based on past experience are tremendous tasks where a computer is not available. Suggest a method that does not involve the use of the computer.

14. Some merchants may feel that the mathematics and procedures discussed in this chapter are too complicated for them to use. Nevertheless, what concepts can they develop from the discussion to improve their timing of reorders and their setting of reserves?

20

THE PLANNING AND CONTROL OF FASHION STOCKS

It is fitting that the final chapter in this treatment of retail merchandise management be devoted to the planning and control of fashion merchandise in both apparel and home furnishings. Fashion stocks are the most complex of all classes of merchandise; they are also the most critical for the merchant because of the tremendous choice of styles, materials, colors, and resources. The expression of this choice and taste level is a major factor in the store's image. In addition, the risks in fashion merchandising are much greater than in staples and provide profit opportunities that frequently make it possible for a store to stock many less profitable lines deemed necessary for a balanced assortment.

The list below presents the major characteristics of fashion merchandise. The key element is the first: its fast-changing nature. The life span of a style may be very short; the features that make it of interest to customers are often elusive; and there are thousands of similar items from which to choose. Some styles, called *fads*, are in fashion for even less than three months and then quickly lose customer acceptance.

PREDICTABLE ELEMENTS OF FASHION MERCHANDISE

In spite of difficulties, the merchant must predict if he is to buy. Fortunately, there are certain characteristics of fashion merchandise that enjoy repetitive demand, such as the distribution of garment sales by size. These are found even in a high fashion dress department. Thus, by determining the repetitive elements in fashion goods, predictions on a basis of past sales are possible.

MAJOR FEATURES OF FASHION MERCHANDISE CONTRASTED WITH STAPLES

- Life span short
- Predictability difficult
- Style and color more important than function
- Assortments broad
- Many purchases by the customer on impulse
- Value to a considerable extent subjective
- Relatively little assurance of availability of reorder from the resource

---

While the degree of predictability varies with each merchandise line, the following characteristics are generally repetitive: classifications and sometimes subclassifications or types, price lines or ranges, materials, colors, and sizes. Open-to-buy is commonly calculated in units for each price range within a classification, and sometimes for each material also. The quantity needed in each color and size within a line can be determined with considerable accuracy by calculating the percentage distribution of sales in the past corresponding selling period.

CLASSIFICATION

As defined in chapter 14, a classification is a major subdivision within a departmental grouping. The end use or function of an item determines its classification. *An item in one classification shall not be substitutable for an item in another classification.* Thus, in a boys' department, underwear and coats comprise two separate classifications. In a dress department, cocktail dresses, because of their social end use, are commonly classified separately from other dress groupings. Relative customer demand for goods in each classification is nearly constant and can accordingly be predicted. Often, subclassifications can also be predicted, such as sleeveless versus long-sleeve shirts in a misses' shirt classification.

PRICE

Because a store attempts to cater to certain income groups, it can be predicted that the average price within a merchandise line will remain relatively constant over a year or two. A dress department's average sale will vary little over the short run. Once this norm is determined, it is not difficult to determine with considerable accuracy the probability of future demand in lower and higher ranges, and even at specific price points.

MATERIAL

Customer acceptance of various materials, such as the leathers and fabrics that enter into the construction of shoes, tends to follow a pattern. Even in a high fashion dress department the sale of different weights and types of fabric recur with considerable seasonal regularity. For example, cottons sell well in summer, wools in winter, and satins for the holidays. A correctly balanced stock gives the proper emphasis to these fabrics at the appropriate times.

COLOR

Basic colors retain their relative position in total sales over a considerable period of time. Some exhibit seasonal regularity. Green and rust, for example, are usually in demand for ready-to-wear early in the fall; black and white in the summer; and pastels and light background prints in the spring. Novelty colors, called *high shades*, are less predictable, but the ratio of sales of all high shades to basic colors is fairly constant, providing a guide as to how many high shades to buy.

SIZE

The distribution of sales by size is fairly constant, at least over the short run. In the case of clothing, it may vary slowly over the long run due to changes in the proportions of the human body.

But the size distribution of the past season is a valid predictor of the demand in the coming season.

NONPREDICTABLE ELEMENTS OF FASHION MERCHANDISE

Although the future distribution of sales within each of the characteristics discussed above is predictable on a basis of past experience, the acceptance of an individual style number,[1] or of a particular *look*[2] available in similar styles, is often not predictable. Every style number offered on the market is a composite of design, material, pattern, color, and size, all fashioned for a particular end use and offered at a price. Public acceptance of the package of elements that constitute a style number is highly uncertain, and the intuitive judgment of the buyer must be relied upon. However, where a certain style incorporates a popular design, a popular material, a popular pattern and color, in a popular size, and at a popular price, it is much more likely to prove a successful seller than would a style that fails to include this composite of characteristics. Sometimes a particular style embodying such characteristics proves to have an extended life over a number of seasons.

THE MODEL STOCK PLAN

By identifying the predictable elements in the demand for fashions, the merchant is able to make an assortment plan, or *model stock plan*, as it is commonly called.[3]

DEFINITION

A model stock is an assortment of merchandise broken down into such predictable factors as classification, price, material, color, and size in accordance with customer demand. In planning a model stock, the attempt is to achieve maximum sales from the merchandise investment. Sales and stock information obtained through a unit control system is necessary if a model stock is to be planned intelligently,

---

[1] A style number is a product of one manufacturer with distinctive characteristics, particularly in reference to composition and design. It is commonly available in different sizes and colors and sometimes in finish.

[2] A *look* may be defined as a group of style numbers that are similar in appearance but that differ in detail.

[3] The model stock is also a useful concept in preparing a stock assortment for staples.

but care must be taken to be guided by current trends rather than solely by last year's sales pattern. Also, the planner should avoid the mistake of trying to keep stock in exact proportion to sales. For example, a store may have three classifications, all three of which require the same number of price lines and sizes. Sixty percent of the sales may be in class A, 30 percent in class B, and 10 percent in class C. If the total stock is distributed in these proportions, the assortment in class C will be very small and probably inadequate to achieve even the 10 percent sales expectancy. Conversely, in class A, the assortment may be larger than necessary to satisfy virtually all customers. Normally, the stockturn in the large classifications should be higher than that in the small classifications, provided the assortment needs in both are similar.[4] The following might be a good distribution:

Class	Planned Unit Sales	Planned Unit Stock	Stockturn
A	600	250	2.4
B	300	150	2.0
C	100	100	1.0
Total	1,000	500	2.0

EXAMPLE OF A MODEL STOCK PLAN

Tables 20.1 and 20.2 indicate the development of a model stock plan for a sweater department. Of a total planned stock of $60,000 for August 1, $7,000 may be allotted to promotional merchandise brought in for special sales in August and $3,000 may be assigned to leftovers from spring and early summer sales. Thus, $50,000 is made available for the department's model stock of fresh goods needed for the regular late summer business. This is broken down into classifications, roughly in proportion to sales with the considerations discussed above in mind.

Table 20.2 presents the unit model stock plan for one of the sweater classifications, broken down by material and price. Breakdowns by color and size may also be made, but as already indicated knowledge of the relative importance of colors and sizes can be applied during the buying procedure, without including these elements as a part of the formal plan. The figures presented are suitable for a large dominant department or women's specialty store.

In determining the units within each type and price, the planner will make adjustments, if necessary, in his mathematically pre-

---

[4] See chapter 12 for the relationship between stockturn and sales volume.

TABLE 20.1   Model Stock Plan by Classification—Women's Sweater Department

I.	TOTAL DEPARTMENT DOLLAR STOCK AUGUST 1		$60,000
	(From seasonal merchandise plan)		
II.	MAJOR BREAKDOWN		
	Promotional merchandise (for back-to-school sale)		$ 7,000
	Carry-over (slow-selling spring styles)		3,000
	Model stock		50,000
	Total		$60,000
III.	CLASSIFICATION	DISTRIBUTION OF TOTAL MODEL STOCK	
	Cardigan	40%	$20,000
	Poncho	25	12,500
	Dressy	15	7,500
	Shawl	10	5,000
	Vest	5	2,500
	Coat sweater	5	2,500
	Total model stock	100%	$50,000

TABLE 20.2   Model Stock Plan for the Cardigan Classification of the Sweater Department—Total $20,000

TYPE (Material)	Price	Units[a]	Dollars
Synthetic (50%)			
	$14–15	170	2,500
	16–17	365	6,000
	18–19	80	1,500
		615	10,000
Wool (40%)	Price	Units	Dollars
	$16–19	115	2,000
	20–26	210	4,800
	27–33	40	1,200
		365	8,000
Cashmere (10%)	Price	Units	Dollars
	$20–29	20	500
	30–39	35	1,200
	40–50	7	300
		62	2,000
TOTAL		1,042	20,000

[a] Dollars divided by the average of each price range and rounded off to the nearest unit of five except for the last item.

pared plan to assure adequate assortments from the customer's point of view. For example, he will question whether 7 cardigan cashmere sweaters in the $40-to-$50 range will provide enough sizes and colors to satisfy the probable demand at that point. He will also question whether 365 units are really needed at the point of greatest customer demand: synthetics in the $16-to-$17 range.

While most staple merchandise may be subject to only one or two changes a year in the composition of the assortment, there is much greater need for frequent changes in the fashion assortment plan. This is prompted by the four major seasons and by the frequency with which new lines make their appearance in the wholesale markets. Thus, model stocks must be adjusted for key dates within a season. For the fall and winter season, for example, the first model might be set for August 1, the next for the start of the peak selling period in October, and another for a much smaller stock for the end of the season in January.

CONTROL OF FASHION STOCKS

Both staple and fashion goods require planning and they both require control. But the control tends to differ in two respects: First, fashion stocks must be reviewed more frequently, usually every week, whereas most staple stocks do not require such frequent attention. Second, the control of fashion reorders is generally based on a heterogeneous unit, usually a price line within a classification, whereas each different item in the staple stock assortment may require separate control.

The model stock plan is the basis for an order control that will keep stock balanced to sales expectancies, but it is not to be followed rigidly. As each season progresses, adjustments need to be made.

THE CLASS-PRICE RECAPITULATION

Once the elements in the assortment plan have been designated (classifications, materials, and price points, for example), a report is set up to recapitulate the unit sales to date and current stocks in each breakdown, such as women's wool cardigan sweaters in the $16-to-$19 range. The report may be prepared weekly or monthly. Current sales are compared with those of last year, and a sales plan for the coming period is set or revised. Current stocks on hand are compared with planned stock levels. The proper stock levels between the dates for which model stocks have been set can be approximated from the stockturn goal. For example, if the annual goal is six turns, the stock on hand at any time should roughly approximate the planned sales total for the coming two months.[5]

THE UNIT OPEN-TO-BUY PLAN

The next step is to translate the information on the class-price recap into a plan of action. This is called a unit open-to-buy plan, or simply a buying plan. Figure 20.1 shows a composite class-price recap and an open-to-buy plan for a month. As indicated, it is commonly prepared for each classification or subclassification and for each price line or zone, but it may also be used to plan orders for styles that are frequently reordered, called *runners*, and also for colors.

The figures appearing on the form are designed to determine the unit open-to-buy for July that will provide the model stock set for August 1 as determined in the plan, table 20.2. Columns 1, 2, 3, and 5 are self-explanatory. The outstanding orders in column 6 represent only orders for current delivery, not orders that may have been placed for delivery in August or later. The figure set in column 4 is based on the experience for the corresponding period last year (column 3) and a comparison of current sales with last year's sales for the period just completed. In the example, the June increase of 10 percent is applied to last year's July sales of 36 to give a projection of 40. Planned stocks for August 1 (column 7) come from the model stock plan (table 20.2). The OTB (column 8) is calculated as the sum of the figures in columns 4 and 7 minus the sum of the figures in columns 5 and 6. This OTB figure is also expressed in retail dollars in column 9.

If delivery can normally be obtained within two weeks, the buyer may decide not to order all of his period's OTB at once, holding some of it for perhaps ten days so that his reorders may take account of the actual stock situation by style number, size, and color as July sales unfold.

MAXIMUM STOCK METHOD OF FASHION CONTROL

Another possible way to control fashion stocks, one well suited to the computer, is to build up the stock commitments at frequent

---

[5] See "weeks' supply method" in chapter 16 where objections to maintaining the stock in a constant ratio to sales are discussed.

UNIT OPEN-TO-BUY

Department: _Women's Sportswear_

Stock on hand, beginning of period: $50,000

Planned stock, end of period: $60,000

Department OTB at retail: $35,000

Period: _July 197–_

Date plan made: _7/1_

Class & subclass	Price lines	1 Sales L.Y. June	2 Sales T.Y. June	3 Sales L.Y. July	4 Pl. Sales T.Y. July	5 On hand July 1	6 On order July 1	7 Pl. Stocks Aug. 1	8 OTB July	9 $OTB July	10 To Buy Now
Wool cardigans	$17.50	50	55	36	40	80	24	115	51	893	36

FIGURE 20.1   Open-to-Buy Plan

reorder intervals to a so-called maximum. This maximum is similar to that described for staple stocks in chapter 19 but includes one more element, the basic stock. In controlling a single staple item, the reserve is provided simply to avoid running out of stock, but in planning for a grouping of items there must be an additional reserve to provide for a basic assortment.[6]

Here is an example of how the OTB in a certain class and price may be calculated: Two weeks may be allowed for delivery, and reorders may be placed every week. The sales at the end of the first four weeks of the season may be 96 units, and the normal seasonal variation may indicate that 12 percent of the season's sales are usually made in the first four weeks. The season's forecast, then, is 800 units. Normally the cumulative sales at the end of seven weeks are found to be 22 percent of the season's total. Thus, 10 percent of the total season's sales should occur in the coming three weeks that cover the delivery and reorder periods. This is 80 units.

The maximum includes not only sales expected in the delivery and reorder periods, which are 80, but also a reserve to protect against stock depletion caused by chance factors and an additional assortment reserve to assure a basic stock of styles, sizes, colors, and quantities within the price and class. The normal reserve would be about 21, and the additional reserve to provide a basic assortment may be set at 144 on a basis of the buyer's judgment.[7] The maximum, then, is 80 (the delivery and reorder period quantity) plus 21 (the normal reserve) plus 144 (the basic assortment reserve).[8] These total 245. If at the end of the fourth week 170 units are on hand and 27 on order, the commitments are 197, calling for 48 more to be ordered during the current week. Some of this quantity will be assigned to the style numbers selected for reorder on a basis of their superior performance record, and the rest will be used in the purchase of new styles. If size and color reports indicate that certain sizes and colors are in short supply, these will be ordered more heavily than others.

---

[6] The basic assortment should not be confused with the model stock. It is the lowest point to which the stock in a category should be permitted to fall, in the planner's estimation, without seriously interfering with sales opportunities. It must protect the assortment of style numbers, colors, and sizes in minimum depth. The model stock is considerably larger. (Mathematically, the basic stock should equal the model stock less the reserve to protect against depletion and less the sales expectancy to the date set for the model stock.)

[7] See chapter 19, where the reserve to provide 99 percent protection against depletion is set at 2.3 times the square root of the sales for the delivery plus reorder periods. In this example, these sales are 80 and the reserve is 2.3×9, or about 21.

[8] The size of the basic assortment may not remain constant; it may change from one part of the season to another.

SELECTION OF STYLES WITHIN OPEN-TO-BUY LIMITS

Within the limits set by the model stock plan and the resultant open-to-buy limits for each classification, type, and price, the fashion buyer must present a wide assortment of styles and looks. These must continually be adjusted to the dynamic changes in customer demand. At this point, the buyer can no longer wholly depend upon mathematical analysis; he must instead depend on astute judgment. For example, if a buyer of moderate-priced dresses has computed an open-to-buy of two hundred units of polyester knit two-piece dresses at twenty-five dollars, he must decide on the particular style numbers he is to include. He may review his current stock and find enough "hot" styles to limit his open-to-buy to reorders of these numbers, but he may find some of them unavailable in the market. He is likely to decide to replenish much of his stock with new styles. He will try to detect the particular customer preference for a look and attempt to adjust his stock to that demand with quick and accurate orders. What make this challenge even more formidable are the economic facts of life of the ready-to-wear industry. That is, one cannot expect the manufacturer to prognosticate much more accurately than the retailer. He also generally offers a wide assortment of styles in his line, and he too must hearken to the dictates of the ultimate judge—the customer. Therefore, he too cannot risk having a tremendous investment in back-up stock for every style he ships. What few units he may still have available will go on a first-come-first-served basis to that merchant who detects the trend first and reacts quickly with a reorder. But the chances are good that one's competition will receive the same merchandise at or about the same time. In fashion, then, it is "the survival of the fastest."

THE STYLE-OUT

Having the stock properly balanced by classifications and price lines does not necessarily make fashion leadership. Stocking merchandise that reflects the customer's preferences does. To detect this trend, some merchants employ the *style-out* technique. Its operation is quite simple. A buyer selects out of his stock the top-selling five or ten dresses, for example, in each classification. He then studies and compares them, attempting to detect a common denominator or feature that makes the items best sellers: a particular soft feeling to the fabric, a certain woven pattern, a color shade, a collar style. Often, in a large store, several different store buyers for the various classifications within a category such as dresses will compare trends at various price lines. If a strong trend is detected, all buyers may purchase styles exemplifying the trend. The store may then undertake a big promotion on that one look, resulting in the type of advertisement that presents one fashion look featured in three or four departments in the store.

CONTROLLING STYLE NUMBERS PURCHASED

Except where the computer has been introduced, many buyers keep control cards for each style purchased, as described in chapter 18. The initial order is recorded in units. Subsequent entries for each style are made when the units are received and when each unit is sold. The buyer reviews these cards at frequent intervals, at least every week, and attempts to decide early in the sales history what action, if any, to take. The possible alternatives are:

1. To reorder the style
2. To transfer it or a part of it to another selling unit of the organization, such as a branch
3. To attempt to return it to the seller
4. To mark it down
5. To give it special promotional attention
6. To leave it alone, permitting the stock to sell out, or at least to defer action until a later date

In making his decision, the buyer must be aware of a peculiarity of fashion merchandise: The rate of sale is largely dependent upon the number of items of the style first introduced into stock. Since usually all the stock of the style, in its various sizes and colors, is exposed to the public, the resultant sales bear a close relationship to the total presented. Thus, if thirty-two units of a style are put on the racks and eight sell the first week, the chance of selling eight the second week are not as good. It is more likely that 25 percent of the remaining quantity will sell; this is about six of the remaining twenty-four, and the third week only four or five are likely to sell. However, if a style has been introduced early in the season, it may show little movement in the first week or two and then pick up as the season progresses. Thus, considerable judgment is required in making a decision as the styles are reviewed.

To analyze continuously the movement of every one of the many different styles carried in stock, often running into the hundreds or even thousands, would be a time-consuming task for a person with many other executive duties. Accordingly, a system called *man-*

agement by exception has widely been introduced. The clerk who maintains the style control cards or the computer that registers the history of each style in its memory is instructed to call the buyer's attention only to those styles that are accumulating a record considerably better or poorer than normal. These may represent only 10 percent of all the styles in stock. The rest do not require the buyer's attention until a subsequent review indicates the need for action. Where manual controls are maintained, the clerk usually attaches a colored tab to the edge of control cards of styles that have achieved well above average performance and a tab of another color for those that have fallen well below standard. Thus, the buyer inspects only those style records tabbed—those that require action. If the computer is used, it is programmed to print out daily or weekly reports only on the styles in each of the two groups—those with exceptionally high performance and those with poor performance.

PERFORMANCE LEVELS

The practical problem is to set the performance levels at which each style is to be reported for attention. To do this intelligently, it is necessary to group all those styles that are competitive and to set average performance levels for the group. The grouping may represent a price line or range within a classification, such as misses' cocktail dresses in the twenty-five-dollar range.

Rate of sale basis for evaluation. The most common method of evaluating style performance is the rate of sale. For example, the average rate of sale for each of the styles within a certain classification and price line may be eight the first week in stock, fourteen during the first two weeks, and eighteen during the first three weeks. A style that sells at close to this average rate will *not* be spotted for review. The clerk or computer may be instructed to report styles that sell more than fourteen the first week, twenty-four the first two weeks, or thirty the first three weeks as exhibiting outstanding performance and probably in need of reorder. Conversely, a style with sales of three the first week, four the first two weeks, and five the first three weeks might be reported as slow selling at the review date at which sales drop to the critical level set for that time.[9]

[9] Another method of setting performance indexes for each style is to calculate the markup return on the investment in each style on a weekly basis and cumulatively during subsequent weeks. The dollar markup on the quantity sold the first week in stock is divided by the cost inventory of that style at the first of the week. At the end of the second and subsequent weeks, the markups

QUANTITY OF STYLE REORDERS

The question of how many to reorder of a style exhibiting high performance is a difficult one. Reorders larger than the initial order are often indicated, provided that the goods will be received before the height of the selling season. A series of small reorders is dangerous because size and color assortments would then probably be inadequate. "Going to the well too often" with frequent small reorders has often led to heavy markdowns, with the last reorders arriving while the season is on its wane.

CENTRAL CONTROL OF STYLES

Buyers for multi-operations usually have an advantage over the buyers for individual stores, since the aggregate volume on individual styles is sufficient to avoid large chance variations in sales. Thus, performance standards can be developed with greater confidence. When a reorder is decided upon for a style with a high performance, the buyer may decide how much to ship of each unit when he places the order, but a better balance can be realized if the distribution is decided upon just before the vendor ships or even after the shipment is received at a central distribution point. The allotment to each store then is made by a distributor who is guided by current information of each store's stock condition in each classification and price line and how well each unit has done with the style number to date.

PERIODIC FASHION REPORTS

In addition to (1) the sales history of each style, with size and color breakdowns generally included (maintained on style control cards or in the computer's memory), and (2) a weekly class-price report covering both sales and current stock on hand, it is essential to have

---

and the first of each week's cost inventory figures are accumulated and the cumulative percentages calculated.

Upper and lower limits are set for styles in each classification. For example, the upper limit for the first week's results may be 12 percent and the lower limit 2 percent. This means that any style that achieves a return on its investment of 12 percent or better during its first week in stock is a candidate for reorder, and any style that achieves a return of 2 percent or less may be subject to prompt clearance.

While this method seems complicated, a computer can be programmed to apply it effectively and print out the styles each week that are in need of immediate attention either for reorder or for disposal.

a number of periodic reports prepared. The major reports are the following:

1. A vendor report monthly or at least once each season that shows the activity of all styles bought from each vendor. The sales, receipts, customer returns, and returns to vendor are often included as well as the initial markup, the markdowns, the inventory, and the stockturn realized. This report is most useful in the evaluation of vendors and in deciding which of them deserve special attention in the near future.

2. A size report, monthly or seasonally, for each classification or group of related classifications, that gives the sales in each size and a comparison with the year before. This provides a guide for determining the proper proportions in which to order sizes. It is not necessary, however, that the size scale be universally followed. Some styles are better suited for people who wear large sizes than for those who wear small ones; also it is more important to have ample stocks in the popular sizes than in the end sizes, where few sales will be lost if the stock becomes depleted.

3. A color report, at least monthly, for each classification or group of related classes, that shows sales by color for the period and cumulative throughout the season, also a comparison with last year. If the last year's figures are carried a few months ahead of the current point in the season, the changes that occurred last year may assist in adjusting the color assortments. The value of this report is similar to that of the size report, but the changes in demand for various colors are much more rapid than those for sizes.

4. An age-of-stock report that lists every week or month all the styles and number of individual items on hand that fall within various length-of-time categories, such as one month to two months, two to three months, three to six months, and over six months. This report identifies styles that are in need of clearance with various degrees of urgency.

SPECIAL SITUATIONS

BIG-TICKET ITEMS

In the home furnishings field particularly, there are many high-ticket items that are sold largely from sample, and there is no need to maintain a stock level in the store by reorders or fill-ins. These include much furniture, some draperies, bedding, major appliances, and some sporting goods such as boats. These products are often finished to the specific requirements of the individual customer, such as fabric for furniture and draperies or extra equipment in other lines.

The goods are often shipped to the consumer directly from the factory or are stocked in the manufacturer's warehouse. If stocked in the store's warehouse, goods would have to be controlled there in much the same manner as has been suggested in this and the preceding chapters.

For such merchandise, the major control problems have to do with the control of (1) the communication process between the selling floor, the vendor or warehouse, and the customer inquiry office and (2) the timing of delivery to customers.

Samples on the selling floor should carry tickets that correctly report the current stock available. If the customer has a choice of fabrics or extras, the availability of these must be known to the salesman and also the length of time required to prepare the goods to the customer's specifications and to make delivery.

It may also be desirable to assign each separate piece in the warehouse a register number and to specify on the price ticket the particular piece to be delivered as well as the style number. This assures the prior sale of the units first put into stock and avoids the creation of a stagnant reserve that depreciates.

SEASONAL COMMITMENTS

There is a considerable amount of merchandise sold at retail that is neither staple reorder merchandise nor fashion merchandise. Some of this must be committed for on a basis of estimates as to requirements three months to nearly a year ahead.

In some of the hard lines such as toys as well as in men's and boys' wear, the buyer has to anticipate most of his season's requirements on a basis of unit control records of the corresponding season last year. For example, he may estimate that he is likely to sell in the fall and winter season 300 boys' woolen suits at thirty-five dollars. If he has an assortment of 90 on hand at the beginning of the season and wants 100 on hand at the end of the season, his planned purchases will be 310 suits. Next, he will decide whether any of these can be obtained as fill-ins at short notice from resources to which he gives substantial advance orders. If he estimates this figure at 65, he will plan to order 275 in advance of the season. He will specify delivery dates depending upon the type of suit and his estimated monthly requirements. In this instance, the unit open-to-buy is for the season and is the difference between the total estimated requirements and the sum of the orders already placed at any given time.

The breakdown of the seasonal orders to specific style numbers, sizes, and colors depends upon experience during the same season last year and the buyer's estimate of changes taking place. The sales activity near the end of the season last year often gives the clue as to what will be demanded during the coming season.

LIMITATIONS OF PAST STATISTICAL RESULTS

Statisticians enamored with the computer age have tended to assume that if sufficient correct information about past performance is fed into the computer, reliable forecasts will be made. But certain psychological studies of top business executives reveal that these men do not base their decisions solely on an analysis of the past or even upon specific knowledge of certain future events. Instead they depend to a considerable degree on intuition or hunches which seem to grow out of valid extrasensory perception. An intuitive merchant may "know" how much will sell and how much to reorder even better than a computer that is fed all data available about the past and is also programmed by the most advanced statistical techniques.

The problem of balancing inventories is of major concern to retailers, one that is not usually going to be solved by the use of packaged computer programs. Management must learn to weigh the results of every unit of merchandise investment against the costs. It has recently been estimated that companies could reduce their stocks of goods on hand $33 billion through better inventory control.[10] Overreliance on the computer will do no more than maintain the *status quo*. The goals in inventory control must be defined more precisely by management.

QUESTIONS FOR DISCUSSION

1. Is the probability that a new style will develop into a runner increasing or decreasing? Why?
2. What difference may there be between a model stock and a basic stock?
3. Suggest a style feature that runs across classifications and price lines that deserves special analysis today.
4. Why is it possible to apply the maximum method of OTB to composite groupings of merchandise but not to individual style numbers?
5. Is it true that the majority of style numbers in stock need no special attention by the buyer at any given review date? Defend your answer.

[10] See *Physical Distribution* Report No. 6, Drake, Shean, Stewart & Dougall, Inc., 330 Madison Ave., New York, N.Y. 10017.

6. What basis of determining the performance index for an individual style number would you recommend for a dress shop?

7. (a) How do the duties of a merchandise distributor differ from those of a buyer or merchandise manager?
(b) Does the position of distributor seem to warrant a relatively high salary?

8. (a) Are there fashion reports other than those listed that you think should be prepared on a regular basis?
(b) Are all the reports listed really necessary?

9. Are the statements made by a sample of customers in regard to their present intentions of their future buying likely to prove reliable in forecasting fashion trends?

10. How would you control the replenishment of big-ticket warehouse stock?

11. In the case of toys, how would you determine what proportion of your estimated seasonal requirements to order months ahead? Of men's outerwear?

12. To what extent will scientific analysis replace intuition in the selection of fashion merchandise?

13. How would you describe the goals of inventory management?

14. With reference to the model stock, figure 20.2, what would be an appropriate distribution, within the total presented for each price range, to sizes and colors? It is suggested that provision be made for 5 different sizes and 3 to 4 colors or color combinations in each. More than one style may be provided for.

BIBLIOGRAPHY

I. BOOKS

Buyer's Manual, rev. ed. National Retail Merchants Association, 1965. (Also a Study Guide by Mary D. Troxell).

FILENE, EDWARD A. *The Model Stock Plan.* McGraw-Hill, 1930. Reprinted by the B. Earl Puckett Fund for Retail Education, 1968.

GARBER, HAROLD, and SEYMOUR HELFANT. *Retail Merchandiisng and Management with Electronic Data Processing.* National Retail Merchants Association, 1966.

GIST, RONALD R. *Retailing Concepts and Decisions* (Part 2), John Wiley, 1968.

GROSSMAN, LOUIS H. *Department Store Merchandising in Changing Environments.* Graduate School of Business Administration, Michigan State University, East Lansing, 1970.

HOLLANDER, S. C. *Retail Price Policies*, 2nd ed. Graduate School of Business Administration, Michigan State University, 1959.

KRIEGER, MURRAY. *Practical Problems in Retail Merchandising.* National Retail Merchants Association, 1970.

LEWIS, R. DUFFY. *How to Keep Merchandising Records.* Fairchild Publications, Inc., 1960.

MCNAIR, M. P., and A. C. HERSUM. *The Retail Method of Inventory and LIFO.* McGraw-Hill, 1952.

NELSON, RICHARD L. *The Selection of Retail Locations.* F. W. Dodge Corp. (Now F. W. Dodge Division of McGraw-Hill), 1958.

OXENFELDT, ALFRED R. and others. *Insights into Pricing.* Wadsworth Publishing Co., 1961.

PESSEMIER, EDGAR A. *The Management of Inventories in Supermarkets.* Washington State University, Pullman, Wash., 1960.

RACHMAN, DAVID J. *Retail Strategy and Structure*, Part IV. Prentice-Hall, Inc., 1969.

Retail Impact—Inventory Management—Program and Control Techniques —Application Description, 4th ed. International Business Machines Corp., 1967.

SCHOTT, ALBERT I., and H. A. TURETZKY. *Retailer's Guide to Merchandise Classification Control.* National Retail Merchants Association, 1969.

THOMPSON, DONALD L., and D. J. DALRYMPLE. *Retail Management Cases,* Parts VI, VIII, and IX. The Free Press, 1969.

WINGATE, JOHN W., and J. FRIEDLANDER. *The Management of Retail Buying.* Prentice-Hall, Inc., 1963.

WINGATE, JOHN W., and H. E. SAMSON. *Retail Merchandising.* South-Western Publishing Co., 1968.

WINGATE, JOHN W., E. O. SCHALLER, and I. GOLDENTHAL. *Problems in Retail Merchandising,* 5th edition. Prentice-Hall, Inc., 1961.

II. NRMA MANUALS*

How to Analyze a Selling Department, 1960.

Leased Departments—Rates, Policies, and Expenses, 1965.

Merchandise Control and Budgeting (revised ed.)

NRMA Standard Classification of Merchandise (2nd ed.)

Ordering Guidelines: A Buyer's Aid for Better Inventory Control, 1968.

Planning Your Store for Maximum Sales and Profits.

Profitable Merchandising of Men's Clothing, 1967.

Putting Classification Merchandising to Work, 1967.

Retail Accounting Manual, 1962.

The Retail Inventory Method Made Practical, 1971.

Stock Shortage Control Manual, 1967.

III. ANNUAL OPERATING RESULTS

Department Store Merchandising and Operating Results (MOR), (Current results in four volumes) National Retail Merchants Association.

Men's Store Operating Experiences—Annual Business Survey, Menswear Retailers of America, 390 National Press Building, Washington, D.C., 20004.

The Super Market Industry Speaks, Super Market Institute, 400 North Dearborn Street, Chicago Ill. 60610.

Note: Many other trade associations compile and publish operating data from time to time.

* National Retail Merchants Association, 100 West 31st Street, New York 10001.

INDEX